LBJ'S TEXAS WHITE HOUSE

LBJ's

TEXAS WHITE HOUSE

"OUR HEART'S HOME"

Hal K. Rothman

TEXAS A&M UNIVERSITY PRESS • COLLEGE STATION

Editing, design, and composition

copyright © 2001 by Texas A&M University Press

Manufactured in the United States of America

All rights reserved

First edition

The original, unedited text of this book was written under contract
to the National Park Service and is in the public domain.

The paper used in this book meets the minimum requirements
of the American National Standard for Permanence
of Paper for Printed Library Materials, z39.48-1984.
Binding materials have been chosen for durability.

Library of Congress Cataloging-in-Publication Data

Rothman, Hal, 1958–
    LBJ's Texas White House : "our heart's home" / Hal K.
Rothman.—1st ed.
        p. cm.
    Includes bibliographical references and index.
    ISBN 1-58544-141-4 (cloth : alk. paper)
      1. Johnson, Lyndon B. (Lyndon Baines), 1908–1973—
Homes and haunts—Texas—Texas Hill Country. 2. LBJ Ranch
House (Tex.) 3. Ranch life—Texas—Texas Hill Country.
4. Texas Hill Country (Tex.)—Social life and customs—20th century.
5. Presidents—United States—Biography. 6. Lyndon B. Johnson
National Historical Park (Tex.) I. Title.
E847.2.R68   2001
967.4'64—dc21   2001001839

In memory of Eileen Barras

For Bob and Yvonne Cole

CONTENTS

ILLUSTRATIONS

ACKNOWLEDGMENTS

This work was initially sponsored by the National Park Service. LBJ National Historical Park superintendents Melody Webb, A. D. Jones, and Leslie Starr Hart extended their cooperation and support. Former Chief Historian Ed Bearss deserves a special thank you. Ed graciously shared his own research on the park, providing insights from his long experience in the system. Park Historian John Tiff provided us with the benefit of his long experience at the park. Regional historians Neil Mangum and Art Gomez generously assisted in the day to day administration of the project and contributed greatly with their own observations on the work. The staff at the park and at the LBJ Library in Austin were remarkable in their willingness to guide us through the enormous volume of paper that held the keys to this story.

Dan Holder also deserves special acknowledgment. As the lead researcher on the project, he organized the information, kept track of countless oral history tapes and other sources, helped in the preparation of the outline, and copyedited and commented on the entire project. The assistance he provided helped make the project run smoothly.

As always, my family deserves more than the thanks I can possibly convey here. Their patience and willingness to tolerate my absences provide the time that allows me to undertake such projects. Words can not convey the depth of my gratitude.

LBJ'S TEXAS WHITE HOUSE

Introduction

On November 22, 1963, on board Air Force One preparing to depart for Washington, D.C., a shaken Lyndon Baines Johnson stepped before his friend Judge Sarah Hughes and recited the oath of office of the Presidency of the United States. Hours before, President John F. Kennedy had been shot in Dealey Plaza in Dallas, Texas, and pronounced dead at Parkland Hospital. His body and his blood-spattered widow, Jacqueline Bouvier Kennedy, were aboard the plane, as were numerous Kennedy aides. The tragedy shocked the nation. It was a particularly terrible moment for Johnson and for Texas as well. Kennedy had come to the state to help heal a rift in the state Democratic Party and restore his popularity there. After the day in Dallas, the Kennedys had been expected as guests at the Johnsons' ranch in the Hill Country, slightly more than two hundred miles south of the airport where the new president stood. As the swearing in ended, President Johnson was whisked to the capital to commence his duties amid the collective mourning of the nation and the world.

In an instant, a transfer of power and leadership had occurred not only in the nation but in the world as well. The suave but perplexing Kennedy—the boy president, war hero, and symbol of a renewal of the nation; the first Roman Catholic ever to hold the highest office in the land—had been replaced by a historically more common sort of president, a man of the backwoods who fashioned himself able to lead by intelligence, skill, cunning, and will. Like Andrew Jackson and Abraham Lincoln, Johnson came from humble origins; like them, he fashioned a persona that brought him success in politics sometimes at the expense of personal goals and public image. A throwback, a man of modest rural roots in an age of urban and military leaders in the White House, Johnson embodied a kind of empathy for ordinary people that belied his tough, manipulative, win-at-all-costs exterior.

The source of that empathy, as well as of nearly everything else about the character of Lyndon Johnson, was the Texas Hill Country from which he came and to which he perennially sought to return. The hilly area west of Austin, called the Edwards Plateau but more commonly known as the Hill Country, had been home to his family for nearly one hundred years when he became president. Despite his claim that he was "a creation of Congress," Lyndon Johnson was truly a product of the Hill Country. Even his detractors recognized the impact of the place on the man; Robert Caro, whose caustic, scathing, and often one-sidedly negative multivolume biography of Johnson delves extensively into his personality, argues that Johnson "came out of the Hill Country *formed,* shaped—into a shape so hard it would never change."[1] While Caro dramatically overstates the impact of his home region on Lyndon Johnson, his charge includes a kernel of truth. The Hill Country had great meaning to the thirty-sixth president of the United States. It symbolized what Johnson thought best, most meaningful, and most trying about the American experience: the ability to meet a rugged natural world on its own terms and emerge, over time and through repeated effort, equal to the task if not entirely victorious. Simultaneously, the Hill Country became a crucible for Johnson, in which he sought to prove not only his own worth but that of his family as well.

This hardscrabble place and Johnson's experiences in it also accentuated every fear and insecurity in the man. This place made him, strengthened him, and gave him the traits he needed to succeed in the contentious world of national politics. Like many from similar backgrounds, Johnson recognized that any lack of fortitude on his own part could quickly lead to a return to the Hill Country in circumstances similar to those experienced by his father, turn-of-the-century politician, farmer, and businessman Sam Ealy Johnson, Jr. Lyndon Johnson retained the deepest kind of attachment to the world from which he came and immense pride in his family's accomplishments. When he returned to his home place, he wanted his return to be in the style of the leader he had become.

Johnson's ranch on the Pedernales River in the Hill Country, the place his wife called "our heart's home," became the primary representation of that style. Eventually known as the Texas White House, it embodied his complex relationship to his past and to the American people. Born less than a mile from the ranch, which belonged to his grandparents at his birth, Johnson grew up with emotional and psychic ties to that particular piece of land. After he and Lady Bird Johnson purchased it in 1951, the ranch came to reflect both Johnson's southern ancestry and his western aspirations. Its regional image belied Johnson's thirty years as a politician with a national identity. The ranch became a symbol of Johnson—his presidency, his roots, and his belief in the ability of people to achieve their dreams. The Texas White House reminded Americans of the rural roots of their nation at a moment when political strife and discord seemed an urban phenomenon, cities coming to embody the worst about America. The ranch reflected cherished American ideals. To foreign dignitaries, it provided a window into a dimension of American culture they could not find in the cities of the Eastern Seaboard. Wearing the ten-gallon Texas hats of lore, they encountered an outlook that was uniquely American, albeit mythically so.

Johnson's ascent to the presidency showcased the ranch. It became his retreat, just as John F. Kennedy had Hyannisport and later, Richard M. Nixon had San Clemente and George H. W. Bush had Kennebunkport. Johnson's attachment to the ranch complex assured that affairs of state would be conducted there, increasing its importance as well as public awareness of it. There he made decisions of vast import: to run for the presidency in 1964 and not to seek reelection in 1968. There he came in the aftermath of solving tough crises such as the steel strike of 1965; there he came to recuperate from illness; there he rested during the nightmare of early spring and summer 1968, when the assassinations of the Reverend Dr. Martin Luther King, Jr., and Robert Kennedy seemed to rend the remaining fabric of the nation. In the iconography of the time, Johnson and his ranch were inseparable. His gangly appearance and Texas twang made him the modern incarnation of the mythic man from Texas. Reporters from the East fed this image, never understanding the man and his Hill Country, never grasping the pull of the place and the personal and political power and sustenance Johnson drew from it.

During his presidency, there was no more important place than the Texas White House for the Johnsons. There they could truly come home from the fast-paced whirl and intense political life of Washington, D.C. In his heart a man of the Hill Country, the president freed himself of the burdens of Capitol Hill politics as he handled the details of the ranch. For him, it served as a hideaway and a place for renewal as well as a showplace for visiting dignitaries. Entertaining there enhanced both his power in negotiations and his sense of his role as a country gentleman. The Texas White House gave him a vantage point he did not feel he had in Washington, D.C.

It was to this ranch and to his roots that Lyndon Johnson returned after he left political life in early 1969. In his retirement, the ranch became his primary focus, its daily activities serving as a substitute for the political life the dynamic leader so loved. On the Pedernales, the retired president could do what he best liked to do: run things. The ranch rejuvenated him in retirement, allowing him to exit public life with a purpose while maintaining the kinds of activities that he found most fulfilling. The press, with which he had had so much difficulty as president, misinterpreted Johnson's desire to be out of the limelight. The press regarded Johnson's reluctance to attract attention in retirement as a sign that he was worn, tired, and defeated. Johnson himself finally had the opportunity to act, talk, dress, and live as he pleased.

During Johnson's years as president, visitors from all over the world were entranced by the ranch on the banks of the Pedernales. The magic of the place captured many as they watched the Texas-orange sun disappear behind the horizon, its beams shimmering on the waters of the river. Johnson's famed Texas barbecues were the talk of the international political set, his favorite musicians time and again playing country, western, swing, and popular music for an array of international leaders and dignitaries. The Texas White House captured the spirit of the man and his time, with all its double-edged promise. For that reason, the day-to-day workings of the ranch offer great insight into the character of Lyndon Baines Johnson.

CHAPTER 1

Buntons, Baineses, Johnsons, and the Hill Country

U.S. 290, the road that leads west from Austin into the heart of the Texas Hill Country, seems to travel upward. Passing through the southwesterly sprawl of Austin and on through Dripping Springs, one of the many gateways to the Hill Country, the highway winds toward a line of hills on the horizon. The vegetation is sparse and intermittent, a combination of various kinds of brush that spread with awesome speed. During much of the road's ascent, grass is scarce, with xeric range forage, dirt, and rock the predominant ground cover. At the highest elevations, live oak trees, spread out against the ground instead of tall and straight as in the more humid climes to the north and east, provide shade. Animals graze, but to even the most casual of observers, each animal requires a great deal of land to fill its belly daily.

To anyone who looks at the region from an economic perspective, this is, in the words of Texas author laureate John Graves, "hard scrabble country."[1]

To someone of a romantic bent, the Hill Country presents an entirely different picture. At the crest of the line of hills—the great tabletop called the Edwards Plateau—the Hill Country seems to be a magic kingdom, a Xanadu, a place different from the rest of the world. The sky is close and low, as if the Hill Country were above the clouds and close to the heavens. The rich blue coloring overhead is clear and refreshing. The world stretches before a traveler's eyes, vision given greater acuity in the seemingly thin air of the hills. The close sky and the ragged hills create an endless space, one not bound by the rules and conventions of the rest of the world. The Hill Country can be a seductive place, a place that attracts observers with its raw beauty and pulls many into its distinct rhythms.

For those born in the region, such as Lyndon Baines Johnson, the thirty-sixth president of the United States, the Hill Country has an eternally strong pull. It is a place defined by its people and their values, shaped and molded by generations. Yet it is a difficult place, one of broken dreams and struggle as well as beauty. It teaches hard lessons that translate well in the rest of the world. What is real in the Hill Country is what someone can touch, decidedly not what they can dream, and that endemic pragmatism offers a strategy for success in the wider world. But the Hill Country never releases its grip on people such as Lyndon Johnson. His home region got under his skin and stayed there, reminding him of the essential truths of American life. The Hill Country became and remained the place where Johnson most wanted to prove himself; the place where validation of his efforts had the greatest personal meaning; and the place to which he returned to look inside himself, evaluate options, and make hard choices both personal and national in character.

Despite its stark beauty, the Hill Country is harsh and unforgiving; it crushes the weak and the foolish and challenges and often defeats even the strong. Its limitations are great, and its power to hold people in a kind of stasis is almost magical. It is "home" in a manner uncommon among American locales, a place to which to return, not merely one from which to depart. People can leave the Hill Country, can triumph over its drudgery and limits, but they always return, in failure or success, to the roots that the character of the place demands from them. The people of the Hill Country are deeply rooted in its thin soil.

Native peoples understood this region as a result of their millennium-long life within it. From a time in the distant past, the Tickanwatick, known to modern scholars as the Tonkawa, roamed the Balcones Escarpment and the Edwards Plateau, living a prehorse hunting and gathering life. Living on the edge of the vast bison range, which expanded until the seventeenth century A.D. and stretched from Tennessee and northern Alabama to the Rocky Mountains, the Tonkawa used skins for their tepees and winter robes. Their ceremonial practices were typical of the people who inhabited Texas before the coming of the Anglos: they tattooed their bodies, organized themselves into clans and moieties, and developed a civil and military leadership structure. Some early European observers perceived them as bellicose; as any hunting and gathering people would, they fought all intruders to protect the resources vital to their survival. Their systematic mobility and small population, which was a function of the limits of their region, made the Hill Country a place where they could live.[2]

By 1500 A.D., the Tonkawa faced Native American adversaries. From the north, Athapaskan peoples descended onto the southern plains, effectively limiting the range of their southern neighbors such as the Tonkawa. Called Apaches by the Spanish, the Athapaskan peoples divided into eastern and western groups. Those to the west became the "Apaches du Navaho," the Navajo. To the east, they became the Lipan, Jicarilla, Palomas, and Carlanas Apaches, the terrors of the plains to everyone they encountered for almost a century. In the 1700s, the Shoshone-speaking Comanches descended from the Rocky Mountains to destroy the eastern Apaches. Astride the horse, the great transformative instrument of the seventeenth and eighteenth centuries, these newcomers captured the bison plains for themselves, driving away Apaches and Tonkawa alike. In the aftermath of the Comanche onslaught, some eastern Apaches looked to the ineffectual Spanish government of New Mexico for protection. The Tonkawa became scattered along the Balcones Escarpment. The plains had been called the Apachería; the new name of the region became the Comanchería, in honor and fear of the people who dominated it from astride their horses.[3]

The Spanish who settled Central Texas in communities such as San Antonio de Béxar felt the arrival of the Comanches as surely as the Tonkawa did. After grappling with Apaches fleeing the southward advance, the Spanish faced the Comanches and later their allies, the Kiowa. In 1790, well into the heyday of Comanche dominance of the southern plains, these two Native American groups formed an unlikely alliance at the behest of a trader. The weak hold of the Spanish on their northern territories; the attention elsewhere of Spanish and, after 1821, Mexican policy; and sparse settlement of areas north of San Antonio in effect turned the Hill Country into a Comanche province.[4]

It was to this land that the ancestors of Lyndon B. Johnson came. Typical of the first Anglos in Texas, they were descended from earlier settlers of the American South: Georgians, Tennesseans, Kentuckians, and others. In this migration, Southerners spread both west and north, across the Mississippi River and the Ohio River, creating farms and plantations using the methods ingrained by the experiences of the generations that preceded them. Their repertoire, born of a preindustrial culture that depended on wood for shelter, fuel, and other necessities, echoed the expansion of Anglo-Europeans throughout North America and reflected the goals of individualism tempered by community standards. The objective of individual economic accomplishment stood apart as a predominant value, particularly among the people from the southern uplands, who were a dominant current of Anglo migration into Texas.[5]

This objective offers a prism into the psyche of the people who came to the Hill County. Both sides of Lyndon Johnson's paternal family, the Buntons and the Johnsons, produced fiercely competitive individuals who sought success and felt little compunction about showing their attributes to others. The Bunton personality, described by Johnson biographer Robert Caro as a "pride so strong that some called it arrogance" coupled with a "fierce and flaring temper," produced bold, paternalistic, self-possessed, and sometimes heroic people who were physically statuesque. John Wheeler Bunton, a bona fide hero of the Texas Revolution and one of the signatories to the Texas Declaration of Independence, was a great-great-uncle of Lyndon B. Johnson. The president's great-grandfather, Robert Holmes Bunton, was equally tall, broad, and impressive. After fighting in the Civil War for the Confederacy, he and a brother began to participate in the cattle trade. In post–Civil War Texas, feral steers available for the taking were worth forty to fifty dollars a head at the railroad terminus in Abilene, Kansas. When a nephew returned penniless after losing the price of fifteen hundred head to cardsharps, Robert Holmes Bunton is purported not to have said a word. He did, however, change businesses, in no small part as a result. The two Bunton brothers stopped driving cattle themselves and began to rent out their pastures to passing herds. As the cattle trade became less profitable, this decision proved prescient. While those bringing herds to the railroad depots had to take the going market rate, pasture along the way remained a steady source of income, its value not subject to the whims of the market. His ranch perched just shy of the Hill Country itself in the town of Lockhart, Robert Holmes Bunton became a wealthy man.[6]

The Johnson ancestors were flamboyant risk takers from the outset. Typical of the early westward migration out of the South, the Johnsons moved westward by generation. Beginning in Oglethorpe County, Georgia, Johnsons appeared in western Georgia and Alabama before arriving in Lockhart, Texas, around 1846. Exuberant and impulsive, they left the soft plains of Central Texas behind when they ascended to the Hill Country in 1856. Deemed by biographer Caro as "dreamers, romantics, and idealists," fierce-tempered, proud, and impractical, the Johnson clan settled the spectacular but limited Hill Country, with one ancestor boasting that they would become the richest family in Texas.[7]

The Hill Country was different than the humid plains of East Texas and much of the American South. Higher in elevation and much drier, with only a few perennial streams, the region deceived incoming Anglo-Americans. To even the trained eyes of people who made their living from the land, the Hill Country looked as if it could support a plethora of economic activity. In reality, the tall grasses of the region were an illusion resulting from ten thousand years of cyclic fire and nomadic use. Rainfall was sparse and too erratic to support unirrigated agriculture for long. The Hill Country was one of many places in the arid parts of the American West that looked appealing but delivered much less than first impressions promised. While the Johnsons briefly succeeded with cattle and fared well for a short time in agriculture, the Hill Country lacked the resilience of humid climes.[8]

There were sections that offered greater potential than the rest of the Hill Country. The valleys surrounding the few perennial rivers—the Pedernales, the Blanco, the Guadalupe, and the Medina—were lush and idyllic. It was in the valley of the Pedernales that the Johnson clan settled, ostensibly offering themselves shelter from the limits of this semiarid place that they did not yet understand. This valley made up a "peculiarly favored subsection" of the Hill Country, one in which prosperity was easier to find than in much of the surrounding region.[9] But for people such as the Johnsons, who settled in this river plain dreaming of great wealth and its attendant status, which the land simply could not provide, the attributes of their valley were only a springboard to greater things.

The Hill Country was hard on such dreams. Although the river valley offered the basis for long-term preindustrial sustenance, the larger region did not. Its limited attributes meant that prosperity would be fleeting, and the instinctively arrogant Johnson clan had no interest in limitations. The Johnsons tasted success but could not hold on to it. On the peripheries of American society, lacking railroad lines to transport products to markets around the nation and the world, the Texas Hill Country and its people—both as a result of and in spite of their skills—would always remain outside of the prosperity of late-nineteenth- and early-twentieth-century American society.

Into a family that experienced all sides of this predicament Lyndon B. Johnson was born on August 27, 1908. His father, Sam Ealy Johnson, Jr., had been a barber and had taught in the one-room schools of the Hill Country before he was elected to the Texas legislature at the age of twenty-seven in 1904. A populist long after the demise of the People's Party, he articulated the slogans that so threatened the Texas oligarchy. Sam Johnson was a "man of the people" in the best Texas turn-of-the-century sense. He was loyal to the hard-working people of the state instead of to the railroads and other interests that ran it. While in Austin, he quickly earned a reputation as a talented legislator; the campaign he engineered that persuaded the state to purchase the Alamo in San Antonio was only the most symbolic of his triumphs. But in a legislature corrupted by money from lobbyists for oil companies, banks, and utilities, Sam Johnson stood apart. Instead of letting the lobbyists pay his way, as they did for so many state legislators, he drank and caroused on his own limited money—more limited after financial reverses in 1905—and acquired the respect of many for his fervent populist stand.[10]

By the time he married Rebekah Baines of Fredericksburg in 1907, Sam Johnson had learned important lessons about politics, economics, and life. Continued financial reverses in cotton futures forced him to decline his district's request that he run for a third term in 1908. Because he had resisted the entreaties of lobbyists and the corporations that supported them, he received no sinecure and few of the perquisites routinely dispensed to former legislators in turn-of-the-century Texas. Instead of a job that paid better than his meager legislative salary, Sam Johnson received nothing—no offers, no opportunities. By the time his first son was born, he had moved his family to the Johnson family homestead, a small three-room Hill Country dogtrot cabin a short distance from the Pedernales River, by the standards of the day a comfortable abode, and had begun to farm.[11]

Sam and Rebekah Johnson's new farm was located in the center of the holdings of the Johnson-Bunton clan. Sam Johnson's parents, Sam Ealy, Sr., and Eliza Johnson, were the closest neighbors, living a little more than one-quarter of a mile away; his aunt and uncle, Frank and Clarence Martin, soon purchased a home farther down the road. Other Johnsons and Buntons abounded in the vicinity. Like many rural families of the time, this was a close-knit extended group that enjoyed all the large events and even the smallest of celebrations together. Their relationships were firm, reflecting the mores and norms of the Johnson clan.

For Sam Johnson's new wife, the Hill Country was a shock. Rebekah Baines Johnson had been raised in a different manner. She was the daughter of a prominent Hill Country attorney, Joseph Wilson Baines. Educated and pious, the elder Baines passed on characteristic, turn-of-the-century Texas Baptist virtues to his family. His daughter attended Baylor Female College, now Mary Hardin Baylor College, in Belton, Texas, and Baylor University in Waco, Texas, working in the bookstore there after her father's own financial misfortunes made the Baines family just another failed southern family. Rebekah Baines Johnson retained the refinement of her youth, and her adaptation to life as a Hill Country farm wife was difficult and torturous. Although she had ample help from her own relatives and the surrounding Johnson clan, whom she sometimes found loud and coarse, she occasionally found the strong sense of community that pervaded their lives—at least as long as the family lived along the Pedernales River—distasteful and oppressive.[12]

In this world, the young Lyndon Johnson was both a precociously intelligent and a famously spoiled child. Indulged by his parents as the oldest child and the center of attention of a large extended family, he was a personable child who sought to "woo and win the affection" of the people around him. From birth he was his mother's favorite; she doted on him and nourished his aspirations throughout his life, although some have suggested that her affection was conditional, alternately given and withheld. Lyndon Johnson cherished the attention and affection he received, once remarking that there was more than love, that there was "a special feeling, something we felt when we looked at one another." Some have called him a "Mama's boy" as a result of this closeness—a contention enhanced by his frequent solicitations of his mother's advice even after his election to the U.S. Senate—but there was also a rougher and independent side to Johnson, which emerged during his childhood. In a frequent ploy that the adults around him perceived as a strategy to gain attention, he "ran away" so often that the family hung a bell on the porch so that Rebekah could call the men from the fields to help look for him; relatives as much as one-half a mile away would see a little figure trudging by and return him home. As likely as not, he would return on another errand known only to himself later the same day or the next. With the Junction School less than two hundred yards away, the four-year-old Lyndon was also drawn to the children who passed by the house on their way to school and by the sound of children playing in the schoolyard. He tagged along, as did thousands of other children around the nation and the world who experienced this informal kind of child care, and his mother arranged with the teacher, "Miss Katie" Deadrich, to allow him to stay. The teacher remembered him as charming and friendly although petulantly demanding and sometimes egotistical.[13]

The Junction School retained the feeling of an extended kinship network. Some of the students were related to the young Johnson in one way or another, and these relationships smoothed Johnson's transition and allowed him to play a privileged role at the school similar to the one he played within his immediate family. Instead of finding himself and his self-defined role mocked by strangers, he experienced a supportive network that reinforced the roles he played at home. Dressed in a white sailor suit, a cowboy outfit, or a red Buster Brown suit, Lyndon looked different from his farm-clothed peers; even when he wrote his name, he made it larger than the rest, using capital letters big enough to cover two blackboards. Perceived as a child with special attributes almost from birth, he was able to extend that distinction into a slightly wider setting that would have seemed vast to a four-year-old. His position on Miss Katie's lap during reading confirmed what the young Lyndon Johnson believed about himself: he was entitled to special treatment that others did not receive.

For a child of the Hill Country, of strong lineage but often limited financial resources, these were circumstances that enhanced personality traits and ties to place. As a child, Lyndon Johnson felt himself the most important of his generation, among an extended network of relatives, but not so important that he did not need to struggle for that preeminence. Biographers have attributed his basic insecurity to the birth of his siblings, who arrived regularly until the last, Lucia, was born in 1916. His attention-seeking ploys—the running away, refusing to read unless he was on Miss Katie's lap—reflected a child who sought security but found its permanent presence elusive. Although Johnson later reported unhappy memories of his childhood to biographer Doris Kearns, his experiences early in life demonstrated his essential needs and his ability to create a strategy to achieve them and bound him tightly to any community as long as he had a prominent role in it.[14]

After the family moved from the farm to Johnson City in 1913, a distance of approximately fifteen miles, the differences between the Johnsons and their neighbors became clear. The Johnson family stood out in the Hill Country; Sam Johnson was worldly and knowledgeable, and Rebekah Johnson was refined and educated. Sam Johnson, according to some who knew him was "a very friendly . . . very down-to-earth man, a man who attracted people and knew how to deal with people." Lyndon Johnson remembered his father as a "warm man, [who] loved people, while my mother was sort of aloof." Johnson City was a small town where everyone knew everyone else, and the successes and woes of each were part of the fabric of the community. It was an easy place to be noticed, but the price of having lofty goals was high in such a small town. The Johnsons were firmly ensconced in the economic and social leadership of the region throughout the 1910s, but their position did not shield them from critical and sometimes envious neighbors.[15]

As the son of a respected family, Lyndon Johnson continued to enjoy special status, but in Johnson City, he learned about life outside his immediate family. With nascent intelligence and a canny understanding of the world, the young Johnson successfully found a niche with boys older than himself. By the age of nine or ten, when his peers were playing marbles in the street, Johnson began to shine shoes in the local barber shop, the venue where local men met to talk. Some Saturday afternoons he sat reading a newspaper and discussing current events with the men who gathered at the barber shop. Like his father, he loved, in the Hill Country phrase, "politicking": the discussion of events that was common currency where men gathered, as well as a dinner-table staple in the Johnson home. At the age of nine, when his father reentered politics, again running for the state legislature, young Lyndon sat on the floor in a bedroom adjacent to his parents' bedroom and avidly listened to discussions of strategy. He also attended a session of the legislature with his father in 1918, canvassing the district on the way to and from Austin. For a boy possessed of a yearning for status and power, who intuitively understood the hierarchical relationships of the world of politics, the experience was idyllic and exciting.[16]

There was another side to the young Johnson, a side nurtured and pro-moted by his mother. Refined by Hill Country standards, Rebekah Baines Johnson was, in the words of her sister-in-law, "always dignified" and, some said, pretentious. Even Johnson City seemed primitive to her. Rebekah Johnson loved books and started Johnson City's first "literary society," where she taught local youngsters poetry and "elocution," the elusive art of pub-lic speaking. She taught the girls social skills as well, offering after-school lessons in her parlor. Rebekah Johnson seemed to have something to offer the community that no one else did: a sense of the proper, the graceful. Lyndon Johnson received the same lessons from his mother. He adored her and sought to please her, learning to spell at her knee and taking much of his sense of what was decent about the world from her.[17] From his fa-ther, he learned to interact in the world of politics, to negotiate, to maneu-ver, and to support principles; from his mother he learned both to aspire in the world and to appreciate its nuances. In his manner, he took after his father; in the way he understood the world, he clearly followed his mother. This was a potent combination.

In the memories of those around him, the young Johnson loomed larger than life. "It might have been small politics" discussed in front of the bar-ber shop, Albert Wierich, who knew Johnson as a boy and maintained a lifelong association with him, remembered. "But thinking about him now, he probably had in mind bigger politics than we ever give a thought at that time." Even those who disliked Johnson or who were ambivalent toward him regarded him as a special kind of product of the Hill Country. "Lyndon always had to be in on everything," Emmette Redford, a Johnson City native who later became the president of the American Political Science Association, recalled. "In any argument, Johnson *had* to win. He *had* to." This marked him as unique.[18]

The exhilaration of success in the town was short-lived, as Sam Johnson's financial reverses again limited the family's horizons. Fifty years after its settlement by Anglo-Americans and German immigrants, the Hill Coun-try remained hardscrabble country, a trap for dreamers and pragmatists alike. People who saw its natural resources as a road to prosperity were sooner or later bound to come up against the hard realities of the region. Despite the overwhelming respect with which nearly everyone in the Hill Country regarded Sam Johnson, his business ventures continued to fail. He bought out his siblings' interests in the family farm on the Pedernales River in 1919 after the death of their mother, and he and his brother Tom tried to make a living raising cotton. They purchased the land in 1919, at the height of the post–World War I land boom. American agriculture had been invigorated by the war, and crop and land prices soared. The reality of the postwar era, however, saw the return to the market of crops from areas destroyed or cut off during the war, and American agriculture returned to the economic doldrums that had been characteristic of it since the end of the Civil War. The same year that Sam Johnson produced his first cotton crop, European cotton again became available, lowering the price the product fetched. In 1922, changes in the agricultural market overwhelmed this farming enterprise, and Sam Johnson and his brother busted. They sold the farm and found themselves saddled with as much as forty thousand dollars in debt, an enormous sum for the time and place.[19]

The demise of Sam Johnson's agricultural enterprise echoed a theme that was repeated through generations of the Bunton, Johnson, and Baines families and that was equally apparent in nearly any other Hill Country lineage. Sam Ealy Johnson, Sr., had endured the same experience, leaving a slew of debts, as had Rebekah Baines's proud family. After her father, Joseph Wilson Baines, died, her mother, formerly the wealthiest woman in the town of Blanco, was reduced to renting rooms to students at the Southwest Texas State Teachers College in San Marcos, at the foot of the Hill Country. As had their parents and grandparents, Sam and Rebekah Johnson toppled in their own esteem, if not always in the estimation of their neighbors.

There were ramifications for the Johnsons that extended beyond economic circumstances. Sam Johnson had been the well-loved incorruptible legislator who defended the interests of the people. He wanted to pave roads, build schools, and regulate utilities, all advantages for the ordinary people he championed. Long-time Texas congressman Wright Patman routinely referred to him as the "best man I ever knew."[20] But that status did not offer the means to earn a living. Despite a network of family, political friends, and others who cushioned the fall, the demise of his dreams in cotton was hard on Sam Johnson and damaged the family.

These were difficult times for the Johnsons. "It was hard for them to survive," Father Wunibald Schneider remembered Lyndon Johnson saying of his family. Sam Johnson had always been a harsh disciplinarian, and the changed circumstances reinforced his need for control; Lyndon Johnson remembered that his father would "take a razor strap and just whip the hell out of us." His drinking increased, and with it increased the characteristic irresponsibility of those who find solace in the muddled sentiments that emerge from a bottle of spirits. Life in the family became chaotic as Rebekah Baines Johnson repeated a pattern begun during earlier illnesses and often took to her bed in protest against her husband's excesses. On occasion, food became scarce, and the children's clothes were rarely pressed and sometimes not even laundered. One Christmas, there was nothing to eat in the house until Tom Johnson arrived with a turkey and a sack of potatoes. Lyndon Johnson saw his father's fall and resented its impact on the family. He felt an obligation to take care of his mother that he articulated from early in life, and the situation required more cooperation than any previously indulged youth could be expected to provide.[21] When Lyndon Johnson's father was able to find work as the section foreman of a road crew on the Austin-Fredericksburg highway that he had worked so hard to fund in the legislature, this political patronage position, which eventually allowed him to employ his son, completed Sam Johnson's descent from respected leader of the community to someone of diminished status.

The new circumstances affected different members of the family in disparate ways. Sam Houston Johnson said of his father that "though he was never a wealthy man, our daddy was always able to provide for his family, sometime more lavishly than others but never bordering on poverty." Younger than Lyndon Johnson by six years, Sam Houston Johnson was preadolescent at the most difficult time in his family's life and presumably less attuned to economic hardship. Yet his recollection indicates that while life in the Johnson house was hard during this time, at least for one of the children it was not unbearable.[22]

During the 1920s, the Hill Country retained only the most marginal of people, those with little capital, less education, and fewer marketable skills than their peers elsewhere. The decline in land quality and agricultural prices had been consistent since the 1870s. Only World War I briefly altered the pattern. Long before Sam Johnson's difficulties, the Hill Country had become a place of terrible drudgery, "out of the Middle Ages," one woman from the region recalled. Even for the most skilled, educated, and affluent of its residents, failure, defeat, and frustration typified the Hill Country experience. The Johnson City of the 1920s remained a place out of time. Elsewhere in the nation, particularly in urban areas, electricity was a common feature of homes, more and more of which were heated by coal and natural gas each year. In Johnson City, a part-time electrical generator provided the little electricity available. Radios were battery powered, washing machines used gasoline when they existed at all, and kerosene mantle lamps and Coleman and Aladdin gasoline lamps provided what little light anyone had as dusk fell. To stay warm, people cut wood for their fireplaces. It was a hard place that aged people quickly and made them resentful, particularly when circumstances delivered a "comeuppance" to people who challenged local norms by their pretensions to the better.

The difficulties that accompanied the financial reverses that Sam Johnson and his family endured were typical of small-town life. Such communities offer safety in the norm. People exceed local standards at their own risk, for those who choose to toe the line have made a decision to reject risk and the opportunity that accompanies it in favor of the warmth of home and homeplace. Such security is highly prized, but it can be economically, socially, and culturally limiting, a reality not lost on community members. Anyone from such a place who tries to exceed the norm, to grow beyond the psychic boundaries of the community, will feel the pull of the place; as long as they succeed, they will retain local respect. When they fail—particularly if they live in diminished circumstances within the bounds of the community, as did the Johnsons—they become figures held up for pity and sometimes contempt in a manner particular to the web of a small town. For the proud Johnson clan and their eldest son, favored since birth and accustomed to special status, the demise of the family enterprise was a brutal fate.

For Lyndon Johnson, the transformation of the family into supplicants as his adolescence began was a cruel twist. The pillars of his world were shaken. His father, whom he previously had idolized, became marginal, still meriting the respect and love of his son but sometimes enduring the scorn of his neighbors. His adored mother, the most important influence on his life, fared little better. The women of Johnson City saw her as someone who would not recognize the fate of her family and who could not take care of her own children, an attitude that was hard for her proud son to bear. At school in the country, in Johnson City, and in a preparatory academy in San Marcos for which his parents had scrimped to afford the fee, Johnson showed all the traits of adolescent rebellion. He "liked to rebel," his brother recalled, defying his parents openly at home, evincing the tyrannical authority of any youth with power but bereft of the responsibility for its application, and breaking any rule or standard held out in front of him. Even his own grandmother believed he would end up in the penitentiary. Some of his choices were typical of those made by young people. He ran with a rowdy crowd and, on more than one occasion, snuck his father's automobile out for late-night escapades. Twice he wrecked the family car. Other manifestations were blatantly offensive. Lyndon Johnson refused to haul water from the well for the family's use, a difficult and physically demanding task that fell to his mother if he could not be persuaded that it was his responsibility. This defiance made his father apoplectic. No more egregious insult could be offered in a family that required the labor of all even to approach completing the tasks necessary to run the household.[23]

The combination of the loss of his family's prestige and position with his personal traits, the symbiotically linked pride and insecurity, helped make Lyndon Johnson the man he became. One biographer notes that his need for attention and his mode of ingratiating himself were not in themselves unusual; what made Lyndon Johnson unique was the way in which he approached these emotional needs, with a fervor and an intensity that were unparalleled. Johnson himself noted his own insecurity when he told Doris Kearns that "my daddy always told me that if I brushed up against the grindstone of life, I'd come away with far more polish than I could ever get at Harvard or Yale. I wanted to believe him, but somehow I never could." Another biographer sees his mother's alternately offered and withheld affection as central to this phase of Johnson's development.[24] The economic collapse of the family brought out in the young man an overwhelming need to succeed at any cost that manifested itself in every subsequent aspect of his life. It drove him to defy his parents and to ignore their plans for him; to work rather than to go to college; to embark on an escapade to California, where he worked as a law clerk for his cousin Tom Martin; and to assert his independence and with it his sense of self in myriad ways. Ever after Lyndon Johnson needed to prove his own worth, most of all to himself.[25]

This intense desire to succeed at all costs is typical of those who have the intelligence and fortitude to leave declining or moribund small towns for the outside world. The people who left places such as Johnson City in the 1920s were few and far between. When they left, they had at stake not only their economic future but their status, self-esteem, and entire relationship to the world from which they came. The fierceness people such as Lyndon Johnson evinced reflected the tangible consequences of failure. If they failed, they had to return in disgrace to the places they had sought to exceed. Lyndon Johnson was well aware of the price of this kind of failure: he had seen it in the lives of his own father and mother.

The young Johnson found many ways to overcome his lack of status and personal appeal, to lead, and to move toward the success he craved. He had been a successful high school debater. When he finally went off to college after resisting it for almost three years, he created a powerful if not always well-liked persona for himself. He finagled his way into the graces of the president of Southwest Texas State Teachers' College during his first five weeks on campus, receiving a job that had not existed before his arrival on a campus where status was determined by the kind of job a student held. At the time, he had not even been formally admitted to the college, but his silky-smooth means of ingratiating himself with older people worked once again. The faculty at the college and the parents of Johnson's friends found him winning.[26] Johnson's success, however, came at the expense of genuine personal popularity and the respect of his peers. His complicated status on campus reflected the resentment directed toward someone who saw bigger issues and dreamed larger dreams than most of the crowd. Entwined with that resentment was a reaction to Johnson's manipulative nature. Fear of Johnson and distrust of his ways were best expressed in the sobriquet attached to him: "Bull" Johnson, which derived from what was perceived to be the value of his words.[27]

From this Hill Country crucible, Johnson moved on to new challenges, driven by the same feelings that had propelled him out of Johnson City. Biographer Robert Caro has suggested that the "Lyndon Johnson of college years was the Lyndon Johnson who would become President. He had arrived at college that Lyndon Johnson. He came out of the Hill Country *formed,* shaped—into a shape so hard it would never change." This, however, belies the complicated changes that occurred in Johnson's thinking, in his ways of working with and around people, in his perspective, and in myriad other aspects of his personality and thinking.[28] As are most human beings, Johnson was a product of his life experiences—of his family, their values, and the extended kinship network that had saved him time and again; of the limits of the Hill Country; of the problems his father experienced; and of all the other events and circumstances that shape an individual's life. To say that in the late 1920s he was all he could become is to apply a deterministic system to human beings that ignores the growth and change that everyone experiences and from which most learn. There were patterns that persisted in his life—intrinsic core features of his personality and value system that remained constant—but Johnson's rise to power, and his eventual decision to remove himself from it, reveal a suppleness that the raw youth from Johnson City simply did not possess.

Johnson left the Hill Country as one of its people, something he grappled with until economic and political success allowed him to return home as an affluent leader. Even in San Marcos, on the edge of the Hill Country but tied to the wealthier, more humid lands east of the Balcones fault, Johnson recognized that he was marked by his upbringing. To a certain degree, he felt betrayed by his family's loss of status; to an equal degree, that loss served as motivation. "The things that you think are defeating him," Johnson once told press secretary George Reedy of Arkansas senator and Rhodes scholar William Fulbright, "are the very things that are putting him up there."[29] Lyndon Johnson might very well have been speaking of himself. His youth had forged in him unbreakable ties to place, but before the young Johnson could exorcice the demons of his past, he first had to triumph, return to his place of origin, and then reconcile himself with his family's past.

Johnson's experiences as a teacher began while he was still a student. His impecunious condition and extravagant spending habits at school drove him to seek a temporary teaching permit granted to teachers' college students with sophomore standing. He accepted a position teaching on the "wrong side of the tracks," in the Welhausen School in the town of Cotulla, ninety miles south of San Antonio and sixty miles from the Mexican border. As was typical in Texas from the end of Reconstruction until the 1960s, Cotulla had a segregated school system. White and Hispanic children were separated, as white and African American children were elsewhere in the nation. The "Mexican schools," as schools such as Welhausen were called, differed little from the sadly equipped "separate but equal" schools for African Americans that took more than twenty years of Supreme Court decisions and changes in federal law to dismantle. The schools were designed not to educate but to warehouse children while their parents worked. Any aspirations to better lives that children in such schools showed were routinely quashed, and in a hurry. Such schools taught Spanish-speaking children their purported "place" in mid-twentieth-century Texas and little more.

Lyndon Johnson set out to change this in the little town of Cotulla. Approaching the education of these forgotten children with the fervor and zeal that had become characteristic of him when he thought a task was important, he accomplished the impossible: he made a difference. Unlike the five local women who made up the rest of the school staff, Johnson treated the post seriously. Appointed principal of the school, he arrived early and stayed late, provided a role model of great fervor and intensity, and injected a combination of spirit and order. He arranged for activities with other schools, set up baseball games and track meets, and cajoled parents who needed the income from every minute of their workday to take time off to drive their children to these events. Seeking to upgrade the use of English among his students, he instituted schoolwide assemblies in which students were forced to participate. Debate, declamation, and spelling bees became characteristic of Johnson's school. The children, even the ones he had to discipline, loved him for his passionate interest in their lives, as did their parents and most of the teachers who found themselves working for the precocious college student. By all accounts, no one could have done a better job than Johnson did that year in Cotulla.[30]

Johnson's motivation at Cotulla has been described as merely the desire to receive a letter of recommendation from the superintendent to assist him in seeking his next job.[31] This transparent explanation belies the reality of Johnson's accomplishments in the hopeless little town. Securing even an outstanding recommendation required far less effort than he put into the school and could have been as easily achieved with the ingratiating techniques Johnson so successfully practiced on President Cecil Evans at the teachers' college in San Marcos. The young Johnson clearly felt real compassion for these people, who were even poorer than those he knew in the Hill Country; when he arrived at the school, he was told that no lunch hour existed because the children did not have lunches to eat. To secure a good letter, he did not need to tutor the janitor in English, to purchase a book for him to use from his own limited funds. Nor did he need to regard the classroom and extracurricular activities with the gravity he assigned them. Cotulla touched Johnson. There in that lonely little crucible, he was a teacher of the kind immortalized in lore and memory; a link in the unending chain of inspirational teachers; and a forerunner of remarkable individuals such as Jaimé Escalante, the near legendary 1980s high school teacher who taught advanced mathematics and science to inner-city teenagers and was immortalized in the movie *Stand and Deliver.* Johnson shared something with the people of Cotulla. He too knew what it was like to start from behind, and he sought to convince them that they could overcome such humble beginnings with sheer hard work. This idealistic sentiment stemmed from his own insecurities and his personal feelings for the people of this little place, not from any utilitarian sense that he could rise in the world as a result of his actions there.

Cotulla also allowed Johnson to continue his role as rebel in a subtle and discreet manner. In 1920s Texas, the effort he expended on Spanish-speaking children was an affront to the hierarchical mores of his time and place. Such an effort would be seen as a waste by the community at large. Johnson's work in Cotulla, however, reflected the populist spirit imbued in all the Johnsons by Lyndon's father, the idea that people were at their core equals and that little people were entitled to the same benefits as big corpo-rations. While this view had the sympathy of large swaths of the Texas public, in the corporate-dominated legislature and in other agencies with authority it remained anathema. By acting out this populist doctrine in what his wife later called "one of the crummiest little towns in Texas," Lyndon Johnson paid a sort of homage to the traditions of his father and his family.[32]

In Cotulla, Johnson was a model teacher and administrator, but he was also a young man alone. Important in the town because of his role and status, he still had immense gaps in his personal life. His first post–Johnson City High School relationship, with Carol Davis, the daughter of an im-portant San Marcos merchant who taught that year in Pearsall, Texas, thirty-three miles away from Cotulla, had begun to cool. Left alone, Johnson was gnawed at by his insecurities, as would be the case for even the most self-assured and self-confident twenty-year-old. He derived his sense of worth from the place and the feelings of its people toward him, engaging in the same kind of emotional manipulation that some biographers attribute to his mother. Nevertheless, he gave his all to a community that had never before experienced anything like his dedication. Cotulla and its Hispanic children were special to him because he was special to them.

Johnson's return to San Marcos after a year in Cotulla marked a change in his life. Emboldened by his ability to motivate in the classroom, he returned to campus full of ideas about politics and power. Through an organization called the White Stars—invented to counteract the power of the athlete-dominated Black Stars, which refused to have Johnson as a member—he inverted the social hierarchy of campus politics; brokered the school elections; and became a "Big Man On Campus," albeit not always a popular one. This was his first direct experience with electoral politics, but to his peers he seemed to have been born with the knowl-edge he brought to the process. His ability to compromise in politics first became evident in San Marcos, where his knowledge and acute sense of political processes allowed him a measure of control atypical in campus politics.[33]

He soon transferred this knowledge to the realm of real politics, in effect becoming a political operative at about the same time he became a high school teacher. In July, 1930, while Johnson was still enrolled at San Marcos, he and his father attended a political barbecue and "stump speaking" outside the Central Texas town of Henly. Before the widespread ownership of radios, such political events were the primary way to reach small-town voters. Among the scheduled speakers was the Texas governor, Pat Neff. But the governor did not appear when introduced. As legend has it, just before the master of ceremonies, Texas state representative and state senate candidate Welly K. Hopkins, was about to declare a default, Sam Johnson nudged his son and sent him forward to speak on behalf of Neff.[34]

This first public political speech had all the virtues of such spontaneous events and presumably many of its flaws. One account suggests that Johnson spoke loudly and "a little bit squeaky like an adolescent." One biographer presumes that he spoke in generalities. But from all accounts, he was a powerful speaker, possessed of oratorical style and a little bit of flair, and the audience received his words in a positive fashion. Hopkins came over to meet the young man. The two talked, and soon after Hopkins enlisted Johnson in his own campaign, giving him responsibility for Hays County, with its county seat of San Marcos, and Blanco County, Johnson's home county. In what he expected to be a tough race, Hopkins won the Democratic primary—tantamount to a general election in Texas during the first half of the twentieth century—by more than two thousand votes.[35]

Hopkins attributed much of his success in the primary campaign to Johnson's efforts. The young man used his White Stars associates from San Marcos to pass out leaflets in every small town in the district, to stir up crowds when Hopkins spoke, and generally to advance Hopkins's election. Johnson served as the de facto campaign manager for the two counties, lining up venues such as the election-eve rally held in Old Main on the Southwest Texas State Teachers' College campus. Only Johnson, with his close ties to the notoriously apolitical President Evans, could have arranged this location. Evans, the most respected man in the area, even sat on the podium in a tacit endorsement of the candidate. Johnson "did a magnificent job for me," Hopkins remembered.[36]

This entrée to politics suggested a rapid rise for the young Johnson.

He had successfully orchestrated a campaign for a district-wide office on the force of his savvy. The word traveled quickly in Texas political circles, and Johnson became known as the boy wonder of Hill Country politics. In the general election, he helped secure the Hill Country for Edgar Witt, a candidate for lieutenant governor, after campaign manager William Kitrell thought there was no chance of victory in the area. But the realities of the Depression meant that job opportunities were scarce, and Johnson needed to earn a living. He taught briefly in Pearsall before taking a job at his Uncle George Johnson's school, Sam Houston High School, in Houston, Texas. There, with the energy he displayed in politics and teaching, he took the school's debate team to the city championship and almost pulled off an upset win in the state finals. But his real calling remained politics.[37]

In 1931, the opportunity to exercise that calling finally appeared, and in an instant, Lyndon Johnson was on his way to Washington, D.C., to fulfill his personal quest. He went as the assistant to Richard Kleberg, himself an unlikely choice for the U.S. House of Representatives but a descendant of a line of Texas moguls. Heir to one-quarter of the immense King ranch, Kleberg was a dilettante and raconteur, a man possessed of that special conceit that belongs only to those born and bred with substantial wealth. His best political quality was his electability in an area of the state known as "Kleberg Country." Disinterested in politics, Kleberg hired Johnson as his private secretary—the position now called administrative aide—and effectively turned the office over to the young man.[38]

From the office of an absent and disinterested congressman, Lyndon B. Johnson began to build what would become an enormous power base in American politics. Developing his practice of cultivating people in positions of power, of providing service to Texans who requested it, and of making sure that everyone knew who the affable young man contributing to their success was, Johnson fashioned the beginnings of a political empire. His willingness to help people extended beyond the limits of Kleberg's district; he offered the congressman's assistance not only to the people of his district, in places such as San Antonio, a city then labeled the "mother-in-law of the Army" because so many soldiers met their wives there, but also to people throughout the state. Johnson's oft-remarked-upon unusual political ability came into play in Washington, D.C., as it had in San Marcos and on Hopkins's and Witt's campaigns. Johnson revived a moribund organization called the "Little Congress," made up of congressional employees, and turned it into the basis of his power among congressional assistants.[39]

Johnson inserted himself close to the heart of the New Deal, the enormous package of reforms enacted by the administration of Franklin D. Roosevelt. In the new climate, with the emphasis on government spending to prime the pump of the American economy, Congress was responsible for much patronage. Johnson's unimportant and uninterested congressman, with his attendant lack of seniority, received fifty patronage jobs to dispense. The average congressman might receive four or five; a powerful committee head could have as many as forty. With Kleberg absent, dispensing the patronage that Johnson himself created in his time in Washington, D.C., became his personal obligation and opportunity. Nor was the young man unknown at the Capitol. No less a personage than United States Postmaster General James A. Farley, the powerful personnel director of the New Deal, knew Johnson and even expressed fondness for him. In 1932, Johnson even challenged the patronage goals of Vice President John Nance "Cactus Jack" Garner and orchestrated a strategy that defeated him. Within a few years of his arrival in Washington, D.C., Lyndon Johnson had defined a role for himself in national politics.[40]

He also had the good fortune to be present as the New Deal gathered momentum. It was the kind of policy that spoke to Johnson's populist roots; to the beliefs of his father, Sam Ealy Johnson, Jr.; and to the experiences of his family in the Texas Hill Country. The Depression had brutal consequences across the nation, particularly in the Fourteenth Congressional District, which Kleberg and Johnson represented. Its two main industries, the military bases of San Antonio and agriculture, were hard hit by the economic catastrophe. Lyndon Johnson's drive to power was intrinsically linked to the needs of the constituency in South Texas.

Characteristically, Johnson's approach was pragmatic. Johnson persuaded Kleberg to loan him and two assistants, Gene Latimer and L. E. Jones, his former debate stars from Houston, to Maury Maverick for Maverick's 1934 campaign for the new Twentieth Congressional District seat, which had been carved out of Kleberg's district. No one more antithetical to Kleberg's views could have been found; Maverick was a utopian and—both in Texas and after his arrival in Congress—a radical. He was another in the long line of people who appealed to Johnson's ties to his roots, to his sense of what ought to occur in American society. Johnson's persuasiveness made this odd pair of positions possible, and he helped Maverick engineer a plurality in a second primary in August.[41]

At the same time, the list of people who knew Johnson and for whom the young congressional assistant could do something continued to grow. Dan Quill, a labor leader whom Johnson had drawn to his camp, became postmaster of San Antonio. Nueces County attorney, former Texas state senator, and noted Austin powerbroker Alvin J. Wirtz, a resident of neither the Fourteenth Congressional District where Kleberg served nor Maverick's Twentieth District, secured important appointments in Washington, D.C., with Johnson's help. Although Johnson was only a "mere" congressional assistant, he became an important contact in the capital for anyone in Texas who needed entrée into the world of national politics.[42]

About the same time, Johnson's personal life took a new direction. Although he had had a steady girlfriend in high school, he had never been popular with women. At San Marcos, where women outnumbered men three to one, Johnson was the target of mocking contempt for his inability to get a date even after he became one of the few students with his own automobile. After the end of his relationship with Carol Davis, he apparently lacked steady female companionship for an extended period. Passing through Austin in September, 1934, however, he discreetly invited a young woman to breakfast the following day as he prepared to take an acquaintance of hers on a blind date. Although she planned to skip the breakfast, Claudia Alta "Lady Bird" Taylor was waved into the restaurant where Lyndon Johnson awaited. According to legend, he proposed marriage on the first date, and a whirlwind courtship began. They married on November 17, 1934, before Lady Bird turned twenty-two.[43]

Lady Bird Johnson proved to be a tremendous asset for her ambitious but socially unsophisticated husband. She was a charming person, shy to a fault but imbued with the grace of southern gentility and the hospitality of Texas. She made their apartment comfortable and homey for the many friends, acquaintances, and contacts that Lyndon Johnson brought home, usually without calling ahead to warn her. Among the guests was a valuable contact who shared Lady Bird's characteristic shyness—Sam Rayburn, a powerful congressman well on his way to holding the position of Speaker of the House of Representatives. A bachelor who feared loneliness more than anything else, Rayburn was consumed with his solitude until Lyndon Johnson and his new wife began having him over, first for dinner and later for Sunday breakfast. Taciturn and grim Sam Rayburn was charmed by the Johnsons—by the sincere sweetness and shyness of Lady Bird and by the filial behavior of her husband. Over time, Lady Bird became Rayburn's favorite of the two, a reality Johnson understood and used to tug at the emotions of this solemn man. The relationship became one of Johnson's most valued, and except for a period of estrangement in 1940 and 1941, it lasted the remainder of Rayburn's life.[44]

The relationship with Rayburn also helped propel Johnson out of his role as a congressional staff member and toward his next objective. Johnson had been planning his subsequent position from the day he accepted his job with Kleberg. He persuaded the congressman to put him forward as a candidate for the presidency of the Kleberg-dominated Texas College of Art and Industries—Texas A&I—in Kingsville, Texas. He was also offered a position as number two lobbyist for General Electric at the princely salary of ten thousand dollars per year. Johnson, however, was not offered the Texas A&I position, and he declined the lobbying job because he thought it would make it impossible for him to win state-wide electoral office in Texas. His sights were set on political goals.[45]

With Rayburn's insistent help, Johnson landed a job as Texas state director of the new National Youth Administration (NYA), an inspiration of Eleanor Roosevelt's designed to put young people to work in public service projects. The twenty-six-year-old Johnson was a surprise choice. He was the youngest director selected among the forty-eight state programs, and he was the only one without prior administrative experience. Marshaling college friends, recipients of his patronage, and former students from Houston into a staff, he began to devise a program that would put twelve thousand young people to work across the vastness of Texas. After weeks of suggestions that failed to meet one or another of the important criteria—that the jobs be applicable statewide across the eight hundred miles of Texas and that they function in a manner that would allow 75 percent of the cost of the projects to be spent on workers' salaries—someone on the staff conceived of the idea of roadside parks. These picnic areas would have a number of functions: they would allow people a place to stop and eat at a table off the often shoulderless, narrow, two-lane roads over much of Texas; they also would improve highway safety, providing a place for drivers to pull off to sleep or relax. After the state highway department agreed to furnish land, materials, and vehicles to transport the young workers, the program met NYA salary allotment requirements. The program was a stroke of genius that created much opportunity, considerable loyalty, and a great deal of patronage that Johnson could wield.[46]

The NYA was also the start of what would later become Johnson's Texas political machine. From his NYA post, Johnson was able to use the patronage he had begun to dispense as Kleberg's secretary. From there it was a small step to begin to galvanize support for a run at a congressional seat. Passing up opportunities to acquire statewide power, Johnson prepared to seek a national position. When that opportunity came with the February 23, 1937, death of Congressman James P. "Buck" Buchanan of the Tenth Congressional District, which included both Austin and the Hill Country, Johnson was more than ready.[47]

He went into the campaign for the special election determined to win and with the financial backing of powerful interests in Texas. Through Alvin Wirtz, Johnson received access to Herman and George Brown. Heads of a multimillion-dollar construction company, Brown and Root, the two brothers aspired to even greater construction projects. The three business-men needed Johnson's support for the construction of a chain of Hill Coun-try dams—the Browns for the way in which such a project would move them up in the world of construction, Wirtz for the positive impact the dams would have on his power base in the utility industry. In the enthusi-astic Johnson, they found their candidate. Despite Johnson's relative unfa-miliarity to most of the large district and Herman Brown's fierce suspicion of a candidate who openly espoused New Deal doctrines, the combination of energy; of financial resources, both Lady Bird's and Wirtz's; and of sheer determination in campaigning worked. Although he lost thirty pounds of body weight in his vigorous campaigning, almost destroyed his voice, and landed in the hospital with an inflamed appendix, Johnson won the elec-tion. In a winner-take-all situation, he received the largest number of votes of any of the eight candidates but less than 30 percent of the total cast. He had galvanized rural backcountry voters of the district, and by all accounts they were responsible for his triumph.[48]

The congressional seat was clearly a stepping-stone for Johnson. He had bigger plans, as well as a strategy to accomplish them. Johnson's vocif-erous support of President Franklin D. Roosevelt and his Supreme Court–packing plan at a time when the plan was unpopular won him a photo session and a two-hundred-mile ride with the president during a Roosevelt trip to Texas. In the photograph taken at the time, Johnson and Roosevelt reach across Texas governor James "Jimmy" Allred to shake hands. Johnson later had the photograph altered to remove Allred and displayed and made famous the self-serving version of the photograph. As had many older men before him, Roosevelt quickly became fond of the new congressman. With this powerful ally, Johnson had access to the world of New Deal insiders, and he became an associate and personal friend of many of them. Johnson developed relationships in the nation's capital in the same manner that he had in San Marcos.[49]

Johnson invested in this effort for at least two apparent reasons. The first was to advance himself—to have the power and status he craved and to win the respect that he feared had eluded him throughout his life. The second reason was to be a part of implementing the programs of the New Deal and, not incidentally, to bring to fruition projects that helped his constituents and his powerful sponsors. Chief among these projects during his first term in the House was the Marshall Ford Dam, later renamed the Mansfield Dam, on the lower Colorado River. The first-term congressman's influence was wide and strong enough to arrange the authorization of this major project, which helped his constituents and his political patrons alike.[50]

The dam and an additional appropriation to enlarge it became the basis of Johnson's power. No less a Washington, D.C., power broker than Thomas G. "Tommy the Cork" Corcoran later remarked that Johnson's "whole world was built on that dam."[51] It established him with all sides of his Central Texas constituency, assured widespread support for his election to a full two-year House term in 1938, and created the context that could permit a run at the U.S. Senate when a seat became available.

The two most important people behind Johnson were Herman Brown and Charles E. Marsh, a southwestern regional newspaper mogul, major businessman, and bankroller of legendary Texas oil wildcatter Sid Richardson. Together Brown and Marsh, both self-made men, had more than enough power to get Johnson where all three wanted him to go: to positions of more power and responsibility. Marsh exposed Johnson to the trappings of real wealth at his Virginia estate, Longlea, enticing the young congressman with the benefits of a luxurious life. At Longlea, Johnson and Marsh's paramour, Alice Glass, may have engaged in a long-running affair. The world of glitz and glitter attracted Johnson, but wealth was clearly not his sole objective. It was at Longlea, biographer Robert Caro suggests, that Johnson's aspiration to the presidency of the United States first became clear. Amid the beautiful hills of Virginia, the congressman declined a characteristic Marsh offer to allow him to purchase enough of a West Texas oil business to make Johnson a millionaire. "It would kill me politically," George Brown recalled Johnson saying. Oil interests would not have hurt Johnson in Texas. They could only have been a problem in a race for a national office.[52]

By 1941, Johnson was ready to make a run for the Senate, and the death of Morris Sheppard, the senior U.S. senator from Texas, opened the way. Just as he had sought the seat of a deceased congressman in 1936, Johnson again sought to move up the political ladder without challenging an incumbent. In this case, he faced three candidates with statewide recognition—Governor W. Lee "Pass the Biscuits, Pappy" O'Daniel, formerly a radio entertainer; state Attorney General Gerald C. Mann; and Congressman Martin Dies, chairman of the House Committee on Un-American Activities—as well as a host of other oddities who paid the filing fee. Although "Pappy" O'Daniel initially demurred, Dies and Mann seemed to be genuine opponents who could beat Johnson. But Dies ran an ineffectual and lazy campaign with no statewide organization of any substance and failed to remain a serious candidate after his strong initial showing. A former football hero at Southern Methodist University, the incorruptible Mann was a perfect candidate for Texas. He had served as a pastor during law school, was handsome and clean-cut, and radiated sincerity. Mann, however, had two weaknesses: he lacked the organization and financial support that Johnson had built, and he failed to understand that spending the campaign traveling from town to town by himself or with one assistant would not get him elected. Despite early polls that placed Dies and Mann far in front of Johnson, the money and organization behind Johnson quickly changed the conditions of the race.[53]

Then, during the week of May 15, 1941, Pappy O'Daniel announced that he would run for the Senate seat. An ironic creation of the media in a state that was still overwhelmingly rural, O'Daniel had parlayed a career in the flour business into a role as the lead radio personality in Texas. Mastering the art of deception that mass media communications allowed before the 1960s and Watergate made the press and the public cynical about the pronouncements of any public figure, O'Daniel, a shrewd businessman, was by 1937 a millionaire. When he decided to run for governor that year, pundits treated his entry into state politics as a joke. O'Daniel had not paid his poll tax and so was ineligible to vote in his first race for the governorship. But with his understanding of rural people and the media, O'Daniel touched a chord with the Texas public. His first political rally in Waco was the largest ever seen in Texas. O'Daniel won the gubernatorial election without a runoff and was reelected by an even larger plurality in 1940.[54]

After O'Daniel's announcement, a fierce campaign ensued for the U.S. Senate seat. O'Daniel was a master of carnival campaigning, offering a stage show complete with hillbilly bands, theatrics, and sermon-like homilies that appealed to rural people. Johnson, who had previously scorned such tactics, now embraced them and organized his own theatrical revues, in effect seeking to "out-O'Daniel" the governor. Johnson had begun the campaign trying to look senatorial; he finished it as a showman and master political tactician in his effort to defeat the best campaigner in Texas political history.[55]

The chicanery that had prevailed throughout the campaign eventually determined the winner. Johnson and his supporters had worked to nullify efforts to adjourn the Texas state legislature, preventing O'Daniel from leaving Austin to campaign. The legislature remained in session for a month after O'Daniel announced for the seat. Ten days before the election, O'Daniel had still not been out on the campaign trail. Johnson's operatives also worked to convince O'Daniel's supporters that the governor could do them more good in Austin than in Washington, D.C. Both sides bought ballot boxes, a common practice in midcentury Texas—Johnson in San Antonio and South Texas, O'Daniel in the East Texas counties that had been Martin Dies's stronghold as long as he was a viable candidate. O'Daniel supporters, with the assistance of powerful opponents who wanted the governor out of Austin, arranged for the purchase of the votes in these counties; additional votes were reported; and in the end Johnson lost by 1,311 votes.[56]

The defeat must have been devastating to a man who saw his dreams so close, but Lyndon Johnson remained indefatigable. If the theft of the election made him more cynical, it also made him more determined. He retained his seat in the House, kept his close ties to the Roosevelt administration, and continued to maneuver for position when the next chance arrived. Johnson repaired the falling out he had had with Sam Rayburn, joined the military to fulfill a pledge he had made during the 1941 campaign, passed on the chance to run against Pappy O'Daniel for a full term in the Senate in 1942, moved away from the New Deal toward a brand of politics that the political powerbrokers of Texas could support, and waited impatiently for his next chance.[57]

It came in 1948, when Pappy O'Daniel decided to leave the Senate. O'Daniel's successor as governor, the popular Coke Stevenson, was positioned for a run for the seat; so was Johnson. A fierce, intense campaign followed, in which Johnson was the underdog to Stevenson after the primary, losing by seventy-two thousand votes. But a runoff between the two was necessary, as Stevenson failed to garner a majority of the vote. During the campaign, Johnson invented techniques that would become typical of the postwar era. He used any available technology to get his message out; he was the consummate modern politician, traveling by helicopter to as many as ten county seats each day and addressing dozens more towns from the air with a loudspeaker. Johnson also remanufactured his political stance, moving much closer to the center of the Democratic Party than to the New Deal wing that had supported him through the 1930s. He also engaged in characteristically tough campaigning, using his allies and keeping his opponent off guard. Johnson's antiunion and anticommunist fervor put Stevenson on the defensive and made the runoff that followed Stevenson's primary victory an extremely close race.[58]

The conclusion of the 1948 election remains shrouded in mystery and myth. Officially, Lyndon Johnson was elected U.S. senator by a margin of eighty-seven votes, earning him the derogatory sobriquet of "Landslide Lyndon." Those votes, delivered by South Texas political bosses, were probably fraudulent. It was clear that Johnson had learned from his experiences in 1941 that he could not depend upon an accurate accounting of votes. All of those who have written about Johnson agree that the decisive votes were stolen and that Johnson supporters held the seat through sheer political muscle at a specially convened meeting of the state Democratic Party. They disagree on the significance of the theft. Biographer Robert Caro portrays the election as a battle between good and evil, with Johnson as the corrupted opportunist and Stevenson as the true Texan, unsullied by modernity. This view, however, belies some of the more vicious aspects of Stevenson's personality: his racism, his isolationism, and his reactionary politics. Robert Dallek carefully outlines the vote augmentation of both camps. Even the sympathetic Paul Conkin agrees with the substance of the vote-stealing charges. Johnson's detractors of all political stripes have pointed to the story as evidence of the flaws they have detected in his character. J. Evetts Haley, a historian and reactionary who in 1964 published a skewed study, *A Texan Looks at Lyndon: A Study in Illegitimate Power,* foreshadows Caro's approach to the 1948 election; the liberal Ronnie Dugger, editor of the *Texas Observer* and a confidante of Johnson during the White House years, portrays Stevenson in a far more realistic manner but comes to similar conclusions about the election. "Possession is the first nine-tenths of the law," writes Dugger, "and politics is the tenth." It was political power and its exercise that brought Lyndon B. Johnson to the U.S. Senate.[59]

Reaching the Senate, Johnson, in his own mind, had finally arrived. The Senate was not the House of Representatives; Johnson was one of ninety-six rather than one of the multitudes in the House. No longer did he have to worry about ending up as an elevator operator, a fear he had expressed during his terms in Congress. In the years between 1941 and 1948, the Johnsons had become wealthy, the purchase and improvement of an Austin radio station, KTBC, contributing greatly to their economic success. Lyndon Johnson had reached the stature he had long sought.[60]

Johnson threw himself into his Senate career with the same energy that had characterized his first terms as a congressman. Within two years he became Senate whip, within four minority leader, and a mere six years after he was sworn in, Lyndon Johnson became majority leader of the U.S. Senate. This meteoric rise was made more significant by virtue of the seniority system in the Senate. Johnson's rise confounded many Senate watchers, for he successfully circumvented the hierarchy of the institution. By the early 1950s, Johnson was a recognized force in the Senate; he was an up-and-coming Democratic star.

At the same time as he rose to power, Johnson perfected his role as consummate insider. Senator Richard B. Russell of Georgia was the master of the Senate, and Johnson succeeded in rapidly developing a close relationship with him. Johnson also became very friendly with two other new members, Senator Robert Kerr of Oklahoma and Senator Clinton P. Anderson of New Mexico. Through Russell, he became tied to a group of approximately ten southern and western senators who provided much of the leadership and controlled most of the committees in the Senate. After he had entered this tight-knit group, the road to Senate leadership was cleared of obstacles.

Now wealthy, Johnson also sought the trappings of the office. Russell, Kerr, and Anderson were all wealthy men. Russell had a southern-style country estate. Kerr had a ranch, as did Senator Wayne Morse of Oregon and many other senators. By this time, the Johnsons had tired of Austin. The radio station did not require their day-to-day input, and when Alvin Wirtz died in 1951, there were fewer reasons for the Johnsons to live in town. Still possessed by memories of his youth and the stark beauty of the Hill Country and still driven by a need to prove himself to the flinty-hard people of his home region, Lyndon Johnson, with his wife, began to search for the right place, a "home" worthy of the man he had made himself.

This search had many implications for Johnson's life. It reflected the importance of the Hill Country to him, the significance of showing his success to the people of the place where generations of his family had failed. Johnson had exceeded the norms of Johnson City and the Hill Country; he had forged a life for himself and his family as he linked the Hill Country to the rest of the state by providing it with electricity and other necessities of twentieth-century life. By returning there to reside, Johnson meant both to locate himself in the place most important to him and to remind those who had denigrated his father, mother, and grandfather that Johnsons were and always had been people of substance. For Lyndon Baines Johnson, the pull of the Hill Country was complicated indeed, its draw uniting many variables in his life.

CHAPTER 2

Buying
the Family
Ranch

By the time Lyndon B. Johnson was sworn in as U.S. senator from Texas early in 1949, he had established a reputation as a seasoned, powerful, and astute politician. His reputation as a legendary fund-raiser was only enhanced by his victory. Johnson's campaigns were among the best financed in the nation. More than a decade in the U.S. House of Representatives; experience in the New Deal; and close relationships with the pinnacles of power, including individuals such as Sam Rayburn and Franklin D. Roosevelt, gave Johnson national influence that far exceeded that of a typical first-term senator. A political machine in Texas that included Herman and George Brown of the construction firm of Brown and Root, powerbrokers such as Alvin Wirtz, and after the 1948 election close ties with the political opera-

tives of the Rio Grande Valley made Johnson very much more than a political survivor. He had come a long way from the Hill Country, from his
experiences in San Marcos and Cotulla, but in his mind he still had a great
distance to travel.

At the swearing in, alongside fellow first-term senators and Democrats
J. Allen Frear of Delaware, Paul H. Douglas of Illinois, and Robert S. Kerr
of Oklahoma, Johnson intuited the need to find a place for himself in the
Senate, the elite club of ninety-six men that was the most exclusive governing body in the United States. Johnson had grappled his way to the Senate,
but success there was predicated on a different set of values and behaviors
than those of a campaign or in the House of Representatives. Entry into this
club of peers conferred a level of prestige that a seat in the House did not. Its
leaders had long tenure, seniority, and prestige based on term after term of
service. Johnson's ability to play the role of son, as he had first with Rayburn
and later with Roosevelt, seemed likely to serve him well in the Senate.

He had also entered the Senate as the result of a pivotal election, a
watershed of change in American society. The 1948 election was the first
post–World War II presidential election, the first to meld the practices and
assumptions of the past with the new realities of the postwar United States,
the first in sixteen years without the dominant political presence of Franklin
D. Roosevelt. It was a time of great change in American society, near the
beginning of a twenty-eight-year period of unparalleled economic prosperity, a time when Americans across social, class, and caste lines received
greater opportunities as their expectations rose. It was also an era of rapid
technological change, and keeping abreast of that change proved problematic in myriad ways. The 1948 presidential election became most memorable for the photograph of reelected president Harry S. Truman holding
aloft a copy of the *Chicago Tribune* with a headline mistakenly proclaiming
his defeat. Pollsters had used telephone books to poll voters and thus reach
their erroneous conclusion, wrongly assuming that everyone in the nation
subscribed to a telephone service. A significant portion of Truman's support came from a segment of the population that could not or did not use
the telephone.

In contrast to the newspaper's mistake, Johnson had used his understanding of the impact of technology to further his 1948 campaign for the
Senate. He devised sophisticated multiple statewide polling strategies that
were designed to detect issues to which voters would respond, and his polls
far exceeded in number and in depth the ones used by other candidates.

After being slowed by an operation to remove a kidney stone, Johnson resorted to campaigning by helicopter, another technological innovation, to get his message out in his campaign against former Texas governor Coke R. Stevenson. He clearly understood the key feature of postwar politics—the need to disseminate a candidate's message, image, and perspective quickly and widely—as well as a more sullied but crucial aspect of postwar politics, the negative campaign. Johnson made both part of his political repertoire.[1]

When he won the election by the slenderest and most contested of margins, Lyndon Johnson entered a political venue primed for change. The Senate class of 1948 was as different as the population that had elected it. Eighteen new senators took office, fourteen of whom were Democrats. Besides Johnson, a number of other new electees from across the country, including Kerr, Douglas, Hubert H. Humphrey of Minnesota, Estes Kefauver of Tennessee, Russell Long of Louisiana, and Clinton P. Anderson of New Mexico, arrived in the Senate chambers for the first time. Johnson regarded them both as peers and as competitors. The derogatory sobriquet "Landslide Lyndon," attached to him as a result of his eighty-seven-vote margin over Stevenson, separated him from other newcomers. He initially reveled in this, for it proved him a political competitor, a feature of his character of which he was particularly proud. Nor did he stand out in the Senate class of 1948 as the only incoming senator who had been accused of impropriety; the reactionary Robert Kerr of Oklahoma faced charges that he had exceeded the three thousand–dollar state limit on campaign spending by sixty-two thousand dollars. Despite the controversies surrounding Johnson, and to a lesser degree Kerr, the influx of new blood represented the changing experiences of the nation, the ascent of World War II veterans, and the passing of leadership from one generation to the next.[2]

The Senate retained its hierarchical features. Leadership in the chamber depended on the seniority for which senators strove, on a slow and steady rise through legions of individuals with more than two or sometimes even more than three terms of service. The Democratic majority had been solid since 1932. Many of its members had entered in the Franklin D. Roosevelt landslide that year and had grown up during the New Deal and the war. They prized their status and position and expected newcomers to wait in line for their turn at leadership.

Lyndon Johnson, however, had not run for the Senate to wait in line. He "took to the Senate as if he'd been born there," his aide Walter Jenkins remembered. "From the first day on it was obvious that it was *his* place—just the right size; he was at his best in small groups . . . with ninety-five others, he *knew* he could manage that." His political ties and experiences in the House gave him valuable seasoning and relationships that he put to use. He was appointed to the Armed Services Committee, chaired by Senator Richard Russell of Georgia, who was considered by many the most powerful man in the Senate and an individual who typified the kind of people with whom Johnson sought to develop firm relations. Described as "reserved, formal, conscientious, and gifted," Russell was, like Rayburn, a lonely bachelor. The Johnsons brought him into their family, now including two young daughters, who called the senator "Uncle Dick." As early as Thanksgiving 1949, Russell came to Texas to visit the Johnsons. Warm relations between the new senator and his powerful superior on the Armed Services Committee followed.[3]

During his early years in the Senate, Johnson had to serve two sometimes contradictory masters: the conservative and almost reactionary Texas electorate and the Senate club that could give him a major national reputation. With his characteristic aplomb, he negotiated this very fine line, appealing to the strident anticommunist and antilabor sentiment in Texas while positioning himself for the more centrist pose that leadership in the Senate required. The relationship with Russell helped him straddle the demands of his constituents and his personal aspirations of leadership.

Johnson's friendship with Russell revealed more than his characteristic need to ingratiate himself with older and more powerful men. It also reflected the new senator's desire to belong, and belonging in the Senate was no small accomplishment. The Senate was a politically diverse but socially conservative club. The men who made up its membership had come from all walks of life, and the combination of ambition and ego that had helped them reach their office and its accompanying privileges made the sociocultural standards of the chamber daunting. Most senators were wealthy men. Even in the 1940s, it took much money and support to reach the Senate. Personal and family fortunes as well as association with the leaders of powerful industries were usually the underpinning of successful senatorial campaigns. Unique in American politics for their remarkable longevity, senators celebrated a kind of inbred insularity.

The level of affluence in the Senate was particularly dramatic. Newcomer Robert Kerr was an extremely wealthy man, a member of the famous Kerr Oil Company family; Clinton P. Anderson had built an insurance empire in New Mexico. Older senators also had substantial assets. Many were descended from the makers of the great fortunes of the post–Civil War industrial expansion. Others relied upon more newly made wealth. Although not given to the displays of ostentatious wealth that have come to characterize American politics since the 1940s, members of the Senate wore their affluence openly and proudly. Many treated the office of senator as the accomplishment of a lifetime, a pinnacle of achievement that set senators apart from other elected officials.

The Johnsons' economic fortunes had improved during the 1940s. After Lyndon Johnson's political career stalled, he sought to alleviate the financial problems that had dogged his life. With money inherited from Lady Bird's father, the Johnsons purchased a radio station in Austin, KTBC, that had previously been limited by its frequency location at the crowded end of the radio dial and by the restrictions on its license, which forced it off the air at sunset. Using his connections in the federal bureaucracy, Johnson succeeded in having the restrictions lifted and the location of the station frequency moved to the opposite and opening end of the dial. The radio station became the beginning of an economic empire in mass communications that allowed Johnson to note in 1948 that his family was worth more than one million dollars.[4]

Among senators, this was an average fortune, but compared to men such as Kerr, Johnson was not really well-off. What made him exceptional in the "club" was his ability to work the organization—to meet and develop relationships with its leaders and to understand the roles necessary for rise in the Senate and be willing to play them. His cultivation of Richard Russell was archetypical. Russell was widely considered the most powerful person in the Senate. Of all the new senators who sought to curry favor with the Georgian, Johnson developed the closest relations and as a result acquired power more rapidly than any other newcomer. This trait—the ability to build power by working the members of the Senate—caught the eyes of the most astute observers there. One Senate colleague described Johnson as "an intensely ambitious man, anxious to get power and hold on to it, a rather curious mixture of pragmatism and idealism."[5] In this, Lyndon Johnson differed from other elected officials. He understood the intricacies of power and relationships in a way that most others did not and desired the rewards of their exercise far more than anyone else could. Much more than displaying the trappings of wealth, this was his way of belonging.

Johnson's understanding of power led to a meteoric rise in the Senate. In spite of the fact that his initial seat was in the back row of the Democratic side of the chamber, the customary position for newcomers, and in spite of the number of senators with greater experience ahead of him, Lyndon Johnson quickly rose to positions of leadership. He benefited from the Republican victories in 1950, which slashed the Democratic majority in the Senate from twelve to two. After the election, he became the Senate Whip—the assistant majority leader—a position that prior to his arrival had been largely ceremonial. Johnson turned this circumscribed position into a powerful one. His extraordinarily rapid rise to even the initially minor position of whip reflected his long-standing desire for power and his need to belong.[6]

The social trappings of the Senate required a kind of public pronouncement of stature to confirm membership. Ownership of land, preferably in the form of a country estate, was a preferred way to announce arrival. Johnson had first recognized the sociocultural importance of a country estate during visits to Charles Marsh's Longlea. There, as he mulled over an offer that could have made him a wealthy man, he could see the physical advantages that wealth gave. A place in the country was a great symbol of power, proof of the owner's ability to dictate terms to others. All who came to such a place arrived at the behest of the owner and in essence owed a favor for the visit. It was a social venue, one in which the owner could promote a budding relationship without giving away any of the power or control Johnson so craved.

All powerful people, it seemed to the still sometimes naive Johnson, had such retreats, places where their dominance was secure. His benefactors, Herman and George Brown, owned Huntland, where Johnson would be overcome by his heart attack in 1955. In the Senate, many important people had their own estates. Russell had a country estate in rural Georgia; Kerr, Anderson, Senator Everett Dirksen of Illinois, and Senator Wayne Morse of Oregon all owned large farms or ranches. In the halls of the Senate, they could put aside political differences and discuss their common avocation of owning property. Nor was the postwar generation bound to the hills of Maryland, Virginia, and the other central states of the East Coast that surrounded Washington, D.C., in the way their predecessors had been when they sought locations for their properties. With the advent of air travel, places far away could serve as more than out-of-session homes. Such retreats could become important parts of political images and, even

more significantly, of the kind of posturing that was an integral part of the
process of becoming powerful in the Senate. Such political maneuvering
was clearly within Johnson's capability. Full membership in the social side
of this elite club, Johnson believed, required a piece of land he could call
his own.[7]

For Lyndon Johnson, the selection of such a place reflected both the
pull of home as well as a way to conquer once and for all any remaining
insecurities about his place in his home town and in the Hill Country.
Beginning in 1948, he and Lady Bird searched for a country home to purchase near Stonewall or on the Pedernales River. Johnson wanted, suggests
biographer Paul Conkin, to be close to the land and people he knew and
revered.[8] His various residences in Washington, D.C., and Austin had never
really been homes in the most meaningful sense. For Johnson in particular, they had simply been stops on the way up the ladder—places of little
significance and meaning; places to rest, eat, sleep, and occasionally relax.

His desire to return to the Hill Country also reflected a strategy to overcome Johnson's insecurities about his past. Never a man to be humble
about success, Johnson had attained the opportunity to return in triumph
to the town where he had been raised, to a town that had been alternately
wonderful and hard to his family, a town that had seen his family's successes and problems. Lyndon Johnson had prevailed. He was a U.S. senator, one of only ninety-six individuals in the highest legislative body in the
land. No one, including his personal tormentors—the people who had
been pleased when the Johnson family experienced hard times—could say
that he was not a success. Returning to the Hill Country demonstrated
crucial truths Johnson sought to prove over and over again: that he was
worthy of his heritage and that it was not the successes of the Johnsons and
Buntons but their failures that were the true aberrations.

The ranch became the vehicle through which Johnson planned to gain
full status among his peers during his first term in the Senate. Besides
reflecting Johnson's need to be admitted into the club that made up the
core of Senate leadership, the ranch gave him pragmatic assets as well. The
other landed senators shared a bond that masked political and party differences, that gave them an avenue of discourse that transcended politics and
conferred a kind of equality upon their extrapolitical interactions. With
Russell, the most powerful man in the Senate, at their head, these landed
senators set the tone of debate in the early 1950s. Initially Johnson was
outside that immediate circle, but his close relationship with Russell gave

the younger man the opportunity to join this clique. Purchase of a ranch allowed Johnson to mimic the status of the senators he sought to emulate, in effect to pretend to be their equal despite his short term of service. It secured a place among these peers for this fiercely ambitious young senator.

In the Hill Country, a mere three-quarters of a mile from the dogtrot cabin where Johnson was born, the Martin place continued to deteriorate. Since 1909, it had belonged to Lyndon Johnson's Aunt Frank and Uncle Clarence Martin, Sam Ealy Johnson, Jr.'s sister and brother-in-law. Clarence Martin was a prominent Hill Country attorney when he and his wife purchased the house and he later became a judge. The largest dwelling owned by any member of the Johnson clan along the Pedernales River, the home was a center for family events. Lyndon Johnson recalled that some of the fondest memories of his youth were set in the Martin's stone-and-frame house. His emotional ties to the place were strong. When Johnson was a child, he and his extended family celebrated holidays and held summer family reunions there, and the young Johnson and his siblings were often called upon to declaim or recite poetry in front of the fireplace. At Christmas, relatives congregated around the house, the youngsters shooting off firecrackers and playing with Judge Martin's hunting dogs. Lyndon Johnson remembered the place as "the *big* house on the river." A year after he married Lady Bird in 1934, he brought her to the Martin place for a visit when he showed her the Hill Country on their return to Texas. It attested to the prominence of his clan. The house in the grove of trees set back from the Pedernales River had special resonance in his life.[9]

By the time the Johnsons next visited the property, in the fall of 1950, fifteen years that had changed their lives had passed. Johnson had become a congressman and then a U.S. senator, and the Johnsons were no longer the impecunious young people they had been in the 1930s. Many changes had also occurred along the Pedernales River. Clarence Martin died in 1936, followed in 1948 by his hard-living son, Tom Martin, Lyndon Johnson's benefactor during his interlude in California and later his political opponent after the younger Martin's return from the West in 1940. After her husband's death, Frank Martin continued to live in the house but had difficulty keeping it in good condition. By the time Lady Bird saw it in 1950, the once beautiful property, the "big rambling house on the Pedernales," seemed ramshackle and dilapidated. It had "gone down, down, down." To her, it had become "a Charles Addams cartoon of a haunted house." During this 1950 visit, when former senator and National Security Council Resources Board chairman Stuart Symington and his wife, Evie, accompanied the Johnsons, Lyndon Johnson suggested to his aunt that she move into Johnson City, where many of her friends resided and where she could easily reach a physician. Several weeks later, much to Lady Bird's shock, Lyndon Johnson exclaimed of the ranch: "Let's buy it!" Lady Bird Johnson later wrote that she should have known what her husband had planned.[10]

The transaction to acquire the property went smoothly, for any problems had been solved before Lyndon Johnson sought to purchase the ranch. Prior to Tom Martin's death in 1948, Aunt Frank Martin had deeded the land to him and her daughter-in-law, Lela Martin, in return for a life estate. After Tom Martin's death, his mother sought to regain full title to the property. Possibly at Lyndon Johnson's behest, she successfully challenged her daughter-in-law's claim, and this paved the way for the senator to gain the 240-acre ranch in exchange for a lifetime right to the Sam Johnson house in Johnson City and a $100-per-month stipend for the rest of the older woman's life.[11]

The Martin place was so dilapidated at the time of the purchase that it had only its setting facing the water as an advantage. Despite the beautiful view of the Pedernales, the property could not have produced sufficient income to support Aunt Frank. Without Lyndon Johnson's intervention, the property likely would have further deteriorated. Although people in the area suggested that Lyndon Johnson maneuvered his cousin-in-law out of the property, the end result seemed fair to everyone. Lela Martin apparently received compensation for the property; Aunt Frank Martin had long coveted the Johnson City house; and Johnson received the house on the river, the raw material from which to fashion a country estate.[12]

The property the Johnsons acquired had a typical Texas land history. The house was located on the headright claim of Rachael Means, a widow and a native of Georgia who was listed as a resident of the Sabine District in the first Texas census, completed between 1829 and 1836. She; her son William; his wife, Francis; and their two small children had made the long trek typical of early Texians, as they were then called, perhaps hoping to acquire some of the land that was advertised as free for the taking within the empresario grants given to men such as Moses Austin and Stephen F. Austin. William Means fought in the Texas Revolution, rising to the rank of colonel. He was assigned to guard the baggage at the camp opposite Harrisburg during the Battle of San Jacinto, the battle outside of modern Houston at which the Texians avenged the Alamo and the massacre at

Goliad, routed the Mexican army, and opened the way for their victory over Mexican president General Antonio López de Santa Anna. The Means's residence in Texas during the revolution qualified them for grants of patents of land from the Republic of Texas, and on April 30, 1845, Rachael Means was granted Survey Tract Number 6 on the Pedernales River, a section of approximately 4,605 acres. The illiterate Means made her mark with an *x* to convey power of attorney to her son to sign the land grant documents.[13]

The land she acquired was adjacent to a number of other claims that abutted the Pedernales River. Most of these had been land grants issued by the Mexican government during its brief tenure in Texas. Land grants in the Hill Country served as outposts, barriers against the *indios barbaros,* the Comanches and Kiowas who terrorized Spanish and Mexican Texas. The Spanish had used such grants and settlements in New Mexico against the Utes, Navajos, and Apaches, and the Mexican government had sought similar protection for its citizens in Central Texas. The residents of these grants, particularly north and west of San Antonio, were often magnets for raids by marauders, an effective by-product of a settlement strategy that was designed to use the residents to keep attackers away from major communities. The Texas Revolution transformed both the meaning and the legal standing of these grants, and by the 1840s they were in jeopardy as a result of the dramatic influx of Anglo-American settlers. The "Texas game"—the principle of governing by populating—obviated previous laws and customs and rapidly overwhelmed Spanish Texas. As Anglo-Texans pushed into the Hill Country, the precepts of their culture had already been institutionalized in the new republic.[14]

During the 1840s, Anglo-Texans pushed up the rivers into Comanche country in the Hill Country and western Texas, forcing a geographic extension of the confrontation between two proud and vain peoples, the resident Comanches and the incoming Anglo-Texans. Grants to citizens of the Republic helped create community in rural Texas and also provided a barrier and sometimes an inviting target for Comanche raiders. The homesteads along the Brazos, Trinity, and Little Colorado Rivers were crude. To European travelers, they seemed uncivilized, but the people who were willing to brave such conditions served an important function as they laid the basis for state institutions. Life was always hard for people who lived on this periphery.[15]

The Means family did not reside long on the Pedernales, and within a generation, the property passed to other hands. In 1872, Martha Means, one of Rachael Means's heirs, conveyed the right to sell the land to B. Marshall Odum of Austin, the son of Rachael Means's daughter Margaret Means Odum. On May 11, 1876, Odum sold the deed to a two-thirds interest in the Means property, Survey Tract Number 6 in Gillespie County, for $12,000 to C. C. Howell, who conferred it to George B. Zimpelman twelve days later for the same sum. With the purchase, Zimpelman appears to have concluded an arrangement that had begun some years before. In 1869, no taxes were paid on the land, but in 1870, six years before the deed to the property was transferred to him, Zimpelman began to pay taxes on 3,070 acres of the original Means grant, the two-thirds portion later transferred to him. Zimpelman continued to pay the taxes on the tract throughout the 1870s. Whether he resided on the land or even visited it remains unclear, but a new generation of owners had taken control. During his ownership of the property, Zimpelman, an Austin attorney, temporarily resided in Mexico, and he empowered his attorney and possible law partner, James V. Bergen, to handle his affairs. The transfer of land away from pioneer families was a by-product of the growth of Texas and of the hard lot of its subsistence livestock farmers in the Hill Country and elsewhere. Such transfers also negated the social goals that underlay the idea of land grants in Texas. Absentee ownership was not something the architects of the Texas Revolution expected.[16]

In the spring of 1882, the property again changed hands. Through Bergen, Zimpelman sold 650 acres to William Meier, who with his wife and four children had migrated from Germany to Texas. A generation after the initial Adelsverein—the German protective society begun in the 1840s that was sponsored by idealistic Prussian noblemen dedicated to founding a new fatherland in America—German surnames had come to predominate in the Hill Country. The Meiers appear to have been relatively late arrivals; at least one of their children was born in Germany in 1870, while the other three were native Texans, placing the arrival of the family thirty or more years after the first round of Germans embarked on their journey to the New World. The Meiers reached a settled world, for the so-called Indian menace had been subdued a decade before. But the fortunes of Hill Country people and their land had begun to decline in the early 1870s. By the 1880s, prosperity for most family economic units was a distant memory. The Meier family agreed to a purchase price of $1,950, payable in three installments of $650 during 1882–84, and settled their new property.[17]

As did most agricultural people of the time, the Meiers supplied the majority of their own needs. William Meier built a one-room log cabin for his family, and in the fall of 1882, the six Meiers moved in. They were typically poor rural people. The one-room home had no kitchen. Cooking took place in a skillet over an open fire behind the cabin, and one daughter remembered potatoes as the staple of the family diet. School was an infrequent luxury for the Meier family. Most days, the children worked in the cotton fields alongside their father.[18]

Like most family farmers in the last quarter of the nineteenth century, the Meiers made little economic headway. They lacked access to the transportation networks that could distribute what they grew, for railroads had not yet reached the Hill Country, and the prices for most crops continuously fell because of the increase in production that resulted from the mechanization of agriculture and the expansion of international agricultural trade. The Meiers were small-crop farmers, increasingly anachronistic on the American agricultural scene. The family acquired independence but little wealth during their first years in the Hill Country. So difficult was their situation that Meier was unable to pay Zimpelman in a timely manner. Only in 1890 did he secure a release of the lien from the previous owner after selling 300 acres of the farm in two separate transactions and producing the final $1,000 he owed on the land.[19]

By the early 1890s, the Meier family had begun to steady their economic situation. In 1894, William Meier—by then know as "Stinkanzer" or "Polecat" Meier because of an incident in which he brought home a stinking skunk that he thought was a kitten because of his lack of a sense of smell—granted a 50-acre plot to his daughter Ida Meier Degel and his son-in-law Wendelin and another plot to his son, William. At about the same time, Meier and his wife, Wilhelmina, contracted to have a stone house built on their property. Three local men constructed the house, which took a little more than a year to build, and it was ready for the wedding of the Meiers' youngest daughter, Clara, in January, 1896.[20]

By the turn of the century, the first generation of Meiers to live on the property could see that their time was short. They continued to divest themselves of their property, giving away all their land to their children but keeping a lifetime estate on the rock house. William Meier, Jr., purchased most of the land and bought out his sisters as a result of an agreement with his parents. Two years later, he agreed to pay his parents $200 per year for the duration of either of their lives as a belated consideration of the arrangement that transferred the farm to him. Within one year, he had paid his parents a lump sum of $800 and absolved himself of further obligation.[21]

The Meiers believed they owned the property free and clear, but the heirs of Rachael Means sought to contest this ownership. As in many other similar cases that involved the transition from Spanish, Mexican, or Texas Republic–era ownership, the plaintiffs contended that only a portion of the property had been sold, but subsequent owners had come to believe that they owned the entire tract instead of the two-thirds shown in the documents from the 1870s. A lawsuit was filed in Gillespie County court that challenged the rights of some of the owners of portions of Survey Tract Number 6, the Meier clan among them. In an extended legal fray, the Meiers and a number of other defendants were vindicated.[22]

This process of challenges to title was only unusual in this instance because the plaintiffs and defendants were Anglo-Americans. Throughout the Southwest, the change in jurisdiction from Spanish to Mexican to, in Texas, Texican and finally American systems of law created loopholes that often worked to divest prior owners of their land. Racial origin was a frequent consideration in what often seemed an organized legal process of confiscation. In California, the Gold Rush of 1849 served as a precursor to the divestiture of many old Californio families of their large Mexican-era grants; in New Mexico, the Mexican War led to a seventy-year period during which Spanish-speaking residents of the state lost much of their land in American courts, received little compensation, and found no legal remedies. In Texas, the experience of Juan Seguín—an important military figure in the Texas Revolution and later mayor of San Antonio, who along with other Tejanos was forced from his land and run out of Texas largely because of his Mexican heritage—illustrated the torturous transition and the difficulties inherent in it.[23]

Between the death of the elder Meiers and 1909, the property twice changed owners. In September, 1906, Charles Wagner, Jr., of Burnet County purchased the stone house, 350 acres of the property, and a range of farm implements, household equipment, and other goods for $8,500. Before he was to take possession of the farm on January 1, 1907, Wagner sold it to a Blanco County rancher, James G. Odiorne, for $8,300. Wagner's decision to sell so quickly suggests that financial or personal reverses had forced him to give up the property. Odiorne and his family moved to the property and lived there until early 1909, when Clarence Martin purchased the ranch, which was adjacent to his wife's parents' homeplace.[24]

With the Martins' purchase, the property ceased to have value simply for what its fields produced. Clarence Martin's extensive law practice and his later appointment as a judge provided the source of family income and prestige. Instead of being the home of poor and marginal farmers or even of more affluent ones, the property now belonged to people of means, the family of a prominent regional attorney. It acquired a kind of status, a condition that almost one-half a century later increased its attractiveness to Lyndon Johnson.

In 1909, the stone house appeared much as it had immediately after its construction in the 1890s. A frame addition to the north side had been added about 1900, making the Meier property one of the most impressive in the region, but the stone portion remained the defining structure on the property. Neighborhood dances and other social events were often held at the house, reflecting its social importance.[25] As befit the stature of an attorney and gentleman farmer such as Clarence Martin, the house he and his family acquired already had local significance.

In 1912, the Martins enlarged the house, adding a two-story frame wing connected to the rock house by a front porch and central rooms. This more than doubled the floor space in the home, allowing the Martins to have a music room and a parlor. It also helped make the home the center of family activities on the Pedernales, the place where the young Lyndon Johnson, his parents, and many of their relatives in the Pedernales Valley congregated.[26] The great fireplace and raised hearth that fronted it gave the front room a type of grandeur that was unparalleled in the typically more modest homes along the Pedernales River. For Lyndon Johnson, this particular room was the scene of many family events he later remembered with great fondness.

From 1909 until the middle of the 1930s, the ranch house was home to a prosperous Hill Country family. Clarence Martin served as a judge, and members of the Johnson clan continued to reside in the immediate vicinity of the house. When Lyndon Johnson brought his new bride to the Martin place in 1934, he was following what had become family tradition: he was taking Lady Bird to the nicest, most genteel place within the extended familial network of Johnsons in the Hill Country, the best location from which to show off the Hill Country and his extended family's prominent position in it. Looking out at the river from the well-appointed house of that era must have confirmed the impression that Lyndon Johnson always sought to put forward: the Johnsons were people of substance.

After Clarence Martin's death in 1936, however, the Martin place began to decline. Alone, Johnson's now-widowed Aunt Frank, more than sixty-five years old, could not properly maintain the house and its surroundings. Throughout the late 1930s and the first half of the 1940s, she had a difficult time finding able farmhands. Even after Tom and Lela Martin, her son and daughter-in-law, returned to the Hill Country in 1940, the situation did not improve. Tom Martin had been a heavy drinker most of his life and remained unable to oversee activities at the property effectively. The work was too physically strenuous for Frank Johnson. Income from her fields and pecan orchards declined, and she could not undertake the repairs necessary to maintain the property. Hired help came and went, working mostly ineffectually and without supervision. After fourteen years without close and able management, the once stately place had become rundown and ramshackle.[27] Under the circumstances, Lady Bird Johnson's reaction to the house in 1950 was probably generous.

To those close to Johnson, his purchase of the ranch seemed an unusual choice for a man as driven by politics as he. The property was isolated, and communications to it could be tenuous. Johnson would not have ready access to information at his new home, and from it he could not easily and quickly get to the seats of power where he could work his political magic. Just months before attorney, political powerbroker, and Johnson political mentor Alvin Wirtz died of a heart attack at the University of Texas–Rice University football game, he told the young senator, "Lyndon, I wouldn't fool with that old house." Hearing of the purchase, Speaker of the House Sam Rayburn remarked, "Now he'll have something to talk about besides Congress."[28] To those who understood his seemingly insatiable urge to engage himself in the person-to-person persuasion of politics, the choice of the Stonewall ranch as the location for a permanent home did seem unusual.

But the ranch had political and personal meaning for Senator Johnson. Wealthy Texans always had ranch property, and in the Senate owning an estate was always an asset. As Johnson emerged as a force in the Senate, the ranch served as a combination of confidence builder and calling card that helped him announce his arrival. In his mind, it pushed him toward peer status with the more powerful members of the Senate, with whom he sought relations. Johnson recognized the ranch as a political asset as well as a piece of his personal heritage. For the newcomer, his ownership of the property mirrored the established status of men two terms his senior. At a very young age he shared not only the political office of such veterans as Russell but also the trappings of these older, more established individuals. For the junior senator from Texas, the ranch was a major step in making the transition from the subservient, obsequious, and sometimes sycophantic role of professional son to that of peer.[29]

The ranch also provided Johnson with a place to "recharge his batteries," as Lady Bird Johnson became fond of saying. Lyndon Johnson had begun to experience health problems, usually associated with dramatic campaigns. In his first run for the House in 1936, he entered the hospital on election eve with an appendix that nearly burst. He began his successful Senate campaign in 1948 with a severe kidney stone. Johnson almost left the race because of the malady, but a trip to the Mayo Clinic in Minnesota allowed a difficult removal of the stone. Even in doubled-over pain, Johnson debated the political cost of leaving the state for medical treatment; he did not want even the slightest implication that Texas doctors were not sufficiently competent to treat the condition. Nor was Johnson a man who took good care of himself. He smoked too much, regularly enjoyed alcohol, ate erratically, and pushed himself beyond any reasonable limit. Johnson simply did not like to rest. By the early 1950s, and particularly after the unexpected death of Wirtz in 1951, Johnson had begun to worry about the relatively short life spans of the men in his family. The ranch gave him an environment where he could decompress, where he could rest without feeling that he needed to take political action somehow and somewhere. Instead, from the time of his purchase of the property, he immersed himself in the details of the ranch, learning every aspect of ranching and ranch management. At the ranch he found solace and peace, commodities in increasingly short supply as he advanced in the world of politics.[30]

The ranch also provided an important link between his past and his aspirations. Johnson had grown up, if not on the ranch, in its immediate environs. He knew the people of that region personally and well, and they knew him—his precociousness, his bluster, and his failings as well as his many positive traits. Johnson had been humiliated by his father's economic demise, by the disregard with which the Johnson family had been treated in the aftermath of the collapse of the family cotton enterprise in the early 1920s. Seeing himself as important almost since birth, he could not stand the loss of stature that accompanied the Johnsons' fall from economic prosperity. As Lyndon Johnson's father became the target of pity and sometimes cruel mockery, the younger man's resolve to prove the family's tormentors wrong must have grown. For as proud a man as Johnson, the purchase of the ranch after his election as U.S. senator served as vindication of the family's presence in the Hill Country.

The ranch also reflected beliefs very close to Johnson's heart. He did believe, as he told his Mexican-American students in the dusty town of Cotulla, that in America people could rise on their merits. His purchase of the ranch and the cleansing of the stain on his family heritage were in his own view surely proof of that belief, demonstrable evidence that people could rehabilitate themselves and their families by a combination of will, work, and intelligence. The ranch was a symbol; proof of the rewards of perseverance; testimony to the fact that if someone worked long enough and hard enough, he or she could put the miseries of the past permanently behind them and reach new heights. This view was a forerunner of the perspective that would later become national policy in Johnson's Great Society programs.

The purchase of the ranch also signaled a homecoming for Johnson, a return to the place in the world that had the most meaning to him. Lyndon Johnson above all was a man of the Texas Hill Country. That place and its vagaries, its erratic rainfall, its poor soil, and its tight-knit sense of community shaped him—made him perhaps not into a form so hard and distinct that nothing could change it, as Robert Caro argues, but shaped him nonetheless. Coming home to the old Martin place, ever after the LBJ Ranch, the old stone house that held bright and warm memories for Johnson, was an expression of the importance of place to Americans. The country along the Pedernales River was Lyndon Johnson's homeplace; when he bought his ranch there, he articulated a kind of rootedness that seemed at odds with the mobility of the United States in the aftermath of World War II.

His letters about the Hill Country reflect that sense of rootedness. Late in the 1950s, Johnson wrote his mother from Washington, D.C., that he "long[ed] to be back in the Hill Country where there is good sunshine. I want to be roaming up and down the river with my beagle dog as I did when I was a boy." This combination of nostalgia, of a feeling of belonging, and of the widely held sense that his physical health had improved because of his purchase of the ranch demonstrated that in Johnson's own mind at least, he had truly come home.[31]

The purchase of the ranch gave Johnson one more piece of the many he believed he needed to make a run for national power. In his own view, it defined him as a national leader, providing the trappings with which to surround ambition, the roots from which to sell himself and his views to the larger world. First in the Senate and later to the public as a whole, Johnson would have to present himself as a fully rounded person with all the attributes necessary to manage the many responsibilities that accompanied leadership. The ranch enhanced Johnson's belief that he possessed those qualities. His ownership of the property served to begin to erase whatever fears of failure he had internalized from his family's experience. Buying the ranch made Lyndon Baines Johnson whole in a manner that no other single material acquisition or accomplishment ever did. The distance to leadership and power was considerably shorter after the purchase than it had ever been before.

CHAPTER 3

The Senate Years

Creating a

Mythic Place

from an

Actual One,

1951–60

The LBJ Ranch, as the Martin place soon became known, rapidly assumed genuine significance in the life of Lyndon B. Johnson. Besides providing him with a place to rest and clear his head, the ranch symbolized Johnson's aspirations and became the place he used to hone his political image. Possessed of an all-too-typical American family history of dreams linked to subsequent difficulty, Johnson departed for the U.S. Senate with a self-imposed stigma equal in size to his immense pride. The purchase and renovation of the ranch were important steps that served to erase the shortcomings of his upbringing in relationship to what he and the rest of the nation perceived as the background of most other senators. Inordinately adept at defining himself as what he believed the public wanted him to be and sophisticated at managing his image, Johnson believed he could become what he owned and could make what he owned into what he wanted to be.

The ranch had immense political potential as well. On the ranch in his home Texas Hill Country, Johnson managed a feat that bordered on the impossible for most American politicians: he reinvented himself in the space of a few short years. Johnson used the symbolism of the ranch to remake his political image into one so malleable that he could employ its different and ofttimes contradictory facets without even a hint of overlap. Under the guise of gentleman rancher in the Senate, he transformed himself from Texas politico to national leader, from man of a region to man of the nation, tied to the mythical iconography of the self-made man that the Western films of the time so dramatically represented.

Johnson's rise to national power coincided with the postwar moment, when "western" came to mean national in character. As Johnson emerged on the scene, the nation was undergoing a transformation in its values, with the West coming to be seen as the site of its creation myth, a status reflected in film and culture. From *Red River* in 1945 to *How the West Was Won* in 1962, the Western harbored national fears and aspirations. In the postwar climate, the Western disguised and replayed social, cultural, political, and other tensions, making some problems palatable and solving others in different contexts. Not only did this make the Western popular, it enhanced the meaning of western expansion as a part of the national consciousness. The American West became a parable for American society, the challenge that Americans faced in the past that offered ways to face, address, and solve new tensions in the present. Americans could return to their *sipapu,* their point of mythic origin, to find the tools and the strength to face the confounding tensions of the modern world. At the same time, the inexorable shift that led John F. Kennedy to be the last American president to claim northeastern origins for more than forty years began. Population, then momentum, then national culture shifted westward—to the Sunbelt, to states such as Texas and California. A new American power—based in the baking sun and not in the cold, wet Northeast—emerged. Johnson was its prototype, his ranch its emblem.

In this, Johnson plugged into a nostalgia for an older America, lost to the post-1945 world but characteristic of the American sense of self. Westernness, as embodied in the LBJ Ranch, connoted authenticity, self-reliance, and frontier spirit in an age before the nation treated such topics with cynical scorn. Johnson announced himself as an American myth in a changing society, a man who came from the region to which the nation aspired. It was a deft trick, melding the country-gentleman style of Senator Richard Russell and others with an announcement of national status that emanated from Johnson's tall Stetson hat. Here was an American truth, Johnson's ranch claimed, a reality more real than the overcoats and top hats of the Northeast. Americans embraced this idea as a rock in a changing society, melding it with the need for continuity best expressed in the everyday emphasis on business that characterized the 1950s.

Over time, the ranch served an even more important function. It allowed Johnson to remake himself from Southerner to Westerner, from a man of the old and, by the middle of the 1950s, seemingly decadent and atavistic South to a representative of the West, a region aglow with new development in the post–World War II era. This gave him an crucial asset in his reach for national prominence. In American iconography, the image of the South as a failed aristocracy was sectional; nationwide, the South retained its reputation as the most backward part of the nation, the most resistant to change and the most out of step with postwar realities. As the Dixiecrat third-party effort of 1948 demonstrated, the South firmly placed region ahead of nation and states' rights ahead of national interests in what had become an era of national goals. The southernness that had gotten Johnson elected in Texas became less useful as he became more established in Washington, D.C. He needed it to get into the inner circles of the Senate, for leadership remained a southern club, but its significance ended there. A southern image, while vital to a place in the club that Johnson strove so hard to join, was of increasingly marginal use on the national stage. As he became a leader in the Senate during the first half of the 1950s, Johnson gradually replaced his southernness with westernness, adding the so-called freedom, honor, and dignity of purported western individualism to his repertoire of imagery. A cynical student of Johnson might note that he assumed the traits widely attributed to Coke Stevenson, his opponent in the 1948 Senate race, both at the time and by subsequent biographers. The self-portrait of Johnson as a mythic "True Texan" became possible in no small part because of the ranch and its connotations.[1]

This transformation was crucial to Johnson's development as a national political leader. As Johnson became first a lukewarm and later an unabashed advocate of civil rights for African Americans, he distanced himself from the South and its leaders. To do so required that he transform his image and the meaning of his ranch from what noted historian William E.

Leuchtenberg has called the "taint of magnolia" to a new "horse-riding, gun-toting, shootin' 'n' huntin' Lyndon Johnson of the Hill Country."[2] This was a dangerous step for a politician from Texas, a state that considered itself heir to both regional traditions.

Texans have always had it both ways when it came to regional identity, but none so much so as Lyndon Johnson. They have been southerners when it suited their purposes and westerners when expedient, managing this convenient bifurcation well into the post-Vietnam era. The eight-hundred-mile wide state includes several geographies and topographies and many kinds of economic and cultural regimes. It supports both southern-style humid-climate economic practices such as cotton growing, which began in the piney woods of East Texas and reached as far west as the Balcones Escarpment in Central Texas, as well as the grazing economy that dominates the sparsely populated, dry plains of West Texas, the famed Llano Estacado of ranching lore. The trick for Texas politicians with national aspirations has always been to balance the demands of both western and southern constituencies by subtle manipulation of the differing symbols of each culture. Before Johnson, no Texas politician succeeded at this except the intractable John Nance "Cactus Jack" Garner, who spent thirty years in the House of Representatives and two years as its speaker before becoming Franklin D. Roosevelt's vice president in 1933. Garner combined the traits of successful Texas politicians: longevity and archetypical Texas xenophobia. He played on the electorate's pervasive sense that the state had been treated badly since the end of the Civil War in order to reach national office. Garner, however, was a rare commodity. Most other Texas politicians either fell squarely in one camp or the other, like the decidedly western and self-limiting Stevenson, or were too idiosyncratic for a national position, like Governor James Hogg.[3]

Early twentieth-century Texans often eschewed national political leadership, feeling it morally inferior to power in the state on nationalistic and ideological grounds. Texans often saw their state as a nation, considering themselves Texans first and Americans second. They pointed to their decade as a republic and to the "choice" of their leaders to join the Union, and they reveled in their mythology of individualism and independence. If they manipulated their past to serve their ideological purposes, they were no different than residents of California or New York, extolling virtues, ignoring shortcomings, and shaping place-born myth. Texans became exceptional only in their xenophobia, in their deeply held conviction that anything Texan was better simply by virtue of its place of origin. As devotees of the doctrine of states' rights, the people of Texas were sure to elect only those who saw state leadership as more significant than a role in Washington. Before 1920, no self-respecting Texan would have traded a prominent role in Austin for one in Washington, D.C.; few even had the chance, and anyone who sought such a chance might be suspect except in the most extreme circumstances.[4]

The rise of Sam Rayburn and the ascendance of long-serving Texas congressmen and senators to congressional leadership in the Democratic landslide of 1932, however, inaugurated a new attitude among state politicians. As Democrats with many years of service in Congress, Texas representatives were the greatest beneficiaries of the Roosevelt ascendance. Garner became vice president, and Texas congressmen assumed the leadership of a number of committees important to the state. Another Texas magnate, Houstonian Jesse H. Jones, rose during the New Deal to become Secretary of Commerce in 1940. As they experienced the largesse that the New Deal provided through the various committees controlled by Texans, state politicians and their electorate began to reconsider the significance of service in Washington, D.C. As Texas's representatives in the nation's capital brought home projects that were financed through means that taxed other states more heavily than Texas, the value of national service in the formulaic understanding of Texas politicians increased.[5]

By the 1950s, Texas was the most powerful state in Congress. With Sam Rayburn as Speaker of the House, Lyndon Johnson on the rise in the Senate, and Dwight D. Eisenhower—born in Texas, raised in Kansas, and retaining an affinity for the Lone Star state—in the White House, Texas was well represented in the distribution of federal largesse. As Johnson grew more powerful, ascending through the positions of leadership in the Senate, the power of the state grew and reached an apex. D. B. Hardeman, Rayburn's principal aide, called the decade from 1951 to 1961 "the peak of Texas influence in Washington, D.C."[6]

But Texas politicians with national aspirations still had to serve two distinctly different and often antithetical constituencies. Politics within the state continued to require an antigovernment, know-nothing stance to assure success at the ballot box; anything else made initial election difficult and reelection nearly impossible. But after the beginning of the New Deal, the pose that enticed Texas voters severely limited a winning candidate once in Washington, D.C. Texas conservatism was different from forms of conservatism elsewhere in the nation. Even the rare moments of Texas liberalism were politically different, bordering more on libertarianism than on any mainstream form of the liberal thinking of the era. Successfully negotiating the national/Texas dichotomy and framing the attitudes of the state in a manner palatable to a national audience remained primary considerations for Texas politicians who sought roles of national leadership.

Lyndon Johnson developed the most successful strategy for this balancing act. Described by his many biographers as a man with malleable principles—as a liberal nationalist; as a sometime conservative; as a sometime liberal—Johnson emerged as a political chameleon who could manipulate his image in a manner more typical of the 1980s than of the 1940s and 1950s. He clearly intuited the ways in which to develop ties to powerful government and private-sector interests. He understood how to make himself useful to anyone with great power or influence. He also had great currency with ordinary people, the "plain folk" who made up the Texas electorate. He defeated the first of the great mass-media-age Texas politicians, Pappy O'Daniel, in the 1941 Senate race before O'Daniel could steal the election from him; in an even more fierce campaign and election, he probably took the 1948 Senate election away from Stevenson, a pre-electronic media politician considered the greatest Texas campaigner of all time. Johnson understood and sympathized with common people and delivered the perquisite power his position provided to them as well as to the rich and powerful. This ability to simultaneously serve different masters while appearing to maintain political independence set him apart from more typical midcentury politicians in Texas and in the nation at large.[7]

The value of the ranch as a symbol could not have been readily apparent when the Johnsons returned to Stonewall to look at their purchase late in 1951. Lady Bird's haunted-house description seemed even more appropriate than it had in 1950; nearly two more years of limited maintenance had made the already dismal condition of the property even worse. Although the Johnsons had acquired the property on March 5, 1951, their plans to renovate it were delayed by the Korean Conflict, which kept Johnson, as a member of the Senate Armed Forces Committee, busy. At the end of October, almost eight months after the purchase was finalized, the Johnsons arrived at the ranch and began to assess its future. The conditions they saw would require an ongoing stream of expenditures.[8]

The arrival of Senator and Mrs. Johnson in the Hill Country gave the region a rare commodity: a homegrown celebrity to pair with Admiral

Chester A. Nimitz of nearby Fredericksburg, Texas. As in many small towns and rural regions, local news was regarded with far greater importance than all but national events of the utmost gravity. When the Johnsons finally arrived at their new home, local reporters Art and Elise Kowert, owners of the weekly *Fredericksburg Standard,* dropped by for an extended interview. In it, Johnson revealed a complicated plan for the ranch that articulated goals of status and community and hinted at his potential national leadership.[9]

In keeping with the image he was in the midst of creating, Johnson took responsibility for the ranching and farm operations. As a young man, Johnson had done some agricultural work on his father's various enterprises, but hoeing cotton had never been something he enjoyed.[10] The ranch, however, was different. Because ranching was the mythic Texas profession, the fodder of regional lore, it held special status. Owning a large tract of land signified arrival not only in Texas but in most of the nation. Despite its 245.82-acre size, which made it a small spread by Texas standards, Johnson's ranch permitted him to appear as a member of the landed gentry and attached an importance even to manual tasks such as fixing fences that agricultural field labor never enjoyed.[11]

Ranch work also strengthened the ties between Johnson and his Hill Country neighbors. By discussing his need to fix fences with the Kowerts, he took a step toward belonging in his old community. He also discussed technical needs and planned improvements with C. A. Stone, the Gillespie County agricultural agent; Stone too had to keep his fences in shape, had to worry about early frost, had to rely on neighbors for advice. The house the Johnsons had purchased was close enough to the original family homestead and graveyard that Johnson could make the case that he had come home. This was no dalliance, his demeanor and attitude in the interview seemed to say. He was home, near to the land his family had cultivated, near to where his ancestors were buried.[12]

The ranch helped him to heal any remaining old wounds and to return home not only as a success but as one of the community. The Johnsons had been the most proud—and in some ways the most arrogant—of the people of the Hill Country. To their neighbors, they seemed unable to accept the limits of the region and its communities, unable to live within the bounds created by harsh environmental conditions and limited available technologies. The Johnsons strove for more; that they succeeded and failed with equal frequency cast aspersions on their character. But ownership of the ranch property, as one of two leading political officials who represented the state, created an aura that Johnson craved. His roots and experiences in the Hill Country drove him to need local affirmation, a commodity the ranch could provide.

Johnson's plans for the LBJ Ranch were impressive by the standards of the region. In November, 1951, he had seventy-five acres planted in winter wheat and another twenty-five in clover. He expected to break and seed another one hundred acres in clover before winter. He had recently purchased twenty-five head of Delaine sheep from a Johnson City man and planned to add thirty head of cattle in the near future. Peach trees to complement the existing pecan trees were also on the agenda for the ranch.[13]

The ranch had more symbolic than economic value in the early 1950s. The Johnsons made their money in media, and radio and television stations remained the primary source of their income. The ranch was, in the words of biographer Paul Conkin, "an indulgence . . . open only to people of wealth."[14] It had been purchased to furnish an image as well as to allow Johnson to return to his home country as a success. As an economic endeavor, the ranch was a poor substitute for other Johnson ventures. The return on ranching enterprises was so meager that a spread many times larger than the acreage on the Pedernales River would not produce enough to support a family.[14] But owning the ranch property did make Johnson one of the people of the Hill Country, affording him the country home so crucial to his view of the accouterments of successful national politicians. The value of the image of the ranch far exceeded any monetary benefit for the Johnsons.

Johnson kept a close eye on his ranch even from Washington, D.C. A. W. Moursand, his close friend, regularly wrote to keep Johnson abreast of affairs at the ranch. Mundane details of such things as cattle branding, the hiring of handymen for outlying properties, weather reports, and similar matters were staples of their correspondence. Although loath to make decisions about personnel changes from far away, Johnson made his wishes clear. Always a hands-on manager, whether in politics or in his personal affairs, he ran his ranch from afar. "I am not completely happy with everything that goes on and has gone on at the farm," he responded to Moursand in 1954, with a telling description of the property, but he indicated that changes would have to wait until he was again in residence.[15]

At least for the *Fredericksburg Standard* article, Lady Bird was designated "chief" of the house and grounds. This aspect of the renovation of the property was far more daunting than transforming the land into a working ranch. The house and the grounds were in horrible condition. Electrical wiring was exposed, the roof continuously leaked during rainstorms, and planking on the upstairs porch was rotten. A simple and battered picket fence surrounded the house, and vestiges of the days before indoor plumbing, including a boxed-in well beyond the southwest corner of the fence, remained.[16] The house and the grounds clearly required major renovation and ongoing care.

Lady Bird's initial efforts involved the grounds. Early in November, she and an Austin landscape architect marked for removal trees from the live oak and pecan grove between the house and the river. A tree surgeon arrived to take out the dead limbs. Grapevines came out, and consistent upkeep of the property began. The front lawn was seeded with Saint Augustine and carpet grass, and a fountain in the middle of the yard was removed because it no longer functioned. A new approach road to the house was laid out. Lady Bird ordered the plaster removed from the exterior walls of the building to reveal the limestone underneath. Through his attorney, Everett Looney of Austin, a long-time associate, Johnson secured water rights to impound two hundred acre-feet of water each year to irrigate his acreage and had a dam built to create a small swimming hole. Located in front of the house, the swimming hole also provided a lakelike view from the porch, another of the amenities that Johnson sought. The Johnsons had a raft built and moored with chains in deep water. The first steps in redeveloping the property had begun in earnest.[17]

The house itself was a much bigger and longer-term problem. It clearly required daily care and a hands-on presence. Everything about the old Martin place revealed fifteen years of declining maintenance. Little had been done to the buildings since the 1920s, when the state of the art in facilities was decidedly different than it was during the 1950s. Although the Martins had installed the best available plumbing and fixtures for their day, by the early 1950s these were quaint anachronisms; many years later, Lady Bird Johnson wished she had kept the old claw-foot bathtubs and pull-chain commodes that had been in the house before the renovation. Although Lyndon Johnson typically wanted everything accomplished immediately, he had to return to Washington, D.C., when Congress reopened session in January, 1952. The renovation of the house was "put on the back burner," Mrs. Johnson recalled.[18]

The transformation of the property proceeded after Lady Bird's relocation to the Hill Country in February, 1952. Along with the two Johnson daughters—Lynda, then eight, and Lucy (later Luci), about five—she came, as she said, "pretty reluctantly."[19] In a reprise of Rebekah Baines Johnson's experience in almost the same place forty years before, she was alone in her husband's homeplace. By the 1950s, there were many fewer Johnson relatives along the Pedernales. Perhaps the lack of nearby relatives was a blessing; the Johnson clan and its coarse behavior had been a source of consternation for Johnson's genteel mother. Lady Bird had other reasons to be unsure about the move. She loved her house in Washington, D.C., and had not even completed its redecoration. As always, however, she made do. Without her husband, Lady Bird threw herself into the renovation of the property.[20]

The catalyst for the house renovation was the hiring of architect Max Brooks of the Austin firm of Kuehne, Brooks, and Barr. Brooks brought in an associate architect from his company, a young man named J. Roy White, who became a close and valued friend of the Johnsons and the primary architect for all of the work on the house and grounds in the course of the subsequent thirty years. White was the firm's period-detailing expert, specializing in mantels, porches, cabinets, and similar features. Lady Bird Johnson described White as "one of my life-long best friends," a tribute from one with as many close friends as she, and he served the Johnsons for the remainder of his life.[21]

When White arrived, the house "had never seen an architect," Lady Bird Johnson remembered. Built by local country people, it had been designed in what has been deemed the vernacular American style. Made of indigenous materials and conceived on a different scale than the Johnsons required, additions had been built throughout the first half of the twentieth century in the haphazard way of rural America. Its rooms were more functional than aesthetic, and they were decorated in a dated but typical rural manner. The living room was "dark and not inviting," in Mrs. Johnson's estimation, with panel wainscoting, "putty-colored" walls, and dark oak beams. She suggested as a way to begin that they rip off the wainscoting and paint the room—beams, ceiling, and walls—white. This would remove the gloominess she felt in the room and serve as a prelude to full-scale renovation.[22]

From February until July, 1952, the house underwent comprehensive renovation. Every room was redone. Walls and partitions were added, floors and floorboards replaced with oak, and brick repointed and replaced. Bathrooms were added and redone, closets were built into bedrooms, and the porches were restored. Marcus Burg, a Stonewall builder, took over the work after another contractor abandoned the project, and with his foreman, Lawrence Klein—a native of the Pedernales Valley who had once been a student at the Junction School—in control of day-to-day affairs, the work proceeded. Klein was familiar with the property, for he had undertaken a number of maintenance projects at the house after Clarence Martin's death. As the lead on-site person, he managed the project to completion.[23]

On July 12, 1952, the Johnsons moved into the refurbished house. The family did not own enough furniture to fill their new house, so Lady Bird Johnson purchased an entire household of furniture from an elderly woman in Washington, D.C., and had it shipped to the ranch. The house glistened from the renovation; its floors sparkled with fresh varnish, the walls shone with fresh paint, and the outside porches no longer sagged. With "cattle grazing in front and the pretty green fields in the background," the ranch presented "quite a picturesque scene," Josepha Johnson wrote her brother. The two Johnson daughters, Lynda and Luci, soon learned to swim in the river their father had dammed. The old Martin place had become every inch the house of a U.S. senator, exuding power and importance. Only its location tied it to the people and experiences of the Pedernales Valley. In August of 1952, Lyndon Johnson marked the property as his own. In the wet cement of a walkway near the south gate, he took a sharp stick and wrote, "Welcome to the LBJ Ranch."[24]

With the completion of the renovation of the house, Lyndon Johnson had defied the axiom of American author Thomas Wolfe and returned home. Except in geographic terms, that home was not the place it had been. Instead it was an image, a sense of self that Johnson carefully crafted. Mobility had characterized the first fifteen years of his political career. The Johnsons had lived in apartments and houses in Austin and Washington, D.C., bouncing among them with regularity. They were all transitory places—certainly to Lyndon Johnson and in all likelihood equally so to his wife, who had to set up her home time and time again and endured the brunt of the frequent moves. The purchase of the property along the Pedernales River ended this motion for the Johnsons. All other addresses, including 1600 Pennsylvania Avenue, would be temporary by contrast.

Although Lyndon and Lady Bird Johnson had both grown up in small rural towns, the return to country life was different for them. For most of the preceding twenty years, they had lived in Washington, D.C., or in Austin, where conveniences were close at hand and they were surrounded by people. Friends, political acquaintances, and business associates could reach them in an instant. Early in his Washington, D.C., career, Lyndon Johnson was notorious for bringing home dinner guests without informing his wife. The ranch was different; it was quiet and remote, and any activity that occurred had to be generated by the Johnsons. Something as simple as a loaf of bread required a round trip of more than twenty miles, and the only connection to the outside world besides the road was the telephone. The pace of life was decidedly slower, and in the manner of rural people, when visitors came they stayed much longer than their urban counterparts. The rhythms of the ranch were different, and for the Johnsons, the new residence required adjustment. Certainly Lady Bird in particular must have experienced moments of loneliness, particularly during Lyndon's frequent absences.

There were also natural hazards with which to contend along a remote river. On September 11, 1952, hard rain pelted the Hill Country, continuing through the night and into the next day. Lyndon Johnson was scheduled to deliver speeches in the Rio Grande Valley and San Antonio, and because Lady Bird was not well, Mary Rather, one of the staffers, was sent to the ranch. Rather drove Johnson to his commercial flight in San Antonio on the morning of September 12. On her return, she found she could not cross the high waters of the Pedernales River to reach the ranch. She returned to Fredericksburg and tried to cross a bridge there, but it too was closed. Floodwaters isolated the ranch.

Lady Bird and her daughter Luci were by themselves at the ranch. Eight-year-old Lynda had gone to school on the bus that morning, and Luci was delighted to be alone with her mother. She soon sensed that her mother was concerned by the rain and the rising river. When the telephone went out, the worry became apparent. The water crept up through the grove below the house and began to cross the road about fifty feet from the house; Lady Bird spoke of saddling a horse and riding to higher ground. Soon "Cousin Oriole" Bailey, who lived nearby, came sloshing through calf-deep water in her boots. Other neighbors seeking shelter followed. The Johnsons' house was at a higher elevation than those of most of their neighbors. By the time Lady Bird Johnson served everyone tomato soup and cheese sandwiches in the afternoon, the flood had begun to crest. Late in the afternoon, Lyndon Johnson returned. He flew from San Antonio to the nearby Wesley West ranch, and a light plane took him to the LBJ Ranch, landing in an open stretch of field. His five-year-old daughter thought her father had come to rescue everybody.[25]

The flood crested overnight, and the next morning Mary Rather returned to assure that everyone was unhurt and to assess the damage. Many of the pecan and live oak trees in the grove in front of the house had been up-rooted, and flood debris was strewn across the lower reaches of the property. Foreman Julius Matus's car and the butane tank at his West Quarters had been swept downstream by the flood. Lady Bird Johnson told Mary Rather that the water had reached within a few feet of the fence in the front yard. Most of the bottomland fences on the main ranch property were destroyed. A number of the neighbors, whose homes were closer to the river than the ranch house, experienced even more significant flood damage.[26]

The people near the Johnson ranch at Stonewall were not the only ones to suffer during this flood. Along the Pedernales River in Gillespie County alone, floodwaters damaged an estimated fifteen thousand dollars worth of property. At Stonewall, more than twenty-three inches of rain fell in a twenty-four-hour period, raising the river forty feet.[27] But rural people were accustomed to such disasters, and the presence of the Johnsons in the Hill Country during the flood and Lady Bird's characteristic graciousness and hospitality during difficult times helped assure their place in the loose rural community. The senator's family had experienced one of the difficul-ties of Hill Country life with their neighbors, and Lady Bird's grace in a pressure-packed situation helped persuade local people of the family's per-manence in the region. As a result, the Johnsons became more a part of the community.

Lyndon Johnson had other expectations for his ranch. As he rose in the Senate, from whip to minority leader to majority leader in the brief span of five years, the ranch became a significant part of the image he projected to state and national constituencies. With the completion of the renova-tion of the property and cleanup of the flood damage, the ranch became an important showcase for Johnson. He brought political friends and al-lies—as well as those he sought to cultivate—to the ranch. Once there, he always showed them around, brought them back to the house, and com-pleted the business that had led to the visit in the living room or den, if it had not been conducted during the tour of the ranch. With a considerable sixty-five-mile distance to Austin and spare bedrooms in the house, many visitors stayed the night at the Johnson ranch.[28]

Informal but staged entertainment also was offered during the 1950s. The primary form of gala entertaining that Johnson enjoyed was the western barbecue, the first of which was presented in 1953.[29] As did many of the other formalized activities that Johnson treasured, barbecues linked his heritage in the Hill Country with his aspirations as a politician and a leader. These meals became mythic, more so as the Johnsons found the caterers, musicians, and entertainers on whom they depended to make these productions serve his purpose.

Johnson liked a western atmosphere, Richard "Cactus" Pryor, a comedian, long-time KTBC employee, and Texas wit who later served as master of ceremonies for many social functions at the ranch, recalled. Coal-oil lanterns and checkered tablecloths, bales of hay, old iron washtubs full of melted butter in which to dip corn on the cob, and other western-style accouterments were typical. The servers were dressed in western clothes. The ranch grounds were manicured for these parties. After a few events were held in other locations, the Johnsons ultimately decided on the grove of trees on the north bank of the river—about two hundred yards east of the house and against the river's banks—as the best location for the barbecues. Once the right place had been selected, barbecues became a frequent event.[30]

Johnson was feeling his way toward the best combination of uses, actual and mythic, for the LBJ Ranch. The rest of his family lived there when he was not in Washington, D.C., and when Congress was not in session so did Lyndon Johnson. He was in residence almost half of 1953 and 1954.[31] Johnson engaged in ranching in a limited way, as much for the meaning of the activity as for any profit that derived from it. Ranching had begun to take on an entirely symbolic significance, becoming a representation of an acceptable national image for an aspiring senator as well as a source of his power. At the ranch, Johnson was in control. From the instant that the first visitor arrived, he drove guests around and showed them what he wanted them to see. Under the guise of showing visitors his spread, Johnson could do what he did best: talk to someone one-on-one and obtain the acquiescence he craved.

Johnson continued to refine his leadership skills in the Senate. The decline of the Truman administration after 1950 provided an opportunity for him. The Democratic majority leader, Scott Lucas of Illinois, and the whip, Francis Myers of Pennsylvania, both lost their seats in the November election. Their losses and the small Democratic majority cleared the way for an inexperienced senator, not up for reelection in 1952, to become the new whip. Johnson stood ready, and with support from his friend Robert Kerr of Oklahoma, he won the seat.[32]

The powerless and thankless post of whip became the catalyst for transforming Johnson's approach to politics and his understanding of his role as a senator. Prior to winning the post, Johnson felt he primarily represented his Texas constituency; afterward, he felt more responsibility for Senate Democrats and, in a minor way, for the functioning of the Senate and the party as a whole. The post gave Johnson a claim on the party. He had served it in its time of need. It also solidified his reputation in Texas as a major power broker. In the end, the whip position gave Johnson a national position that allowed him to broaden his horizons realistically and made the ranch and the image it created even more important to him.

His political fortunes seemed to run inversely to those of his party. When the Republicans won control of the Senate in the 1952 election, Johnson became the minority leader of the Senate. This was another post with relatively little power that Johnson was able to expand, and his performance garnered the respect of his Democratic colleagues. When Tom Connally, the senior senator from Texas, retired before the 1952 election, Johnson replaced him as the senior Texan in the Senate and used his position to bind the new senator, Price Daniel, to him. Johnson developed a reputation as a powerful strategist and a consensus builder among Democrats and received equal recognition for skilled political maneuvering on the other side of the aisle.[33]

When the Democrats recaptured the Senate in 1954, Johnson ascended to the position of majority leader. The Democrats held a one-vote margin of forty-eight to forty-seven. The one vote remaining belonged to Senator Wayne Morse of Oregon, a ranch owner and an independent who had once been a severe critic of Johnson. He had abandoned the Republican Party two years before and had nearly registered as a Democrat earlier in 1954. Morse lost his committee appointments and his positions of leadership when he left the Republican Party, and Johnson, in return for his support, in effect returned his seniority to him.[34] This was one of the many steps Johnson took to consolidate power and Senate support in the majority leader's chair.

Johnson's position as a majority leader responsible for a minute plurality required relentless intensity, and from January, 1955, when the new Congress convened, Johnson gave such an effort. The physical toll on him was enormous, and his personal habits did not help. He smoked at least three packs of cigarettes each day, drank more alcohol than usual, missed lunch every day he did not have an engagement, and frequently did not take time for dinner. Inexplicably, he also gained considerable weight, reaching 225 pounds. As the session neared an end in early July, it caught up with the forty-six-year-old Johnson. On the way to Huntland, George Brown's Virginia estate, for the Fourth of July weekend, Lyndon Johnson suffered a major heart attack.[35]

The heart attack was the most severe health crisis of his life, and it forced significant changes in the way he lived and operated. Johnson almost died the night of the heart attack, instructing his wife to tell his tailor to hold most of an existing clothing order but to "go ahead with the blue suit. We can use it no matter what."[36] The next day, the chances of his survival remained equal to those of his passing away, and he spent the next five weeks in the hospital. He turned Senate leadership over to his hand-picked whip, Senator Earle Clements of Kentucky, and returned to the Texas ranch to regain his health.

Johnson's fierce desire to lead and his physical problems were uncomfortably juxtaposed. He was young to suffer a major heart attack, even by the standards of an era when hard-living men of his age often succumbed to health problems, but he had not yet achieved what he set to accomplish. Lady Bird and his physician agreed that if he returned to the Senate he would not behave any differently than he had in the past. They were also sure that, as Dr. James Cain, his personal physician, remarked, if Johnson "were sitting on the porch at the LBJ ranch whittling toothpicks, he'd have to whittle more toothpicks than anybody else in the country." They correctly assessed that politics had been Johnson's life and that as a still relatively young man, he would have little reason to live without them.[37]

The enforced regime at the ranch greatly strengthened Johnson. Discharged from the hospital on August 7, 1955, long after the congressional session ended, he told reporters that he would be "as good as new in January," when Congress reconvened. On August 27, his birthday, he flew to Fredericksburg to return to the ranch. Mary Rather remembered him as "the thinnest thing you had ever seen, and his clothes were just hanging on him." But back in the Hill Country, away from the pace of Washington, D.C., and Congress, he could build up his strength.[38]

The months at the ranch after the heart attack were notable for the changes in Johnson's behavior. His official physician, Lt. Comdr. J. Willis

Hurst, gave specific instructions for Johnson's recuperation. The senator was to have no worries. Lady Bird played an important role in monitoring his affairs. "Whatever Lyndon did, Lady Bird did," Rather recalled. Awakening to the sound of a Jersey cow mooing to be milked each morning, Johnson often had breakfast under the trees on the lawn. He became a fanatic about his diet during his recuperation, losing more than 40 pounds until he reached 177 pounds. Johnson also became closer to his family than ever before, playing cards with his school-age daughters and delighting in getting to know them. Willard Deason, his college friend and long-time employee, noted that he "had time to talk and visit with them," instead of simply kissing them and running on to the next of the never-ending series of political meetings and events. "He moved into a more nearly normal family relationship," Deason remembered. Johnson "realized the value of having hours" with the two girls.[39]

The enforced rest at the ranch was also a catalyst for the next stage of its renovation. A gloomy attitude had descended over the family, and Lady Bird Johnson noted that "it was very clear one might as well spend what one had and not wait for later, because there might not be any later." One of the first additions was a large kidney-shaped swimming pool and a cabana, an addition planned before the heart attack but built in 1955 primarily to help Johnson maintain a regular exercise routine. He sat in a lawn chair and watched the large hole become a pool. When it was completed and Johnson wanted to swim, he would order everyone into the pool to join him.[40]

He did not rush back to politics, although those who spent time with him knew that he thought about it. He had to decide whether to return to Washington or to resign and stay at the ranch. Despite his health, Johnson knew better than anyone what drove him. Everyone around him was aware that the heart attack would not in and of itself create limits for a man as driven as Lyndon Johnson. He would not work less hard because of the illness, a reality that forced him to choose between his health and his profession. At some point Johnson made his choice. As his health improved, his political activity increased. Although the addition of a telephone and a walkie-talkie radio by the pool helped keep him in an outside hammock, the communications equipment also meant that he was back into his mode of constant political maneuvering. He made only two speeches that fall. One introduced Sam Rayburn; the other was an important thirteen-point, New Deal–style policy address titled "A Program with a Heart" that he made before fifteen hundred people in a packed gymnasium in Whitney, Texas, in October. That speech announced his return to politics and raised his standing throughout the state.[41]

As Johnson's health continued to improve, telephone calls went out to national news correspondents. After the middle of October, magazine and newspaper reporters were frequent visitors to the Pedernales Valley. On October 15, 1955, television and radio personality Arthur Godfrey; Frank "Scoop" Russell, vice president of the National Broadcasting Company (NBC); William S. White, a Pulitzer Prize–winning journalist from *The New York Times;* and Gerald Griffin, Washington, D.C., correspondent for *The Baltimore Sun* arrived at the ranch to spend the weekend. Their visit indicated that Johnson planned a return to Washington, D.C., in the very near future.[42]

As Johnson recovered, politicians began to visit the ranch, and sometimes it seemed as if the Senate was in the process of moving its chambers to Stonewall, Texas. Democratic senators Stuart Symington of Missouri, Hubert Humphrey of Minnesota, Kerr Scott of North Carolina, J. William Fulbright of Arkansas, George Smathers of Florida, Estes Kefauver of Tennessee, and Robert Kerr of Oklahoma all came during the fall of 1955, as did Speaker of the House Sam Rayburn and Governor Adlai Stevenson of Illinois. By Thanksgiving, Republicans had joined the procession; the Republican Senate whip, H. Styles Bridges of New Hampshire, and his wife joined the Johnsons for the holiday weekend.[43]

Even during his recuperation, Johnson showed his penchant for using the ranch as a strategic asset. Just prior to the visit by Stevenson and Rayburn on September 28, 1955, President Dwight D. Eisenhower suffered a severe heart attack. After a speech by Stevenson in Austin, he, Rayburn, Grace Tully—a former secretary to Franklin D. Roosevelt who had become a Johnson staff member—and Newton Minow—a Stevenson political advisor who would later become chairman of the Federal Communications Commission—drove to the ranch. They arrived late at night, expecting to find the Johnsons asleep, but the recuperating Johnson had stayed awake to greet them. It was a moonlit night with a gentle breeze, Mary Rather recalled. The guests arrived after 10:30 P.M., and Johnson stayed up and talked with them for more than an hour.[44]

Typically, Johnson sought to keep the press at a distance during Stevenson's visit. He wanted to make sure that reporters did not think that he, Stevenson, and Rayburn were "plotting how to take over the government while Ike

[was] dying," Minow remembered. George Reedy advised him to allow the press on the ranch to cover the visit, but Johnson demurred. He even sought to have them removed from the fence at the edge of the ranch, but Reedy prevailed on him not to contest the press there. Reedy told a distraught Lady Bird Johnson that while he "was pretty good with the press, [he could not] keep them off of a public highway." By morning, Johnson had devised a new strategy. Rather than bar the press, he planned an early breakfast and invited his guests and the reporters who followed them on a tour of the ranch, dispelling any notions of a secret cabal. The ranch backdrop diffused the political tension surrounding Eisenhower's illness.[45]

By the time Johnson returned to Washington, D.C, when the congressional session opened in January, 1956, the ranch had acquired an important place in American politics. Johnson's illness and his position as majority leader had made the ranch a place to which other Democratic politicians felt the need to come to pay a sort of homage. In particular, with the election year of 1956 approaching and the Democrats in dire need of Johnson's political skills, the power Johnson had consolidated in the majority leadership was a necessity to any aspiring Democratic presidential candidate. To receive access to that power required going along with Johnson. Even the powerful and idiosyncratic Estes Kefauver recognized the importance of Johnson's support. During Kefauver's visit, Johnson awoke the Tennessee senator at 4:30 A.M. for a deer-hunting jaunt. When Kefauver responded slowly, Johnson yelled, "I was about to come out for someone else for President if you don't get down here in ten minutes." Kefauver understood the veiled threat contained in the jest; within ten minutes, he and Johnson were in the heated pool on their way to a morning of deer hunting.[46]

The time at the ranch reinforced the physical limitations of the property to both Johnsons. "Never will a home be finished," Lady Bird Johnson lamented, and with her husband's predilection for rapid decision making and his need to have the place in constant motion, the construction, improvement, and renovation of the ranch and house were ongoing. During the spring of 1956, Johnson asked his brother-in-law, Birge Alexander, to prepare plans for a new addition, a single-story structure to be appended to the east end of the property. Built later that year, it included the expansion of the master bedroom; of Rebekah Johnson's bedroom and bathroom; of the Johnsons' dressing room; and of the Gay room, the upstairs parlor. This addition made the house noticeably more spacious and comfortable.[47]

Johnson's long stay at the house also made other deficiencies more apparent. The lack of office space was one major problem. During Johnson's recuperation period, the living room began to change into an office. Mary Rather's desk sat in the southeast corner, and after a while, Lady Bird's desk was claimed by another secretary. By 1957, the living room more resembled a working office than part of a home. Telephones rang constantly, and the room was crowded and hectic. It was clear that formal office space was essential.[48]

At the Johnsons' request, J. Roy White designed an office addition for the west side of the house, atop the location of the old hand-dug cistern. Workmen filled in this last vestige of life before indoor plumbing as they began construction of the twenty-eight-foot by twenty-eight-foot structure. Designed to accommodate three desks and a couch, the office had a number of aesthetic features. The beautiful, hand-oiled knotty pine walls were especially attractive, but as long-time ranch foreman Dale Malachek noted, Lyndon Johnson maintained "a highly functional office." Aesthetics were incidental.[49]

The renovated ranch became an essential part of the image and reality of Johnson's rise to national leadership. As he had done with the whip post, he made the majority leader's position far more important than it had been in more than a decade by his consolidation of power. The "Johnson Treatment," as his ability to persuade, cajole, manipulate, and outmaneuver other senators came to be known, heightened his effectiveness.[50] The seemingly endless pilgrimages of politicians to Texas during his illness accentuated the significance of the ranch. The LBJ Ranch had become as well known and as central to American politics as the retreat of any senator. All of this contributed to Johnson's idea of himself as a national leader instead of a regional politician.

The ranch became the symbol of this transformation, which was crucial to any aspiration to higher office that Johnson harbored. Born and bred a southerner, a Texan descended from the historic oligarchic traditions of the state, Johnson faced twin image problems with a national audience. Although westerners had begun to assume the presidency, beginning with Iowan Herbert Hoover and followed by Missourian Harry S. Truman and Kansan Dwight D. Eisenhower, there had not been a southern president since immediately following the Civil War, and that president, Andrew Johnson, ascended as the result of an assassination and almost lost his office at the hands of an angry Congress. Lyndon Johnson's rise to statewide power required him to play the part of a southern politician, as in his first Senate speech, an anti–civil rights diatribe that filled eight pages in the *Congressional Record.* But the rhetoric he used and the issues he supported in state elections became a liability on the national scene.[51] Johnson began to counter those limits when, as minority leader, he allied the Democrats with Eisenhower against the rabid right wing of the Republican party, but the subtleties of such a stance were largely lost on the voters of the nation. Johnson remained a Texan—a nationality unto itself—and a southerner in the eyes of most Americans.

The post–World War II era damaged the already marginal stature of the South in American society. Since the end of the Civil War, the rest of the nation had regarded the South as the defeated section and the most backward region of the country. Its people were the poorest in the nation, the industrialization that brought economic prosperity to the North by the late nineteenth and early twentieth century developed slowly in the South, and southerners were generally perceived as quaint and anachronistic. After World War II, questions of race relations also figured into an increasingly negative image of the South. Although Americans were generally ambivalent about civil rights for African Americans, the war against fascism spurred such comprehensive changes in American society that the old rules about the limits on different races no longer reflected the understanding of the majority of the nation. The trenchant South stood against such changes, its stand reinforced by its Dixiecrat swing in 1948. That stand isolated the South in the national political culture, but the region was still a valuable prize for aspirants to national office.

The West had a different image, much closer to the one Johnson sought to project. Westward expansion had become the American creation myth, reinforced in film and legend as the region's history melded with the sentiments of the nation in the 1950s. The West seemed new and invigorated, individualistic and expanding, with the promise of prosperity for everyone. In the immediate postwar era, the region was booming. During the war, people moved to California and the West Coast to work in the defense plants, and hundreds of thousands of soldiers passed through on their way to the Pacific Theater; afterward most stayed and many more came. A ten-dam package for the upper Colorado River—the Colorado River Storage Project—promised enough water and electrical power to fuel an economic boom as far north as Utah and the western slope of Colorado.[52] The population of western states grew, infrastructure benefited from developments such as the interstate highway system, and the region seemed on its way to full status in the national partnership. The West seemed destined to recapitulate the promise of the nation.

The West held the future, the South the past, and Johnson sought a future in national politics. The LBJ Ranch became a symbol as well as a home, transforming Johnson from someone tied to the Old South into an individual affiliated with the mythic West and with all the promise contained in that concept. In this reinvention of self, Johnson mirrored the "galvanized Yankees" and the recalcitrant southerners who left rather than accept new circumstances and resettled in far West Texas and the West after the Civil War. They too seized the chance to reinvent themselves and shed the burdens of their past; they too enjoyed an opportunity to remake their lives in a wide-open geographic and cultural setting rather than a limited, regional context.

A number of Johnson's actions in the late 1940s and early 1950s reflected not only his symbolic westernness but another current within the man: the egalitarian strain that had been so evident in Cotulla. In one instance, the little Texas town of Three Rivers refused to allow a local burial service for a Mexican American soldier who had been killed in the Philippines during World War II and whose remains were repatriated in 1949. Johnson took the side of the man's family, arranging interment in Arlington National Cemetery after the town refused to accommodate the family even under pressure from the senior U.S. senator of the state. According to D. B. Hardeman, Johnson was outraged by the conduct of the town and took its behavior as a personal affront. The ceremony, in which the soldier, Felix Longoria, was posthumously awarded full military honors, was his way of rectifying what he saw as a wrong.[53] Although detractors regarded the burial as a cynical publicity stunt, the incident reflected Johnson's deep-seated personal beliefs about honor, loyalty, and obligation to those who sacrifice, which the country associated with its westward experience.

The ranch became the most important symbol of Johnson's reinvention. Perhaps he recognized how well the western image played in Texas. He was certainly aware of the significance of the history and imagery of the region during the 1950s. Coke Stevenson, his opponent in the 1948 Senate race, was the type of flinty, hard-eyed person that had become the westerner in the American mind, and this persona played extremely well in Texas politics. With the advent of the era of great and glorious Western movies, often featuring the actor John Wayne, a ranch became a symbolic and culturally familiar setting to Americans. On television and on the movie screen, the West became the crucible of American values, the ranch the setting in which these values were forged and honed.[54] Johnson's ownership of a ranch—part relic, part myth—enhanced his position and prestige with an electorate that increasingly took its values from mass media.

Beginning in 1954, with the *Brown v. Board of Education of Topeka, Kansas, et al.* decision by the U.S. Supreme Court, race became a primary factor in American politics. The migration of African Americans to the North as a result of the two world wars and their expanded presence in northern cities, as well as technological changes in cotton-growing and cotton-picking, made racial questions, previously regarded as a sectional concern, into national issues. After the breaking of the color line in major-league baseball by Jackie Robinson in 1947 and the desegregation of the military, ordered by Truman in 1948, protection for segregation in statute slowly but inexorably crumbled. The Brown decision was the culmination of a long series of court cases that in effect isolated southern politicians, forcing them to go headlong into the massed forces of change.[55]

Johnson's astute political sense and his native sympathies allied him with the changes of the postwar era. Although in the first years after his election to the Senate he had acted as if he were a "true southerner" in order to ingratiate himself with Richard Russell and the Senate club, his rise to power mirrored an emerging political independence. Some northern liberals thought of him as a populist, socially liberal in the nonpolitical sense of the word but trapped by the conventions of his state and office. Despite the stance opposing civil rights that he had taken since 1937, Johnson could see the changes coming in race relations. He had also supported the concept of opportunity for all people for a long time. He had grown up poor and feeling left out, and as his experience as a teacher in the "Mexican" school in Cotulla showed, inclusion was one of Johnson's goals.[56] As the national political climate surrounding race relations grew increasingly charged, the ranch became an important vehicle for assuring Johnson's national status and his claim to a heritage that was not rigidly southern.

The most prominent feature of Johnson's majority leadership was the way in which he held the political center. Particularly on matters of race, he successfully negotiated a path between McCarthyite Republicans and Dixiecrats on one side and northern liberals such as Senators Paul Douglas and Hubert H. Humphrey on the other. This position took him far from the mentorship of Senator Richard Russell, a diehard segregationist from

Georgia, and helped Johnson establish a national bearing. Johnson's identification with the West became increasingly apparent in the middle of the
1950s. He and Tennessee's two senators, the maverick Kefauver and Albert
Gore, Sr., were the only southern senators who refused to sign the Southern Manifesto, formally titled the Declaration of Constitutional Principles,
an election-year ploy by southern senators in 1956 to associate civil rights
with subversion.[57]

Positioning himself for a run at the presidency in 1960, Johnson played
a strategic game. He opposed the manifesto by privately arguing that it
would only drive African American voters in crucial northern states into
the Republican Party; he was proven correct in the 1956 elections, when
larger numbers of African American voters supported the Republicans than
at any time since the election of Franklin D. Roosevelt in 1932. This kind of
pragmatism, instead of a hotheaded emotional response to the *Brown* decision, reflected his national aspirations and his increasingly western affilia-
tions and image. Southern senators did not hold his actions against him.
They recognized that he had to play a leadership role and that he had aspirations to national office. Sitting on the porch of his ranch, Lyndon Johnson
had fewer commitments to the political past and could see the future more
clearly than could many of his more senior peers in the U.S. Senate.

Johnson's orchestration of the passage of the Civil Rights Act of 1957
demonstrated his pragmatism in the most difficult of venues. Senate rules
allowed individual senators almost infinite ways to delay legislation, and
on the subject of race southern senators felt backed up to the wall. As a
result, civil rights legislation was often stillborn in the Senate. Johnson
later considered the passage of the 1957 bill his greatest legislative achievement, but his detractors among civil rights supporters thought he gutted
what might have been a miracle. Again, his success depended on finding
the middle so thoroughly missing in Congress when the subject of race
came up in. In his pragmatic way, Johnson defined the issue in political
terms. If the Democrats did not pass a civil rights bill during the session,
Johnson believed, they would pay for it at the polls in the 1958 elections.
He quietly circulated the word that the Senate would pass a civil rights bill
during the session, and southern senators needed to decide what kind of
bill they could grudgingly accept.[58]

Again Johnson acted in the definitive manner of a mythic western
rancher, a man given not to emotion but to sheer determined pragmatism.
The bill that passed the House on June 18 provided for a new commission

on civil rights and a new assistant attorney general specifically to handle civil rights issues. In Part III, the bill's most controversial section, the Justice Department was granted the power to enforce the provisions of the Fourteenth Amendment, effectively gutted at the end of the nineteenth century, by filing injunctions against states and school districts that did not comply with the *Brown* decision. This put the force of possible physical federal intervention behind the Supreme Court ruling. Such a weapon held over the South threatened to isolate the region, Johnson told southern senators, and he effectively forged a compromise in early July after a week of difficult maneuvering and countless Senate amendments. The bill that finally passed, and that Eisenhower reluctantly signed, was emasculated in the view of its critics, but it was a start.[59]

The Civil Rights Act of 1957 confirmed the trend that had begun with Johnson's purchase of the ranch. In one dramatic gesture, Johnson gave up a twenty-year career as a segregationist, a career of playing to his vocal but narrow home-state constituency. With the Senate majority leadership and the passage of the bill, he ceased to be a regionally oriented Texas politician. With the ranch to prove his credentials, he made himself into a national figure based in western myth. Johnson forged an interregional political consensus that held the center, enhancing his national aspirations and lining Johnson up with the future rather than the past. Although he seemed more involved with the politics than the morality of civil rights, Johnson was the only legislator in the United States who could have constructed the coalition to pass even the watered-down bill of 1957. Despite the limitations the compromise created, Eisenhower signed the bill. Much of the South refused to accept the new dictates. Two days after the bill became law, Governor Orval Faubus of Arkansas ordered the National Guard to prevent nine African American students from enrolling in Central High School in Little Rock. Federal intervention ensued.[60]

In no small part, Johnson was able to negotiate this compromise as a result of his changing image. Although he still depended on the conservative Texas electorate for his Senate seat, Johnson was beyond its reach. By the time he needed to run for reelection in 1960, he planned to be searching for higher office as well. The Texan had become a national figure with an image tied to the West. He was the Hill Country rancher who led the Senate, the man whose honey jars at his ranch bore the LBJ Ranch logo and who bought silver beaver Stetson hats, three hundred at a time, to give to important visitors. Southern politicians seem not to have resented greatly the transformation of their old ally, although in a number of instances Russell and other powerful southerners threatened Johnson by reminding him of the electorate in Texas. Johnson's political pragmatism worked well during this era. His experience in the Senate and his ability to seem simultaneously to represent many points of view gave him great currency.[61]

His ranch and its meaning played an important part in solidifying Johnson's national image as he planned his path to national office. As the South erupted in conflict in the aftermath of the *Brown* decision and with the emergence of the Reverend Dr. Martin Luther King, Jr., during the Montgomery bus strike of 1955, Johnson publicly became even more of a westerner. He spent considerable time at the ranch even after his recovery from the heart attack. His public interests changed, as he published articles about the specific problems ranchers faced and about the need for greater public understanding of ranching. More and more often, Johnson was photographed on horseback or in a Stetson hat and boots.[62] This image accentuated the centrist stance he favored as majority leader, allying him with a different set of concerns than those of the South.

The ranch had also become home to the Johnsons, a place to which both loved to return. Buying and improving the ranch enabled Lyndon Johnson to "have a big comfortable house that meant a lot to him," Lady Bird Johnson recalled in 1972, "to his spirit and to his heart." Johnson himself was even more explicit when he remarked that he found it "almost necessary to return to Texas" after time in the nation's capital. "This country," he remarked of the Hill Country in 1957, "has always been a place where I could come and fill my cup . . . and recharge myself for the more difficult days ahead." The Johnsons continued to spend as much time at the ranch as they could. After Congress adjourned in August, 1953, the Johnsons spent five months at the ranch. After the 1954 recess, the family again lived along the Pedernales River until Congress reconvened after the new year. In 1955, the heart attack kept Johnson there throughout the fall, and in 1956 and 1957, he spent most of the months of August, September, and October and about half of November and December there. The couple felt at home along the shimmering river. "I am enjoying the ranch," Johnson wrote in 1957," the swimming pool and the dove hunting," but he also added an increasingly complex communication system to facilitate his long-distance political maneuvering.[63]

The ranch also became a social setting for the Johnsons, a place where they loved to entertain not only politicians and social leaders but friends and family as well. They showered their friends with hospitality, bringing an unending stream of people to visit and spend a night or two at the ranch. Lyndon Johnson hated to be alone, and the steady flow of names recorded in the ranch guest book reflected not only that but also the range of political and personal friends and acquaintances of the Johnsons. Beginning in 1956, the register showed more friends than politicians, but as always with Johnson, these categories overlapped considerably. The Johnsons held a continuous string of social affairs, most small and personal, to complement the occasional barbecues and other functions for larger audiences.[64]

The ranch was also the location of important family functions, such as Rebekah Baines Johnson's seventy-sixth birthday celebration on June 26, 1957. The aging mother of the senator already was aware she had cancer. In her long life, she had seen her cherished oldest son rise to positions of unforeseen national power and yet retain his filial commitment to her. She had watched over him throughout his life, and the two maintained an ongoing correspondence. As she aged, Lyndon Johnson reversed their roles and took care of her. The birthday celebration, limited to close friends and family, was an example of this.[65]

The ranch also became a place where the family could relax, where Lyndon Johnson had control of every aspect of life in the manner he desired. Johnson's heart attack in 1955 highlighted the importance of the ranch. In its aftermath he was forced to relax, to breakfast on the porch or in the trees by the river, to—in the words of aide George Reedy—"spin his dreams," and the experience reminded Johnson that the ranch was more than a symbol. Before the heart attack and despite his evident feelings for the place, the ranch was as much for show as it was for inhabiting in any genuine way. As Lyndon Johnson recuperated and became reinvigorated there, his ties to the place and region were both strengthened and transformed as a result.

As Johnson's power and significance in politics grew and as the routine at the ranch became established, the Pedernales River became the location of a range of official functions. The first official visitor was President Adolfo Lopez Mateos of Mexico, who came during a ten-day state visit to the United States and Canada. Sharing a rural background and an interest in teaching with Johnson and regarding the Texan as a likely future national leader, Lopez Mateos sought out Johnson in the mid-1950s. After Lopez Mateos's election as Mexican president in 1958, Johnson visited the new leader in Acapulco, and the two men developed a friendship; "they had gotten along astonishingly well," George Reedy, who began working for Johnson in 1951 and became his press secretary at the White House, remembered. A stop at the Texas ranch to reciprocate Johnson's visit was important enought to Lopez Mateos to make it part of the state trip. After a state dinner in Washington, D.C., in October, 1959, Lopez Mateos went to Canada and then returned to Mexico via Texas, where the climax of the tour was to be a Hill Country barbecue at the Johnson ranch.[66]

The preparations for a party of such proportions and significance required greater expertise and organization than any previous endeavor at the ranch. Throughout Johnson's years in the Senate, and particularly after he became majority leader, the ranch had served as a backdrop for a range of political and political-social events. The parade of important politicians who arrived in Texas to pay their respects during Johnson's recuperation from his heart attack set a new tone for the symbolic meaning of the ranch. At first, the barbecues Johnson offered were trials, offered to constituencies that would be thrilled for the invitation and likely to overlook any shortcomings. Others were ceremonial events, chances to be seen for both Johnson and his invitees. One such planned event, a barbecue Johnson wanted to offer for outstanding college students as part of his effort to respond to the launches of Sputnik I and Sputnik II by the Soviet Union, offered him a public relations coup and a chance to cultivate future supporters, as well as an opportunity to develop the barbecue procedures for future use. His staff canvassed caterers throughout the Hill Country in an effort to find the best barbecue for the money, seeking to build relationships that could be useful in designing affairs of state. For the students, an invitation to the home of the majority leader of the U.S. Senate was a significant honor, and even if a few things might go wrong, such a night would remain memorable.[67]

By the time the planning for the Lopez Mateos visit to the ranch began, the staff had a great deal of experience with both state events and barbecues. But planning for the visit of a foreign head of state required additional measures. Lady Bird Johnson played an active role in the arrangements, selecting both the location of the barbecue and the menu. After the guest list was finalized and the visit protocol established, Johnson's staff had to work out arrangements for the president's retinue and the Mexican press that would accompany the president. Questions of security had to be addressed. New phone lines had to be added, the proper wines selected— Justo Sierra, Lopez Mateos's aide, thought that his president would prefer an American claret over an imported wine—and numerous other details handled. Sierra informed George Reedy that the Mexican press regarded their president's informal visit with Johnson as the most meaningful part of the trip. The other formal events were of far less significance, in their cultural understanding of politics. The needs of the American press had to be addressed as well, and with the shortage of space in Johnson City, the question of their location loomed large.[68]

The arrival of President Lopez Mateos in Texas was a gala event. On Sunday, October 18, 1959, the airplane carrying the president and his party landed at Bergstrom Air Force Base in Austin, Texas. The welcoming committee included Senator and Mrs. Johnson, Governor and Mrs. Price Daniel, Mayor and Mrs. Tom Miller of Austin, and Col. Frank E. Marek, the commanding officer at the Air Force base. After a ceremonial greeting, the president and his party were escorted to helicopters for the short jaunt to the Hill Country. Lopez Mateos; Johnson; Daniel; Mexican ambassador Antonio Carillo Flores; Sim Gideon, the general manager of the Lower Colorado River Authority; and Mexican Brig. Gen. José Goméz Huerta were passengers on the first of six helicopters required to take the party to the ranch. The one-hour flight toured the highland lakes of the Hill Country and the many dams along its waterways. By early afternoon the party arrived at the ranch.[69]

The barbecue began shortly after the arrival of Lopez Mateos. Held in the oak grove on the north bank of the Pedernales, near the low-water dam, the event showcased the Texas Hill Country, the ranch, and Johnson's growing political importance and aspirations. Johnson opened the program, speaking briefly and introducing President Lopez Mateos, who praised the "Good Neighbor" policy in which the U.S. government engaged. Lopez Mateos's assistant translated his remarks into English for most of the audience. After the brief program, the guests sat down to eat barbecue in the tents. The event was a full-fledged state affair, with a guest list that included former president Harry S Truman, Speaker of the House Sam Rayburn, Secretary of the Treasury Robert S. Anderson, and four other official U.S. representatives. "The whole thing was typically Texas," wrote Wes Izzard of *The Amarillo Daily News,* as the fusion of the various ingredients of Johnson's personality, aspirations, and image showed the press the image Johnson wanted to put forward.[70]

Late in the afternoon, after the barbecue and the departure of the press and most of the guests, Johnson took Lopez Mateos on a tour of his ranch.

Across the pastures of grazing cattle, by the old pecan and live oak trees, the two men rode and talked. This was a highlight for both—Johnson showing who he was and creating the setting in which he most liked to do business and Lopez Mateos establishing ties to the man he expected to be the next president of the United States. A formal dinner with a few guests followed. After a leisurely breakfast the next morning, the Mexican president and his entourage departed for Austin. The Johnsons joined the group there for lunch and escorted them to Bergstrom Air Force Base for their departure to Mexico City. This ended a weekend that Hill Country old-timers called "the biggest celebrity laden event in the 114 years history of these parts."[71]

The Lopez Mateos visit increased the stature of both Johnson and his ranch. "Friendship—warm and genuine—downed all the language barriers," one newspaper reporter wrote. The Mexican president told his countrymen that his "crusade of good will" had been a success. American officials concurred. "Congratulations on a job exceedingly well done," U.S. Ambassador to Mexico Robert C. Hill wrote to George Reedy on October 29, 1959. "President Lopez Mateos returned to Mexico with the feeling that they had received an extremely fine reception in Texas and that Senator Johnson's hospitality should go about bringing a better understanding in Mexico about Texas." Hill also wrote Johnson that the visit to the ranch was "a truly significant climax to [Lopez Mateos's] very successful visit to the United States." Truman described the Johnsons as "perfect hosts," a sentiment that clearly touched Johnson. The Johnson ranch had been the home of first a regional politician and then a national leader. After the Lopez Mateos visit, the ranch was a national showcase, the place that helped persuade the nation that Texas was truly one of its states, a place worthy of the candidate for national office that Lyndon B. Johnson planned to become.[72]

There were obvious and subtle signs of Johnson's changing aspirations. At the Lopez Mateos barbecue, a banner reading "Lyndon Johnson sera presidente" ("Lyndon Johnson for President") hung in the trees. The Senate had become stale to Johnson. He had accomplished all he could in the club of peers, and as the Democrats sought to reacquire the White House in 1960, they became less interested in the kind of bipartisan accomplishments at which Johnson excelled and more in the obstructionism that preceded an expected reconquest of the White House by the party out of power. Johnson's growing number of critics successfully boxed him into a narrow role, defying his legendary power, and he began to see his effectiveness

limited. The Senate ceased to be fun in the way it had been earlier in the
decade, and Johnson set his sights higher and contemplated his chances.[73]

The ranch had symbolic significance for Johnson, but a run at national
office would require physical changes there as well. The catalyst for these
changes was the Lopez Mateos visit. The travel arrangements for the visit
were an immense problem, not only because of the difficulty involved in
getting the Mexican president and his entourage to the ranch but also with
regard to the sleeping arrangements, the transportation of the press, communications, and other issues. In 1959, the ranch was not set up to accommodate national events. Although Johnson had scaled his career beyond
Texas politics, the ranch was still designed for regional affairs. But soon
after the Lopez Mateos visit, a new standard for the ranch was established.
Symbolic of its new level of significance was the construction of a 3,570-
foot airstrip, where Johnson could land his newly purchased airplane.[74]

The Lopez Mateos visit also confirmed Lady Bird Johnson's suspicion
that the family had been living "too modestly." All the ranch had to quarter the visiting head of state, his wife, and Eva, their seventeen-year-old
daughter, was a suite of three bedrooms and one bath. While this was
acceptable for typical dignitaries and friends, for heads of state and other
distinguished visitors the accommodations were insufficient. Plans for expansion were soon underway. Lady Bird Johnson later recalled that Lopez
Mateos's visit hastened a project that the Johnsons would have undertaken
in the near future in any event.[75]

In many ways, the Lopez Mateos visit to the LBJ Ranch provided a
catalyst for the next stage of its transformation. By the end of the 1950s,
the ranch had become an important political icon for Johnson, a symbol
of what he had become politically and a representation of what he had left
behind. The purchase of the property began as a way to initiate Johnson
into the Senate club, to make him a peer in the chamber of peers. Perhaps
building off of the regional success of Coke Stevenson, who seemed to the
Texas public the embodiment of a western man, Johnson expropriated
that set of symbols for his own use. By the time he returned to the Senate
after his heart attack, the ranch had become the home of an important
national politician, the majority leader of the Senate. The parade of political figures who had visited during Johnson's recuperation attested to that.
By the end of the decade, with Johnson's political aspirations expanding to
meet his broadening horizons, the ranch had become a place with national
meaning.

The Lopez Mateos visit illustrated the great importance of the ranch as a symbol as well as its shortcomings for the next stage of Lyndon Johnson's career. Lady Bird Johnson once sighed, "Never will a home be finished," and—in part because of Johnson's restless spirit and in part because of the continuing redefinition of his political goals—she was quite correct. The Lopez Mateos visit was the end of one era and the beginning of another. The LBJ Ranch had become a place of national significance rather than merely the home of a regional leader, and as such, it would have to be remade both physically and symbolically. Remaking the ranch went hand in hand with Lyndon B. Johnson's efforts to design a political persona that would sustain a run for national office.

CHAPTER 4

The Vice President's Ranch

B y the end of the 1950s, Lyndon B. Johnson was prepared for the next stage of his career, his first genuine effort to run for national office. After a decade in the House of Representatives and more than another in the Senate chambers, the funnel to the peak of power had narrowed considerably. Johnson had been an integral part of the Senate leadership for almost a decade, building strong alliances that he expected would serve him well in an effort to secure the Democratic nomination for the presidency. He believed he had the stature, experience, and leadership capacity to be effective as the top official in the land.

Throughout the 1950s, Johnson had managed the symbols so crucial to his political aspirations in an astute manner. The run-down ranch he purchased in 1951 had been an important part of the creation of his national image. It had been first a ticket to membership in the inner club of the Senate—a symbol of Johnson's leadership and the vehicle through which he achieved his cultural transformation from southerner to westerner—and finally a backdrop for high-level political negotiations and the location of affairs of state. As Johnson readied himself for the move to higher office, he prepared his ranch, symbolically and physically, for the demands that inevitably would follow.

Late in the second Eisenhower term, Johnson positioned himself for higher office. Although widely perceived as inordinately capable, he carried many liabilities; his southern roots in particular loomed large. Even Republican presidential aspirant Richard M. Nixon recognized Johnson's abilities, but he questioned whether the electorate would support him. "If [Johnson] had only one strike against him, he might make it," Nixon told reporter Carroll Kilpatrick in 1958. "But I don't think he can with two." Although some believed a run at the presidency was Johnson's life-long goal, in pragmatic terms he recognized that he had to accomplish many political objectives before he could become a legitimate contender in anyone's mind but his own. Much of the 1950s had been devoted to the task of counteracting any negative impressions of Johnson the public might hold: his centrist position, his power-brokering in the Senate, and his anti-southern stance on the Civil Rights Bill of 1957 were all evidence, which the public easily interpreted, of the efforts of a national leader rather than a regional politician tied to the needs of his immediate constituency.[1]

Johnson had feinted at the presidential nomination before 1960. In 1956, he came to the convention in Chicago as a favorite-son candidate, nourishing a slim hope that Adlai Stevenson could be thwarted, but he recognized that the Democratic ticket had little chance that year. In the end, Estes Kefauver, Johnson's rival in the Senate, secured the vice presidential nomination over Massachusetts Senator John F. Kennedy, a prospect that seemed to disturb Johnson only a little. The Democratic ticket was trounced at the polls in 1956, but as always, the defeat of his party enhanced Johnson's standing. After Eisenhower was sworn in for a second term, Johnson's position as a leading contender for the 1960 Democratic nomination was secure. During Eisenhower's second term, Johnson again turned the precarious Democratic position to his personal advantage. Between 1956 and 1960, he accomplished much of the groundwork necessary for a serious run at the top spot on the ticket. A range of commentators, including

Eisenhower, publicly announced that they regarded him as a leading presidential candidate.[2]

Throughout early 1960, Johnson inexplicably refused to declare his candidacy for the presidential nomination. He teetered ambivalently as others made headway, citing his health, the negative impression the majority leader of the Senate would make by campaigning while Congress still had work to do, and other factors. Along with a number of other Democrats, including Hubert Humphrey, Kennedy, Johnson's old friend Stuart Symington, and the perennial Stevenson, Johnson was considered one of the leading candidates for the presidential nomination, but unlike the rest, he remained in Washington, D.C., to run the Senate. The others hit the campaign trail with a zeal that reflected the imminent change in the occupancy of the Oval Office. Johnson even ignored Sam Rayburn's announcement that a "Johnson for President" office would open in Austin in October, 1959.

Johnson's biographers have all speculated on this seeming abandonment of a goal that was so close at hand. Conkin argues that Johnson lapsed into one of the periods of inactive lethargy that were paired with his hyperactive engagement and that he was intimidated by the prospect of running without an established national base. The success of the Democrats in 1959 and 1960 had hampered Johnson's ability to lead in the Senate. His critics began to get the best of him, and sensing the end of an era, Johnson became frustrated and contemplated retirement. According to Conkin, he may have meant it. Other biographers, such as Robert Dallek, have intimated that Johnson felt he deserved the nomination and waited to be drafted, expecting the party to come to him in the manner that he had demanded of supplicants all through his adult life. Johnson had a "limited understanding," Dallek states, "of how important style was in a presidential candidate and White House occupant." Whatever the cause, his refusal to declare himself a candidate limited even the remote chance that he would secure the nomination.[3]

At the very last moment, three days before departing for the Democratic convention in Los Angeles, Johnson announced he would run. "The old Johnson came back to life," Conkin grandly suggests. The greatest prize was too close to ignore. But he had given up the entire campaign season, during which John F. Kennedy had successfully positioned himself as the front-runner. Johnson faced an uphill battle. After months of playing down his interest in the nomination as potential rivals toured the country, Johnson sought to pull together disparate support in a figurative instant. Kennedy, a Roman Catholic, had emerged as the leading candidate; he and Johnson had different but enormous liabilities. Kennedy's religious faith was an issue throughout the campaign, as was Johnson's regional origin.[4]

The most unusual aspect of Johnson's behavior in 1960 was his reluctance to chase the nomination. The 1960 campaign seemed remarkably similar to other situations in which Johnson had advanced his political career. As a politician, Johnson had never defeated an incumbent. He secured his House seat after the death of its previous denizen and successfully won the Senate race after the retirement of his predecessor. No giant killer, Johnson benefited greatly from the type of circumstances that prevailed in 1960. Yet when they arose that year, he demurred. His lack of willingness to engage political rivals was the cause of much surprise in political circles. Johnson had never before been reticent about pursuing his ambitions.

The Los Angeles convention was typical of political affairs, with much back-room politicking and deals made left and right. Although Johnson may have expected the Democratic Party to rally around him, in reality Kennedy had such an immense lead that he was the likely candidate even before the convention opened. Hubert Humphrey also had an outside chance to secure the nomination. The vice presidential slot remained available. An effort to arrange the post for Humphrey, whose own rivalry with Kennedy had turned unfriendly during the West Virginia primary, failed. At the convention, Philip Graham, the publisher of *The Washington Post,* and one of his top political correspondents, Joseph Alsop, secured a five-minute interview with Kennedy during which Graham suggested that Johnson be selected as the vice presidential nominee. Kennedy immediately agreed, Graham later recounted, leaving him "doubting the easy triumph." As Graham pressed his case, Kennedy informed the publisher that he had decided on Johnson because of the southern support Johnson brought to the ticket. After Kennedy was nominated, the Massachusetts senator officially named Johnson as his running mate.[5]

The emergence of the "inverted ticket"—by experience and age—with Kennedy at the top and Johnson as the running mate offered important insights into the changing character of American politics. Until the 1960 election, American politicians had followed a number of unwritten rules: place of origin, seniority, and an extension of the reverence for experience expected in the chambers of the legislature were important prerequisites in building a ticket. A long record was extremely helpful as candidates sought to communicate to the public. But as Johnson himself demonstrated in his 1948 senatorial campaign, the advent of broad-based mass-communications networks changed the nature of politics. Image had replaced demonstrated performance as a foundation for a candidate's appeal.[6]

Television, which had become an important medium by 1960, was more powerful than any previous form of communication. It could beam an image of an individual into millions of homes in an instant. But for many traditional politicians, there were drawbacks to this mode of communication. Accustomed to a different manner of speaking—in fact to different ways of thinking about reaching voters—they were confounded by the new technology.[7] Nor did television help anyone with idiosyncratic or regional characteristics. Television seemed to amplify an individual's traits or flaws, highlighting their most visible aspects and framing them almost as caricature.

On television, the Kennedy-Johnson ticket had enormous advantages. The photogenic Kennedy, despite a regional northeastern accent in speech, conveyed a personal warmth across the airwaves that his Republican opponent, Richard Nixon, did not. David Halberstam has aptly described Kennedy as "the first television president." Johnson's features, particularly his enormous ears, seemed a political cartoon on television screens, but his Texan and southern way of speaking coincided with a large segment of the American public that did not respond to Kennedy's northeastern accent. The resulting combination was powerful, and in the 1960 election the Kennedy-Johnson ticket won by a small plurality.[8]

The campaign offered another opportunity to highlight Johnson's western image, and as always, the ranch was central to that endeavor. The Hill Country and the West had become embodiments of Johnson's new national persona. By 1960, he had been distancing himself from the South for almost a decade; after the 1956 campaign and the Civil Rights Bill of 1957, Johnson presented himself to the national public as a western man, unencumbered by the legacy of the South. With the South appearing to be in a struggle between its history and its future, with its politicians increasingly marginalized but its electorate of vast importance, Johnson's western image and his long ties to the South were twin assets to Kennedy and the Democratic ticket.

The issue of religion loomed large throughout the campaign. Johnson's southern ties helped counter the strident denunciations of those who opposed Kennedy because he professed Catholicism. With the selection of Kennedy as the party's nominee, Johnson's Texan, southern, and western roots had become even more valuable. In a still parochial America, not yet homogenized by mass communication and readily available and seemingly instantaneous travel, Johnson seemed more typically American than Kennedy in large sections of the country. While the Democratic Party might not have been ready for a candidate with rural roots in Texas, coupling such an individual with a Catholic from the Northeast seemed a good political strategy. Johnson understood his role. He had to deliver the South and defend Kennedy against gratuitous attacks on his faith and character.[9]

In a changing America, Johnson's western posture was an asset of tremendous value. The West had a different image, as a place of reinvention and self-realization, and it appealed to Americans more broadly than did the South, with its racial problems and seemingly feudal economic and social situation. Johnson sounded southern but acted increasingly western. The ranch and its accouterments—the consistent stream of stories about it since Johnson's days as majority leader—contributed to his revitalized image. The site created an iconography mimicked across the nation. In one instance in Boston during the campaign, Johnson was met by a group of Italian-American women, all "absolutely overpowered by these great big [cowboy] hats," Elizabeth Rowe remembered.[10] The cowboy hats represented a shared Americanism that transcended region, an American pose that obviated ethnic and religious differences. In effect, the ranch and the values its western mythology represented became a part of holding the political center against Nixon in 1960, a way of speaking to the South in southern terms while packaging the same message as a representation of the West for the rest of the nation.

Johnson assiduously defended Kennedy against attacks on his Catholicism, a strategy that had particular resonance in the heavily Protestant religious culture south of the Mason-Dixon line. He frequently mentioned John Kennedy's brother Joseph P. Kennedy, Jr., who was killed as his plane went down during World War II. In the copilot's seat next to the young Kennedy sat a young man from New Braunfels, Texas. Johnson reminded audiences time and time again that as the two young men fell heroically to their deaths, no one asked what religion they professed. This seemingly western mythic trait—judging an individual by their actions instead of their words or beliefs—had great resonance. If a Texan and fellow Southerner could accept a Catholic, could argue that if a man was fit to serve in the military and sit in the Senate he had to be fit for the White House, so could the rest of the region. At the same time, Johnson's Stetson and the innumerable scenes of him on horseback captured in newspaper and magazine photographs played an important role in persuading the rest of the public that the number two man on the ticket was not a real Southerner. In a close election in which almost 67 million votes were cast, this combination of action and image contributed to the Democratic ticket's 112,881-vote margin. Considering Johnson's importance in carrying much of the South, Texas, and California, Kennedy's postelection trip to the LBJ Ranch a week after the Johnsons came to Florida to see the Kennedys was more than a mere gesture.[11]

But for Johnson, the triumph was hollow. He had settled for the second highest office in the land, shy of his genuine objective of the Oval Office. He had much of which to be proud. Texas had voted Democratic in a presidential election for the first time since 1948, and the 1960 election helped remake the American political landscape. But rather than shortening the distance to what he hoped to achieve, ascension to the vice presidency in a younger man's presidency could easily have meant that Johnson had gone as high as he would go. As the returns came in, Johnson only smiled for the photographers. One account called him "demonstrably morose," and one of his secretaries recalled that after the victory was secure he "looked as if he'd lost his last friend on earth," a sentiment that accurately described the ambivalence of a man who had previously hoped that on November 8, 1960, he would be the one elected president rather than vice president.[12]

The Kennedy visit to the Johnson ranch eight days after the election underscored the complicated nature of Johnson's new position. Although the vice president's mood improved after the night of the election and he was typically hospitable, the arrival of Kennedy, a few of his staff, and the flock of reporters signaled a new moment for Johnson at his ranch.[13] The ranch was Johnson's place of power; there he controlled everything, made all the decisions, held close the power. Now his new superior, the president-elect of the United States, had dropped by to pay a visit. It was a classic situation, in which Johnson's desire to best anyone—particularly anyone who was part of the Northeastern liberal establishment—had to be muted.

During the visit, the new president and vice president engaged in a day of deer hunting. In many situations, Johnson regarded such hunting trips as a way to enunciate the superiority of a rural upbringing and experience with the land. He reveled in taking inexperienced people hunting, helping them prepare to shoot and then disrupting their aim, laughing it off as an enormous joke. Only the most skilled ever managed to hit a deer. Such seemingly childish behavior allowed Johnson to prove himself more accomplished and somehow more entitled to lead. Kennedy's visit acknowledged the president-elect's appreciation of Johnson's contribution to the campaign. After a 6:00 A.M. breakfast of hominy grits, home-cured bacon, home-baked bread, orange juice, and coffee, the two left on a seven-and-one-half-hour hunting excursion that began even as rain threatened. During the day, both men shot the two-deer limit. In Johnson's case, the results were attributable to experience; in Kennedy's to, in the words of reporter Joseph R. L. Sterne, "a streak of fabulous beginner's luck." Johnson brought down a buck more than six hundred yards away, a feat that Kennedy, who had never been deer hunting but who had considerable experience with weapons, called "the best shot I have ever seen." Kennedy's aides described the president-elect as a "crack shot," and Johnson was similarly laudatory of Kennedy's expertise. The president-elect himself joked that the number of his missed shots was "executive privilege."[14] Yet for Johnson, this was a new role. Even in the privacy of their limousine, beyond radio range and accompanied only by presidential advisor Kenneth O'Donnell and Torbert MacDonald, a U.S. representative from Massachusetts, Johnson could not embarrass the new national leader as he could newsmen, friends from the Senate, and other visitors to the ranch.

The Kennedy visit was illustrative of the problems inherent in the vice presidency. As the two men "sat up late after eating charcoal-grilled sirloin strip steak," they discussed the issues that faced the country. Johnson had showed Kennedy his stock and his fields during the visit, and after the sumptuous southern dinner, agriculture and ranching were the primary topics of their conversation. This was an area that Johnson had made his own, but again he had to defer to the younger man. For the first time at his ranch, Johnson was not in charge, not in control. The "crack shot" from Massachusetts set the agenda and even the tone in the sprawling living room of the ranch house. Despite his widely acknowledged significance in the triumph of the ticket, the proud Lyndon Johnson had to accustom himself to a subservient role in a younger man's administration. The change was apparent from the outset of the visit. When Kennedy arrived, Johnson met him wearing an enormous Stetson. The president-elect quipped in response to Johnson's greeting, "I could see you if you took that hat off." In his home country, on his home place, Johnson shed his Stetson, his symbol of westernness and independence, in an instant.[15]

This simultaneous increase and decrease in stature weighed upon Johnson. After the Kennedy visit, the ranch returned to its daily rhythm. Cattle and sheep grazed, the low-water bridge was again open to local traffic, and the large Secret Service contingent departed.[16] But the tone of the place had changed. Instead of reflecting Johnson's power and leadership, the ranch now reflected his ironically subordinate status as the second-in-command of the most powerful nation in the free world. The Johnsons returned to the ranch for the 1960 Christmas holidays in the manner typical of the family, but that year the vice president–elect was preoccupied. His new office was a powerless, limiting position, in many ways less valuable than the majority leadership he would abandon when inaugurated. Despite Kennedy's efforts to develop a rapport to promote closeness between the first and second families, Johnson still felt the potential to be left out. This feeling was acute, for it was a sentiment of which he was keenly aware as a result of the experiences of his youth. Johnson used the holidays to devise a strategy for overcoming the inherent powerlessness of his new position.

The vice presidency was a new and different role for Johnson, more ceremonial than his majority leadership and less alive with the machinations of politics. For a skilled legislative broker, it must have been something of a disappointment; the vice president had little influence and even less power. Johnson's predicament was compounded by his uncomfortable position in the Kennedy administration. During his visit to the ranch, Kennedy had predicted that Johnson would become "the most effective vice president in history," but even that distinction had dubious connotations. Although the Kennedys included the Johnsons in all the White House social events and the president kept the vice president involved in every major political decision—except, as Kennedy later noted, the Bay of Pigs fiasco—Johnson still felt he remained on the fringes of decision making. His expertise was necessary, but around the Kennedy White House, Johnson did not fit in. The new president surrounded himself with people like himself. Eastern, well-educated, from fashionable backgrounds, they were unlike the rural and often self-conscious Johnson. Conversely, Johnson regarded many of the individuals in the Kennedy White House as inexperienced and often incompetent political and legislative maneuver-ers. Despite his expertise with Congress, Johnson was kept out of the process of crafting legislation on many occasions. When he tried to offer assistance, he usually wound up feeling rebuffed. The new vice president felt his insecurities exacerbated during the Kennedy presidency.[17]

But Johnson respected Kennedy's political sense and accomplishment, respected the challenges they had overcome to win the election, and he played the role of vice president. He refused to become a John Nance Garner—a disloyal vice president who undermined his president, Franklin D. Roosevelt, whenever the opportunity arose. Instead, Johnson worked hard for the new administration. The Johnsons sold their previous home in Washington, D.C., and purchased a mansion called The Elms. They turned it into an official residence, preparing it for the lavish formal entertaining required of the office. In a role that limited his most valuable skills and reined in his instincts, Johnson endured.

The demands of the vice presidency continued to drive the transformation of the LBJ Ranch. Johnson's new role increased the ranch's importance as part of an image of America projected to the nation and the world. The ranch now represented the nation's aspirations as well as Johnson's, and the press and foreign visitors could point to it as a mythic version of the American experience and the roots of the nation. Johnson's ranch continued to be tied to an iconographic American heritage, its attributes expressed as a colloquial representation of the creation myth of the nation. The state events that began with the Lopez Mateos visit became more common during Johnson's vice presidency, and the ranch underwent another series of renovations in a seemingly endless process.

The Lopez Mateos visit had highlighted the limited amenities of the ranch house. The Johnsons were embarrassed to have the Mexican president, his wife, and their daughter be forced to share one bathroom during their stay. Immediately after the visit, the Johnsons discussed adding on to the guest rooms. Following the inauguration, early in 1961, the Johnsons again contacted J. Roy White and requested that he draw a plan for altering the east wing of the second story of the house. White's drawings reflected the Johnsons' desire to change the guest bedrooms into suites to accommodate the stream of important guests likely to visit during the vice presidential years. Dressing rooms and bathrooms were built into the Green and Gay rooms, creating suites that were ready for use by the summer of 1961.[18]

The vice presidency allowed Johnson to play a role in international relations that he had never before experienced. Prior to ascending to the vice presidency, the time he had spent overseas was limited. He had last been overseas in 1945; since then he had visited only Mexico outside the borders of the United States. In 1960, Johnson could be characterized as an amateur in matters of foreign culture and even provincial in his outlook on the rest of the world. He did bring some advantages to the informal position of roving ambassador that was part of the vice president's duties. His rural background amid the poverty of the early-twentieth-century Hill Country prepared him for the economic and social state of the Third World and offered him insight into its many predicaments. Johnson understood poor people and ambition, and he respected practices that developed the land: agriculture, animal husbandry, and similar economic endeavors. Poverty, in his view, was a correctable problem, one solved by a combination of the application of technology and the hard work of poor people. At the moment when Americans propagated the "Green Revolution"—a package of technologies designed to further the expansion of agriculture, particularly market crops, throughout the world—Johnson's view of remedies to poverty and official American attitudes nicely coincided. Johnson's personal traits—his gregariousness; his willingness to shake hands, to mix in crowds, to kiss babies, to taste raw fish—gave him a popularity that more refined and effete American leaders never achieved with the public in the Third World.[19]

His first trip, to a celebration of the independence of Senegal, a former French colony in West Africa, in April, 1961, demonstrated all the characteristics of Johnson overseas. The role of vice president restrained him at home, but overseas he could behave with the reckless abandon to which he was accustomed. Warned by the American ambassador that he should not go among the people of Senegal without gloves because they were dirty and diseased, the bare-handed Johnson plunged into the crowds in Dakar anyway, shaking hands, giving away souvenir pens, visiting homes, and drawing comparisons with Texas. In one instance, he saw immense baskets of peanuts and remarked to Lady Bird, "Why, it's just like Texas." On another occasion, Johnson left the sleeping ambassador and toured the city himself. He arose at 4:30 A.M. to visit a fishing village, where he discovered that the per capita income was about $100 per year. He told the people that when he was young, the per capita income in rural Texas was about $180 each year but that improvements had since raised it to $1,800. In the determined eyes of an African mother of eight, Johnson saw the "same expression I saw in my mother's eyes when she, the wife of a tenant farmer, looked down upon me and my little sisters and brothers, and determined that I should have my chance and my opportunity, believing that where there was a will, there was a way." This sentiment made a similar rise for the people of Senegal seemed foreordained.[20]

Johnson's foreign travel continued. During a 1961 Asian jaunt, he visited Saigon, South Vietnam, Bangkok, Thailand, New Delhi, India, and Karachi, Pakistan, with brief overnight stays in Manila, Taipei, and Hong Kong. At each stop he continued to visit markets, leaving reporters behind in Bangkok while he toured the Klong, the water market; meeting crowds in Manila; and being mobbed by admirers in Karachi. In India, he kissed Lady Bird inside the Taj Mahal and gave a Texas yell there to test the echo, gestures that violated decorum and shocked both the American retinue and his hosts. Long-time Johnson aide Walter Jenkins recalled "thousands and thousands of people lining the street [of Karachi] to the point that we had to stop and let them open the way."[21]

Stuck in the crowd in Karachi, Johnson got out and began his customary practice of shaking hands. To one side stood a man with his camel, an individual with "an unusual face, a very fine face, a sort of Santa Claus face that looked like a tremendous amount of humanity," George Reedy recalled. Johnson conversed with the man through an interpreter, making the off-the-cuff remark that he hoped the man would someday have the opportunity to see the United States. Johnson continued to the palace for talks with Mohammed Ayub Khan, the leader of Pakistan, and forgot about his encounter with the camel driver. But the following morning, the Pakistani newspaper *Dawn* featured an article lauding the vice president. "He reaches out to the man with no shirt on his back," the paper insisted, reporting that the bazaars of Karachi were filled with talk of Johnson's invitation to the camel driver, Bashir Ahmed, to come to the United States and stay at the Waldorf-Astoria Hotel in New York City.[22]

While the episode could have turned out to be an embarrassment for Johnson and the United States, a quick response averted the problem. After he returned home, Johnson was informed by the U.S. embassy in Karachi that while he might not have intended to invite Ahmed, all of Pakistan regarded his remarks as an invitation to the camel driver. Johnson groaned and endured the prospect of this unlikely visitor. A detachment from the U.S. embassy was sent to Ahmed's mud hut in Karachi to formally invite him to visit, but when they arrived the camel driver was gone. Pakistani police had taken him away, preferring that the Pakistanis who attracted the attention of the U.S. press were educated members of the elite, not illiterate camel drivers. The issue seemed closed.[23]

Despite such unusual situations, Johnson's international excursions were part of the development of the social role of the second family. The responsibilities of the vice president were often limited to formal and ceremonial events. Visits had to be reciprocated, and the second family played an important role in entertaining foreign dignitaries in the United States. Beginning in 1961, the Johnsons often hosted affairs at The Elms in Washington, D.C., but continued their practice of saving their best and most genuine entertaining for the LBJ Ranch.

The first guest at the ranch to experience Texas vice presidential hospitality was Chancellor Konrad Adenauer of West Germany, who arrived in April, 1961. Texas retained a mythic hold on many Europeans. The work of nineteenth-century German author Karl May presented a fictionalized but enticing view of the West that was part of the cultural milieu for German youth before the rise of Hitler. As did many other young Germans of his day, Adenauer dreamed of seeing the legendary places of the American West. Texas, with its heritage of fierce independence and its large German population, was first among these places. During a visit to the United States two years before, Adenauer had expressed his interest in visiting Texas to Johnson, who was glad to oblige. Adenauer and his daughter, Libeth Werhahn, flew from Washington, D.C., to Texas on Sunday, April 16, 1961, transferring to a helicopter at Bergstrom Air Force Base in Austin. Landing in Stonewall, the party attended a special Mass officiated by Father Wunibald Schneider at Saint Francis Xavier Church. To accommodate Adenauer, Father Schneider had to circumvent church rules that prohibited saying Mass after noon. The German chancellor "was a very strict Catholic and he wouldn't miss Mass for anybody," Father Schneider recalled Johnson informing him. "No matter what happens, I'll say Mass when Adenauer comes," the priest responded after his bishop agreed to the plan. After the Mass, a helicopter took Adenauer and his entourage to the ranch for a barbecue.[24]

For the Adenauer visit, the Johnsons prepared a sumptuous spread in the classic Texas style. Two huge tents were set up in the grove near the river, a hedge against a Texas spring rainstorm. The tent floors were carpeted, and the interior "looked sort of like a rich Turk's harem," KTBC employee and Texas humorist Richard "Cactus" Pryor recalled. Mary Kooch of Green Pastures in Austin catered the affair, trucking in the "fixings" and barbecuing some of the ribs over an open grill outside the tents. Ham, potato salad, Texas-style baked beans, cole slaw, pickles, and Texas toast rounded out the menu. A crowd of between four hundred and five hundred gathered to greet the chancellor, who arrived in a sleek Johnson convertible after the helicopter landing scared the horses that were supposed to pull the chancellor in a surrey. The affair presented, Pryor recalled, "a pretty fancy spread."[25]

After the meal, which was quite popular with the guests, a program followed. Cactus Pryor had driven the entertainment—a duo called Tommy and Sandy, who along with Arthur Godfrey later became the nucleus of the Serendipity Singers, and two chemical engineering majors from the University of Texas who were fine singers—to the ranch. Although he thought he was "just functioning as a chauffeur," Johnson's executive assistant, Elizabeth "Liz" Carpenter, told Pryor that Lady Bird Johnson wanted him to serve as master of ceremonies. "I immediately acquired an almost lethal attack of stage fright—tent fright, I guess you'd call it," Pryor remembered, "and then when she signaled that she wanted the entertainment, I went on in. . . . There were more brass than I'd ever seen assembled in one place in my life." Ambassadors, generals, and other dignitaries dotted the crowd, and even the irrepressible Pryor was intimidated. Without a microphone, he meekly asked for everyone's attention not once but twice. Everyone continued talking. Finally, he recalled, "I shouted out in my best Texas voice, 'Simmer down!' And they did." Pryor introduced the acts and told some jokes, which Adenauer's translator conveyed to the chancellor while Pryor waited, and the afternoon was judged a success. During the ceremonies, Johnson presented Adenauer with a modified Stetson hat.[26]

Adenauer and his entourage continued to Fredericksburg, the home of Adm. Chester W. Nimitz, the World War II hero. Nimitz had flown back from California to meet the chancellor, and although his wife became ill and remained at the ranch, he enjoyed the barbecue and joined the group for the trip to Fredericksburg. At Gillespie Fair Park, more than seven thousand people awaited the chancellor, who marveled at the tremendous reception, gave a brief address, and repeatedly remarked on his excitement at finally visiting the Hill Country. The party returned to the ranch for a private dinner that consisted of the Johnsons, the Nimitzes, and Adenauer and his daughter. The next day, the chancellor left Texas after a brief stop to address the state legislature in Austin. It was, he told the representatives, a genuine pleasure to visit Texas.[27]

As a result of Adenauer's visit, the symbolic value of the ranch became apparent to many who had previously ignored its potential. The ranch was not in the iconographic "boondocks," as some of the Kennedy White House staff had assumed. Johnson's Texas roots and the way he presented them at the ranch had tremendous pull even for people of other countries. The American West and its ranching, its barbecues, beans, and chuck wagons, had a cross-cultural resonance that allowed even those raised in other parts of the world to participate in an American myth made universal by popular fiction and the movies. Foreigners could see their preconceived vision of the "real America" in the vistas, settings, entertainment, and libations of the LBJ Ranch. For Europeans, this was all especially poignant; it resonated with the myths they held about the American West. Adenauer's visit began a universalization of the ranch, its transformation from a place of continental iconography to one of international symbolic meaning.

The ranch was also a highlight of the state visit of Field Marshal Mohammed Ayub Khan of Pakistan, whom Johnson had visited earlier in 1961. Pakistan played a crucial geographic role in Cold War politics. The United States sought an ally on the Indian subcontinent. The insistent nonaligned status of India, the other substantial state in east Asia, and the religion- and territory-based rivalry between the two nations made the Pakistanis attractive to American foreign policy experts. In no small part, the location and strategic importance of Pakistan accounted for Johnson's visit to Karachi and were contributing factors in Kennedy's invitation to Ayub Khan. After a state visit to Washington, D.C., that included a candlelight dinner on the lawn of Mount Vernon, the home of George Washington, in rural Virginia, Ayub Khan flew to Texas on July 15, 1961. He visited the Alamo, in San Antonio, where he participated in a wreath-laying ceremony, and then continued by helicopter to the LBJ Ranch.[28]

Typically, Johnson offered a Sunday barbecue in honor of Ayub Khan as the highlight of the visit, with other smaller activities preceding and following the affair. Ayub Khan arrived on Saturday evening. A fifty-person dinner at the ranch that evening included a number of influential Texans. Educated in England, the Pakistani leader was quite secular. He spoke the English language with fluency and aplomb and understood western ways. The Johnsons were able to organize a sophisticated entertainment program without worrying about offending Ayub Khan's mores. Pryor, who again served as master of ceremonies, remembered Ayub Khan as a "very happy fellow" who "laughed very easily." On an evening graced by a stunning full moon, the Johnsons provided a candlelight dinner on white linen tablecloths for their guests. Among the visitors were Secretary of State and Mrs. Dean Rusk, Secretary of Defense and Mrs. Robert McNamara, Texas Governor and Mrs. Price Daniel, and other Texas dignitaries. Aquatic teams performed, and an Australian, Diana Trask, who was then appearing on television's *Mitch Miller Show,* sang. Wearing a blue gown and bathed in the light from a blue spotlight, she sang "Blue Moon." Cactus Pryor remembered the evening as "a very romantic setting."[29]

The barbecue the next afternoon drew more than five hundred visitors to the ranch. "The planes came in from all over the Southwest," Pryor recalled, "jets—swarming around like turkey buzzards coming in for landings." Among the guests were more than fifty-five Pakistani students studying at Texas colleges. One of Johnson's favorite entertainers, Eddy Arnold, the "Tennessee Plowboy," sang, as did regional celebrity Rosalita of San Antonio, and a mariachi band played. Pryor again served as master of ceremonies, standing on a raised dias adorned with red, white, and blue bunting and flying the United States and Pakistani flags. Johnson presented Ayub Khan with a saddle, three Texas-style hats, a pair of spurs, and a leather-trimmed hunting jacket and then inexplicably took the Pakistani leader away in a golf cart. Eddy Arnold began singing to the backs of the guests' heads as everyone's eyes followed the two departing leaders. Pryor recalled that Arnold was "a little bit miffed" at his treatment.[30]

Ayub Khan's secular bearing and experience with the larger world helped avoid what could have become an uncomfortable international incident. On the menu along with barbecued beef and chicken was barbecued pork—a taboo for any devout Moslem, a threat to the status of any Moslem leader who might sample it, and potentially an inadvertent insult. Although the pork ribs were not on the trays offered to the Pakistani guests, even their appearance on the menu could have been considered an affront.[31] Ayub Khan's worldly experience and his sense that he was among friends allowed him to consider the offering of the meat as simply a mistake on the part of the Americans, and an incident that could have been extremely embarrassing was avoided. Johnson's Texas background gave him charisma and had symbolic value, but it also contained limitations.

Johnson and Ayub Khan had a great deal in common. Both enjoyed hunting and were excellent marksmen; both, according to Liz Carpenter, "loved the land, loved the countryside." The shared outlook of the two men became clear during their conversation. "How much rainfall does your country have?" Johnson asked Ayub Khan in his typical measure of the nature of a people. As the leader of a country with vast arid regions, the general could respond with an answer Johnson appreciated. After the barbecue, Johnson took Ayub Khan on a drive across the ranch, and the two men discussed a range of subjects as a friendship began to grow. Among the topics was the camel driver from Karachi, whom Johnson insisted should be brought to the United States for a visit.[32]

Bashir Ahmed, the camel driver, posed an ongoing problem for the Kennedy administration. Johnson's "promise" to him had to be fulfilled, or the Americans would seem to have reneged on a meaningless promise that could have ramifications for foreign policy. The visit was set for October, 1961. There were problems beyond the timing. Ahmed was illiterate and unskilled in the ways of the diplomatic and official world. He had never been to the West, never seen its customs, and the modern world contained many features that would shock a devout Moslem. Press coverage of the trip also posed problems. The cynical American media would likely have a field day with this ordinary representative of a populous protoindustrial nation. Ahmed's visit ran a real risk of becoming a farce. Newspapers assigned their humorists to cover the trip, potentially turning the gesture of the invitation into an event that could be offensive in a personal sense and might also seem to mock the Pakistani people. Despite Johnson's contention that the United States "need[ed] on our side the camel drivers of the world," the attitude of the American press remained a sensitive issue.[33]

Ahmed's visit had to be closely managed. Johnson and his staff repeatedly informed the press of their obligation to treat Ahmed gently in their reports. Johnson told reporters that he thought it would be "cruel and foolish to poke fun at him in print," reminding them that not only was Ahmed a personal guest of Johnson's but that he represented the type of people in the world who Americans wanted to support their goals in the international arena. Henry B. Gonzalez of San Antonio, a friend of Johnson, echoed these sentiments with Lady Bird Johnson and Liz Carpenter at his side during a political rally in San Antonio just as Ahmed arrived at Idlewild Airport in New York City. Lyndon Johnson met him there and whisked him off to Texas, in no small part to control press access to someone nearly everyone believed was an unsophisticated visitor. Liz Carpenter was enlisted to play "nursemaid" to the visitor. Planned events were kept to small groups, and for a time during the visit Johnson simply kept Ahmed away from reporters.[34]

During the visit, however, Ahmed astounded Americans with a kind of grace and charm that they did not expect from a Third World camel driver. Treated as if he were a minor celebrity, Ahmed marveled at the United States and its many attributes. Serendipitously he became an archetypical foreign guest, albeit one possessed of considerable appeal and charisma. He became a public relations dream for Johnson and his staff. Ahmed had great personal presence. He was "extraordinarily gentle; he had this marvelous face," George Reedy remembered. "And he was a devout Mohammedan and didn't drink. He was past the age where he would chase women, if he ever had chased women. He really loved small children, and they responded to him. He handled himself with considerable dignity." An adept interpreter made the camel driver sound well spoken, witty, and innocent in a manner that Americans liked but could hardly emulate. "Smoother than a camel," Ahmed remarked of his horse ride on one occasion. He also demonstrated what Americans regarded as simple dignity. "Perhaps my body is weary but my heart will never tire of the friendship I have seen," he told reporters assembled in Washington, D.C. "When I sat atop my camel I thought I surveyed the world, but I had not seen one handsbreadth," he said from atop the RCA Building, overlooking New York City. He also had a profound innocence that enticed Americans. When he saw the coverage of his arrival in New York on television after he had reached the LBJ Ranch, he exclaimed with wonder: "How can I be here when I am there?"[35]

The ranch served a dual purpose during Ahmed's visit. Johnson used it when he sought to hide his guest from the press; at the same time, the operations of the ranch were comprehensible to Ahmed in a way that American cities and customs were not. The ranching enterprise fascinated and awed Ahmed. Its machinery and what seemed to the guest to be a large number of animals were beyond his experience in Pakistan. Johnson used Ahmed's interests and his control of access to his ranch to manage the visit. Instead of showing Ahmed the United States, Johnson initially brought many aspects of Texas and American culture to him. As Ahmed became more comfortable and Johnson's staff recognized that the visitor could charm the American media, the vigilance that characterized the first stages of the visit relaxed.

The vice president treated Ahmed to a tour of Texas and a glimpse of Texas history and culture. Texas philosopher and folklore laureate J. Frank Dobie and famed Texas historian Walter Prescott Webb explained the history of the region to Ahmed, who responded: "Well-said words are like

golden plums in silver bowls." Upon leaving the ranch, the Johnsons took
the camel driver to the Texas State Fair in Dallas. After Lyndon Johnson
bid him farewell, Ahmed continued to Kansas City, where he toured the
headquarters of People-to-People, the organization that had handled the
tour arrangements; saw a cattle auction; visited the Truman Library in
nearby Independence, Missouri; and shook hands with former president
Harry S Truman. "For every white hair on his head, there has been a troubled
day," Ahmed said of the former president.[36] When he left to return to
Pakistan, Americans wistfully watched this modern version of the natural
man leave their midst.

Bashir Ahmed's visit remained a curious moment in Johnson's long political career. Lyndon Johnson must have invited thousands of people to
Washington, D.C., as he shook hands across the country and the world,
but as one of his aides remarked, "we thought it was just as well that of all
those thousands of people, maybe tens of thousands that Mr. Johnson
invited to Washington, only one ever showed up." Ahmed possessed the
kind of charisma and bearing that made for a good human-interest news
story, something Johnson acknowledged during the visit when he finally
removed restrictions on contact with the press. In effect, at some point
Johnson decided that the camel driver could handle media attention, and
what had seemed an ordeal became a very pleasant and valuable public
relations experience.[37]

The relationship between the United States and Pakistan improved as a
result of Johnson's endeavors. The Ahmed visit was a stunning success with
both the American and Pakistani publics. Ayub Khan and Johnson had
much in common, and after the field marshal's return to his palace at
Rawalpindi, Johnson showered the Pakistani leader with mementos of the
trip. "I have not yet got over the tremendous hospitality kindness and
friendship you showed to me during my visit to your great country," Ayub
Khan wrote after his return. "May I say again how impressed I was with
your sincerety [sic] and wisdom?" Ayub Khan was also pleased that Ahmed
"conducted himself with poise and dignity . . . the basic qualities of our
people, however uneducated they may be." Pakistanis marveled at Johnson's
generosity with Ahmed; across the Pakistani nation, "it tended to break
down any existing wall of suspician [sic]," in the estimation of a member
of the military guard at the U.S. embassy who traveled throughout the
country. Everywhere he and his entourage stopped, the talk was of Ahmed.
"In every teahouse all over Pakistan, they were talking of nothing else when

[Ahmed] was here except his visit," Liz Carpenter recalled. "It was page one every day. . . [it allowed the U.S.] to identify with the man on the street and the peasant instead of the professor." In Pakistan, the vice president was referred to as "Friend Johnson Sahib." Americans and Pakistanis drew closer as a result, achieving an important diplomatic goal for the Kennedy administration.[38]

During the vice presidency, the ranch increasingly became a focus for formal social affairs in the informal Texas style. With barbecues as the centerpiece, Johnson often brought an array of visitors to the Hill Country to experience regional color and hospitality. The ranch offered an all-purpose destination for dignitaries visiting Texas—a chance to charm anyone with gracious hospitality, a stunning rural setting, and the feeling of a down-to-earth experience. Visitors loved the ranch. During October, 1962, the Johnsons hosted a delegation of Latin American ambassadors from the Organization of American States (OAS) meeting in San Antonio. Brought in by bus, the delegates enjoyed an early afternoon cocktail party on the front lawn. After a lunch served among the trees, Johnson presented his visitors with "Honorary Texan" certificates and took them on a tour of the ranch. By late afternoon, the OAS delegates were on their way back to San Antonio for their banquet; Johnson rode a helicopter down to join them and gave the banquet address.[39]

As the stream of dignitaries to rural Texas continued, the more formal barbecues functioned in a similar manner. When the Johnsons hosted United Nations ambassadors for a barbecue at the ranch in April, 1963, "Texas twang and clipped British" accents were juxtaposed, Cactus Pryor remembered. "The first thing that struck you was the contrast: The Oriental and the Occidental, there were Paris frocks and Levis." Liz Carpenter also noticed the contrasts. "The world really shrunk in my eyes," she remembered. "Seeing saried women from the Far East in a remote part of Texas was a whole new ballgame." The ambassador from Ceylon, now known as Sri Lanka, arrived dressed in a traditional gown and wearing the Stetson that Johnson had given him. Johnson's cousin Oriole Bailey asked Washington, D.C., socialite Perle Mesta what she did. "Well, I give parties," Mesta said after a moment's thought. "You mean that's all you do?" Mrs. Bailey inquired. "Yes, that's about all I do," Mesta replied. "My, that's a funny way to carry on," Cousin Oriole remarked. More than two hundred guests joined the twenty-five United Nations representatives for a noon barbecue, followed by a shooting exhibition, a bullwhip champion displaying her prowess, and a comedy by the Geezinslaw Brothers.[40]

Throughout the many barbecues, the tangy aroma of meat on the grill permeated the ranch grounds. Texans took great pride in their barbecue, and Johnson sought only the best for his affairs. For major events, Johnson hired Walter Jetton, the famous Fort Worth barbecue impresario, who would bring his chuck wagon and portable barbecue pits to the ranch. By nine o'clock on the morning of any event, the smell of pork ribs, beef brisket, and simmering chicken would "convince your stomach that breakfast had been days before," Pryor recalled.[41]

The ongoing flow of visitors required continuing changes to the ranch house. After the initial redesign inspired by the Lopez Mateos visit, two further additions took place. The bedrooms and bathroom in the west wing, previously used by live-in servants, were remodeled into two guest suites and became known as the Carnation rooms. By January, 1962, that work was completed. That same year, the dining room, kitchen, and the ancillary areas nearby were also remodeled. A tool room and utility room were added, and the carport was redesigned.[42]

By the end of 1962, nearly two years into his vice presidency, Lyndon Johnson could look at his ranch and see more than a work in progress. In the decade during which the Johnsons had owned the property, the house had been redone to accommodate their growing need to host visitors, and the ranch had played an important role in the creation of a national image for Johnson that had contributed to his ability to secure the vice presidency. During the vice presidency, the ranch had become an international meeting place, an evocation of an America far different than the swirl of Washington, D.C., society. Even more important, the ranch had become home to the Johnson family. It was a far cry from the early 1950s, when floodwaters trapped Lady Bird and Luci in the ramshackle house. Throughout 1962 and 1963, the Johnsons made a series of ongoing trips to the ranch for personal and public affairs. The ranch provided time for relaxation from the busy, world-traveling schedule of the second-in-command of the free world.

Typical of the Johnsons' trips to the ranch was the Christmas vacation in 1962. From early December to early January, 1963, the Johnsons were at their ranch in the Hill Country. Arriving on December 7, Lyndon Johnson remained at the ranch until January 5. He was only away for three days, once for a brief trip to Austin and Fort Worth and once for a two-day return to the nation's capital. His first morning at the ranch, he breakfasted with his old friend and neighbor A. W. Moursand, and in time-honored Johnson fashion, the two drove around the ranch. During the afternoon, they went boating on Lake Granite Shoals, and the pattern continued throughout the holidays. Hunting and boating were regular activities during the entire trip.

In Lyndon Johnson's life, business and pleasure were always intertwined. During this stay at the ranch, a steady stream of political friends and acquaintances came by. Old Johnson friend and Texas governor-elect John Connally visited, as did Texas politico Dolph Brisco. A contingent from Georgia, including Governor Ernest Vandiver, Governor-Elect Carl E. Sanders, Senator Richard Russell, Judge Robert Russell, and Georgia state senator and state Democratic Party chair J. B. Fuqua, arrived to enjoy the hunting. The parade of guests and social events continued; twenty-six visitors enjoyed dinner at the ranch on December 27. By the time Johnson returned to Washington, D.C., to preside over the opening of the U.S. Senate on January 9, 1963, he had spent nearly a month in the element in which he was most comfortable.[43]

Throughout the first ten months of 1963, the pattern continued. Johnson returned twice in February and for a week in March and spent at least half of April and May at the ranch. Beginning in late June, he spent forty of the next sixty-one days at the ranch, leaving just prior to his birthday at the end of August. During these frequent jaunts to Texas, Johnson attended to a number of ceremonial functions inherent to his position. A barbecue for Finnish Ambassador and Madame Richard Raphael Seppala took place in late March. During the Easter recess, Johnson addressed the graduating class of Johnson City High School as a favor to the superintendent, Kitty Clyde Ross Leonard, his high school sweetheart. Johnson attended the Gillespie County Fair, where his Hereford herd made a "clean sweep" of the division. Ranch foreman Dale Malechek, hired in January, 1962, earned most of the credit for this success. In the evening, Johnson would stroll down to "Cousin Oriole's place" for conversation.[44] Such a rhythm was characteristic of Johnson's visits home, both for political and personal reasons. It kept Johnson close to the people of his region and state, served to further illustrate the image he had worked so long to develop, and gave him the only kind of relaxation he could tolerate: busy, mobile, and involved.

As the winter of 1963 approached, the LBJ Ranch had become an important place in American political culture. Johnson's uses of it had been largely successful; it was a far different place than it had been in 1951, both physically and symbolically. The renovated and reconstructed house had acquired an important position in Johnson's vice presidential activities. Besides simply being Johnson's home, the ranch had become a window into the ways of leadership, a guesthouse to the world. It showed the world, from national leaders to camel drivers, the "real America," a place where people worked with their hands and with the land, where Americans' ties to the way the rest of the world lived were far closer than they might seem on a trip to Manhattan Island or Washington, D.C. At his ranch, Johnson could show dignitaries from other countries that not all of America was highways and skyscrapers, that Americans operated in a manner and on a scale that the rest of the world could understand. He could talk about how recently the people of rural Texas had been as poor as those of the Third World, and visitors from around the globe could see what he meant. He could show them the land and animals, vestiges of a preindustrial American economy that resonated with people in developing countries. For visitors from developed nations, the ranch evoked an American past that was mythologized around the world. The ranch symbolized a kind of reality, a brand of history, that Americans and their guests found pleasing. It highlighted a type of heritage that Americans claimed closely but from which most had grown distant. Lyndon B. Johnson's ranch reminded Americans of their mythic and actual roots in a way that no city could.

The Johnson family in front of the main house of the LBJ Ranch, Christmas, 1955.
Courtesy Lyndon Baines Johnson Library

An aerial photograph of the LBJ Ranch, circa 1959–60, showing the main house and pool, the Martin garage, the hangar, and airstrip. Courtesy Lyndon Baines Johnson Library

(From left) *Harry S. Truman, Sen. Lyndon B. Johnson, President of Mexico Adolfo Lopez Mateos, and Speaker Sam Rayburn during Lopez Mateos's visit to the LBJ Ranch in October, 1959. Courtesy Lyndon Baines Johnson Library*

(From left) *Mercury Seven astronauts Scott Carpenter, Gordon Cooper, Alan Shepard, and Virgil "Gus" Grissom visit Vice President Johnson at his ranch on April 25, 1962. Courtesy Lyndon Baines Johnson Library*

Ludwig Erhard, chancellor of West Germany, visits President Johnson at his ranch in December, 1963. Photograph by Yoichi R. Okamoto, courtesy Lyndon Baines Johnson Library

Gustavo Diaz Ordaz, president of Mexico, is shown around the main house of the LBJ Ranch by President Johnson in November, 1964. Photograph by O. J. Rapp, courtesy Lyndon Baines Johnson Library

The front of the main house of the LBJ Ranch, taken in January, 1965. Photograph by Cecil Stoughton, courtesy Lyndon Baines Johnson Library

President Johnson drives his Lincoln Continental down the runway at the LBJ Ranch on January 15, 1965. Photograph by Yoichi R. Okamoto, courtesy Lyndon Baines Johnson Library

President Johnson sits in his Lincoln Continental parked next to an airplane on the runway at the LBJ Ranch in January, 1965. Photograph by Cecil Stoughton, courtesy Lyndon Baines Johnson Library

Cattle graze on the LBJ Ranch, with the hangar and aircraft in the background. Photograph by Yoichi R. Okamoto, courtesy Lyndon Baines Johnson Library

President Lyndon Johnson drives his Lincoln Continental full of guests around the LBJ Ranch in the summer of 1966. Photograph by Yoichi R. Okamoto, courtesy Lyndon Baines Johnson Library

President and Mrs. Johnson swim in the pool, with the main house of the LBJ Ranch in the background, in the summer of 1966. Photograph by Yoichi R. Okamoto, courtesy Lyndon Baines Johnson Library

The Birthplace home, part of the Lyndon B. Johnson National Historical Park, in a photograph taken on August 16, 1968. Photograph by Mike Geissinger, courtesy Lyndon Baines Johnson Library

Israeli prime minister Levi Eshkol talks to President Johnson during his visit to the LBJ Ranch on January 8, 1968. Photograph by Yoichi R. Okamoto, courtesy Lyndon Baines Johnson Library

Spiro Agnew (left) *and Richard M. Nixon talk to President and Mrs. Johnson during a visit to the LBJ Ranch on August 10, 1968. Photograph by Mike Geissinger, courtesy Lyndon Baines Johnson Library*

President Lyndon Johnson among the wildflowers on his ranch. Photograph by Yoichi R. Okamoto, courtesy Lyndon Baines Johnson Library

CHAPTER 5

Creating the First Remote White House

L yndon B. Johnson's ascendance to the presidency following the assassination of John F. Kennedy inaugurated a new era for the nation as well as for the ranch on the Pedernales River. In the throes of a cataclysmic tragedy, the nation mourned its lost leader and turned to its new one with decidedly mixed emotions. Johnson himself had to be perplexed by the whims of fate; in a terrible instant, all he had wished for had come true, but through the most bizarre and horrifying of circumstances. Unable or unwilling to secure the office by election, Johnson faced the much harder task of earning it through action—under the microscopic watch of the nation and the world. He would have to prove himself worthy of the mantle he had inherited rather than won, a gargantuan and daunting task in the late autumn and winter of 1963.

The tragedy brought out the best in Johnson. In the period immediately following the assassination, his most statesmanlike qualities, his leadership ability, and his desire for conciliation stood out of the fear, turmoil, and dashed hopes of the nation. The assassination in Dallas offered a frightening specter, for the president had gone to Texas, in the words of Kennedy aide Kenneth O'Donnell, "as a faith-healer" to mend a fight among Texas politicians that posed problems for the Democrats in the upcoming 1964 elections. With the stain on the nation emanating from Texas, Johnson had to demonstrate not only his own worthiness but that of his hallowed home state as well. Among his gestures were personal letters to each member of the deceased president's immediate family, a blanket request to all Kennedy cabinet members to stay on, and his insistence at walking behind Kennedy's caisson to Arlington National Cemetery despite the objections of security professionals. His willingness to expose himself to potential danger as well as other kindnesses to the Kennedy family inspired a long and laudatory handwritten note from Jacqueline Bouvier Kennedy, the president's widow. "Thank you for the way you have always treated me—the way you and Lady Bird have always been to me—before, when Jack was alive, and now as President," the grieving Mrs. Kennedy wrote. Her testimonial to Johnson's consideration spoke volumes about the new president's manner in these difficult circumstances. "To me, Johnson's conduct in that period . . . was perhaps his finest hour," said Charles Roberts, *Newsweek* contributing editor and White House correspondent. "He couldn't have been more considerate, not only of Jackie but of all the Kennedy people. He was thoughtful. He was thinking ahead."[1] This gracious caliber of leadership marked the transition period to the new Johnson administration.

For the nation and the world, the transfer of power to Johnson was fraught with peril. Here was a new American leader, older and more mature, yet rural and seemingly less polished than his slain predecessor. Undoubtedly Johnson was a man of substance, but he was of a different appearance and manner than Kennedy. Johnson was a large man "with preposterous ears and a Texas twang," biographer Merle Miller wrote—a different sort of image than that projected by the suave and stylish John Kennedy.[2] The iconography of leadership changed in an instant, from the rough and tumble touch-football games on the lawn at Hyannisport to the more bucolic, more homey, but more geographically distant and culturally remote setting of the LBJ Ranch.

The presidency became the signal moment in the history of the ranch. The dilapidated place that had belonged to Johnson's aunt and uncle, Frank and Clarence Martin, became an essential part of the political infrastructure of the nation as well as a symbol of healing. In the aftermath of the assassination of Kennedy, when the nation was racked by paroxysms of sorrow and doubt, the symbolic importance of the ranch setting grew. More than ever before, the ranch on the Pedernales River harkened back to a "better" America, a more placid, more sturdy, less tendentious American past. It was clearly Texan at a moment when Texas was tainted, a symbolic joining of the best and the worst at once. Transformed into a combination of command post and getaway for the leader of the free world, the ranch became one of the headquarters of decision making for the nation and the world. It became a pragmatic, functional, efficient place, even as it represented a less complicated past.

With Johnson in the presidency, the ranch developed new importance that far surpassed its role as the vice president's estate. What had largely been a retreat of ancillary importance became the second most significant location in the nation after the White House. The little stone house and its many additions had become the home of the president of the United States, a symbolic significance for which Johnson had long been preparing the ranch but that caught him and the nation by surprise. The development of the ranch in the previous decade had become, in an instant, only the precursor of a more fundamental transformation. Indicative of the change was the new name that the press and soon everyone gave the Pedernales property: instead of the LBJ Ranch, it became the Texas White House.

Johnson felt a level of comfort at his ranch that he enjoyed nowhere else, a sentiment crucial to the reinvention of the ranch as a remote White House. "The best place to talk to a man is on your own ground," Dale Malechek reported being frequently told, and others, especially McGeorge Bundy, encouraged Johnson to utilize the ranch as more than his home. Johnson believed he had more control on the ranch, "more willpower to influence people there," in Malechek's words, and with his deep-seated need to have people around him, he enjoyed having people visit the ranch. The fusion of the ranch as both place of business and home ground fit with Johnson's political and personal philosophies.[3]

The president required a range of services and facilities that were unavailable even to the vice president, and Johnson's predilection for spending time at his Texas home meant in essence that a second communications, security, protocol, and administrative structure parallel to the one in Washington, D.C., had to be established at the ranch. Johnson loved his ranch and spent as much time there as he could, but as president he required all the support systems necessary to perform the duties of his office. The geographic location of the ranch created logistical problems for planners. Johnson was the first U.S. president from the South since Woodrow Wilson left office in 1921 and, despite his rural roots in a region known for its degree of urbanization, the first genuinely Sun Belt and western president in the nation's history.[4] His ascendance was a precursor of fundamental changes in the signs and symbols of American society and politics; it created numerous problems simultaneously that forced his staff to improvise, to invent solutions.

Johnson's manner of running the presidency and his needs were different from those of any of his predecessors. With a home far from Washington, D.C., and strong filial ties to his home state, Johnson lacked the luxury of the proximity of Kennedy's Hyannisport or the desire for a farm at Gettysburg or for the federally owned retreat at Camp David. Chauvinistically, he wanted to be in Texas whenever possible. He would often tell Lady Bird to be ready to leave for Texas in less than one hour, but both were so devoted to their home state that she barely objected to the lack of notice. This fealty to state or region of origin was a common trait in American politics. But Johnson was the first president from a distant state who could have the desire to spend a great deal of time at home accommodated. Meeting his needs required something new and different on the American political landscape. Johnson's presidency created the first remote White House, the first time in American history that a leader of the nation could meld a desire to be far from the nation's capital with the demands of leading the country.

As was the case in his first Senate campaign, Johnson had to invent the processes that would allow him to accomplish his ends. In 1948, he had enlisted technology as the way to spread his message. Besides inundating the state with political advertising, Johnson hired a helicopter and flew from town to town. The aircraft itself generated great interest in rural Texas and created a venue from which to spread his message. In the 1948 campaign, Johnson foresaw the future of communications.[5] His use of technological campaigning foreshadowed its later importance.

At his ranch, Johnson also anticipated future developments in the use of various forms of communications media. He installed the systems that allowed him to make his Texas office into a second Oval Office, enabling him to govern far away from Washington, D.C. The ranch became "an extension of his office," in the words of Maj. James U. Cross, who piloted Johnson's plane and later served as armed forces aide to the president.[6] In this, Johnson served as a model for later developments in communications protocol and procedure. Politicians had utilized radio and television communications since the first availability of these revolutionary technologies; as happened to some silent-screen stars with the coming of synchronized soundtracks in the movies, some politicians, in particular Senator Joseph McCarthy of Wisconsin, were undone by the image television projected of them. Johnson understood how to use new forms of communication better than most politicians. He was the first president truly to utilize postwar technology to govern rather than to campaign, to understand its implications for the way the nation could be run and to use it to implement policy. This gave him the option, in fact the choice, of governing from afar, of utilizing his home in a manner that no previous president could.

Johnson's frenetic pace of governing required a significantly enhanced infrastructure at the ranch. Every aspect of the place—from roads to communications systems, from security and housing to the airstrip—had to be rethought and redesigned after Johnson became president. In the immediate aftermath of the Kennedy assassination, presidential security became the paramount concern, but as the outlines of the Johnson presidency became clearer, a full-scale physical transformation of the property along the Pedernales River began to take place.

The development of communications facilities was a primary consideration. Johnson was the president who, in the words of *Newsweek*'s Charles Roberts, "made the [tele]phone an instrument of national policy," who brought the dependence on communications so characteristic of modern government to the presidency. "He could practically crawl through that [telephone] wire," George Reedy remembered, and it was essential to his way of conducting business. Johnson spent as much as eighteen hours a day on the telephone. By 1958, Johnson had a telephone in his automobile, an amenity that attracted much attention because it was so rare. He was the envy of his peers; when Senator Everett Dirksen, a curmudgeon about new technologies, finally had a telephone installed in his car, he called Johnson to inform him. "Wait, Ev," Johnson is purported to have replied. "I've got to answer my other line." Johnson also had a phone with a thirty-five-foot cord in a metal box on a post in the backyard of his

Austin home. He could talk in the yard and even walk into the house with this cord.[7]

Telephones were more than necessary for Johnson; they were elemental. For the ranch to serve as a remote White House—a place from which the president of the United States could conduct national and international business—required those wires, the creation of an infrastructure previously unequaled in the Hill Country and uncommon anywhere else in the country but within the highest levels of business, government, and the military. Assembling its various components required the application of significant resources and the efforts of numerous organizations and government entities.

By November, 1963, the LBJ Ranch had already undergone a range of infrastructural transformations since the Johnsons purchased it in the early 1950s. In his first years at the ranch, Lyndon Johnson had found the Stonewall telephone exchange insufficient for his needs. He had only one telephone line, and in particular, he wanted better long-distance service. He contacted Ira W. "Stormy" Davis, a long-time Southwestern Bell Company manager who had supervised the installation of the private branch exchange (PBX) used at the "Johnson for Congress" headquarters in Austin during the 1946 campaign. This was the first instance of the use of a private PBX in Texas. Under Davis's supervision, Southwestern Bell provided a long-distance trunk line along the Pedernales River for Johnson, as well as a private toll line connecting the ranch with nearby Johnson City. Davis recalled that Johnson needed the new lines because there was only one line through Stonewall, and "people kept the [long-distance] line tied up to such an extent that the senator had great difficulty in making and receiving long distance calls." Johnson paid $36.63 every month for each of twenty-two extensions at the ranch.[8]

This first stage of communications development, in place by the middle of the 1950s, soon became obsolete as Johnson's responsibility grew. Improvements in company capability and Johnson's nomination as vice president created both the ability and the need to provide more comprehensive service. In August, 1960, Southwestern Bell offered the ranch four Austin lines and one Stonewall line to meet Johnson's long-distance calling needs, supported by a total of sixteen long-distance circuits from facilities located in the center shed of the hangar. Eleven six-button handsets and an emergency backup generator were also installed. The Southwestern States Company, a regional concern, provided local service for the ranch.[9]

Lyndon Johnson had been a heavy user of the telephone throughout his political career, and the limited capabilities of the ranch during the early 1950s barely slowed him. In every photograph ever taken of a Johnson office, a telephone is visible; in Johnson's world, telephones were located on desks, on mantels and dining room tables, under desks, by couches, on window sills, and even in the bathroom. Numerous photographs of the man show him glued to the telephone handset. As majority leader of the Senate, Johnson required eleven separate local and long-distance telephone lines at the ranch. These were in use most of the time, either by Johnson himself or by one of his ever-increasing number of secretaries and assistants. When he became vice president, he increased the number of phone lines at the ranch to fifteen to accommodate the growing demands of his office.[10]

The changing demands on the ranch during the vice presidency prompted the rearrangement of facilities. The Johnsons needed more space to accommodate visitors, staff, and official personnel, and they requested that the Southwestern Bell facilities be moved out of the hangar. A new structure, known as the "O" carrier building, was constructed next to the airstrip to house the telephone equipment. It remained in use for that purpose until after the Kennedy assassination.[11]

During most of Johnson's vice presidency, six telephones were located on the first floor of the ranch house. Three of these were in Johnson's office at the west end of the house, with one each in the living room, den, and master bedroom. Two additional handsets were on the second floor: one in the upstairs master bedroom and the other in administrative assistant Mary Margaret Wylie's bedroom. The bath house by the swimming pool also contained a handset. Special telephone service was added for visiting dignitaries or during barbecues or other social events to which members of the press were invited.[12]

Johnson also used the television as a major source of information. He was notorious for having three televisions, each tuned to one of the three major networks, on at all times in the Oval Office and in his bedroom at the White House. But the ranch in Stonewall was well beyond the range of most conventional television signals, an ironic predicament for a family that owned a major media network in Texas. Until the late 1950s, television reception at the ranch remained poor. In 1960, Johnson ordered a fifty-foot-tall television antenna installed. "This tower—though highly functional," Lady Bird Johnson remembered, "was the bane of my life—

aesthetically. Lyndon finally moved it for me." The tower was relocated to the Scharnhorst property in 1962 as part of a series of renovations, and it remained the basis for television reception at the ranch.[13]

Throughout Johnson's presidency, television reception continued to be a problem. After nearly two years of intermittent complaints about interference from other signals by the president, Federal Communications Commission officials sought to improve reception at the ranch. The White House Communications Agency and Southwestern Bell drafted a plan to install a new relay station on Hartman Hill, about fifteen miles from the ranch. The cost of the endeavor was estimated to be between $150,000 and $200,000 for the first year and $50,000 for every subsequent year, which dampened enthusiasm for the project. When the cost was coupled with the assessment that even the new relay station could not guarantee consistently better television reception at the ranch, further discussion of the idea was dropped. The effort was deemed unworthy of the bad publicity the cost would generate.[14]

Improving communications reception and transmission at the ranch became a recurring concern of the Johnson presidency. By 1967, efforts to enhance television and commercial and government radio reception and transmissions were again underway. A tower was installed at the ranch to improve both television and radio reception. A base station in Fredericksburg was built, and antennas were added to a Central Texas Electrical Cooperative tower located about one mile from Fredericksburg. A tower was removed from the LBJ Ranch and taken to Riley Mountain, near Llano, to provide coverage in that area. The Riley Mountain location was ideal for reception but unfeasible because there were no rural electric or telephone lines to operate the tower in the immediate area. Only the community of Llano had the appropriate utility infrastructure to support the project, necessitating a new tower location. When the installation was finally erected at Camp Bullis, radio coverage was completed from San Antonio to the south, Austin to the east, through Lake LBJ to the north, and to a line between Fredericksburg and Llano to the west. The television antenna installation was also completed, although occasional co-channel interference remained. Another effort to improve communications between the ranch and the outside world fell short of optimal results.[15]

The Secret Service also made demands on radio transmission in the area. Col. Jack A. Albright of the White House Communications Agency secured numerous written agreements for government use of several radio installations across the Hill Country and Central Texas. Albright made fixed-term arrangements for the use of a number of locations, including Packsaddle Mountain, Hartman Hill, Westley West Tower, the Fredericksburg Co-op Tower, and Camp Bullis, but Secret Service officials noted that the arrangement did not meet their needs. They preferred agreements made on an "indefinite basis," Thomas L. Johns of the agency informed W. Marvin Watson, a White House aide. "These communications facilities should be available to the Secret Service as long as the Secret Service has a responsibility compatible to this area." Efforts were made to accommodate the needs of the Secret Service.[16]

Before the Johnson presidency, transportation to the LBJ Ranch differed little from that to the rural ranch of any influential individual. The main road, which crossed the river by the Junction School, was a typical Texas rural road. Called "farm-to-market" roads, these were usually blacktopped by the 1960s, but they were designed for farm trucks and farm machinery. Most had slow-moving traffic, and negotiating them during planting, harvest, cattle roundup, or hunting season could be difficult. Yet such roads sufficed for Johnson while he served as senator and vice president.

After the 1952 flood, Johnson had considered adding an airstrip to the property. Not only would it save him time in his hectic political travel schedule, but it would also provide a means to rescue his family should a severe flood again occur. During 1955, a 3,570-foot asphalt landing strip to handle light aircraft was constructed, and after he learned to select aircraft of the right size to have piloted in, the airstrip became a significant time-saver for Johnson. He regarded transportation in the most utilitarian terms and was impervious to the dangers involved in riding in low-flying helicopters and small planes. Maj. James U. Cross recalled that Johnson expressed a curiosity about the technological side of flying but was more interested in rapidly reaching his destination. Even the death of two of his pilots in a 1961 plane crash in the Hill Country did not deter Johnson from his insistence on flying even the smallest of craft in the worst of weather.[17]

Security procedures prior to Johnson's presidency also reflected the combination of importance and marginality associated with the vice presidency. During Johnson's vice presidential years, Secret Service agents were not stationed at the ranch except during Johnson's visits, and there were no permanent facilities designated for their use. Agents would arrive a few hours before the Johnsons to assure that there were no unauthorized people on the property and that no dangers to the Johnsons' safety existed.

Initially, Secret Service operations were located in handyman Lawrence Klein's old shop, and in some cases, Secret Service vehicles served as temporary command posts. A General Services Administration (GSA) trailer for Secret Service operations was placed north of the ranch house during the first year of the Kennedy administration. Plumbing and sewer connections were added, and the trailer became the center of security operations during the vice presidency.[18]

In the aftermath of the Kennedy assassination the ranch became the presidential residence, and the rules of its administration changed. Security of the roads, the infrastructure, the landing strip, and communications became preeminent concerns for those responsible for protecting the leader of the nation. At the ranch, this meant developments in each of these areas, upgraded facilities and management systems, and a full-time staff located at the Texas White House even when the Johnsons were not there.

Johnson's dependence on communications made the development of these systems a primary concern. The president needed access to any and all available information at all times, but much of what he needed to know was in Washington, D.C. A secure, coded system of transmission had to be established for conveying information to the ranch. The installation of three trailers immediately following Kennedy's assassination served as a prelude to the creation of a White House communications complex at the ranch. This facility included a communications switchboard and the cryptograph section, as well as quarters for military aides and other personnel on twenty-four-hour call.[19]

Johnson's predilection for the telephone required one of the best communications transmission systems in the world. Despite the installations and upgrades accomplished during the senatorial and vice presidential years, the presidency demanded an entirely revamped telephone system. Southwestern Bell assumed responsibility from Southwestern States for all telephone service to the ranch; the company faced a "monumental challenge," Stormy Davis recalled, in order to have an adequate system functioning by December 12, 1963, the date planned for the new president's first return to the ranch.[20]

Southwestern Bell raced to accommodate the new level of demand. Beginning on December 3, the company erected a steel structure on 4.73 nearby acres leased from Ernest Hodges even before formal arrangements for the property were completed. Within seventy-two hours, the site had been cleared, the foundation dug, and a building erected. A one-hundred-person crew arrived to install the sophisticated new telephone system. Three temporary microwave towers, sent from the American Telephone and Telegraph Company (AT&T), were built—one on Hartman Hill, a second at the Sawyer Ranch, and a third at the new telephone communications building. The microwave system provided 120 channels to Austin. The switchboard was located in a trailer that was placed east of the "O" carrier building. A second trailer, equipped with teleprinters and cryptographic machines, became the communications center. This equipment linked the Texas White House with the White House in Washington, D.C. By December 10, two days before the expected arrival of the new president, the system was operating, albeit primarily from temporary facilities.[21]

A delay in the Johnsons' arrival until December 24 allowed Southwestern Bell to make its temporary setup into a permanent operation. New towers replaced the hastily erected trio. State-of-the-art telephone equipment was installed, including a two-hundred-pair cable "plowed" underground east of the ranch, even though the muddy winter conditions caused as many as eight vehicles to be stuck at one time during the work. Southwestern Bell also established an engineering office in the vacant Johnson City Variety Store building from which to administer its efforts.[22]

By the time the upgraded system was completed, the telephone and communications structure housed enough equipment to service a small city. Power supplies—including a chrome-plated, fifty-thousand-kilowatt emergency generator that had been scheduled for use in the upcoming 1964 World's Fair—filled one-third of the communications trailer. The installation of this auxiliary power unit cost five thousand dollars, while the modifications required to keep the residence in compliance with national electrical code standards cost another two thousand dollars. Seventy-two telephones were installed at the ranch, including one in every room of the house, one in the president's bathroom, and another by the pool and the outbuildings. A radio system, replete with the requisite codes for staff and Secret Service personnel, was established; Johnson complained about the poor audio quality of the secret communications line until he became accustomed to it. A sixty-four "O" carrier line was added to the existing poles between Stonewall and Austin. A loudspeaker system was installed that allowed Johnson to give orders to anyone, in the house or in the pool, at any time. By the end of December, 1963, the Texas White House had a modern communications system that could support the activities of the president of the United States.[23]

With the permanent system established, refinement of the various operations commenced. The Johnson City facility that Southwestern Bell used eventually became the press center for reporters in the Hill Country when Johnson vetoed the idea of such a site at the ranch. Stormy Davis, of Southwestern Bell, spent endless hours accommodating the needs of the president, assuring that the most up-to-date equipment and the best possible service were available and in place. Other equipment had to be kept current as well. Copiers that reflected the latest advances in technology were installed. The network of communications was widened. Johnson's cars and boats at Lake LBJ received radio-telephone capabilities, making it possible to communicate with the ranch switchboard from the water. The television networks volunteered equipment that would be kept at the ranch for broadcasting. Each of the five ranches—the Scharnhorst, Lewis, Haywood, Nicholson, and Jordan House—received underground telephone cable service. Each was also equipped with typewriters for the use of senior staff members who might stay there.[24]

The new importance of the ranch created a range of transportation, traffic flow, and security problems. Before Johnson became president, the old low water road was the primary means of access, although at low water Johnson himself often drove across the dam he had built just west of the house. The old ranch road was not designed to accommodate either the official or the visitor traffic that a president could expect, and a range of improvements had to be undertaken.

One of the first changes was the upgrading of the approach road to the ranch. The ascendance of the new president increased the number of people who sought to view his Texas home. Most of them traveled old U.S. 290, a stretch of two-lane road that passed in full view of the ranch house across the river. It had been turned over to the county when the new U.S. 290 was completed. Early in December, 1963, Texas Highway Department officials approached the White House about resuming administrative responsibility for the stretch of the old highway, and Johnson assented. On December 19, 1963, the highway department appropriated forty thousand dollars for the construction of a 4.5-mile secondary loop from just west of the Blanco County line to the proximity of the ranch. The loop funneled traffic to the ranch off the new U.S. 290, the main artery of Hill Country, and allowed visitors to drive by the ranch, seeing it from across the river. Designated Ranch Road 1, the spur was a valuable addition that helped alleviate security concerns. It funneled traffic by the ranch without allowing people to approach the property. The spur was "most excellent," presidential assistant Clifton C. Carter informed Texas State Highway Engineer Dewitt C. Greer on January 2, 1964. "I am sure [it] will be helpful to the tourists who are now frequenting the area."[25]

The combination of easier access and Johnson's resounding popularity after the election of 1964 resulted in management problems on the new stretch of road. After a hunter tried to spot Johnson through a hunting sight, Ranch Road 1 was closed to the public for security reasons whenever the Johnsons were in residence at the Texas White House. A stream of requests to drive by the ranch while the Johnsons were present reached the White House staff. Typical was a letter from Larry Megow of Houston, who described himself as a "proud grandfather." Megow's son-in-law, an Air Force officer, had flown an escort jet for Johnson during a trip in the Far East and remained stationed there. The officer's wife and five children were visiting Texas during the Christmas holidays, and Megow wanted his grandchildren to see the president's home and take some pictures to show their friends in Florida. Johnson assented, a common gesture for him—particularly for anyone other than the press and during the holidays—and the Megow clan made their trip.[26]

The ranch road also provided proximity for those who wanted to bring a cause or policy to the attention of the president and, via the ever-present press, the nation. An array of individuals used the ranch road and the ranch as a backdrop to promote their causes. In a characteristic incident just prior to Christmas 1966, four Syracuse, New York, protesters tried to camp on secured land near the ranch to complain about the implementation of Johnson's antipoverty programs. The four were members of a group called the James Geddes Organization, which sought to assure adequate housing for the poor. They protested the termination of their funding by the Office of Economic Opportunity (OEO), headed by R. Sargent Shriver, a brother-in-law of former president John F. Kennedy. A Johnson aide, Jake Jacobsen, met with the protesters and explained that they should pursue the issue with OEO officials. The four continued their vigil and were later arrested when they refused to leave an area in which signs denying access were posted. The group was arraigned in nearby Fredericksburg.[27]

The arrests initiated an uproar. Maury Maverick, Jr., the son of an old Johnson friend and a prominent San Antonio attorney who offered his services to the American Civil Liberties Union in Texas, entered the case. Within two weeks, telegrams were received from a number of prominent antipoverty advocates, including Roy Wilkins of the National Association for the Advancement of Colored People (NAACP) and the Reverend Ralph David Abernathy of the Southern Christian Leadership Conference (SCLC), denouncing the arrests of the members of the group, now renamed the Syracuse People's War Council Against Poverty. The incident gave the group press coverage, although the pressure applied through the media was not sufficient to alter any federal decisions.[28]

Johnson remained wary of the press, and his treatment of it at the ranch reflected the often uncomfortable relationship. While he was quite at home with his friends in the media, such as Houston Harte of Harte-Hanks Communications, a Texas-based newspaper chain, the national media received more gruff treatment. In 1964, Chief White House Correspondent John Chancellor of NBC News sought permission to survey the ranch for locations from which the networks could provide improved television coverage. Chancellor proposed that the three major networks join to provide the best available signal and ambience from the ranch. This would entail scouring the property for the best location. On the memo requesting his approval, Johnson rejected the idea and angrily scrawled, "We don't want them at the ranch. We don't provide baby sitting." In contrast, in 1965, when Houston Harte requested permission to send photographers to the ranch to capture its springtime beauty, Johnson personally intervened after aides, wary of allowing even friends to intrude on Johnson's privacy, initially denied the request. Secret Service agents guided the photographers around the property. In accordance with Johnson's instructions, the photographers were kept out of the ranch house.[29]

Johnson's decision to limit press access to the ranch reflected his view of the property. To the president, the ranch was first his home and only then a second White House. The press had no business in someone's home except by invitation, Johnson insisted, and the press certainly would not be allowed to run loose in the White House. The Hill Country had few other distractions for members of the press, and the president was their focus there in a way that he was not in Washington, D.C. This made Johnson even less likely to allow representatives of television networks to roam the property. It would take up the time of security personnel for what Johnson regarded as largely meaningless aggrandizement of the press.

The result was a series of planned "adventures" at the ranch. These were designed to enlighten and entertain the press corps without allowing them free access to Johnson's world. Typical of such endeavors was a proposal from presidential aide Douglass Cater to hold a "reflective backgrounder" at the ranch as 1964 drew to a close. It had been a dramatic year, Cater noted, and an effort to "set the record straight" on the transition to the presidency, the genesis of the War on Poverty, the concept of the Great Society, and the many other issues of the year offered the president the opportunity to help shape the news reports of his efforts. Cater also planned to use this event to pit the White House regulars, the reporters on the capital beat, against their own bureau chiefs, "curbing the arrogance," he wrote, of the reporters. Again, control of physical access to the ranch and control of access to news and information were closely related in the Johnson worldview.[30]

Other parts of the transportation infrastructure were also upgraded to accommodate the president's travel needs. During the presidency, the landing strip was paved and extended to 6,150 feet to allow the president and staff officials to reach the ranch in a Jetstar without stopping in Austin if they desired. Although the air strip was "beefed up a bit" by the improvements, Major Cross recalled, and was long enough for Air Force One, a customized Boeing 707, to land, the Caliche soil base under the runway was not sufficiently stable to support the impact of the plane. The presidential plane, therefore, never landed at the ranch. Cross, the president's pilot, flew a DC-9 to the ranch in place of Air Force One. A portable air tower and personnel to staff it were brought to the ranch from Bergstrom Air Force Base to assist in landing military and private jets during Johnson's stays at the ranch.[31]

Johnson also had a greater need for aircraft and a broader tolerance for the risk involved than did many civilian officials. During 1964, Johnson planned to privately purchase a Beechcraft Queen Air for occasional flights in the vicinity of the ranch. There was no precedent for the use of a private or civil aircraft by a sitting president. Franklin D. Roosevelt had been the first president to travel by air, and military aircraft and crews had been used to transport him and all subsequent presidents. As a result of Johnson's proposed purchase, Federal Aviation Administration (FAA) officials sought to train and qualify his civilian pilots as if they were members of the military and wanted to add additional navigational equipment to the Johnson City Airport, the destination of numerous high-level visitors to the ranch. The planned improvements would be temporary in nature, similar to the ones added to the Gettysburg, Pennsylvania, airport during the Eisenhower administration. FAA officials were nervous about the consequences of a president flying in an aircraft piloted by individuals who did not hold military certification for the plane in question. With Cross's assurance that the FAA move was unnecessary, Johnson was typically cavalier about such demands on his staff.[32]

Turning Johnson's ranch into a second White House required an enormous organization and a great deal of money to assure the safety and security of the president and of the ongoing flow of travelers. Every time Johnson went to Texas an entire retinue of aides and staff members went as well. Cabinet officials and dignitaries sometimes accompanied the president, and on some occasions it seemed to observers that the trips to Texas included a never-ending parade of people and equipment. Cross recalled that "coming to Texas, we'd have forty, fifty people" on the plane. During each presidential visit, the airstrip was busy, as some officials flew in to discuss new business, others departed, and couriers carrying a range of information arrived and left. Each time, government officials in several agencies in Washington, D.C., had to cease other activities and prepare for the movement of as many as one hundred people to the ranch. Johnson flew anyone he could on the presidential plane. Routinely clerks, stenographers, and three shifts of Secret Service agents were on board. "We'd load everybody on that Air Force One," Cross remembered, "and away we'd go."[33]

The Air Force and the Secret Service began to set up the initial ground rules covering travel as early as November 28, 1963. Medical personnel had to be provided in case of emergencies, and helicopter support had to be arranged, along with numerous other details. The effort to assure that the people, information, and tools necessary to run the nation from a remote site were present at the ranch had to be comprehensive. This was a major undertaking. For example, fifty-five staffers flew with Johnson for the Fourth of July weekend in 1965; in another instance, fifty-six members of the press boarded the charter for the January 14, 1965, flight to the ranch, seemingly leaving no one in Washington, D.C., to cover other federal affairs.[34]

Devising economical traveling arrangements for such large numbers of staff proved to be a problem. Although Johnson was gracious about allowing staff on Air Force One and other presidential planes, the routinely higher number of staffers than places available compelled alternate arrangements. Initially, support personnel were transported on the press charter, but by 1965 the practice ceased after complaints of overcrowding by reporters. There was simply not sufficient space for support staff as well as newspeople. Reporters were often outnumbered by more than two to one by White House and military support staff. After June, 1965, a separate military aircraft transported staff, while the press flew on its charter.[35]

Johnson's affinity for his ranch was well known before 1963 and became even more apparent during his presidency. Between November, 1963, and September, 1967, Johnson made forty-two trips to the ranch. Thirty-four of these left from Washington, D.C., while the remainder departed from a variety of locations, including New York City; Atlantic City; Houston; Philadelphia; and Newport News, Virginia. Each trip to Texas required a full presidential entourage, and almost every flight included cabinet officials and other dignitaries as well as members of the press. Typically as many as one hundred people traveled at official expense on each of the trips, requiring significant expenditures to cover transportation.[36]

The cost of the frequent travel to the ranch drew some negative attention from the press and the public. Cost cutters everywhere noted the sizeable number of consistent travelers. Although the criticism was often muted, the expense of travel and the myriad other needs supplied to the Texas White House was high, ongoing, and—in the minds of some—of questionable necessity. Since taxpayers paid the bills, some watchdogs were critical of the White House. In one instance, a report in the *Dallas Morning News* at the beginning of 1964 that fifty new phone lines were to be installed at the ranch at the cost of more than $2.5 million generated complaints from a businessman. Such criticism kept Johnson and his staff fully aware of costs, and they strove to keep expenditures under control. In early August, 1965, the White House Communications Agency reduced its staff for the Texas trips from fifty-three to thirty-three. Switchboard operators were cut from ten to six, radio operators from eight to five, and the Tele-Prompter maintenance staff decreased by half. Later that month, a further decrease in staff went into effect. Permanently stationing one officer and fifteen enlisted personnel at the ranch allowed the decrease in traveling staff. The savings generated by the move amounted to ten thousand dollars per month in travel costs and sixty-four workdays in salary.[37]

Still, the list of official personnel for each trip nearly always exceeded sixty, and questions about the wisdom of such expenditures continued. Approximately thirty-five of the regular travelers were military personnel. When the president's White House staff and their support personnel, family, and guests and other mandatory personnel were included, the government was still flying a large number of people to Texas on a regular basis. Newspapers commented on the practice in an indirect manner. Peter Lisagor of the *Chicago Daily News* wondered where everyone slept and justified the expense of traveling such a "far piece" to the ranch by noting: "Mr. Johnson's friends and associates say it is one of the few places he can relax, if not the only one." The demands of the presidency, however, made the expenditures worthwhile in the opinion of most of the press, and complaints were generally muted.[38]

The combination of the remote location of the ranch and the manner in which Johnson and his staff controlled access to it, and thereby to the president, led to ongoing disagreements with the press. In the early 1960s, the U.S. press was at the peak of its influence. With such names as John Chancellor, Walter Cronkite, Chet Huntley, and David Brinkley, television had become an important medium of communication. John F. Kennedy had held the first live televised press conference in January, 1961, and the various uproars in international affairs during the Kennedy administration, the Cuban Missile Crisis in particular, were covered by television. The Civil Rights Movement was transformed in no small part because television exposed the public to atrocities committed in the name of law and order. The public and the press were still charmed with the new medium, and almost no one was cynical about the impact of the press on the way people understood national and international events. The public did not yet seriously doubt the motives, manners, and so-called objectivity of the people who brought them the news.

Johnson had long been in the forefront of the technological revolution in politics. He had utilized the radio, the helicopter, and other innovations to assess public sentiment, spread his message, and develop his programs. He understood the impact of television more clearly than most politicians. But he also maintained presidential prerogative, closing his ranch to the press and the outside world except by his permission. The result was an uncomfortable truce and occasional skirmishes between the president and the press over the question of accessibility. To some in the press, the Texas White House was a castle to which Johnson retreated to hide from his detractors; from Johnson's perspective, it was his home, and his privacy was of greater significance than the press's right to any news story.

Some members of the press reacted with greater equanimity than others to Johnson's dialectical push and pull with the press. As New Year's Eve 1964 approached, members of the press sought to enliven their time in Texas. On December 28, 1964, the LBJ Ranch received a cryptic but warm telegram that played on one of White House staffer George Reedy's jokes:

"The Society of Prudent (Or Imprudent?) Men and Women, White House Correspondents' Association Division, facing up to the happy prospect that we may be in Texas when the time comes to ring in the new year, is planning a New Year's Eve party in honor of your staff. We would be honored and delighted for you and your family to join us in the festivities . . . at the Driskill Hotel" in Austin. This gesture conveyed both the difficulties of the arrangements for the press, some of whom stayed in Austin, more than sixty miles away, as well as the need for access that Johnson so assiduously controlled.[39]

The control of access to the ranch and the required travel to Texas exacerbated the already uncomfortable relationship between the president and the national news corps. Every one of the forty-two times Johnson traveled to Texas during his first three years in office, the press had to follow, often complaining about the short notice. At first, most found Texas entertaining, but the charm wore thin as reporters found themselves with a generally uncooperative president and a set of rules that limited their access, curtailed what the press perceived as its right to know, and sometimes seemed petty and insulting. When Johnson "came to rest, it was to Texas almost all the time," George Christian remembered. "And [reporters] got tired of coming to the same place." Transportation from Johnson City to the ranch became a focal point of press frustration. The White House Transportation Agency provided an air-conditioned bus from the Johnson City Press Center to the ranch. There was a five dollar per person charge for members of the working press, some of whom had to come from Stonewall to ride the bus. There was no other way for the press to gain entry to the ranch, for Secret Service officials would not admit anyone who did not ride the bus. Garth Jones, the Associated Press correspondent in Austin, vehemently protested this arrangement. "Is this really just a $5 admission charge to the ranch for the working press?" Jones wrote, implying a more sinister motive. Using a renowned Johnson phrase, he finished: "Come, let us reason together, and do something about this." But the difficulties in the relationship remained.[40]

The problems stemmed from two factors. With the reporters kept first in Austin and then in San Antonio, they were far removed from any political action taking place. "On occasion we overworked them here, and they complained about that," Christian suggested. "Sometimes we underworked them, and they complained about that." The location away from the ranch also contributed to the problem. Reporters "complained enough about

Austin," Christian continued; "they'd say, 'well, let's go out and watch them paint the stripe in the street.'" Christian and the staff insisted that while the president was at the ranch, he was relaxing, and "if there was anything important he was doing, we darn sure tell them."[41] It was an impasse born of different styles and cultures.

In the aftermath of the Kennedy assassination, Johnson could easily invoke presidential safety as the rationale for such policies, and protection and security at the ranch remained major concerns. In addition to the heartrending sorrow and numbness it sent through the nation, the Kennedy assassination had provided a terrible shock to the security forces charged with guarding the president. Although there had been attacks on U.S. presidents since the days of Andrew Jackson, there had been no attempts on a president's life since the attack on the White House by Puerto Rican separatists in 1951; Harry Truman was staying at Blair House at the time, while the White House was renovated. No president had been fired upon since 1932, when an attempt on President-Elect Franklin D. Roosevelt in Miami took the life of newly elected Chicago Mayor Anton "Tony" Cermak. In the immediate moments after the attack on Kennedy, security officials assumed that the assassination was part of a worldwide attack on U.S. leaders. No one knew the extent of what had occurred, who was behind it, or whether other political leaders might also be targets.[42] A belated but intense vigilance, which came to characterize the Johnson presidency, followed.

At the ranch, security became a paramount concern. A swarm of new agents arrived to guard the ranch, and expanded facilities for their use had to be established. Guard shacks were set up "straight off the truck," Albert Wierichs remembered. New security fences were located at the perimeter of the property; later, electric entry gates were added. The Hightower residence, originally located south of the Pedernales River and now within the boundaries of the LBJ State Park, had been moved to the main property by the time Dale Malechek arrived to assume his duties as ranch foreman. The house had become the residence of ranch worker Albert "Pretzel" Rodriquez and his family, who had previously worked with the Malecheks at Boerne. The Secret Service took over these quarters, and the GSA took responsibility for converting the quarters into a Secret Service command post.[43]

Security required its own infrastructure at the ranch. The Secret Service needed guard stations to augment the command post. Early in 1964, three small frame structures were constructed, one each at the east and west security check gates and the third at the cattle-guard opening south of the Pedernales River. These allowed control of the entrances to the ranch and, along with the miles of fence that surrounded the ranch, assured that the president's home was secure.[44]

For the Johnsons, being the first family took some getting used to. It meant constraints on personal freedom and a tremendous lack of privacy, as secretaries, aides, military personnel, Secret Service agents, and others moved through the house. Although most tried to be inconspicuous, they were still ever-present. Even a road built for the workers was not sufficient to mask their activities. The strain of constant supervision was evident in the first family. Lyndon Johnson seized every opportunity to leave his handlers and staff behind. When Johnson finally arrived at the ranch on December 24, 1963, for his first visit after becoming president, he got off the airplane and hopped into the car with his friend A. W. Moursand, initiating the practice of eluding the Secret Service that Johnson so enjoyed. "There they went, away to get lost over the horizon," Lady Bird Johnson recalled. Secret Service agents were dumbfounded as the president disappeared from sight. They rushed to their vehicles and followed in hasty pursuit. Presidential affairs were forgotten as Johnson roared away for a little deer hunting and a lot of talking, pursued by the people responsible for his safety.[45]

The presence of all these people was even harder on Lady Bird Johnson than on her husband. She had people traipsing through her beloved house, and changes that she found unaesthetic and unappealing had to be made to the property. On her first trip back to the ranch, she remarked on the "two enormous silver saucers"—satellite dishes for communications. Large searchlights probing the night, Secret Service agents bustling about, guardhouses located at the entrances, and other accouterments of security changed the feel of the place. To Lady Bird, it felt as if she had turned her home over to outsiders.

This feeling was driven home in an incident when Lady Bird Johnson found herself locked out of her own home. The Secret Service insisted that the exterior doors to the house remain locked at all times, and agents developed the habit of locking the doors the instant anyone left the house. During a visit by members of the media, Lady Bird served tea and cookies to the press on the lawn, intending to give them a tour of the house. When she tried to open an exterior door, she was embarrassed to find herself locked out. A chagrined security officer immediately opened the door, but the incident served as reinforcement of the reality that at least as long as Lyndon Johnson was in the presidency, the Johnsons' ranch would be public as well as personal property.

Military officials were keenly aware of the burden their presence placed on the first family. It was difficult to ignore the hardware—the helicopters, airplanes, vehicles, and communications equipment—that dotted the ranch, reminding the Johnsons and their military attachés that the ranch was as much a military installation as a family ranch. By the end of 1965, Cross, recently promoted to lieutenant colonel as part of his new position as Armed Forces Aide to the President, felt compelled to remind the many military personnel stationed at the ranch to be considerate of the first family. Soldiers had been far too visible on the property, and some had used objectionable language in the proximity of the Johnsons, a situation Cross found particularly abhorrent. In January, 1966, Cross strengthened his earlier cautionary words. "I would hope," he informed military personnel, "that all personnel would take particular care to avoid ever offending the privacy of either the first family or any one of the civilians associated with them." Yet their presence and the movement of vehicles continued to remind the family that as long as Lyndon B. Johnson remained in the presidency, their home was an unusual kind of public facility.[46]

Yet despite sharing the ranch with the world, the Johnsons lived in a special place that had transformative qualities. The stunning orange Texas sun shone on the land, and as the light from the sunset twinkled across the Pedernales River, the beauty of the Hill Country calmed Johnson and charmed his visitors. "Out here, you don't think about missiles," Johnson apocryphally told a reporter in an oft-repeated quote. Reporters noticed how differently the president acted at his ranch, and many commented on the impact of the place on the man. "He has made a success here," wrote Arthur Hoppe of the *San Francisco Chronicle*. "He will leave his mark on this quiet land. Here, then, he is secure." Such reasoning, which swallowed whole the mythology Johnson had created about his youth and allowed reporters to feel that they knew the President in an intimate and personal fashion, was an important strategic tool for Johnson. On the ranch, the control he craved was still his, and it showed. "It is almost as though there are two Mr. Johnsons," Hoppe continued. "I, for one, like and admire this Texan far better. And late this afternoon as I walked along the banks of the Pedernales, flushing doves and armadillos, I couldn't help thinking what a shame it is, both for him and for us, that he can't govern the nation from here."[47]

The creation of the remote White House sought to accomplish precisely what Hoppe wished for Johnson. The transformation of the LBJ Ranch into the Texas White House occurred quickly and decisively. The ranch became the site of a branch of government, and the numerous aides, support staff, and security personnel who lived on the premises, as well as those who traveled with the presidential entourage, confirmed the nature of the transformation. The communications system at the ranch was equal to that anywhere in the world, and with it Lyndon Johnson could both visit his home and conduct the business of state. The ranch created a new kind of presidency, one dependent on communications systems instead of proximity to national politics.

This creation of a remote White House was a product of the times and of the individual who demanded it. Johnson had never cared to understand how technology worked, but he could clearly see its possibilities and implications, and with the resources of the presidency at his disposal, he was determined to transform his ranch. What he accomplished only became possible in the 1960s, as the combination of widespread jet travel, improved communications equipment, and other technological advances allowed the transcending of the great distance between the Potomac and the Pedernales Rivers.

As he accomplished this transformation, Johnson again foreshadowed changes in American society. As a westerner, he utilized new amenities in an effort to fuse the demands of the White House with the security and reassurance of the place he loved best. As he brought the two together, he established a trend that later presidents and, after them, the American public would follow. From private jets to second homes to modems that allow access to faraway individuals and sources of information, the type of technological commuting in which Johnson engaged became a typical feature of American life.

CHAPTER 6

The President's Palace

The Ranch

Day-to-Day,

1963–69

L yndon B. Johnson was a perpetual motion machine; everything about his life reflected his desire to be ever in motion. Each morning he rose early with a long list of tasks to accomplish, and he kept his days full. He was also a micromanager of grand design, refusing to delegate even the smallest of decisions. He liked his life busy, and because of his penchant for controlling any situation into which he entered, he made the lives of others around him—including family and employees—equally full of activities and sometimes of misery. At the Texas ranch, this tendency was highlighted in the clearest relief, for there Johnson believed that his right and ability to direct the actions around him were without question. As a result, during his presidency life at the ranch took on a frenetic character, as the property became the stage for a typically Johnsonesque range of purposes. "Rest at the ranch is a misnomer to me," Lady Bird Johnson once wrote, and the pace of activity there supported her recollection.[1]

In part, this freneticism was the result of the incredibly small space at the ranch. Despite the series of renovations and expansions that had begun in the 1950s, the house was little more than forty-five hundred square feet. The famous barbecues were outside, by the river; in case of bad weather they were relocated to an indoor facility, such as the high school gymnasium in Stonewall. The outbuildings and guest houses at the ranch removed some of the pressure for overnight guests, but often there was no space and few activities for many of the people who arrived at the ranch for official, ceremonial, and other functions. Nor could visitors move about freely, for barriers to access existed and Secret Service agents quickly reminded stray visitors and reporters to stay within established boundaries. The airplane hangar served as the location of numerous press conferences, and guests were often left in the front yard as other events in which they were not included took place. A constant flow of people who seemed to have nothing to do stood around on the grounds, watched carefully by Secret Service agents.

Although Lyndon Johnson, as the center of attention, was mostly oblivious to all of this, the conditions at the ranch exacerbated tension between the president and the press. Accustomed to the freedom of movement available in Washington, D.C., if not in the White House itself, and far from home and familiar surroundings, the mostly eastern press found aspects of Johnson's formidable personality even more overbearing during his stays in Texas. Although Johnson was far more likely to speak candidly and let down his guard at the ranch, he simultaneously used his dominance of the place as a way to compel the press to do things as he wanted. Sensing this contradiction and feeling constrained, the press resented Johnson, which was reflected in attitudes expressed in much of the reporting. The negative sentiments made Johnson defensive, which in turn made him less receptive to the entreaties of the press. A push and pull existed throughout the presidency that was reflected personally in press coverage of Johnson. His tactics made the press less likely to give Johnson the benefit of the doubt, which made him less likely to cooperate. As the Vietnam War accelerated and Johnson's famed "credibility gap" became an article of faith for the press, the situation worsened as both perspectives hardened. The result was an ongoing series of misunderstandings and an ultimate stalemate.

Much of this resulted from the dialectic created by Johnson's insistence on running the national government from his ranch. During his presidency, the geographic ranch became two different and overlapping psychic and actual places, each embodying distinctively different rhythms. When Johnson was gone, the day-to-day operations of the property were those of an ordinary ranch, with a significant number of additional personnel in the vicinity. Cowboys and other ranch workers were the most evident people on the place, and the mobile irrigation system and the animals became the center of attention. The Secret Service agents and military corpsmen permanently stationed there watched as Johnson's workers took care of ranch business. No one sought to move the cows away from the house, as Johnson insisted when present, and ongoing maintenance, repair, and other activities took place. When Johnson was present, the entire ranch operated as both a working property and a remote White House. The ranch became a fast-paced, crowded, busy place, full of dignitaries and the professional staff necessary to accommodate them. The Teletypes hummed, and the numerous phone lines were in constant use. Policy makers and reporters seemed to be everywhere, and official pronouncements came by the dozen. As cows grazed and irrigation pipe was installed, decisions that directed domestic programs and foreign policy were discussed. Military couriers handled coded messages as cowboys transported animals to new pastures. Generals and advisors landed at the airstrip while ranch help drove to town for supplies. In effect, two distinctly different places overlapped on the same terrain.

This dual personality made the ranch/Texas White House an unusual place. Part Hill Country intermittently profitable economic enterprise and part national political headquarters, it embodied divergent features within Lyndon B. Johnson's personality—both the feel of his youth and the demands of his position. Hardly a reluctant leader, Johnson reinforced his forcefulness by using the ranch as his headquarters. In this environment, he trusted his instincts more clearly than in the nation's capital. He knew and understood more than those who came from Washington, D.C.; at the ranch he could utilize his experience and expertise to articulate to everyone and anyone who was really in charge. Along the Pedernales River, Lyndon Johnson truly controlled every facet of interaction and discourse, and he never failed to remind visitors, reporters, and friends of this reality.

Again, the dominance so central to Johnson's personality emerged as part of a tactical strategy. The ranch and his homeplace gave Johnson a feeling of security and control so powerful that he was willing regularly to move the national government to the ranch for months on end. This willingness to exercise prerogative let Johnson wield the control that was of great importance to a man of his combination of awesome power and vast personal insecurity. He could insist on a visit to the ranch and everyone *must* follow. The imperative enhanced Johnson's sense of power while simultaneously reflecting his insecurities. That he could and would exercise this privilege reflected his need to remind Americans, their government, and the press of his power. Conversely, as he reminded others of the scope of his power, he diminished its range, especially in the realm of Washington, D.C. Johnson seemed to believe that when he returned to the ranch, he recouped lost power and could then use it more effectively. But the manner of its acquisition and use was alienating.

The pattern of Johnson's presence at the ranch reflected its growing importance in national affairs and ultimately in the national cosmology. The Johnsons' initial post-assassination visit was delayed two weeks. Instead of arriving on December 10, 1963, as planned, the Johnsons did not reach the ranch until the day before Christmas. During 1964, the Johnsons rarely visited before November, the month in which the presidential election took place, when Johnson was elsewhere for only three days. After the election of 1964, a pattern began to emerge that typified the presidency. The Johnsons were usually in residence during July and August, particularly around the president's birthday, August 27. November and December were also favored months for living at the ranch. During the rest of the year, they were present for short times as frequently as possible, when they could get away from Washington, D.C., in the case of recuperating from illness, or when a formal event such as the signing of the Education Bill of 1965 took place.[2] This pattern reflected both the importance of the ranch to the Johnsons on a personal level and increasingly the iconographic meaning that had become attached to it.

Throughout Johnson's presidency, the ranch simultaneously served both public and private functions. Family lunches and official business became inextricably intertwined in the manner of the nineteenth century, when the lines separating public and private spheres were not as distinct as they later became. Friends and family members sat at the table with important visitors, creating a sometimes awkward and always amusing social interaction. This fusion of different aspects of life typified the regime at the Texas White House during the presidency, enhancing its unique role among presidential homesteads until that time. The Texas White House was the first presidential home to be far enough from Washington, D.C., to need all the technological attributes of the modern age in order for the president to be able to administer his responsibilities.

By 1964, the ranch had become considerably different from the haphazardly managed property Johnson acquired in the early 1950s. A succession of foremen had not met Johnson's expectations; some had not understood the need for technology, and others could not accept the constant second-guessing and the seemingly arbitrary decision making in which Johnson engaged. But the president eventually got the results he sought. Under Dale Malechek's guidance, the ranch had become, by 1964, a "nothing-wasted layout that almost glows with care and scientific management," one reporter wrote, and Johnson loved to show it to visitors. "That's what he was proud of, that's what he loved, that's what he came here for," remarked Kermit Hahne. The ranch and especially its cattle were "his life."[3]

At the ranch, Johnson utilized a method that anyone who ever worked with him would recognize. He expected "a dime's worth for every nickel he spends," Malechek recalled, even though the ranch was not an important source of profit for the Johnson empire. Detractors would often refer to the president as a gentleman rancher and a hobbyist, but Malechek, who arrived in 1960 and remained, refuted this idea. The president was interested in cattle as a business and paid little attention to show cattle and the ribbons they won. The first time the ranch made any profit, Johnson jumped up, said "look, the ranch is making money," and ordered his long-time assistant Mary Rather to take the check for three hundred dollars directly to the bank. Malechek observed that ranching was never a hobby for Johnson, since the ranch was an expensive undertaking and Johnson would never have spent a nickel on any hobby.[4]

After he purchased the property in 1951, Johnson sought to increase its operations and develop modern systems that would better support a ranching enterprise. The centerpiece of these activities was the dam, built in 1951, which provided water in abundance, the most crucial need of the ranch operation. When the river was high, the water backed up behind the dam for almost one mile. Irrigation began soon after the construction of the dam, and parts of the property—between the hangar and Oriole Bailey's house to the east of the family cemetery—were consistently irrigated throughout the 1950s and early 1960s. After the arrival of Dale Malechek, the area under irrigation greatly expanded. A manual system of seven-inch pipelines with sprinklers, described by Malechek as "exceedingly large and exceedingly heavy to carry around," was used to irrigate the ranch. The pipes were moved by hand, requiring a great deal of labor.[5]

Johnson's penchant for saving money extended to the irrigation operation. After Malechek's arrival, the ranch continued its established practice of buying used equipment. As neighbors and others bought new and sometimes larger equipment, Johnson was able to purchase their discarded gear. Four- and five-inch pipe was often available. Seven-inch pipe was used for the main water supply or "trunk" lines, while smaller four- and five-inch pipe became the core of the sprinkler system. This "made considerably more sense," Malechek recalled, "because it didn't kill a fellow as fast hauling that around as it did six-, seven-, and eight-inch" pipe.[6] Johnson's desire to keep costs down meshed at least this once with the needs of his ranch staff.

By 1964, Johnson had invested a considerable amount of money developing the ranch into a sophisticated, modern operation, and as a result of his efforts he fancied himself a conservation farmer. Three pumps put twenty-one hundred cubic feet of river water per minute into the pipes that supplied water to the 100 irrigated acres on the ranch. Most of this land was in winter oats, alfalfa, Sudan grass, or coastal Bermuda grass, which Johnson had been among the first to introduce in the Hill Country. The Bermuda grass produced a greater tonnage of hay per acre than other grasses, and the extra feed it generated for Johnson's stock was welcome. About 180 acres were served by terraced pastures and by deep and full human-dug "stock tanks"—ponds to hold runoff and water pumped from wells for various uses, such as watering stock and irrigating crops. One hundred and ten of the unirrigated acres farther from the river were planted in Sudan grass and winter oats, crops that needed less water. These lands were also terraced, the soil treated with nitrogen by the planting of clover and legumes.[7]

The remaining 250 acres—either permanent pasture, replete with native bluestem grasses, or river bottom—comprised the grazing area of the ranch. In the Hill Country, about fifteen acres per cow were necessary. About two hundred Hereford cattle, an essential part of the breeding business Johnson began in 1955, were intermittently pastured on these lands and on other Johnson-owned or -leased properties. In general, the registered stock was kept at the main ranch, and the commercial herd, which sometimes reached one hundred head, was pastured at outlying rental properties. A Devon bull from Senator Wayne Morse's herd was part of the Johnson herd, as were a few Holstein milk cows that served as nurse cows for the Hereford calves. The cows were an aesthetic problem for Lady Bird Johnson, who did not like them in front of the main ranch house, and the Holsteins wore bells, which irritated Johnson whenever the cows approached the ranch house.[8] The sounds of animals, so central to his routine during his recovery from the 1955 heart attack, became just another annoyance during his presidency.

The cattle operation required intensive management, for despite its mythic image, the Hill Country offered only mediocre grazing. The placement of the cattle for grazing depended on the distribution of rainfall, for the semiarid region was known for uneven rainfall even within a very few miles. Assuring sufficient water for stock required the digging of stock tanks and the placement of numerous water tanks. Crops had to be grown for feed, native-grass rangelands were fertilized, and a range of other activities was undertaken to assure the best available forage for the Johnson herd. Such intensive management was necessary to ensure the success of the cattle-raising enterprise.[9]

Johnson valued his cattle operation less for the money it generated than for its cultural and social importance. Johnson did not merely want to walk around in cowboy boots and call himself a rancher, Jewell Malechek remembered. He was immensely proud of the ranch and wanted to make it into a place where other ranchers came to get ideas. Johnson paid close attention to the science of the ranch; specialists from Texas A&M University—agronomists, ranch specialists, and "seed people," who Johnson invited to inspect his efforts and assess new ideas—were frequent visitors. The ranch became a "showplace," Dale Malechek noted; when Johnson "came home, he wanted to come to a working ranch" that reflected the best of the ranching profession.[10]

Commercial cows played an important role in the economy of the ranch. At times the operation included as many as six hundred commercial cows, compared to a much a smaller number of registered animals. "We were out for every dollar we could get out of that commercial calf," Dale Malechek recalled, and although greater long-term benefits could be derived from the registered cattle, the commercial cows formed the backbone of the operation most of the time. This fit Johnson's interests as well; he was far more interested in raising cattle than in showing them and collecting ribbons.[11]

Johnson's presidency made the daily working of the cattle operation at the old location more difficult. When Dale Malechek arrived in 1960, the cattle pens were located close to the main house, between what became Lawrence Klein's shop and the old barn. The pens were small and cramped, but sufficient for the twenty registered cows on the ranch at that time. "You sit there and look at it," Dale Malechek remembered, "and you say 'how in the hell did you ever work anything in that area?' Well, that's where the area was." The influx of people at the ranch as a result of the presidency made working in proximity to the house a difficult task. "With all the multitude of people, there wasn't any way in hell you could operate," Malechek remembered. "There'd be six Secret Service guys from New York had never seen any work cattle before hanging on the pens, leaning over the fence, wanting to see what in the hell you were doing. You couldn't drive a cow through a gate, you couldn't drive a cow through a chute." People were consistently in the wrong place.[12]

The sheer difficulty led to changes in the location of the working pens. Beginning in 1964, pens north of the main house were constructed, followed by the Show Barn in 1966. The new pens were set up to work as many as three hundred head, either commercial or registered breed. The Show Barn, with its larger pens and its distance from the other activities that routinely transpired on the ranch, was an important addition for the cattle operation. Malechek and the other cowboys were relieved finally to have working space away from the center of ranch activities.[13]

By 1964, the ranch operation had also expanded to include a number of leased properties in the vicinity to support Johnson's growing interest in breeding cattle. The most significant of these was the 2,600-acre Scharnhorst place, formally titled the Clear Creek and Granite Knob Ranch, which was used for pasture and deer hunting. About three hundred head of both sheep and goats, animals Johnson referred to as "mortgage-lifters," ran there. The Comanche Cattle Company, Johnson's partnership with A. W. Moursand, owned 4,500 acres in Llano County called the Haywood Ranch. This property was mostly undeveloped. Its primary economic use was pasture, and it also was one of many sites for water recreation. Johnson kept a motorboat there for late afternoon forays on the Llano River. The 2,200 leased acres at Three Springs Ranch were entirely undeveloped and kept in pasture for the herds.[14]

There was also a noncommercial dimension to the sheep raised at the LBJ Ranch. Among the mortgage-lifters—the sheep raised for their wool and for the lamb chops that, as Johnson discovered in a Washington, D.C. restaurant, cost as much as the whole sheep he sold in the Kansas City market—were specialty animals for use in the barbecues so central to ranch life. Foreman Malechek kept about one dozen Barbudal Sheep to provide lamb chops for the president's guests.[15]

The presidency forced Johnson to change some of the patterns of his ownership of his various enterprises. Although he continued to manage the details of his ranching operation, the decision making passed to other hands. The LBJ Company, which owned the ranch as well as the various media outlets and other businesses that the Johnsons held, was placed in a trust administered by Johnson's close friend A. W. Moursand. Although this designation was required by law and expected by custom, it hardly kept Johnson from making decisions about the operations of his pride and joy. Even during his presidency, Johnson was closely involved in business; in the limited time available during ranch trips, Malechek was expected to recount to the president everything that had occurred in his absence and show him any improvements or changes. Johnson's control extended to every facet of the ranch operation; he even required Dale Malechek to have money in hand before the cattle sold left the ranch. His protestations of minimal involvement to the contrary, Johnson remained involved in the day-to-day workings of the ranch throughout his presidency.[16]

But the demands of the office kept Johnson away from his land for much of the year, and in his absence it ran as a working ranch. Dale Malechek was in charge on a daily basis, but even from Washington, D.C., the president consistently looked over his shoulder. Malechek expected and often endured daily telephone calls from the president that lasted as long as three hours, conversations almost always devoted exclusively to the workings of the ranch. At the White House, Johnson received daily weather reports from the Hill Country by telephone or telex; during bad weather, he expected hourly updates. His obsession with the weather was so overwhelming that in press conferences, reporters would ask about conditions at the ranch. Johnson's overbearing manners when it came to the affairs of the ranch made him a difficult man for whom to work. "He was a son of a bitch to work for," Malechek remembered long after the president's death. "One son of a bitch. I'll guarantee you. He expected 110 percent 120 percent of the time."[17]

Always involved, even from a distance, Johnson, with his penchant for hands-on management, immensely complicated the life of his ranch staff.

When Johnson was present, Malechek would have to tuck his plug of chewing tobacco deeper in his jaw and accommodate his employer's demands. The foreman "liked it a lot better when the President was in Washington," Liz Carpenter, who had become Lady Bird Johnson's executive aide, said. Then Malechek only had to endure the long phone calls instead of having the president look over his shoulder as he made every decision. The two had a complicated relationship that often elicited a comment by reporters who wrote of the ranch. The stoic Malechek steadfastly refused to criticize his employer to the press, reflecting Johnson's ambivalence toward the media and Malechek's respect for his employer. Johnson will "give you advice," Malechek once told reporters in a typical cryptic comment, "but he lets you make the decisions—and you better be right."[18]

Yet the pace was different during Johnson's frequent absences. Official personnel stationed there watched as the cowboys took care of the ranch, with some expressing interest. Others simply ignored such nonmilitary activities. The ranch was a busy place, and if the pace slowed at all during Johnson's absences, it was only evident in the level of stress apparent in Malechek. With Johnson gone, everyone could undertake their tasks without the prospect of being watched by a demanding employer who had no qualms about commenting in tough and often graphic language. During Johnson's absences, tension diminished.[19]

Lyndon Johnson's absence also made life at the ranch quieter for Lady Bird Johnson. Demure and always shying away from the limelight, Lady Bird Johnson found the time at the ranch without her husband to be very pleasant, stolen moments from the whirl of the presidency. On the occasions when she found herself at the ranch without her husband, she could fashion a world of her own with only the minimal restrictions imposed by the Secret Service. She engaged in beautification, one of her major interests, during her time at the ranch, leading the local garden club and other civic organizations in arranging the planting of all kinds of flowers. In one instance, donated seed was planted along Ranch Road 1; in another, she arranged for bluebonnets to be planted along the landing strip. She also had English Park and eighty acres on the west side of the Dantz place seeded with wildflowers. It was an idyllic existence for the first lady, very different from life in Washington, D.C., or life on the ranch when the president was home. "Odd, the way I live insulated from the world here, when he is not here," she wrote in her diary. "I never turn on the TV, I do not have a newspaper. But with him the world returns, TV and the newspapers."[20]

The impact of Lyndon Johnson's arrival at the ranch was comparable to the impact of the arrival of a Texas Blue Norther, one of the forceful storms of Texas lore that gather momentum and swoop in from the north at incredible speeds, changing the temperature by as much as seventy degrees in the space of a few hours. Like these storms, Johnson altered the very tenor of life at the ranch. The helicopter or plane with the president would touch down, and when Johnson stepped off, a forceful and demanding presence around whom everything revolved became the dominant force on the property. Johnson's ties to the land were extremely close. When he arrived, what he wanted to see was not the house but the land from which he sprang. "The first thing we do when we get home is to make a tour of the ranch," Johnson was fond of telling reporters. "Before we go to the house, we drive around."[21]

The emphasis on mobility was both characteristic of Johnson as well as a means of asserting his principle that "the best place to talk to a man is on your own ground." On his ranch, people followed his lead; when he hopped behind the wheel of one of his air-conditioned Lincoln Continentals, he set the tone, tenor, and pace of everything that followed. People piled in at his request, and Johnson performed what became a ritual as well as an integral part of every one of his visits to the ranch. He gave a tour of his property. After initial episodes when they were caught unaware, Secret Service agents became accustomed to Johnson's routine and were prepared to follow him. Journalists never quite became accustomed to it, often watching in a cluster as Johnson's vehicle disappeared over the horizon. Johnson may have carefully orchestrated these settings, allowing journalists to be present when he arrived but not affording them the opportunity to ride in what could be labeled pursuit vehicles.[22]

As Johnson settled in, the ranch ceased to be exclusively a working ranch. Although Johnson attempted to maintain a public illusion that the ranch was simply a cattle ranch, the swirl of activity—from Secret Service to Signal Corps, from barbecue to high-level meeting—spoke of a different reality. The pace became more intense after his arrival, as the ranch's agricultural operations ceased to dominate daily life and a swirl of activity that included everyone and centered on the president began. Johnson relished the whirlwind pace and the control he could exert over it. He was in his element, and it showed. Lady Bird Johnson, the most astute observer of the president, noted that despite it all, "somehow, the ranch manages to be restful to Lyndon."[23]

Official functions were another of the staples of ranch life. Cabinet members, couriers, staff personnel, and others flew in and departed regularly, some leaving on the same day they arrived. Despite the objections of the Air Force, which disapproved of the length of the air strip, the cattle's access to it, and its incline, the runway was in frequent use. Helicopters and a range of airplanes touched down with presidential advisors and others. Some celebrities arrived in their own private planes. The traffic amused the cowboys, who had little to do with the governmental activity, but others noticed and commented on the pace. "The airport stays busy, disgorging cabinet members with important difficult decisions, budget estimates, crises," Lady Bird Johnson observed. To her it was "like living in a revolving door."[24] The ranch functioned as the White House, with a constant stream of official and unofficial visitors and a decided ceremonial caste to the nature of activities there.

The weeks following Christmas 1963 set the tone for such circumstances. The first presidential state visit to occur during Johnson's presidency followed the Christmas holiday by a few days. Immediately after the departure of West German Chancellor Ludwig Erhard on December 30, the Joint Chiefs of Staff, led by Gen. Maxwell Taylor and including Gen. Curtis LeMay of the Air Force and Gen. David Shoup of the Marines, arrived for high-level consultations. At the same time, Dr. Walter Heller, chairman of the Council of Economic Advisors, and Kermit Gordon, director of the Bureau of the Budget, were at the ranch, offering counsel on a range of matters. Heller, Gordon, and the president discussed economic policy while hunting deer from one of the Lincoln Continentals.[25]

"These old walls are bursting at the seams," Lady Bird Johnson half complained, and the constant stream of people at the ranch—business leaders, press representatives, friends, cabinet members—demonstrated her point. In a typical circumstance, during the first ten days of "rest" after the 1964 campaign and presidential election, six cabinet members arrived at the ranch to engage in high-level discussions. At the same time, Dr. Frank Stanton, head of the Columbia Broadcasting System (CBS) visited, along with Donald Cook, head of American Electric Power Service, Thomas B. Watson, head of IBM, and Edwin S. Weisl, Sr., an old Johnson friend and political advisor. Johnson was considering the men for places in his cabinet. Within a few days, eleven Iowans—including the president of the national swine growers association, the president of the Iowa Farm Brokers' Association, and the farm editor of the *Des Moines Register*—came to the ranch at the behest of Secretary of Agriculture Orville Freeman. They were all there as friends of a man from Iowa, Richard Juhl, who wanted to give the Johnsons a Yorkshire boar. The President asked Lady Bird what he should do. She replied: "Well, the least you could do would be to ask [the group] to lunch." Eleven lunch guests on short notice inspired Lady Bird to remark, "I think everyone had fun and none of them had the feeling it was an unusual day at the LBJ Ranch."[26]

A similar caravan accompanied the Johnsons to the ranch during Christmas 1964. Half the cabinet, including Secretary of the Interior Stewart Udall; outgoing Secretary of Commerce Luther Hodges and his successor John T. Connor; Secretary of Labor W. Willard Wirtz; and budget director Kermit Gordon, flew to the ranch with Johnson on December 20, 1964. Secretary of Defense Robert S. McNamara and the Joint Chiefs of Staff arrived two days later, followed later in the same day by Secretary of the Treasury C. Douglas Dillon; the head of the Federal Aeronautics Administration (FAA), Najeeb Halaby; and National Aeronautics and Space Administration (NASA) administrator, James Webb. On December 23, 1964, Secretary of Agriculture Orville Freeman, Postmaster General John Grounoski, and David Bell of the Agency for International Development (AID) flew to the ranch. After Christmas, the parade of visitors continued: Health, Education, and Welfare Secretary Anthony J. Celebrezze; R. Sargent Shriver; Veterans Administration head John Gleason; and Housing and Home Finance Agency administrator Robert C. Weaver arrived on December 28 and 29. By the end of the week, nearly the entire cabinet had been in conference at the Texas White House.[27]

This mixing of relaxation and business on the president's home turf came to characterize the Johnson presidency. It fit Johnson's personal style—his desire to be constantly busy, to have people around—as well as his idea of relaxation and fun. Talking politics in the setting of the Hill Country perfectly fit the image Johnson held of himself. As the leader of the nation, he could dictate terms as well as be gracious on his home ground. A hard man to say no to in any circumstance, Johnson began negotiations with a decided advantage in his Lincoln Continental, in his front room, or in the informal setting under the oak tree by the house that the president favored.[28]

The ranch also became the backdrop for official ceremonies. New officials were often sworn in during the president's stays in Central Texas. On a rainy November day in 1965, two officials took their oaths of office in a place unfamiliar to them. That morning, delays kept airplanes from landing at the ranch, and Lady Bird Johnson found herself with fifty reporters on the grounds, awaiting the arrival of buses from Bergstrom Air Force Base in Austin that carried the delayed travelers. Instead of keeping reporters in their vehicles or providing coffee in the hangar, Lady Bird Johnson invited them into the house. When the official visitors arrived, they were greeted by a happy and comfortable press. An old Johnson friend, federal judge Homer Thornberry, administered the swearing in of John Grounoski, the former postmaster general and a descendant of Polish immigrants, as Johnson's new representative to Poland, in front of the fireplace in the living room at the ranch. They then "piled into cars," Lady Bird Johnson wrote, to travel to nearby Hye and see Lawrence O'Brien, of Irish ancestry, take the oath of office as postmaster general in front of the post office, a building with red, white, and green gingerbread trim that one reporter thought could double as a movie set.[29] This juxtaposition of urbanity and Euro-American ethnicity with the hills and people of Texas typified the Johnson administration.

The Johnsons also offered far more informal kinds of hospitality. A parade of guests, personal friends, and relatives all came to the ranch during the presidency, some staying for a few days, others just visiting for an afternoon. They experienced the range of Lyndon Johnson's moods and impulses, the gregarious hand shaking and talking and the whimsical changes in plans. Johnson "loved to show off his land," Liz Carpenter said; "he relaxed by driving across it," and his visitors were compelled to go along. "He always used those automobiles like cutting horses," George Reedy recalled. Johnson would "drive them right across the field." The president's guided tours of his property—the wild rides in his Lincoln Continental with which he entertained guests, carting along newspaper reporters, friends, relatives, and nearly everyone else who arrived at the LBJ Ranch—became legend. A child of rural America, accustomed to the distances of the West, Johnson had a deep appreciation and a primal need for the idea of freedom that American culture invested in mobility. Automobiles gave him the space he associated with the ranch, a way to control what went on around him by staying in constant motion. Away from the routine he found stultifying in Washington, D.C., away from the consistent and oppressive watchfulness of Secret Service agents, Johnson could seize what to a man of his energy was the key feature of existence: the right to roam. Off he would go at speeds of up to ninety miles an hour, off the road, through pastures, and up embankments, to show off his cattle and feel the wind and the power of the engine beneath the hood. He even owned an amphibian car that he loved to drive, ripping into the water and creating waves. Most guests were bored with it by the end of their second ride.[30]

Johnson also used the car rides as a form of political commentary, a way to present his views to people with influence. Noted journalist Stewart Alsop recalled one trip that illustrated the relationship among Johnson, his ranch, and politics. After banging around in one of the convertibles across rocky land and dirt track to reach a herd of cows, the president brought the car to an abrupt halt. He blew the car horn and shouted at the cows to get them to stand. Then he pointed to various cows, compared them to politicians, and discussed the profit he expected to realize from each animal. Alsop likened this behavior to that of Sir Winston Churchill at his country place, Chartwell, where he engaged in the same sort of practice. Churchill compared his prized goldfish to his political adversaries, commenting on their various shortcomings for reporters and visitors.[31]

The informal nature of some of these activities allowed different facets of American society to intersect at the ranch in a manner they never otherwise would. Not only could Cousin Oriole Bailey meet Washington, D.C., socialites, but policy makers from the east could meet the people of the rest of the country. During the post-Christmas 1963 visit of Walter Heller and Kermit Gordon, a group of Texas cattlemen also visited the ranch. In front of the fireplace in the living room, these two distinctly different segments of American society met and talked. The cattlemen weighed in on the question of the War on Poverty, the Kennedy program that Heller had championed and that he, Gordon, and Johnson were then discussing. This "handout," as the cattleman referred to it, was in their view a bad idea, particularly at the projected cost of one billion dollars per year. Nor did Heller's elegant slacks—"city-bought trousers" as they were called in rural Texas at the time—leave a positive impression. Heller recalled that Johnson and the cattlemen made fun of the economists, a ribbing Heller remembered taking in stride. The juxtaposition reflected one example of the importance of the role of the ranch as a meeting ground for different segments of American society.[32]

Johnson's informal hospitality operated on a number of levels. It was relaxation for the president, although most would not recognize this type of activity as anything more than an extension of daily business. There was fun, as Johnson defined it, involved in his stays, and the entire experience included a message for any visitor. The theme of this message was often hierarchical; the relative meaning, significance, status, and worth of all involved figured into the equation. In Washington, D.C., even the president was defined by the world and the people around him. In the Hill Country, however, Johnson was master of all. His control of mobility and of every facet of experience reminded every one of his guests of that mastery.

Although the reports of Johnson's aides and political associates assumed that a hierarchical relationship existed, reporters often had difficulty with the way in which the president treated them and others during times at the ranch. To some it seemed as if he played a game with them, offering them insight as he shut the door, figuratively and literally, in their faces. The administration and its press staff seemed to have too much control of sources of information in Texas, members of the news media thought, and it hampered their ability to perform their job. Reporters in particular recognized that the Johnson they encountered in the Hill Country was a distorted version of the politician they knew in Washington, D.C. Visitors felt, in Alsop's words, "commanded . . . to admire" Johnson's world and by extension the man himself. Although Johnson's close associates were accustomed to the poses the president demanded, as the Johnson presidency became increasingly mired in Vietnam this "admiration by order" turned awkward for much of the press. As Johnson sensed his prestige waning, he instituted stronger measures designed to heighten his control of every facet of the ranch. In one instance, he ordered reporters relocated to San Antonio from Austin in an effort to limit their access to the political gossip that abounded in the state capital. For the most part, such measures backfired, as the force with which Johnson instituted his rules inspired a negative response from the press, whose members had become bored with the Hill Country. Even the skill of such consummate media diplomats as George Reedy and George Christian could not always smooth over the incessant and inherent conflict.[33]

The souring relationships created a tension-fraught geography at the ranch house, a division of the house and grounds into public, private, and in-between spaces. Although the house was little more than forty-five hundred square feet, the property had been built in so many stages that there were de facto different areas within the house. The bedrooms and the guestrooms, places where the family could gather without worrying about intrusion, were off-limits to the press. No one was admitted to the private area except by special request, and few reporters were willing to make such a request. Other places, such as the office and the living room, could be visited when the president allowed. Reporters in effect awaited a summons to such places. Other places took on the character of waiting rooms, where reporters sat and hoped the president would come out and speak to them. It was aggravating and annoying for the press, one more piece of evidence that there was little for them to do even in the inner sanctum in Texas. "They [reporters] had to justify being here," George Christian remembered. "They had a very practical problem."[34]

Again Johnson's penchant for hierarchy was revealed. Retreating from control of the ranch and the grounds, he turned the house into a figurative fortress, a castle to which people were admitted based on their importance to him. In most circumstances, this would not have been problematic; the White House and the nation's capital functioned in precisely this manner. But the situation in Texas was different. The Hill Country was a foreign place to many reporters, and they had little with which to distract themselves there. Some came to regard the trips to Texas as impositions—a sop to the vanity of a president for whom respect was plummeting—and even exiles. The sixty-five miles between Austin and the ranch seemed to serve as a no-man's-land between the press and the president, and the relationship frayed. Treatment and limitations that would have seemed ordinary in Washington, D.C., rankled in the Hill Country.

The limited space at the ranch and the ranch house also meant that events with no relationship to each other often overlapped in time and space. Personal events occurred simultaneously with official events, such as the announcement of appointments and nominations to positions in the government. In a typical instance on September 30, 1967, a private Johnson family photo session and the arrival of an airplane full of dignitaries intersected. For Lady Bird Johnson, this was a difficult situation that required patience, diplomacy, and tact. But on this day, she was distracted from her responsibilities. As the photographer prepared for the session, Lyndon Johnson asked Lady Bird to join him as he met an airplane from Washington bringing Attorney General Ramsey Clark, U.S. District Judge Harold "Barefoot" Sanders, Edwin Weisl, Jr., and Dean Erwin Griswold of Harvard Law School. The dignitaries were "settled in the front yard" with coffee, and the family rushed back inside to try to complete the pictures before Patrick Lyndon Nugent, then about one year old, became too hungry, tired, or sleepy. They were too late; the baby refused to cooperate, and the picture session became a hilarious shambles. Although numerous photos were taken, none look quite right. The baby became madder and madder; his mother, Luci Nugent, looked like "a graven image"; and Lady Bird laughed so hard the tears rolled down her face.[35]

But family events were not all that had to be accomplished that day at the Texas White House. An hour after the attempts to take the pictures, Johnson shepherded the dignitaries waiting in the front yard to the hangar to introduce Griswold to the press as the next solicitor general of the United States. He replaced Thurgood Marshall, whom Johnson had earlier appointed to the U.S. Supreme Court. A press conference ensued, with Yuki, the Johnsons' beagle, roaming in front of the television cameras, sniffing at the legs of the people manning the equipment. After the affair, Griswold was treated to a Mexican dinner in the dining room, a delicacy for the southwesterners present. The spicy food made Lady Bird "flinch a bit" for "our friend from Harvard." Within an hour after the end of the meal, the dignitaries were on board their aircraft on the way back to Washington, D.C.[36]

These kinds of events were particularly difficult on Liz Carpenter, George Reedy, and George Christian, the people who had primary responsibility for the media. Johnson was notorious for operating at his own pace; he and only he would determine when and where things happened, and all the coaxing and cajoling of his staff rarely changed that. Carpenter, Reedy, Christian, and their staffs were left to placate irate individuals; to explain the newly revised schedule; and to entertain and amuse disgruntled reporters, impatient dignitaries, and everyone else. They also had to cultivate leading journalists—Stewart Alsop, Tom Wicker, and others—who were sufficiently important to have individual personal contact with the president. The press attachés had to do everything in their power to assure that such visitors saw the Hill Country in the manner Johnson intended. On one occasion, Stewart Alsop was seated in a floating chair in the ranch's heated swimming pool with a scotch and soda in his hand after a full day of the "Johnson Treatment," the "incredibly potent blend of badgering, cajolery, promises of favors, [and] implied threats" that typified Johnson's efforts to sway an individual. According to George Reedy, Alsop wrote "one of the finest columns I have read about Lyndon Johnson out of that," which is testimony to the success of the staff.[37]

This pace and the multiple events taxed everyone at the ranch—except Lyndon Johnson, who orchestrated them all. Lady Bird Johnson and the staff always seemed to have someone in another room, someone in the hangar, someone on the phone or in the dining room . . . waiting. Lyndon Johnson fluidly moved from place to place, oblivious to the concerns of the staff, who had to manage the guests, and the visitors who awaited him. From Johnson's point of view, he moved from important event to important event;

he moved, as he almost always did, at his own pace, and everyone else, from visitors to press, had to adjust their pace to his. Johnson's whims and desires took on even greater importance in Texas. The limited size and space of the ranch, the small number of other officials present, and the lack of other sources of information, communication, and entertainment meant that anyone who came to the ranch was at his mercy.

Johnson relished this scenario but failed to recognize how it bred resentment, among the press in particular. In an idealistic moment in the history of the nation, as the electronic media established its importance and the print press enhanced its stature, the loyalty and deference Johnson required—particularly apparent because of the circumstances imposed by Johnson at the Texas White House—became particularly degrading from the perspective of the press. This resentment became an underlying theme during the five-year commute that the Johnson presidency became.

CHAPTER 7

A Slice
of Real
America

Showcasing

the Ranch

during the

Presidency

D uring Lyndon B. Johnson's presidency, the LBJ Ranch came to serve many functions. Besides its numerous official capacities—ranging from a retreat to the location of cabinet-level meetings—the ranch was the scene of a grand social life, formal and informal, loaded with political and symbolic significance for both the American public and the people of the world. Affairs of state were held along the Pedernales River, and important national and international personages spent time there, enjoying the beauty of the Hill Country and negotiating with this self-invented gentleman-rancher-turned-president who was as much a creature of the halls of Congress as of the Hill Country of Texas. Against the serene backdrop of the river and the Hill Country, the president reaffirmed his roots in a mythical America that ordinary people could understand and that foreign dignitaries found genuine.

In this process, the ranch again proved to be a malleable tool for the ever-inventive Johnson. As the location of affairs of state, the Texas ranch continued to serve in the role of a remote White House, but such affairs were different from any presidential event ever staged in Washington, D.C. Instead of the formal and sometimes officious tone of the nation's capital, guests at ranch affairs saw a mythologized rural America that emphasized preindustrial relationships: ties of family, of place, and of honor. This attractive image presented only the best of the rural experience, glossing over its poverty and deprivation; Johnson offered this image not only as a view of his ranch but of his administration and worldview as well. It was, as W. D. Taylor of *The New York Herald-Tribune* wrote, "barbecue diplomacy," juxtaposing two words generally perceived to have little in common. Once again, Johnson transformed his ranch to suit his new circumstances. In a typical instance, Horace Busby, a longtime Johnson aide, suggested that the guest list for an affair of state, the 1964 visit of Mexican President Gustavo Diaz Ordaz, "be oriented nationally, not regionally. . . . [This] would win significant national attention—and be a significant political plus in Texas."[1] Again, in the skillful hands of his staff, the ranch came to represent the nation and its values even more than it previously had.

In his quest to project an image of himself as a typical man in extraordinary circumstances, Johnson relied on a specific kind of imagery. An admirer of Harry S. Truman, another "commoner" turned president, Johnson played on the same kind of "plain folk" sentiments that were crucial to Truman's success. Johnson's speech, his actions, his way of thinking seemed to millions of Americans to be much like their own. This president was not a graduate of an Ivy League school nor heir to a great fortune. He spoke colloquially, metaphorically, in the rough and sometimes crude speech of rural America. What he had, Johnson's tone, tenor, and posture announced, he had earned by the sweat of his brow. Johnson affirmed this stance as he utilized the ranch, bringing all manner of people to it and showing them a stereotypical if not altogether real "Texas good time."

Characteristic of social engagements at the ranch was a type of event that Johnson turned into an institution to suit his purposes: the LBJ Ranch barbecue. Usually held in the grove by the Pedernales River, these affairs were renowned for food, music, libation, and the opportunity for discussion that they inevitably included. Despite their pretext of informality, the barbecues were created in a systematic fashion to serve real and symbolic purposes. These events—of which there were almost one hundred during the five years of the Johnson presidency, some entertaining as many as five hundred people—became symbols of Johnson, his presidency, and the real United States so often obscure to the foreign visitors who only saw American cities. Johnson's rural "spread" and his use of it for entertainment enhanced a uniquely American mythology that the world found more appealing than the realities of an urban, industrial nation.. Here was an America seemingly comprised of people who worked for a living, had few if any pretensions, and appreciated and embraced simplicity, order, and community. It was an idyllic vision, necessarily inaccurate but carrying much meaning and symbolic weight.

To Europeans especially, and foreign visitors in general, the ranch served as a symbol of this mythically genuine America, where people were "just plain folk" and a handshake was as good as a written contract. It was as if the world of the Western movie had come to life. The conviviality of the Johnson barbecues and the manufactured ambience of authenticity created a seductive environment that disarmed even the most suspicious of visitors. In this setting, Johnson could work his personal magic and could utilize the charisma that underlay his political career with a style and comfort level that he simply did not possess in the nation's capital. In the setting at the ranch, under the tents from which the aroma of barbecued pork and beef emanated, Johnson seemed at home, genuine in a manner foreign to the Washington, D.C., environment. He was a real American in the real America—a seductive concept for Europeans familiar with American mythology as well as for national leaders from elsewhere around the globe.

The ranch and the Texas experience also served as a backdrop for the enactment of the policies closest to Johnson's heart. The rural setting, with its message of innocence and, in Johnson's manufactured personal history, of poverty overcome, had a certain appeal to the American public. During the cultural revolution that swept the nation during the late 1960s, the rural American past acquired an almost nostalgic meaning for youth that was ironically shared by the older public, increasingly distant from rural roots but enamored of them in an age of rapid change. The family farm was idolized; the rural life, despite the many hardships associated with it even in the most benign accounts, was seen as somehow more pure than the struggle for a living in the city. Rural places spoke of roots and meaning, precious commodities amid the uproar of the decade.[2] That sense became pervasive; any event that called on such symbols played well with a wide segment of the public. The astute Johnson was keenly aware of the cultural advantages of his geographic location and of the meaning that the public and his guests invested in his ranch along the Pedernales River. Johnson utilized this idyllic setting and the Hill Country around it on even the slightest pretext.

In events such as the barbecues, LBJ built iconographic significance for the ranch and the Hill Country. The ranch was a kind of clay to this master of symbolism. The Hill Country property could serve as a stage for the Great Society and its programs, illustrating the poverty typical during Johnson's youth and the need for programs to alleviate the social and economic problems that resulted. This view, this symbolism, was an updated version of New Deal ideology, filtered through rural Texas. Bills such as the Education Bill of 1965, signed in the Junction Schoolhouse, were in a direct line from the construction of the Buchanan Dam in the Hill Country and the creation of the Rural Electrification Administration, pieces of legislation reflecting goals that were at the very core of Johnson's political programs and that demonstrated his success.[3] The barbecues and other major official social events at the ranch reflected Johnson's personal tastes and highlighted the difference between rural, kinship-based sociality and the formal world of Washington, D.C. The ranch became a cultural symbol that represented the "real America" to the television cameras, one that reminded the nation of roots that it had shed but that in times of turmoil it sorely missed.

Throughout Johnson's years in the Senate and the vice presidency, barbecues had been a characteristic feature of entertainment at the ranch. The barbecues "fit LBJ's style," Cactus Pryor remarked, for they expressed the feel of Texas hospitality and entertainment as opposed to the formality of Washington, D.C., high culture. In one instance, Johnson took a group of United Nations ambassadors on a horseback ride around the ranch before a barbecue; Johnson rode a Tennessee Walker, his personal favorite among horse breeds, while the ambassadors, certain that they were no longer in New York City, rode cow ponies. Johnson liked a western atmosphere for the barbecues, with round tables, checkered tablecloths, and coal-oil lanterns. Servers wore western attire, although security officials dressed in their normal business suits. Johnson and his staff strove for an authentic ambience, dictated as much by popular culture's Western films as by the realities of the experience of nineteenth-century Texas. The barbecues "had the look and feel of a chuck wagon dinner," Pryor recalled, something many visitors understood as part of the uplifting, moral, and character-building experience of the mythical cattle drive.[4]

The barbecues became structured, following a clear and distinct pattern that demonstrated and conveyed exactly what Johnson wanted. Through a series of barbecues in the late 1950s and early 1960s, the ranch staff developed a formula that governed everything from the food to the atmosphere. This formula included the caterer, for important events almost always Fort Worth barbecue impresario Walter Jetton; the location in the grove by the river; and the decision to have Cactus Pryor, a long-time Johnson employee and humorist in the Will Rogers tradition, serve as master of ceremonies.[5] The setting by the Pedernales River, the food, and the ambience were Texas through and through.

On some occasions, the barbecues became the setting for a seemingly simple but highly charged historical reenactment. At Johnson's request, hired actors, ranch hands, volunteers, and neighbors would depict a highly stylized settling of Texas, "with the early Spaniards in costume coming down the Pedernales River and the friars and the Indians meeting them," remembered Pryor. Stagecoaches, buckboard wagons, and Anglo-American settlement followed. This format was adapted to each specific guest list. Texans in the audience found a rendition that exalted their traditions, while those from other parts of the nation and the world learned about the history Texans fashioned for themselves from a decidedly Texan perspective. These were, in the words of John Graves, an astute observer of his native state and its people, a "proud and vain people," possessed of a sense of self-righteousness and mission inherited from their nineteenth-century ancestors.[6]

To outsiders, this xenophobia about mythic roots was at once the most attractive and the most repelling facet of Texas. Texans were a breed apart, and nativity in the state created an arrogance and reverence for the Lone Star State that at first seemed quaint to people from other places. Texans were sure that their state was best and brooked little discussion of the merits of the rest of the world, a subtheme in almost any conversation between a visitor and any native. The ranch reenactment reinforced this sentiment in a less abrasive fashion than might have occurred in ordinary conversation. On their home turf, Texans were entitled to enact their myths, and the pageantry of the reenactment and the barbecue became intertwined examples of state heritage.

But Texans also ran hard against other American myths. In the 1960s, Texas was still far from the American political and cultural mainstream, even farther because of its association with the segregationist South in the middle of the civil rights revolution. Although U.S. politics were changing, its symbols remained northeastern in character and origin, its orientation focused on the prosperity brought by industrialization, and its ideas shaped by the concept of a nation rather than by the integrity and domain of an individual state. The press concentrated on New York and Washington, D.C.; what was sophisticated and urbane emanated from the two seaboard coasts, east and west. To many visitors to Texas and the LBJ Ranch—those who saw the reenactment and those who did not—the chauvinism and what could be labeled the arrogance of Texans were poorly masked and thoroughly unjustified.

But Johnson's barbecues often transcended such difficulties in cultural understanding and transmission. The westernness of the barbecues was in a way generic; they represented not only Texas within their form and format but every western place and indeed every Western movie. They called on icons that any American and many educated foreigners understood, symbols communicated to the global village that the world had become, symbols that were abundantly clear to anyone who had ever seen a film about the U.S. West or imbibed the mythos of the nation. As a result of their success at communicating myth in the barbecues, Johnson's staff received a seemingly endless string of requests from individuals and organizations for information about how to stage their own Johnson-style barbecues.[7] At Johnson's ranch, Texas became the West in the same manner that Johnson had made himself into a westerner during the 1950s.

The initial barbecues during the Johnson presidency were even more meaningful in their iconographic impact than previous efforts had been, but they also reflected some of Johnson's overall difficulties with his new office. The senatorial and vice presidential barbecues had been regional in conception, aimed at showing domestic and foreign visitors the culture and attributes of Texas. Presidential barbecues, like any other presidential function, were an articulation of the nation and represented the whole instead of one part of the United States. This meant that the features of such events had to be not only characteristic but extraordinary. Unlike the vice presidential barbecues, which accentuated regionalism and were designed for a national audience only as an afterthought, the presidential barbecues had national and international meaning built into their very structure. The ceremonial and official demands of the presidency diluted the Texas side of the experience, making it conform as much to standards of diplomatic protocol as to those of Texas, the Hill Country, and the ranch.

The visit of Ludwig Erhard, chancellor of the Federal Republic of Germany, was the first major presidential gala in the Hill Country and served to highlight the difficulties involved in this changed symbolism. Erhard spent December 28 and 29 of 1963 in the Hill Country, on the first official state visit to the Texas home of the new president. He came to engage in a serious discussion concerning mutual issues such as the Soviet threat, the Berlin Wall, and other matters of international politics. Some news writers felt this to be a meeting of great importance; "Johnson and Erhard Face Decision Hour," a headline in *The Philadelphia Inquirer* read on December 27, 1963. Other newspapers, such as *The Wall Street Journal*, regarded the visit as an opportunity for Johnson to assert his claim on the presidency.[8]

For Johnson, the Erhard visit was a pivotal moment. The role of West Germany in the postwar world had changed greatly since the late 1940s, and the importance of the country as a bulwark against Soviet expansion had dramatically increased. With the exception of finicky France and its dynamic leader, Charles de Gaulle, western European countries had become staunch U.S. allies, for the threat of the Soviets loomed large. American willingness to oppose the Soviets at Berlin contributed to positive feelings between the United States and West Germany, but the relationship required continuous maintenance in the face of changing Soviet policy. Both Erhard and Johnson had recently ascended to the top positions in their respective countries, and the Hill Country meeting showcased their abilities as statesmen.

After the hectic period in Washington, D.C., following the Kennedy assassination, the Johnsons had finally reached the ranch on December 24, two weeks later than their scheduled arrival. As they left their plane, Lady Bird Johnson could see workmen preparing the facilities for Erhard's arrival. Bess Abell, Lady Bird Johnson's social secretary; Liz Carpenter, press secretary and staff director for the first lady; Pierre Salinger, the White House press secretary and a holdover from the Kennedy administration; and a number of stewards arrived in Texas on December 26 to assist in the preparations. The stewards were housed in the guest house and the Scharnhorst ranch house. Other logistical questions soon arose to be addressed.[9]

At the same time, many of Johnson's advisors began to arrive. Secretary of State Dean Rusk arrived on December 26, meeting with previous arrivals Secretary of Agriculture Orville Freeman; Special Assistant to the President for National Security, McGeorge Bundy; and George McGhee, the U.S. ambassador to the Federal Republic of Germany. Briefings and other preliminary meetings to prepare the Americans for the arrival of the Germans took place. "Two by two and three by three and in groups they huddled with Lyndon and talked, and moved around the ranch," Lady Bird Johnson remembered.[10]

Small groups were a luxury not afforded the first lady, who had to prepare for five busloads of the press—as many as two hundred reporters—that were expected at 2:00 P.M. on December 26. The press had been informed as early as December 15 that they would have little leeway in covering ranch events; they would be quartered in Austin, about sixty-five miles from the ranch, and only reporters on official buses would be allowed onto the ranch grounds. Despite grumbling, the reporters had no option. They had to cover the story, and if the only way they could get to the ranch was in an official bus, then they accepted the need to travel in that manner. But the circumstances did not make them feel warmly toward the new administration.[11]

At the ranch, Salinger acted as "top sergeant," Lady Bird Johnson wrote, herding the passengers from the five Greyhound buses to three school buses for a tour of the fields and pastures. Ranch foreman Dale Malechek served as guide for the lead bus, with Lady Bird Johnson taking the second and the—as the first lady called her—"obliging dear" Lynda Johnson taking the third. Those who were interested in ranching and agriculture were directed to Malechek's bus. Lady Bird and Lynda Johnson told their audiences about the Johnson family history and about buying and renovating the ranch. For most reporters in the presidential corps, it was the first time they had ever seen the ranch. Many were impressed at its beauty, and the enthusiasm of Lady Bird and Lynda Johnson and the knowledge of Dale Malechek were infectious. "You enjoy talking about what you love," Lady Bird Johnson wrote with her characteristic grace, "and I love this place."[12]

After the tour, Lyndon Johnson engaged in a homey kind of gesture designed to quell any resentment members of the press might feel about their treatment. Since many were on their first official visit—for many the first time they had ever seen the Lone Star State—Johnson planned a mini-barbecue for the press. In an effort to curry favor, Johnson took on his persona of an ordinary rancher and, with a dose of Texas hospitality, sought to make the members of the press comfortable. Walter Jetton had already begun to cook for the big Erhard barbecue the following day, and the Johnsons treated the press to a sampling of the barbecue, coffee, and beer. It was a sunny winter day, and everyone settled down on bales of hay near the grove or under the trees to talk. Lyndon Johnson pulled up in his convertible—with the top down—and joined the gathering, bringing along Rusk, Freeman, and Thomas C. Mann, the chief Latin American affairs coordinator. The president stood on a bale of hay and addressed the gathering, and the informal barbecue "turned into an all-around press conference."[13]

The next morning, the German chancellor and his entourage arrived at Bergstrom Air Force Base in Austin. It was a "beautiful blue and gold day," Lady Bird Johnson remembered, with flags flapping in the breeze and the troops lined up to be reviewed. A military band was present, and a red carpet awaited the arrival of the chancellor's airplane. The plane overshot the red carpet, and the dignitaries had to "hop around a few feet," Lady Bird Johnson remembered, to reach the ceremonial entry. After the customary events, including brief speeches by Johnson and Erhard, the almost forty-person official German entourage boarded helicopters and flew to the Hill Country. An eight-car motorcade slowly brought the Germans through Fredericksburg, in the heart of the German-Texan Hill Country. A forty-foot-tall sign reading "Willkommen" graced the entry to the town. After the Germans arrived at the ranch, fourteen of the most important negotiators and leaders were treated to a luncheon, and official talks proceeded throughout the afternoon. A stag dinner for the entourage followed that evening. The guest list of twenty-nine included every major dignitary in both groups. Even Lady Bird Johnson was excluded from the gender-segregated festivities; she stood outside on the porch and listened through the window. The menu of shrimp mousse, filet of beef Texanna, potatoes casserole, and creamed spinach was topped off with pecan pie for desert. Dom Perignon 1955 was the libation of the evening. State gifts were exchanged as Ezra Rachlin—a former child prodigy and native of Berlin, now the leader of the Austin Symphony Orchestra—played the piano and Linda Loftis—a former Miss Texas and a talented vocalist—sang German lieder and, by coincidence, a Puccini aria that happened to be Erhard's favorite. The chancellor, who had trained as a concert pianist, was intrigued and enchanted. After Loftis finished singing, Erhard stood, selected a yellow rose from a vase, presented it to the singer, bowed, and kissed her hand.[14]

One of the gifts that the Johnsons presented to Erhard accentuated the ties between Texas and West Germany. The German influence in the Hill Country was apparent to all observers. "There are few places in America where the German tradition of 125 years ago is so pronounced or so well preserved," newsman and Johnson friend Houston Harte wrote. "Here stand the stone houses laid with trowels brought to this new homeland from the iron mongers of Germany." To add substance to the imagery, the Johnsons had bound a number of poems written by Hulda Saenger Walter, a young German immigrant to Texas during the 1840s whose family settled in Fredericksburg. She wrote of the travails her family experienced in their new land, of how hard they had to labor, and of how they missed their home in Germany. Lady Bird Johnson added a letter to the chancellor's wife with the gift, expressing her regret that Mrs. Erhard had not been able to make the trip.[15] Such a gift reinforced the ties that the negotiators worked so hard to maintain and subtly reiterated the kinship between Germans and Texans. It was a characteristic Johnson gesture, one that was generous and meaningful at the same time that it cultivated relationships.

Sunday dawned clear, beautiful, and very cold, and Lady Bird Johnson gave thanks that the first presidential barbecue, planned as the centerpiece of the trip, was scheduled for the Stonewall High School gymnasium instead of the grove by the river, which was the typical location for such events. According to Liz Carpenter, the decision to hold the event in the gym resulted from Bess Abell's consultation with Dr. Irving Krick, a Palm Springs, California, meteorologist, who had predicted cold weather. The barbecue was central to Johnson's conception of a trip to the ranch, for it allowed the president to highlight the Texas and western traditions that he found had so much appeal. Even the risk of cold wet winter weather could not dissuade him, so after Krick suggested that the weather might not cooperate, the barbecue was scheduled for an indoor venue. Austin interior designer Harold Eichenbaum was engaged to decorate the gym. By Sunday, December 29, workmen had spent three full days fulfilling Eichenbaum's plans to give the gym the authentic feel that Johnson insisted upon for his barbecues.[16]

The Stonewall High School gymnasium was typical of such structures across the nation. In small towns, the gymnasium was a malleable location. It was often the focus of local pride as well as of much activity. The school's sports teams played there, and it fulfilled a social function as well. Gyms served as community centers and meeting places, and within their walls almost every kind of small-town social, political, and cultural event took place. A gym housed everything from community bake sales to school pep rallies, but nothing like this—the arrival of a foreign head of state from the ancestral homeland of many Hill Country residents—had ever happened at the Stonewall High School gym.

The gym was transformed for the event. By the Sunday morning of the barbecue, workmen had spent countless hours hammering and sawing to create an outdoor western atmosphere underneath the basketball hoops and the overhead lights that were covered with wire to prevent errant balls from breaking bulbs. Liz Carpenter added bales of hay to create what she labeled "artistic rustic fashion." Walter Jetton's saddles, lariats, and red lanterns augmented the hay. Even Lady Bird Johnson found the ambience of the gym "transformed; bunting was everywhere," she recalled, and the German flag and national colors adorned the room. A mariachi band greeted the guests outside the door, adding another ethnic flavor of Texas to the event.[17]

After much discussion, Van Cliburn, a distinguished international classical pianist who had been raised in Fort Worth, Texas, had been selected to perform, a choice dictated by Erhard's youthful desire to be a concert pianist. According to Cactus Pryor, Liz Carpenter initially asked him to arrange the typical array of country musicians who had played at previous ranch events. "Liz, wouldn't this be a good opportunity to display to the world that Johnson isn't a hick, a hillbilly, that Texans are something besides cowboys and fiddle bands?" Pryor recalled asking Carpenter. "Why don't we get Van Cliburn down?" "But this is a barbecue," Carpenter responded. "We can't present Cliburn at a barbecue." Pryor persuaded her that nothing would be more beautiful than Cliburn playing under the trees with the Pedernales River in the background, and Carpenter assented. After Lady Bird Johnson approved the idea, Cliburn was engaged to perform. When Cliburn arrived and found he was expected to wear a red checkered shirt and jeans while he played, he balked. His preference was white tie and tails, his typical concert performance apparel. "But Van, they haven't ever seen a tuxedo in Stonewall," Carpenter pleaded. "This is a concert for the chancellor of Germany," he retorted. "But you've never seen Stonewall!" she and Bess Abell shouted back. After much discussion, Cliburn consented to wear a business suit, a compromise that everyone accepted.[18]

The food was typically delicious. Walter Jetton prepared a meal of barbecued spare ribs, cole slaw, and pinto beans, although in his introduction of guests Pryor apologized to Erhard because Jetton had not been able to find a recipe for barbecued sauerkraut. "Plenty of beer," was available, Lady Bird Johnson recalled, served from large barrels made by area resident Harry Jersig. Hot apricot pie and coffee comprised desert, and the almost three hundred guests ate heartily. Interspersed among the international and national visitors and the White House, German, and local press were approximately seventy-five Texas dignitaries. Four Texas state senators and their wives attended, as did Johnson friends and colleagues Homer Throneberry, Horace Busby, Texas Attorney General Waggoner Carr, and their wives. Robert Kleberg and Jay Taylor represented the Texas cattle industry, while Chancellor and Mrs. Harry Ransom of the University of Texas system, legendary University of Texas football coach Darrell Royal and his wife, and Texas folklorist laureate J. Frank Dobie and his wife also attended. Johnson's nearest neighbor, Simon J. Burg, sat at the head table.[19]

As the meal continued, Johnson became characteristically restless and sought to begin the entertainment. Liz Carpenter noticed the president's agitation and rushed to Cactus Pryor, telling him to hurry over and introduce the president. Pryor went to Johnson and requested the microphone. "What for?" asked the president. Pryor explained that he needed to present Johnson. "Why do you have to present me?" Johnson asked. Pryor finally persuaded him to give up the microphone, and the formal program began. There were introductions and toasts all around as Lyndon Johnson introduced the important guests and said a few words about each. According to Lady Bird Johnson, he extemporized all his remarks. Johnson had arranged for Texas-style cowboy hats to be given as gifts to the German entourage and the reporters who accompanied them. The gifts sat in the corner of the gym, awaiting their moment. But the president decided that he wanted each recipient to try his on. The hats were not yet creased, and Liz Carpenter remembered being sent to "whack them in just the right place so they shape up nicely." After two or three tries, it was apparent that she lacked the requisite experience, and Johnson sent A. W. Moursand to join her. The experienced Moursand did most of the creasing as a chagrined Carpenter looked on. Johnson then personally fitted each of the prominent Germans, placing a ten-gallon—or forty-liter—hat on their heads to determine if the Stetsons fit. Erhard's size was perfect, but the first hat Johnson placed on the head of Dr. Karl Carstens, the secretary of state of the West German Foreign Office, fell over his ears and almost obscured his face. After the hats were distributed, everyone awaited the program.[20]

Entertainment, hosted by perennial master of ceremonies Cactus Pryor, followed the meal. A group of young Fredericksburg women presented German folk dances, to the delight of Erhard and his entourage. A folk group, the Wanderers Three, played. The Saint Mary's Catholic High School choir sang songs such as the Christmas standard "Silent Night" in German, ending with a rendition of "Deep in the Heart of Texas." As the strains of this easily identifiable song began, Erhard leaned over to Lady Bird Johnson and whispered, "we know that [one] in Germany, too."[21]

The main musical program was stunning. Wearing his unfamiliar business suit, Van Cliburn played Beethoven's *Appassionata,* a work by Schumann, as well as a number of other selections. Erhard and his entourage appreciated the skill and virtuosity of this accomplished musician. Despite the gravity and formality of the occasion, there were lighthearted moments. Press secretary Pierre Salinger, who had once hoped to be a pianist, took a turn after Cliburn. According to observers, he acquitted himself nicely.[22]

The indoor barbecue was a rousing success. It "all melded well," Pryor recalled; "it jived." The range of music and ethnicity elicited much positive comment, and the sophisticated Erhard truly appreciated Cliburn's vast talents. The chancellor and his party received "a sense of the hospitality of this country in a setting where there were ties of kinship," Lady Bird Johnson wrote, and it seemed to the guests that they had visited an America they had never seen, much closer to the one of mythology than the urban nation most mid-twentieth-century visitors experienced. It seemed to reporters that the atmosphere at the ranch was a good one for international relations. The bridge between Bonn and Washington, D.C., that Johnson and Erhard sought "got off to a new beginning," *The New York Herald-Tribune* reported. "It was favored by the friendly outgoing personalities of the new President and the new Chancellor."[23]

The barbecue also served as a counterpoint to the typical venues in which political discussions and high-level talks were held. Instead of being held in the White House, the hotels, or the drab government buildings of Washington, D.C., this meeting was set among the hills of Texas, the land dry from a lack of rain during the fall and early winter. The venue made the negotiations easier, while making the tone less formal. It moved these leaders from their typical regime into a far less rigid world, and according to the joint communique released after the meeting, the two leaders and their staffs engaged in a series of "frank and far-ranging talks" about common problems. Erhard and his entourage "will have something new to take home to Europe," reporter Houston Harte suggested: a different view of the United States.[24]

Not everyone thought that the event was a complete success. U.S. Ambassador to Germany George McGhee later remarked that although Erhard enjoyed the informality of his Texas visit, the event "appeared to indicate a degree of intimacy which different people perhaps thought went too far. ... [T]he impression given to the Germans is that [the ranch] is a little too intimate for their Chancellor." Although McGhee found the ranch a "congenial" place for a meeting, it seemed to him too informal for the first meeting between new leaders during a stressful transition.[25] Accustomed to the more formal nature of the Kennedy administration, McGhee did not yet recognize how different were the symbols and protocols of the new administration.

The first presidential barbecue differed in tone from any previous one held at the ranch. During his years as senator and vice president, Johnson had used barbecues to accent his regional identity. As a "southern" politician, he initially used the barbecues as a way to highlight his increasing identification with the West instead of the South. The Stetson hats he so often gave as gifts were one example of this transition; the chuck wagon atmosphere so aptly described by Cactus Pryor another. Even during the vice presidency, the themes that ranch events illustrated were regional. The barbecue thrown for President Lopez Mateos of Mexico in 1959 was typical. With its Texan and Mexican flavor, it might as well have taken place on the border between the two lands.

The first presidential barbecue operated under a different set of conventions. Held in the winter, during the only time of year that made an indoor venue necessary, it was created not out of regional spirit but out of national obligation. Erhard's state visit had been planned before the Kennedy assassination and, in the changed climate, had to continue. The West German leader and his new American counterpart had much to discuss. The barbecue had become the social event that underlay substantive meetings, not the strictly social occasion it had often been. The addition of Van Cliburn also changed inferences about the ranch, precisely as Pryor had anticipated. A renowned international talent, Cliburn raised the level of entertainment at ranch events to new heights. Previously, regional or local musicians and entertainers had performed at barbecues; on some occasions, national country and western artists such as the Geezinslaw Brothers had played. Cliburn, however, set a new standard that linked the accomplishments of Texans outside the state to activities within it. This created a new symbolism for the ranch, a western setting with a national and international meaning. Once again, the ranch had been rapidly reconceived to meet Johnson's new status, sense of self, and social and symbolic need.

The barbecue proved as malleable as it had in the past. In an often-repeated process, the presidential barbecues became as typical of official hospitality at the ranch as had their senatorial and vice presidential predecessors. Some barbecues were elaborate, staged, and highly formalized. Others were instantaneous responses to a presidential whim. Election day in 1964 provided an example of a hastily organized barbecue. The week before, the ranch had been the scene of a campaign barbecue, a full-scale production that included a chuck wagon with an "LBJ OR BUST" sign painted on the side. As Lyndon Johnson drove to the polls to vote, he saw the remains of the campaign party. "What's all that junk?" Johnson asked. Told it was left over from the previous week, Johnson paused and then said, "We just might have a barbecue tomorrow for all those reporters who've been traveling with us. Might ask the Humphreys down, too." The plans were underway.[26]

"In view of the poor physical condition of the Fourth Estate," the invitation read, "the President and Mrs. Johnson invite the Johnson and Humphrey traveling press to a barbecue." There were a few stipulations attached to the invitation: "all microphones are off, no crowd estimates will be made, [and] no copy will be filed." The barbecue was designed to be both relaxing for the press and an effort to build bridges for future political use. The traveling press corps had served the Johnsons well throughout the campaign, and the gesture seemed one of friendship, designed to get Johnson's full term as president off on the right footing with the press.[27]

The entertainment at the presidential barbecues reflected the new standards demanded by Johnson's new position. Prior to a presidential summit meeting at Punta del Este, Uruguay, concerning the Alliance for Progress, a Kennedy-era program designed to further relations with Latin America, Johnson invited all the Latin American ambassadors to the LBJ Ranch for a barbecue and other activities during the weekend of March 31–April 2, 1967. The event was to set the scene for the meeting and to allow everyone to become acquainted in an informal setting. The entertainers were a group from Albany, a West Texas town with considerable wealth and a tradition of sending its children to eastern universities such as Yale and Princeton. The town put on an annual pageant called the *Fandango*. It portrayed the settling of Texas in an impressive fashion, in some instances placing as many as 150 people on the stage of a natural amphitheater outside of town. The Albany group was asked to perform the *Fandango* for the ambassadors.[28]

Persuading Johnson that the group was sufficiently professional fell to Pryor. The president doubted the entertainment ability of the group, thinking that they probably appeared amateurish. Pryor agreed that they were amateurs in the original sense of the word—people who performed from a love of their subject—but according to Pryor the group made up for any lack of professionalism with "enthusiasm and quality of composition." Johnson still demurred, and Pryor pushed for the group. "In my opinion," he told the president, "this will be one of the best things we've ever presented at the ranch, and I think we should do it." This forceful approach was hardly typical for Pryor or any other Johnson subordinate, and Johnson apprehensively agreed to the program.[29]

The "Friendship Fiesta," as the party for the Latin American ambassadors was called, was well received, and Pryor's insistence paid dividends. At the April 1, 1967, barbecue, he rated the *Fandango* a "huge success." Johnson watched his audience for the first three numbers, and as he saw their enjoyment, he relaxed and began to enjoy the show. By the end of the program, Johnson was cheering louder than anyone. As the pageant ended, the president and first lady went forward "strictly out of their hearts," Pryor remembered, and embraced the performers, a gesture that the Latin Americans, who attached great significance to the *abrazo,* appreciated. To see the U.S. president hugging common people made a strong impression on them.[30]

In *The Vantage Point,* Johnson rated the meetings at Punta del Este, which took place two weeks later, as an important success. In what he remembered as the most intensive three days of meeting he had outside of a crisis, Johnson forged a new direction in relations with Latin America. He believed that the discussions led to a different understanding between Latin American leaders and the United States, as the agreements reached at Punta del Este clearly illustrated that the United States "would now be a junior partner in Latin American economic and social development," Johnson wrote in his memoirs. He could envision a Latin American common market, a goal that was a cornerstone of the president's policy for the region but that has never come to fruition. While the ranch played no direct role in the negotiations, the barbecue for the ambassadors helped paved the way for Johnson's objectives.[31]

Official state barbecues also carried forward the practices established during the Erhard event. During the week following the 1964 election, President Gustavo Diaz Ordaz of Mexico came to the ranch for a visit, and a barbecue was scheduled. The theme of this event accented the shared border between Texas and Mexico. Mexican and U.S. flags lined the road above the barbecue area. The tables at the barbecue were decorated with flowers and covered with white linen, and piñatas hung from the tent. The 243-person guest list featured every important Hispanic in the Southwest, including U.S. Representative Henry B. Gonzalez of Texas; U.S. Representative Joseph Montoya of New Mexico; numerous state dignitaries; and, seemingly, every important Spanish-surnamed attorney in Texas. National leaders and other figures made the trip as well. Governor Edmund P. "Pat" Brown of California and Gene Autry also attended, as did comedian Milton Berle. Brown was added to the list to emphasize the connections between California and Mexico, while Montoya represented his home state as well as long-time Johnson ally U.S. Senator Clinton P. Anderson of New Mexico, who could not attend.[32]

The entertainment featured an array of cross-border performers. Ricardo Gomez, a talented flamenco guitarist who was also a psychology major at the University of Texas, played. A candidate for Miss Texas 1964, Mary Moore Swink, performed classical Spanish dances "as well as any professional Mexican dancer," in Pryor's estimation. Los Delfines performed with Maria de Lourdes of Mexico City, as did Marimba Ecos de Chiapas of Brownsville, Texas. Clint Harlow displayed his trained sheepdogs; the finale involved monkeys riding the sheepdogs as the animals herded sheep. The featured performer was singer Eddie Fisher, a nationally known singer who was also a strong supporter of the 1964 Democratic ticket and who was thrilled to be invited to the ranch to perform. Fisher became tangled in the microphone cord as he walked up to the stage. Lyndon Johnson jumped up to help him, and Fisher noted that it was the first time a president of the United States had helped him get untangled.[33]

The introduction of a well-known performer such as Fisher again illustrated the differences between presidential barbecues and their senatorial and vice presidential predecessors. Fisher appealed to a national mainstream audience. An urban ethnic who had been married to film star Elizabeth Taylor, he had no prior identification with the West, Texas, or even the

South. Fisher had a national reach that even Johnson's favorite country and western performers such as Eddy Arnold—the Tennessee Plowboy, who had played at the barbecue held in honor of the Pakistani leader Mohammed Ayub Khan in 1961—did not share. The selection of Fisher demonstrated that, in effect, after Cliburn the entertainment at the ranch had adopted the levels of network television and popular culture rather than of the western region of the nation. It was no longer simply entertainment that Johnson enjoyed. The choice of entertainment represented the presidency and was subject to a range of commentary.

There was only a minor political agenda for the 1964 meeting with Diaz Ordaz; the visit was mainly designed to let the two presidents become acquainted and share ideas.[34] Johnson's ties to Diaz Ordaz's predecessor, Adolfo Lopez Mateos, were very close, and the incoming Mexican president felt the need to establish his own relationship with the leader of the powerful nation to his north. The ranch setting, criticized by Ambassador McGhee for its informality as a venue for the Erhard visit, was very suitable for the Mexican president. It was a type of locale familiar to upperclass Mexicans, most of whom owned similar properties, and the setting made cultural sense to them.

The ranch provided an excellent venue for the meeting. The issues the two leaders discussed took the conversations far beyond the level of merely getting acquainted. Trade, immigration, and the final details of the long and complicated El Chamizal settlement topped the agenda. Treating and cleansing Colorado River water before it entered Mexico, the change in river flow that resulted from the opening of Glen Canyon Dam, and the filling of Lake Powell earlier in 1964 also presented important cross-border issues. The issue of Fidel Castro's Cuba loomed large between the two leaders, for Mexico was the only country in the hemisphere that retained relations with what the United States considered an outlaw nation.[35] Again, the backdrop of the ranch and its staged informal atmosphere allowed for productive interaction.

Private events with immense political ramifications also took place at the ranch. These were visits during which the full complement of public activities did not occur but during which the ranch served as the backdrop for important affairs of state. One such visit was that of Israeli Prime Minister Levi Eshkol in January, 1968. Early in 1967, the geopolitical conflicts in the Middle East had begun to intensify. After Egypt closed the Strait of Tiran—Israel's sea access to the Indian Ocean and Asia—to Israeli shipping, war seemed inevitable. When it finally broke out on June 5, 1967, the world was astonished to find the small and vastly outnumbered nation trouncing its opponents. The Six-Day War of June, 1967, ended in a resounding Israeli victory that enhanced the already strong ties between the United States and Israel and dramatically altered the balance of power in the Middle East. The two leaders had much to discuss six months after the stunning military victory.

Johnson sought privacy for these discussions, but he was dissuaded by his staff. Initially the president had planned to invite the press to the ranch during the Eshkol visit, but he changed his mind and planned to bar the press. However, there were consequences to such a change, press secretary George Christian informed Johnson. During such a visit, the ranch served as a seat of government, and barring the press would be tantamount to barring them from the White House itself. By the time Johnson sought to prohibit the press, Christian had already informed the Israeli and White House press corps that they would be permitted to report on the events at the ranch. Rather than pursue a strategy that he believed would generate negative publicity, Christian recommended that the press be allowed on the grounds but confined to the hangar, a longstanding Johnson strategy for keeping the press out of the action.[36] Reluctantly, Johnson assented.

Eshkol and Johnson had much in common. Both were men from lands of little rain, and both had overcome much in their personal and political lives. They had an intuitive understanding of each other. Johnson's favorite question of foreign political leaders had long been about the amount of rainfall in their land; he was, George Reedy reflected, obsessed with water. "After all, when you lived in the Hill Country, boy, you got worried about water because there wasn't much water there," Reedy said. As a man from an arid land, Eshkol could answer with a response Johnson understood and appreciated. The Israelis had invested deeply in transforming their desert into productive agricultural land. This was something Johnson himself sought to do at the ranch with his irrigation systems, something in which he invested much time, effort, and energy. The two leaders began what became a warm friendship.[37]

This commonality in their places of origin was accentuated as the Johnsons drove Eshkol and his wife around the ranch. The Israelis remarked on the similarity of the climate, topography, and terrain of Texas to that of parts of Israel. Texas live oak trees and the olive trees of Israel looked much alike to the visitors, and although much of Israel was closer to sea level than the Hill Country, the vistas seemed remarkably similar. Ephraim "Eppy" Evron, second-ranking diplomat in the Israeli delegation to the United States and a close friend of Johnson, remarked: "[T]he [Hill] country reminded me of parts of the lower Galilee [with its] low hills and trees."[38] During the 1960s, the Galilee and the adjacent coastal plain contained the heart of Israeli agriculture, including many collective *kibbutzim* and *moshavim,* the communally owned agricultural enterprises that at the time produced most of Israel's exports to the rest of the world. Private property owner or member of a collective, these people faced the same kinds of problems with land and water. Both Johnson and Eshkol regarded such problems as having considerable significance, and this helped forge a bond between the two leaders.

As was apparent to the Israelis, the parade of visitors, foreign and domestic, enhanced the symbolic meaning of the LBJ Ranch. It became a place where Lyndon Johnson could illustrate values that he thought important to the American people and that he wanted the rest of the world, particularly foreign dignitaries, to associate with the United States. This was not Manhattan or Washington, D.C., but a mythic "real" America, full of people who worked for a living and gave their word when they shook hands. Johnson was skilled at orchestrating events at the ranch, using people from his own past and station in life to juxtapose with dignitaries to create the ambience of authenticity. The venue and circumstances of such events demonstrated links between the decisions at high levels of government and the needs and desires of ordinary people, a theme chief executives have sought to articulate before and since with varying degrees of success.

Yet the events and the barbecues that were often the centerpiece of ranch activities were hardly spontaneous; often they seemed choreographed with a kind of folksy humor and activity designed to lull visitors into thinking that the American president was less sophisticated and able than he actually was. Cactus Pryor, the self-proclaimed George Jessel of the campfire circuit, played an important role in putting everyone at ease. With his brand of wit and humor, descended directly from the style of the renowned Will Rogers, Pryor seemed uniquely American. The selection of the entertainment, often from Texas but after the Erhard affair always including a national headliner, also reflected the changing iconography of the ranch. Throughout his term in office, Johnson successfully combined the down-home nature of the staged events at the ranch with its natural setting to increase the vast tactical advantages he had in political discussion on his home turf. He could show Texas and then negotiate with other leaders who were charmed by the setting and surroundings. It was a solid strategy that effectively served Johnson and American national interests.

The ranch also served as backdrop for another category of events, those that involved the policies of Johnson's vast domestic programs, usually labeled the Great Society programs. Drawing on personal experience, Johnson used the Hill Country to illustrate the problems of rural America and of the poor. His memories of the Hill Country were of an economically and culturally impoverished place, its conditions not wholly alleviated by the construction of Hill Country dams and the projects of the Rural Electrification Administration. In Johnson's view, these New Deal–era programs had begun to bring his home region into the twentieth century, but when he arrived in office, he realized that much more remained to be accomplished not only in the Hill Country but in the nation at large. The War on Poverty and myriad other Great Society programs were among the results.[39]

Among such programs, education took a preeminent position. Johnson was "a nut on education," observed Hubert H. Humphrey. "He thought education was the greatest thing he could give to the people; he just believed in it, like some people believe in miracle cures." George Reedy agreed: "Johnson had an abnormal superstitious respect for education." His January 20, 1965, State of the Union address made these feelings clear. Of all the programs that Johnson perceived as crucial to the development of his Great Society, the Elementary and Secondary Education Bill, the first of some sixty education measures enacted during the Johnson administration, topped the list.[40]

The provisions of this act typified Great Society programming. The bill initiated the Head Start program, which became a mainstay of preschool education for disadvantaged children, and offered funding for schools, school libraries, scholarship loans, and university extension programs. It tied education to practical goals and objectives and made education the focus of access to opportunity. Johnson strongly believed that education could serve as a great equalizer in U.S. society, a way to lift people beyond the limits of their backgrounds and give them a chance in mainstream society.

The legislative process that underlay passage of the bill was an example of all-encompassing coalition building at its most organized. Recognizing that he had a limited honeymoon period in which to operate, Johnson brought his leading priorities to Congress. He counted on a window of about six months, after which, he told Wilbur Cohen, "the aura and halo that surround me [will] disappear." Working to counter Republican opposition as well as constituencies that did not believe that the federal government should offer funding to parochial schools, Johnson relied on the political skills he had perfected in the House and Senate. The bill passed the House by almost two to one on a roll call vote on March 26, 1965. On April 9, the Senate approved the House bill by a seventy-three to eighteen majority. One of the centerpieces of Johnson's Great Society awaited his signature.[41]

Johnson seized on his personal history as the proper backdrop for the signing of this legislation. The Education Bill was crucial to the future of the nation, Johnson believed, and for the signing ceremony Johnson again brought the nation to his home country as a way to illustrate the importance of the bill. The one-room Junction Schoolhouse, down the road from the ranch, had taken on an iconographic significance. It had come to represent every one-room schoolhouse in the nation, every place that adults associated with fond memories of their childhood experience, every place where people could rise on the basis of their merits—if they had the sort of assistance that Johnson's Great Society could provide.

April 11, 1965, the day of the signing, was a "gold-star" day in their lives, Lady Bird Johnson wrote. The Johnsons had arrived at the ranch late the night before; the signing ceremony was scheduled for the following afternoon. At about 2:30 P.M., two chartered Greyhound buses and several school buses arrived, bringing many of Johnson's former students from his days as a high school teacher in Cotulla and Houston. Among the passengers were two of his closest assistants from his time as a congressional aide, Gene Latimer and L. E. Jones.[42] It was a reunion of a sort that none of the students could have ever expected. The man who had driven them mercilessly but lovingly had proven what he had always asserted: if anyone in America worked hard enough, they could achieve anything to which they aspired.

Around 4:00 P.M., the Johnsons and their entourage arrived at the Junction Schoolhouse. The schoolhouse had become the summer home of a woman from the Hill Country and her husband, who had retired to Oklahoma, and they graciously permitted its use for the ceremony. The Johnsons had the grass mowed, and spring flowers, resplendent in yellow and purple, graced the front steps. Bess Abell had found a number of the old double desks that were typical of such schools and placed one or two out front. "It was an accurate, corny, warm setting," Lady Bird Johnson wrote, a fitting location for a piece of legislation so important to Johnson's conception of the nation.[43]

A crowd of about three hundred witnessed the signing. Among the guests were "Miss Katie" Deadrich Loney, the teacher on whose lap Johnson sat at the age of four in the schoolhouse, and Sam Fore, a legendary South Texas editor from whom the young Johnson had sought political advice. Tourists mingled with former Johnson students, one of whom had flown his Piper Cub airplane in from Yazoo City, Mississippi, for the ceremony. The Johnsons had a picnic table and benches brought from the ranch, and Lyndon Johnson sat at the table and faced the television cameras. Next to him sat Miss Katie. "As President of the United States," Johnson said from the picnic table, "I believe deeply that no law I have signed or will ever sign means more to the future of America." He signed the bill and gave the single pen he used to Miss Katie, who had begun his education a little more than fifty years before. Understanding its personal as well as national significance, Lady Bird Johnson termed the ceremony "a moment to remember."[44]

The Education Bill, Johnson's personal favorite among the legislation he initiated, typified the ways in which Johnson used the ranch to create public symbolism. The signing of the bill intertwined his personal experiences and rise to power with his aspirations for the nation, highlighting a "bootstraps" philosophy that called for a little help from a friendly federal government. This message, of overcoming adversity once opportunity was assured, lay at the core of what Johnson believed and sought to transmit to the nation.

The Hill Country and his ranch were central to that formulation. In his view of the world, these places, with their close sky and broken country, reminded him of essential truths. Lyndon Johnson packaged those truths through barbecues, bill signings, and other events. He used them to communicate a genuine Americanness, based as much in myth as in reality, to the American public and the world. No prior president had his finger so tightly on the myths of the nation, so no prior leader understood how important was the feeling of the lost past that could be recaptured. For none of them had this conscious manipulation of symbols been so important.

To Lyndon Johnson, his ranch was a showcase for what was best about the nation. It highlighted the kind of optimism for which he, his Great Society programs, and indeed his time were famous. Utilizing the ranch as a means to convey the "real" America not only to foreigners but to Americans themselves was a stroke of political genius that in postwar politics, before the ascent of Ronald Reagan, only Lyndon B. Johnson could have achieved. As he invented a history for himself, he invented one for his nation as well.

CHAPTER 8

Eastern Media and the Man from Texas

The Ranch as a Cross-Cultural Experience

L yndon B. Johnson showcased his Texas ranch to illustrate its importance as a symbol of and for Americans. The ranch was both idyllic, emblematic of the country's rural past, and increasingly posh as it was renovated, coming to reflect an old-time American aristocracy. Johnson discouraged neither image, for the power and meaning of the ranch was not lost on this sophisticated manipulator of signs and symbols. Although his public pronouncements often reminded the world of the hardships, fictitious and real, of his youth, he basked in the idea of himself as a landowner, a person of substance. To Johnson, such ownership negated the insecurities of his Hill Country upbringing.

Raised in an era before the idea of individual progress developed any of its 1960s-induced tarnish, Johnson trumpeted his material and personal accomplishments. He was closely tied to an older ethic that articulated and glorified the ability of individuals to rise through their own efforts. Vaguely related to Social Darwinism, this mode of organizing the world was unabashedly hierarchical. Johnson believed that his accomplishments placed him at the top of this hierarchy; he saw the ranch as tangible evidence of his triumphs. In this respect, he took a sometimes undue pride in the ranch and its significance.

By the middle of the 1960s, Johnson's mode of thinking about such relationships had become anachronistic in America's rapidly changing society. This older manner of organizing the world represented a competitive system that seemed not only to embody the opportunity of American society but also to belie it. The enormous affluence of the nation in the post–World War II era inspired widespread optimism and innumerable schemes to level the gradations caused by the very economic system that had created the wealth some sought to redistribute. Recognizing the impact of poverty on people, Johnson paradoxically believed in "helping-hand" measures; programs such as Medicare and a range of antipoverty programs including food stamps and Head Start, designed to assure minimum levels of sustenance for all Americans, were at the core of his cherished Great Society programs. But the same sentiments that supported such programs came to be a part of a complex of values that soon denigrated individual accomplishments and made attitudes such as those of the president seem unsophisticated and sometimes uncouth.

For Lyndon Johnson, the ranch became an emblem of himself and of the nation he sought to serve. He strongly identified with the Hill Country, seeing it as a reflection of himself and himself as a reflection it—of the place in which he was raised and to which he chose to return. Johnson found great power in his rural roots, a strength he sought to transmit to the nation through his Great Society programs. Consciously and unconsciously, privately and publicly, he used the ranch to convey Hill Country sentiments: life was what an individual made of it; personal history and the struggle to overcome it contained vast power that could be translated into any area of endeavor; and American roots, particularly in agriculture and ranching, held the key to a strong healthy character.

As much as Johnson believed these sentiments and sought to communicate them, he had neither sufficient understanding of the meaning of his actions as they would be interpreted by the American press and the public nor adequate control of his public emotions to package properly this formulation for the nation. In many ways, Johnson's actions reflected a different understanding of the relationship between the presidency and the nation than the one held by the press and, through its news product, the public. Most of the public never saw the ranch. People only formed their opinion of it as it was filtered through the television and print media. Johnson expected a kind of respect and consideration from the press; in effect, he wanted to be treated as Franklin D. Roosevelt had been, covered in the manner he chose. By the 1960s, however, this coddling treatment had passed into history, with an inquisitive and aggressive press replacing its more cooperative, even docile, predecessor.[1]

Johnson reacted poorly to this new relationship, for it created a barrier to his method of communication. He sought a news media that would carry his message unquestioningly, that would do the "packaging" of his image for him. When it did not, he became obsessed with the press and its power. By the 1960s, he was clearly aware of the impact of new forms of communication on politics. He saw and understood the ways in which television news and increased newspaper scrutiny changed the public's attitudes, expectations, and opinions.[2] Johnson sought to bend both the press and its coverage of him in his favor. When he could not, he substituted his ranch for himself as the emblem of the power of individualism and will, which he believed the nation needed.

Unlike many modern presidents, who have become increasingly carefully crafted caricatures of their roots, Johnson held a tie to his personal history that was so strong as to obviate his carefully constructed public persona on occasion. Johnson strove to use the ranch to enhance his image as a "man of the people," to demonstrate that he was a common man with faith in the nation and its people. This sentiment drew him closer to Harry S. Truman in image than to any other previous modern American president. Later, only Ronald Reagan would articulate a similar philosophy, but Reagan more resembled the fictional Forrest Gump of Winston Groom's novel and the subsequent film than the pull-yourself-up-by-your-bootstraps Johnson and Truman. Johnson's transformation from an energetic but awkward schoolteacher to a national political leader was paralleled by his move from the little cabin in which he had been born to the family ranch house that he remade into the Texas White House. The process included symbolic contradictions that Johnson never resolved to the satisfaction of the public.

Johnson also used the ranch and what it symbolized to reinforce his image as a man from the country. He fashioned and sometimes fabricated his rural roots until they expressed everything this president thought was positive about the nation. The Hill Country had honed him, made him proud and tough, and given him the tools to succeed in life. On a horse, wearing a Stetson hat, Johnson fashioned himself into an American myth, born and bred in the West, making himself a competitor and, not incidentally, an optimist as a result.

His personality and the ranch were intrinsically linked. In Johnson's formulation of the world, the ranch served as both a precursor and an emblem of success. In this mythic construction, the open Texas land became a crucible, in which life skills and values were learned and sharpened. The discipline necessary to operate a ranch successfully was the same as that required in the larger world, the skills the same combination of knowledge and ingenuity. The ranch reflected those skills. The sleek look of the land, the juxtaposition of irrigation pipes and machinery with the rolling hills, signified a man who had learned his lessons and achieved his goals— an extremely useful image for a man who sat in the highest political office in the land. Johnson's emphasis on utilizing the newest conservation techniques in agriculture and ranching, on using the best knowledge, equipment, and livestock available, showed a man of substance who understood his trade. He was fortunate, in this mythic construction, to live in a land he loved, shaped and made productive by his hand.

His belief in this constructed background gave Johnson a feeling of great power, which underlay the efforts of the Great Society to forge a new and better nation. "The roots of hate are poverty and disease and illiteracy," Johnson told forty of the nation's governors in an off-the-record meeting three days after John F. Kennedy's assassination, "and they are broad in the land." This heroic posture, of a bold and valiant individual fighting against real and powerful forces, characterized Johnson's self-image. He was the man chosen by fate to guide the United States through its most difficult internal transition—through what in the 1960s seemed to be the imminent resolution of its civil rights issues. This sense of destiny gave Johnson great faith and a kind of self-righteousness. No obstacle could be allowed to stand against the forces of right. "There is nothing this country can't do. Remember that," Johnson roared at his cabinet one day in 1965, in response to Health, Education, and Welfare (HEW) Secretary John Gardner's pronouncement that something could not be done. It was an infectious message, which Johnson wholeheartedly believed and communicated to everyone around him. The assistant secretary of HEW, Wilbur J. Cohen, said that "domestically he was doggone close, very doggone close" to proving that anything could be accomplished.[3]

This optimism was a tremendous burden, particularly in the aftermath of the Kennedy assassination. Johnson had succeeded a man martyred, a posthumous figure of epic proportions whose stature in death rose to heights it sometimes attained but never maintained during life. In his formulation, Johnson had to continue the Kennedy legacy while stepping out from the shadows as a hero in his own right. He was a different kind of person than John Kennedy, a person who represented a very different place and indeed a very different time, a reality reflected in the way Johnson looked and acted. One of the cornerstones of his difference was the Hill Country and the ranch that Johnson fashioned there.

As a result, the Texas White House became subject to a much higher level of scrutiny than had occurred during the senatorial and vice presidential years. It was the president's home, far more important than the home of a vice president or a senator, and it seemed to the nation to embody the man. To the press and the immense segment of the public to whom Johnson's symbols were mystifying, the ranch became the best avenue through which to understand the president. It was the entry point into Johnson's world, the portal through which the rest of the nation could catch a figurative and literal glimpse of the newest leader of the free world.

As a result, the ranch became the subject of tremendous media coverage and scrutiny. Each time the Johnsons traveled to Texas, it seemed that the entire Washington, D.C., press corps followed. When the Johnsons went to church in the Hill Country, the back row was always filled with members of the press. Articles with titles such as "Will LBJ Visit Ranch Often?" and "President Flies Back, 'Relaxed' by Texas Stay" graced the headlines of newspapers in the first months of the Johnson presidency, as reporters sought to convey to their readers the meaning of the ranch in Johnson's life. Famed pundit Tom Wicker wrote of the ranch that there, Johnson "reveals the image of a westerner." Johnson's thirty-two years in Washington, D.C., "do not seem to have taken the West out of Lyndon Johnson," Wicker noted, "and that may be a good thing." To Douglas Kiker, a well-known newsman of the era, the ranch was "the measure of the man," the place that held reality for the president. It offered the intimacy in which to conduct presidential business, other reporters recounted, and was a tremendous attraction for foreign visitors.[4] By the end of this publicity barrage, the public recognized that the ranch was special to Johnson and believed it to be valuable to the nation. Whether they learned to understand its meaning in a cultural sense remains unclear.

The initial press coverage of the ranch was sympathetic to the place and to Johnson's need for it. Wicker's article and others in *The New York Times* acted to justify his need for the ranch, implicitly validating the expense of travel there. Kiker was among the many who sought to explain that Johnson needed to be in the Hill Country to be most effective. "He feels for the people. He looks to the future. He gives visitors Texas hats, and, if they seem to like it, a link of deer meat sausage," Kiker wrote. "He is taking a hard look at the United States right now, and appears to be ready to break any precedent—if he thinks that is what is needed."[5] Such statements reflected the success of Johnson in manufacturing the right message about himself during the first months of the presidency. Kiker and Wicker in particular, two of the most influential print journalists in the country, presented Johnson's image as the president saw himself: a heroic individual facing hard decisions, supported by the belief that the values of his experience would guide him to the right solutions.

Johnson's approach to the media had always been warmth to those members of the press whom he considered his friends and outright hostility to those he saw as his enemies. He cajoled, flattered, and attempted to intimidate the press, bargaining with reporters and trying to sway them as he sought to dominate their agenda in much the same way as he did his peers while serving in Congress. He expected reporters and newspaper editors to follow his lead, and in Texas throughout the 1950s, they usually did. When they chose properly, Johnson rewarded them with hospitality, kindness, and confidences. Some, such as Dave Cheavens of the Texas bureau of the Associated Press, were favored with invitations to visit the ranch to enjoy fishing and hunting. Throughout Johnson's presidency, cordial relations continued with friendly members of the press.[6]

By 1967, however, most members of the national press no longer fit Johnson's definition of friendly. Thin-skinned, the president did not like even mild criticism, and by 1967, biographer Paul Conkin states, "he was conducting a virtual cold war with newspeople." Johnson tried to befriend some reporters, and they often responded to the warm and humorous side of the president. The president expected something in return for this intimacy—favorable treatment—but most reporters retained their independence when they wrote about Johnson and his administration. Ronnie

Dugger, a left-leaning Texan and the editor of the *Texas Observer,* opens his critical biography, *The Politician,* by describing this very paradox. "Lyndon Johnson was the president, but he was personal," Dugger reveals. "He took you on directly with his thrust, charm, wit, charge, and parry." Johnson and Dugger enjoyed a close but extremely adversarial relationship. Among the members of the press, Dugger was unique. He was a Texan, and Johnson granted him a kind of leeway he did not allow to people from other parts of the country. They maintained a relationship while others in the media found the White House and the Johnson ranch increasingly closed to them.[7]

Johnson felt that especially during the later years of the presidency and in retirement, the press portrayed him unfairly. Beginning in 1965 with a piece by David Wise in *The New York Herald Tribune* entitled "Credibility Gap," Johnson's administration began to experience a critical press; according to Kennedy and Johnson aide and distinguished historian Eric Goldman, this idea "had certainly been expressed before, and the thought was in the air," but it exacerbated an already tense relationship. After that time, Johnson's relations with much of the press declined. The war in Vietnam greatly contributed to this decline, as did the collision of the new role as guardian of the public interest that the press defined for itself and the static expectation that Johnson held of the relationship between the media and the president. One of the defining moments was a CBS news special report from Vietnam broadcast on February 27, 1968. Walter Cronkite, whom Johnson regarded as the voice of the American people, visited Vietnam in the aftermath of the destructive Tet Offensive. In his television commentary he advocated an end to the ongoing escalation of American involvement in the war. "It seems now more certain than ever," Cronkite concluded, "that the bloody experience of Vietnam is to end in a stalemate." Johnson watched this report on videotape and saw it as a turning point. Although Johnson retained his respect for Cronkite, he regarded the newsman's pronouncement as an extremely negative view of his administration. The power of the modern press was never more apparent, and Johnson regarded it as hostile.[8]

Some of his closest associates did not agree, regarding the difficulties as resulting from the actions and expectations of both the president and the press. Harold Woods, who then administered the LBJ State Park, felt that the press "was pretty generous to [Johnson]. . . . I think it is a function of the press to ridicule the president." Charles Boatner, a long-time Johnson associate who served as city editor of *The Fort Worth Star Telegram* from

1947 to 1961 and was a special assistant to the vice president and assistant to the secretary of the interior, regarded the conflict between the president and the press as an interregional affair. Texas journalists clearly understood their relationship to Johnson, he said; the Eastern press corps did not. Even Liz Carpenter, a staunch Johnson defender in almost every situation, admitted that Johnson "never understood the press and its agenda and sometimes failed to cope with it adequately."[9]

The ranch became a fulcrum of the tension between the president and the press. It was Johnson's mythic place, the one that held not only his real experiences but also the dreams he had for the nation. It was his bastion, and in his view the press did not respect it either as a place or as a symbol. To reporters, the ranch was interesting from a symbolic perspective, as an explication of the president and his worldview, but it was hardly a seminal American icon worthy of the fealty Johnson demanded. The ranch was a manifestation of a president who increasingly seemed at odds with the nation and its self-appointed representatives, the press, a man whose words had to be carefully evaluated before they could be trusted.

During Johnson's presidency, the volume of press questions about the ranch grew to epic proportions. Sensing the importance of the place in Johnson's view of the world and seeking a convenient way to categorize the president, reporters sought to find out as much as they could in an effort to know the man and his land. In this quest, reporters followed topics of interest to the president. Rainfall, the president's obsession, was the subject of frequent queries throughout the presidency, as were other agricultural and ranching subjects from irrigation to market prices. The Johnsons' many building projects at the ranch also attracted media attention.[10] Somehow the details of the ranch seemed to be a way to shed light on the mysteries of the Johnson presidency, to convey what passed for understanding to the public.

Even when doused with the public spotlight, the ranch provided the kind of stability that Johnson craved. In the fall of 1965, Luci Johnson's romance with Patrick Nugent attracted much attention. During the election day weekend, the Johnsons returned to Texas amid an "absolute barrage" of news stories about the romance, as Lady Bird recalled. Lyndon Johnson was "happy and relaxed," Lady Bird Johnson remembered, amid the uproar over reports that Luci Johnson and Nugent planned to ask the president and first lady for permission to marry. During the weekend, the Johnsons, their staff, Birge and Lucia Alexander, and Cousin Oriole Bailey sat down to a dinner that reminded all of them of the special qualities of the ranch, its environs, and the patterns of kinship that defined the people of the Hill Country. The scenario allowed Johnson the kind of peace he craved at a moment of great emotional intensity.[11]

His feeling for the significance of place became one of the best-known characteristics of Lyndon Johnson's personality. Reporters, often from urban backgrounds, frequently remarked on this trait as they searched for a way to understand Johnson, and the Johnsons demonstrated their attachment to the ranch time and again, even judging people by their feelings for the land. The artist Peter Hurd and his wife, Henriette, made a positive impression on the Johnsons even though they did not like Hurd's portrait of the president. It was too large for the Johnsons' taste, Johnson's eyes too dreamy and his hands and body not quite right. "They love so many things that I do, including the land," Lady Bird Johnson wrote in her diary. Johnson himself even accepted a Hurd landscape after the fiasco of the portrait. After returning from the moon, astronaut Frank Borman presented Johnson with a picture of the ranch taken from space, a photograph Borman was "sure the president would want."[12] Johnson's tie to place was strong and clear, reflecting his roots and his values.

Yet there were subtle and frequent inaccuracies in this personal history that Johnson fashioned through the ranch for the press and the public. Although Johnson liked to dramatize the poverty of his youth, Lyndon Johnson's family was not genuinely and historically poor; a more realistic assessment would have placed them among the aristocracy of the Hill Country—William Faulkner characters in their intermittent prosperity and figures from John Steinbeck in their clannishness and interdependence. Lyndon Johnson did not always pull himself up by his bootstraps, as in his mythic formulation. His uncanny and prescient understanding of human beings and a measure of amorality allowed him to fashion a spectacular political career and amass a fortune, but he often bent rules in the process. He once claimed that his great-grandfather had fought at the Alamo, only to be forced to retract the contention. Over time, this personal myth-making opened his official pronouncements, such as remarks made during the Gulf of Tonkin crisis, to greater scrutiny. Often Johnson's statements, both about personal and family history and about political decisions, seemed to reek of embellishment. In the end, the perceived disparity led to a vicious joke about Johnson and his relationship to the truth. In it, Johnson is purported to have been telling the truth when he tugged at his earlobe, had his finger by the side of his nose, or stroked his chin, but not when he spoke. The inconsistencies in his pronouncements had become a crack in the facade of the presidency through which greater and greater suspicion and mistrust eventually flowed.[13]

Throughout the presidency, the media subjected Lyndon Johnson and his pronouncements to increasingly harsher scrutiny. There was ample reason to question what he said; a skilled manipulator of political meaning, Johnson, especially in remarks concerning his personal history, often lacked demonstrable veracity. The president was a master of myth-making disguised as obfuscation. Eric Goldman points to Johnson's view that he upheld American commitments in Vietnam as one example. "In a way," Goldman writes, these were American obligations; "LBJ, being LBJ, transformed those facts to all the way." From the perspective of those who worked closely with him, this was typical of Johnson. "Not only did Johnson get somewhat separated from reality," George Reedy observed; "he had a fantastic faculty for disorienting everybody around him as to what reality was."[14] The rules of the presidential-media relationship also changed. Less laudatory than ever before, the press first shared the optimism of the time, then acquired the cynicism about government actions that came to dominate the nation. Johnson's ability to evade questions and manipulate facts caused concern, for to many in the press this ability did not seem a quality of American leadership.

Nor did Johnson inspire the immediate respect of the eastern media as did the patrician-class Franklin D. Roosevelt or the war hero John F. Kennedy. The twangy accented voice, the big ears, and the colloquial Texas speech and mannerisms provided Johnson no insulation from inquiry and, eventually, caricature and ridicule. Unlike Roosevelt, who was by tacit agreement never photographed or reported in his wheelchair, or Kennedy, whose marital indiscretions were overlooked at the time, Johnson found himself with a press that mocked him and sought to ferret out the truth about any inaccuracy or misstatement that came from him or his aides. Applying more stringent rules meant that Johnson was not granted the leeway that most of his predecessors in the Oval Office had enjoyed.[15]

Although Johnson's behavior contributed to the difficult relationship between the president and the press, larger social forces played an enormous role in defining the ground on which this battle would be waged. Reporting had become more aggressive with the advent of television, as print media fought to retain its share of the market, grappling to find a way to combat the immediacy and the visual advantages of television. Instead of simply conveying the news as they had before electronic media, newspaper reporters now had to analyze its meaning in an effort to ensure that newspapers did more than rehash the previous evening's television newscast. At the same time, the presidency as an institution began an inexorable decline in stature, a slide to which Johnson contributed and that Richard M. Nixon brought to an unequaled low. Johnson himself recognized this reality, observing that when he talked with Walter Cronkite on camera, the two were on the same level, an advantage for the reporter and a disadvantage for the president. Reporting became more direct and less sycophantic, more focused on issues and less aimed at upholding the sanctity of the presidency and the government. Johnson had long recognized the importance of new forms of media, but he had difficulty adjusting to the new tactics, strategies, and approaches of the press. They destroyed the kind of politics he knew and loved.[16]

The tension between the press and the president was exacerbated by conditions at the Texas White House. The ranch was isolated. The nearest hotels were sixty-five miles away in Austin; the closest place where reporters could file a story was thirteen miles distant, in Johnson City. The only way onto the ranch was by presidential leave, always on an official bus. When reporters were on the property, they had no freedom of movement. Only Walter Cronkite could come in his own vehicle, a situation that surely rankled the newsman's compatriots. Nor was this Washington, D.C., where thousands of other stories and sources were available to compete for reporters' attention. "There wasn't much for them to do," press secretary George Christian remarked. "They got tired of coming to the same place." In the Hill Country, there was only one story, and the media's access to it was limited at its very source.[17]

Many members of the press also followed a time-honored pattern of outsiders in Texas. On their arrival, they found Texans and Texas gracious and charming; they marveled at the speech and the manners, found the climate and vistas attractive, and enjoyed what they perceived as quaint local customs. But most members of the reporting corps came from other places, and over time the myths of Texas and its many charms wore thin. The inherent chauvinism, the sometimes unwarranted pretentiousness, and the raw arrogance of many Texans made eastern reporters long for what they considered more civilized places. Away from the two coasts, where the important events of the era happened, and with the difficulties inherent in

covering stories at the ranch, many reporters ended up with negative pre-
dispositions about the state that they sometimes projected onto the president as they reported from the ranch.[18]

Nor was Johnson emotionally or culturally designed for the harsh glare
to which the modern press subjected him. Instead he was accustomed to
the Texas newsperson, who either supported or opposed any politician
and whose stance was assured, whether positive or negative. Johnson had
long courted such individuals, made friends with them, and in the Texas
tradition, they supported or criticized him. But the national press behaved
differently. Seeing themselves as an unbiased, truth-seeking vanguard, they
charged forward with an arrogance spawned by the meeting of technology
and power, bringing a predetermined and set view of the world to bear on
the malleable realities of domestic and foreign policy in the 1960s.[19]

Johnson also thought and spoke in a manner far different from that of
most of the reporters who covered him. Raised in the country, Johnson
spoke the language of rural America—folksy, metaphorical, and sometimes
crude, closer to the basics of Hill Country life. Both real and mythic, such
language reinforced the image that Johnson sought to promote. Unfamiliar with such speech patterns, the press attributed many characteristic rural expressions to Johnson himself, never realizing that he had learned most
of them from the people of the Hill Country. "Lyndon didn't ever say a
word that his pappy didn't—and worse," Wright Patman recalled, but reporters sought to fashion Johnson as the inventor of a range of crude aphorisms. Representative Richard Bolling of Missouri remembered him as "a
crude bastard—barnyard" in his speech and actions. "He didn't change
when he was president," Lois Roberts, the wife of Chalmer Roberts of *The
Washington Post* remembered. "He went right on, didn't try to clean up his
language." In a classic instance of his use of language, Johnson once retorted to questions about why, as Senate majority leader, he had not challenged a speech by Vice President Richard Nixon by saying, "I may not
know much, but I do know the difference between chicken shit and chicken
salad." John Kennedy never talked that way in public.[20]

Johnson's language and some of his actions—such as raising his shirt to
show the scar from his gall bladder surgery in 1966, swimming nude in the
White House pool, and lifting his dog by the ears—seemed to segments of
the press to be behavior unbecoming of an American president. Many
presidents had engaged in similar behavior, particularly during the nineteenth century, but the reportorial standards of earlier eras meant that most

such actions were not widely reported. Johnson was president during a time of different, more intensive media glare, when few barriers to reporting a president's foibles existed. "It was his misfortune to appear," Marshall Frady perceptively wrote in *Harper's* in 1969, "at a moment when he was dismissed for ebullient vulgarities that, had the same facilities for collective scrutiny been around then, would have equally ended Andy Jackson and Abe Lincoln."[21] The result was a characterization of Johnson that more accurately reflected his behavior than that of previous presidents but that on occasion made him appear uncouth.

The press often misread Johnson's actions, mistaking his "innocent robust expansiveness," in the words of Marshall Frady, for boorishness. "It was a mistake," Frady claims, "of the supercilious to react to him as a caricature," to see his outward behaviors as indicative of the depth of the man.[22] Johnson contributed to the sense of the importance of such behaviors by responding to criticism as if the demeaning characterizations had the ability to wound. In the process, he gave such allegations credence that they would not have had without his response.

The result was an ongoing battle between the press and the president, who expected the respect accorded his predecessors. Each time a reporter who had previously offered positive comments about Johnson changed perspectives, the president regarded such stories as comparable to acts of treason. Dan Rather of CBS News, himself a Texan but a man of independent mind, squarely faced the ethical dilemma this situation created. Rather shared a number of Johnson's traits, such as the gnawing sense that easterners condescended to him, but even when Johnson told him that he understood the president and could help him, Rather maintained professional distance, sometimes at great cost to his advancement at the network. In the end, Johnson could not sway him any more than he could the rest of the national press corps, and he remained perplexed. Yet the president's personality and forcefulness were legendary. A generation after Johnson's departure from the White House, rumors that Johnson harangued reporters and editors for what he perceived as negative coverage persist, but scholars who study this phenomenon have come to regard this view as closer to myth than reality.[23] Undeniably, Lyndon Johnson decided that the press could not be trusted, a sentiment that translated into policy, particularly at the ranch. Reporters were kept farther from the action, frequently warehoused in the hangar, and every aspect of covering a story from the ranch became more difficult. A stalemate of negative reporting and curtailed cooperation ensued, to the exasperation of the press and the consternation of the president.

It often seemed to Lyndon Johnson that the press did not respect him and his accomplishments. To reporters, Texas was quaint, and this man who talked in aphorisms was a curiosity. The lack of mutual understanding was obvious to everyone. "I often wonder what these Eastern reporters, these city boys, will remember about their Johnson City interlude—winding over the Caliche hills behind the President who stops to telephone instructions to a foreman about a sick cow or a cattle guard or a fence crew or seeding a pasture," wrote the prescient Lady Bird Johnson in her diary. "It must be as unintelligible as Urdu to them."[24]

The folksy manner of the president among the people in the Hill Country was a mystery to much of the press. During his many drives around the Hill Country, the president never failed to pick up anyone he recognized who was at the side of the road. This often led to Lincoln Continental convertibles full of Hill Country people and the invariable request from Johnson for a staff member to give up a seat in the car in favor of someone else. Although Johnson told such unwilling departees that he would soon return for them, on occasion he simply forgot. One visitor, Ervin S. Duggan, a speech writer whom the president wanted to hire for a position at the LBJ Library, was entirely forgotten. After spending a number of hours in Johnson City, he returned to the Austin airport and flew back to the East Coast.[25]

Such miscommunications typified the problems of easterners in Johnson's Texas. To some of the press and even some of his staff, Johnson's behavior in Texas seemed sophomoric, unbecoming of the chief executive of the nation. In particular, the president's habit of what could be called joy-riding or cruising offended segments of the press. To those with memories of Roosevelt or loyalties to the idea of Camelot and the person of John F. Kennedy, Johnson seemed decidedly not presidential. His antics were undignified, his habits common, and he did not fit the image that 1960s newspeople, engaging in reshaping the political terrain, believed a president should have any more than had Harry S. Truman. But Truman had kept himself in check; he displayed none of the exuberance of Johnson and much of the very traditional moralizing of the rural American middle class.

In contrast, Johnson seemed to these self-appointed shapers of the image of the presidency to be out of control. Reporters wrote of his many automobile jaunts with a combination of respect and mockery, in effect judging his policy decisions solely by his actions behind the wheel. Coverage of these events was tinged by a nostalgia that suggested that this kind of activity reminded reporters that someone from the simpler America who would condone such actions was poorly suited for presidency. A prominent sense that such behavior was beneath a president of the United States pervaded press accounts of Johnson's four-wheeled expeditions.

The coverage of the president and his ranch by the press showed a lack of understanding. Most members of the press corps that covered the president were from urban or suburban backgrounds. Few had any experience with rural America, and fewer still took the time to attempt to understand the patterns of life in the country. "They were fish out of water" in Texas, George Christian believed.[26] In effect, they filtered what they saw in Texas through an urban prism rather than seeking to understand the place and the president on their own terms. Patronizing coverage, exacerbated by Johnson's credibility problems, resulted.

The relationship with the press cooled quickly after Johnson assumed office and remained tenuous throughout the presidency. The mutual lack of trust was reflected in numerous encounters throughout the presidency. These ranged from the nature of coverage of events at the ranch to the interaction between reporters and staff, ranch employees, and other native Texans. Texans comprised much of Johnson's staff, and they sometimes reacted angrily to what seemed to them slander against their state. George Christian, W. Marvin Watson, Bill Moyers, and Liz Carpenter, all of whom held prominent positions in White House communications, expressed frequent distaste at the treatment of Texas and the Johnsons in the national press. Neither group understood each other, and after a certain point members of both groups ceased to try. Texans snickered at the antics of reporters, while the reporters covered Texas in an increasingly patronizing fashion. Reporters were heard to say of their time in Austin, "Let's go down to the barber shop and watch the haircuts"—a sentiment sure to offend any Texan. A man as careful in his choice of words as press secretary George Christian remarked that "some of the press were prima donnaish and didn't mix too well with some of the folks" in Texas.[27]

The problems were apparent to all who were close to the president. In her memoir, *Ruffles and Flourishes,* Liz Carpenter succinctly captures the spirit of this complicated interaction. "Pardner out there it's Marlboro Country," she remarks in a tongue-in-cheek comment, but a tone of bitterness seeped in. The president's brother, the eccentric Sam Houston

Johnson, regarded anti-Texan feelings as an important component of the president's trouble with the press.[28] This was a recurring theme throughout the presidency, but at no time was it more apparent than in the famed "beer can incident" of 1964, in which Lyndon Johnson was cast as a litterbug for purportedly throwing a beer can out of his Lincoln Continental as he drove guests around the ranch.

In her recounting of this pseudoevent, Carpenter presents a wronged president and a vindictive press. Columnist Marquis Childs had sent word that he would like to visit the ranch, and Johnson was pleased to accommodate this venerated writer with roots in Oklahoma and Texas. Johnson took Childs on a convertible ride, filling the automobile with other reporters as well. The terrain, the images, and everything else about the ranch were different from the reporters' prior experiences, which, according to Carpenter, became the source of the rumor. The "Johnson safari around the ranchlands—so strange to [the reporter's] Eastern breeding" became enlarged with each retelling, until rumors that the President tossed beer cans out the window as he drove at reckless speeds were reported in *Time* and *Newsweek.* Carpenter avers that Johnson had only a paper cup of beer on the dashboard, from which he occasionally sipped; when a female reporter complained about the speed at which he drove, he covered the speedometer with his Stetson hat. Others, including Father Wunibald Schneider, indicated that Johnson was an unlikely litterbug in any circumstance; on the Johnsons' walks, they always picked up stray beer cans and other refuse that marred the ranch and the Hill Country landscape. Carpenter believed that the stories damaged Johnson, for they occurred almost at the same time as Lady Bird Johnson began to develop the ideas that would become the national beautification program.[29]

The incident articulated a much deeper gulf between the press and the president: they embraced different value systems that only overlapped in politics. Reporters "couldn't understand why a man would prefer pastures to Picassos," Carpenter writes. Their only response to the "joy [of] blue skies and enough rainfall [or] the beauty of a shiny, fat white-faced Hereford" was to "get out a pencil and pad and make lists of the number of ranches, ranch houses, and heads of cattle." Johnson's pleasure at the ranch was a mystery to Eastern-based reporters, and in Carpenter's view, they did not show sufficient respect for the president's values. She remained certain that reporters behaved differently when they visited the Kennedy and Harriman estates or other properties.[30]

This perceived lack of respect became pronounced as reporters spent more time around the ranch while still learning little of its culture. Even the most simple types of ranch equipment, such as cattle guards—a series of six to eight pipes with small spaces in between suspended over a ditch or laid over a hole in the road—were unfamiliar to them. Cattle will not cross such a contraption. In one incident that left locals chuckling, Bonnie Angelo of *Time* magazine was warned to look out for the cattle guards. She responded: "Why? Are they handsome?" Other reporters tried to walk across cattle guards; some fell through the parallel pipes, again to the great amusement of locals. Lyndon Johnson was purported to have had the best laugh of his presidency when he received a call at the White House that informed him that someone from "*Life* Magazine fell into the dipping vat this morning."[31]

A patronizing dimension in the treatment of Texas and Texans also existed in the reportorial coverage. Much of this was focused on the president's relatives, especially his eccentric brother, Sam Houston Johnson, and Cousin Oriole Bailey. Reporters feasted on the quaint names and seeming backwardness of Johnson's relatives; with first names such as Ovilee and Huffmann, the relatives seemed anachronistic to a press accustomed to the sophisticated and flamboyant Kennedy clan. The stories that followed were not always favorable, and Hill Country people sometimes resented the way they were portrayed in the national press.[32]

Johnson put his older relatives, particularly Cousin Oriole, on display for visitors, enhancing the widely held sense of his ties to the place. A typical visit to Bailey's followed a pattern that seemed choreographed. "Let's go see Cousin Oriole," Johnson would say many nights after dinner, and he would don a cap, zip his jacket, and grab a flashlight. The president and the accompanying crowd would "walk along in the moonlight," one observer recalled, with only the flashlight and the moon to guide them. Occasionally a ranch hand would come up to greet them or the president might stop to look at the roads, his irrigation system, an animal, or something else from the ranch. Secret Service agents blinked their flashlights to keep track of his location. Johnson passed through the guardhouse that marked the east end of his property and strode up to a small house with a screened porch. He "whams the screen door against its frame," Douglas Kiker recorded, "and shouts at the top of his voice: 'Oriole. Oriole.'" Together, she and the president often watched the ten o'clock news before Johnson departed for his home.[33]

Cousin Oriole was one of the many enigmas of Texas during the Johnson administration. She was "quite a lady," medical corpsman Tom Mills remembered. A shy, elderly, hard-of-hearing woman who was a practicing Christadelphian and an avid reader of the Bible, she was everyone's rural grandmother or aunt, both relic and source of wisdom. Her little home looked like that of many ordinary Americans. A television set and white wicker armchairs with padded seats accompanied the bright wallpaper. Red alabaster orioles abounded in the room, highlighted by the overhead light.[34] Her views made Cousin Oriole seem to belong to an earlier time.

Johnson's desire to play with the press, to slyly make fun of reporters visiting Texas, made his presentation of Cousin Oriole a litmus test of reporters' reactions. The president placed her on display for whoever was around. To Johnson, she was fun; to the reporters, she was difficult to comprehend, emblematic of rural America in a derogatory way. Their reading of her often clearly reflected their interpretation of the president. Characterizations of her varied. At one extreme, chief of protocol Lloyd Hand described her in sympathetic terms: she was "well read, literate, a little zany." Paul Conkin, Johnson's most sympathetic biographer to date, offers a different perspective. Cousin Oriole, he writes, was "elderly, ill, lonely, and unaware of patronizing smiles."[35] Johnson saw his cousin as representative of the American people. The press took the view that she was anachronistic, a quaint look into a simpler but essentially useless American past.

Johnson was fully capable of finding a slight in the coverage of his cousin that had not been intended. One of the most well-known Associated Press reporters, Helen Thomas, once wrote a story about Oriole Bailey that George Reedy characterized as "marvelous. . . . It had ten million votes in it easily." Johnson read the portrayal in a different manner, regarding it as patronizing slander directed at his family that made it look foolish. Reedy sought to soothe the president's feelings and smooth over the controversy. The incident again illustrated the gulf between Johnson's and the press's expectations of the nature of coverage of the presidency.[36]

To Lyndon Johnson and the people of the Hill Country, the patterns of the world of rural America had great importance and significant meaning. The traits that defined quality individuals in rural America were different from those of the coasts, and in the Johnson administration those attributes had great power. Acceptance in a Texas-dominated administration required different sorts of rites of passage than might a similar position in a Yale or Harvard University graduate's administration.

One dimension of the difference was Johnson's emphasis on hunting as an important ritual activity. Since the coming of Europeans to the New World, hunting had played an important role in the rites of passage in rural America; the ability to secure game had long been a necessary and desirable skill. An entire culture of hunting that emphasized these skills had grown up before the twentieth century. It pervaded rural life in every region of the country. American heroes such as Daniel Boone were renowned for their prowess; local communities gauged the worth of their young men based on the skills they demonstrated in competitions that utilized the skills of the hunt. Even in the middle of the twentieth century, hunting defined people in places such as the Hill Country of Texas.[37]

By the early twentieth century, however, hunting had developed distinct class differentiations. Hunters who fancied themselves sportsmen, usually members of the genteel upper classes, regarded the activity in a different manner than did those who hunted for subsistence or market or even those who shared the view of hunting as a sport but eschewed the ethic of conservation. State land laws and customs influenced the nature of hunting in individual states, changing a ritual activity to one of privilege. In states such as Texas, where hunting was every man's right in theory but the lack of public land led to a leasing system for private property on which to hunt and created a de facto class system, self-proclaimed sportsmen were few in number compared to those who hunted indiscriminately.[38]

Hunting in Texas and the West was different than in the eastern states. Most western states had fewer game regulations than their eastern counterparts, and the loosely regulated hunting in such states attracted people to violate even the few rules that existed. There were reasons for such minimal restrictions. Besides a tradition that opposed state regulation, a spacious state such as Texas had relatively few people, large populations of deer and other game species, and much territory to hunt. Texas allowed practices that shocked eastern hunters. Shooting an animal from an automobile, a practice banned in heavily populated eastern states, was legal in Texas. So was hunting on Sunday; reporters were amazed, in the words of Merriman Smith, to see a stream of cars bearing field-dressed bucks rolling toward Hill Country towns at noon on Sunday. Even does could be hunted in Texas.[39] To eastern reporters and even to some hunting enthusiasts, the hunting situation in Texas seemed uncivilized.

Lyndon Johnson became a hunter relatively late in life for someone who had grown up in the Hill Country. In his youth, he was "not much of hunter," according to boyhood friend J. O. Tanner.[40] A bit squeamish by Hill Country standards, the young Johnson associated hunting with the aspects of regional life he sought to avoid. It was only after his purchase of the ranch and his admittance to the Senate club headed by Senator Richard Russell that Johnson understood the social ramifications and class dimensions of the sport. During the 1950s, an invitation to hunt at the LBJ Ranch included an offer to further develop a relationship with this rising political figure. Johnson became a competent hunter, and as Mary Rather recounted, he "couldn't bear" to shoot a deer himself, although he "did shoot them for guests."[41] After 1960, an offer to visit the ranch was sometimes a reward for an accomplishment, at other times an affirmation of the status of the invitee, and always an opportunity to discuss issues with Johnson.

Many of the properties Johnson and A. W. Moursand leased for the cattle business were also used for hunting. Johnson leased "deer rights"— a Texas colloquialism for hunting privileges—from other area landowners as well. The Scharnhorst and Haywood ranches were frequent sites of Johnson hunts, and other nearby properties were used on occasion. Johnson also owned a hunting lodge on A. W. Moursand's property, and a constant stream of visitors came to use it.[42] By the early 1960s, hunting had become an important ritual activity at the LBJ Ranch.

Visitors came through the ranch to hunt the deer that roamed the various Johnson properties. During the 1950s, senatorial colleagues came to hunt, Russell prominent among them. Johnson even taught his wife to hunt. Lady Bird Johnson had been excited when Johnson took up hunting because it was the first activity outside of politics that he seemed to enjoy, and she learned to shoot herself, becoming a crack shot. Just after the election of 1960, John F. Kennedy came to the ranch and enjoyed the hunt as he discussed his administration with his new second in command. Mercury astronauts Deke Slayton, John Glenn, and Gordon Cooper were invited for a hunting trip. Prominent individuals were welcomed, as were friends and close associates and their relatives. Political issues of all kinds were discussed in the course of such hunts, the activity and the camaraderie serving as a backdrop for consensus. On one such trip, with Lynda Bird Johnson and George Hamilton in the back seat holding rifles, Johnson and Walter Heller, head of the Council of Economic Advisors, sat in the front seat and discussed whether Johnson should reverse his stand on federal excise taxes.[43]

Johnson's attitudes about hunting changed dramatically after the Kennedy assassination. Before the tragedy, Johnson "lived with a gun in his lap," Dale Malechek recalled. "He was forever ever ever hunting, shooting. After the Kennedy incident, I only remember him shooting a gun one time." Johnson took a different perspective in the aftermath of the assassination, one that was reflected in an exchange with Father Wunibald Schneider. "Mr. President, I'm glad I'm not a hunter," the priest said as they saw a beautiful buck. "Why?" asked Johnson. "You wouldn't let me shoot a buck like that," said Father Schneider. "No," Johnson replied, "they are not for shooting." Albert Wierichs witnessed the same change in the president. "Way back yonder, he liked to hunt," the Johnson City native recounted. "I don't think in later years he ever shot another deer."[44]

At the ranch, hunting served as a way to differentiate people, to assert the primacy of the Texas experience. It became a measure of an individual; for Lyndon Johnson, hunting differentiated among kinds of people. Johnson often judged people by the way in which they handled the outdoor experience. For visitors, particularly those from the North or East, deer hunting in the Hill Country became a rite of passage, a test of the caliber of a man. "He'd invite various people which had never hunted," James Davis, who served as cook and houseman beginning in 1959, remembered. "I guess he got a kick telling them how to hunt."[45]

Robert Kennedy made one such visit in 1959 that illustrated the importance of hunting as an activity that defined character. Although Johnson and the younger Kennedy later became adversaries of immense proportions, in 1959 they still sought some form of accommodation with each other. Similar kinds of hierarchical thinking combined with different backgrounds, great pride, and relatively short tempers to make the younger Kennedy and Johnson a difficult match. Still a Senate-staff member, Robert Kennedy had never hunted before he arrived in Texas. Johnson sought to show his guest the joys of Texas living; hunting the abundant deer was chief among them. Johnson and members of the ranch staff tried to teach Kennedy how to handle a deer rifle, but, as Davis recalled, after the end of the lesson Kennedy still "need[ed] more instructions." When the northeasterner fired at a deer, the gun kicked and hit him in the face. Although Kennedy's shot hit the deer, Davis and the others had to complete the kill. It was a moment that highlighted the differences between a Hill Country background and experience and the younger Kennedy's more privileged background elsewhere.[46] It was certainly a memory that Johnson later relished as his relationship with the younger Kennedy deteriorated.

Most hunts on the ranch were typical Johnson productions. The fleet of Johnson convertibles was the most important ingredient; the president's entourage hunted from what was usually labeled a "motorized safari." Johnson often drove in his Lincoln with A. W. Moursand by his side, usually followed by Lady Bird Johnson in another vehicle, additional cars of reporters or other guests, and a car carrying Secret Service agents and other official personnel. Sometimes Johnson used an old red Ford converted to a "deer-hunting car"; it included a built-in bar. A station wagon driven by the ranch staff, used to carry kill to a locker plant, brought up the rear. Johnson sometimes drove the wagon, but usually not during a hunt with visitors. The convertibles were the most essential vehicles in this motorized parade because they offered the opportunity for an unobstructed shot from within. Their use became a Johnson trademark.[47]

The actual shooting of an animal became a litmus test that allowed Johnson to apply mythic rural and Hill Country values to people from other parts of the country. Those who declined his offer to shoot or who acted as if they felt hunting was an inappropriate activity for the president instantly diminished in Johnson's estimation. Those who embraced hunting enthusiastically, even if without any idea of how to shoot accurately, were perceived by the president as having potential. Skilled and experienced shots received special treatment. Johnson often sought to distract such guests as they shot, increasing the degree of difficulty and making failure a certainty for all but the most experienced with firearms.[48] In the distinction he drew between those with the skill to succeed and those who lacked it, he affirmed the importance of the ranch and its meaning.

This formulation inverted the values that the national press respected. Hunting was a respectable activity, reporters believed, but a little undignified for a president. Many members of the press, raised in cities and suburbs, had little prior experience with the sport and even less of the framework in which to understand it. The assassination of John F. Kennedy produced a revulsion directed at firearms, especially rifles, and reporters reflected that newfound horror. As a result, they responded with stereotypes and clichés, grasping the notion that hunting held an important role in the way the president understood people but failing to go beyond that into full understanding. Most news accounts sounded simultaneously patronizing and bemused at the mysterious activity with which the president confronted his public.

Nor did the American political elite, with its roots in the culture of the East Coast, successfully come to grips with Johnson's predilection for the activity. To them hunting was a relic activity, more appropriate to utilitarian conservationist grandfathers than to the leadership of a changing nation. Other presidents from rural backgrounds, Truman and Eisenhower in particular, reached accommodation with the culture of the East; even those who had not been thrilled by it acknowledged its importance. Lyndon Johnson was different, and the emphasis on hunting as a ritual and a pathway to acceptance reflected his cast of mind.

In this manner, the ranch and activities associated with it became a cross-cultural experience, a place where Johnson's America, mythic and real, touched the America of the press and the two coasts. It was not always a happy meeting ground, and rarely was it a place filled with understanding and appreciation for different ways of living. Often the ranch and the activities engaged in there were indicative of tensions that swirled around the relationship between the president and the press. Even more often Johnson's trips to Texas worked to alleviate his insecurities about life among the privileged in Washington, D.C. In Texas, with a figurative gun in his hand, he could restructure relationships to cast himself as the one with the dominant skills as well as the power he held in Washington, D.C. This assertion of the importance of the ranch was reflected in the way most reporters wrote and spoke of it. As is true of so many anthropologists, their words and thoughts told their audience more about themselves than about what they saw and experienced. Filtered through the prism of their background and values, the Texas White House took on the quality of a foreign country. In many accounts, the strange customs of Texas, its people, and its president were explained in a manner only slightly different from that used to described Pakistan or Egypt.

This fundamentally patronizing characterization revealed the degree to which the ranch was the scene of an ongoing cross-cultural interaction. Texas was foreign to the national press, particularly to the White House corps that produced so much of the ranch coverage, and they treated it as such. The result was typical of cross-cultural experiences: the groups saw each other in action and gained both some measure of respect and some degree of contempt from the interchange. This deeply affected the reports of Johnson carried on television and in the newspapers. In the end, the experiences of the press at the ranch were part of the discontent and distrust that grew during the Johnson presidency. The national press ultimately perceived the ranch through the prism it brought from the East Coast. The foreignness of its portrayal was an essential component in the process that demystified the presidency and led to the fierce inquisitiveness that came to dominate the later years of the Johnson presidency. Unresolved, the struggle for symbolic control and cross-cultural communication and understanding had great consequences for Johnson and the White House.

CHAPTER 9

The Ranch

as a

Haven

The Hill Country had a special effect on Lyndon B. Johnson. As he recounted time and time again in many ways, it was home to him, a place where he could shed the pressures of the presidency, breathe deeply the pure air, and see more clearly the breadth, depth, and ramifications of the issues he faced. His most difficult choices became resolvable in the physical setting he loved, near the grave sites of his ancestors, on the land that he felt to the core of his being. No other place had the emotional impact nor the steadying influence on Johnson that the Hill Country and the ranch did, and nowhere else did the president feel able to manifest the broadest range of his emotions and feelings.

This tremendous feeling for place was reflected in the way both Lyndon and Lady Bird Johnson regarded the ranch. Over and over, the Johnsons referred to the Texas White House as the place where they could "recharge their batteries." The ranch provided solace and clarity, clearing the murkiness of Washington, D.C., for these two Texans, and created the climate in which they could find new perspectives from which to resolve continuing problems. Lyndon Johnson himself best framed the importance of the Hill Country and his ranch when he said, "When I come here and stay two or three days, it's a breath of fresh air; it's new strength. I go away ready to challenge the world."[1]

The ranch served as a haven for Johnson, a place where he could relieve the stresses of national political life, where he could control a microworld in a comprehensive manner to which the larger world only rarely responded. "It was a real retreat for him," press aide George Reedy recalled. "He'd go [to the ranch] and spin all kinds of dreams." Even with the president's busy schedule, Johnson "usually had no set plans" when he arrived at the ranch, Yolanda Boozer recounted. He was there because he wanted to be, there because he needed the special feeling the ranch gave him.[2] In the Hill Country, Johnson could control daily life with the kind of mastery that he had enjoyed in the Senate but that often eluded him in the presidency. On the ranch, Johnson's penchant for managing every detail could be fulfilled; he could establish the peremptory domination of the efforts of his staff for which he was renowned. The ranch was small enough to function in this individualistic and idiosyncratic fashion, returning to the president the sense of control essential to him that seemed to spiral away as U.S. cities erupted in flames, as the war in Vietnam began to consume lives and resources at an ever-greater rate, and as Americans, particularly young ones, expressed their dismay about their society in a range of civil and often extralegal protests. A man who prided himself on his ability to use politics to control people and their behavior, as president Johnson faced a world that did not respond to reason. His ranch and the Hill Country did.

There was also an enormous and powerful personal side to Johnson's feelings about the ranch. He loved the place—loved the spectacular Pedernales River sunsets, the long walks he took along the riverfront, the serenity of the rolling Hill Country, and the proximity of friends and neighbors. The Johnson family graveyard just east of the ranch house had great meaning to him; generations of his ancestors were buried there, including his mother and father. Johnson planned to join them one day, selecting a location next to his mother among the "beautiful trees, so peaceful and quiet," as he often said. The meaning of the ranch also became clear in other ways.

Johnson loved to be at the ranch for his birthday. During his presidency, he spent each birthday there with the exception of 1967. The Johnsons almost always spent Christmas at the ranch, rushing there in 1963 on December 24 so as not to miss the holiday at home. Only in 1968—during Johnson's lame duck period before the inauguration of Richard M. Nixon—did the family stay at the White House for Christmas. The emotional pull of the ranch far outweighed any other material influence in Johnson's life. Only his wife and his mother had a greater impact upon him.[3]

At his ranch, Lyndon Johnson felt secure in a way he did not elsewhere. Although not a man given to conventional definitions of relaxation, he found the Hill Country property able to quiet his worries in ways that no place, event, or person in the nation's capital ever could. Despite illnesses and other health worries, Johnson remained a vigorous man throughout his life. He faced innumerable crises without flinching and was so driven that he thought nothing of routinely working eighteen- and twenty-hour days. Only at the ranch could he focus that energy inward, combine it with his insight and turn it on himself. Only there could he express his thoughts and feelings, his desires and needs, with a precision that was sometimes missing elsewhere. At the ranch, Lyndon Johnson was reflective in a manner that belied the stereotypes of the press, candid in a way that defied the negative characterizations of his veracity. He was at his best on his property, his insecurities quieted by his feeling for the place.

Besides its function as a place for clear thinking, the ranch also served as a retreat. Johnson made trips to the ranch following important and stressful decisions and cataclysmic events, when he needed peace and serenity. He rewarded himself with a trip to Texas after the successful completion of many difficult negotiations; in the aftermath of nearly every major decision he made elsewhere, he jetted to the ranch in a combination of celebration, reflection, and relaxation. In the Hill Country, he could ride with his close confidant A. W. Moursand and other friends and let the tension of his position dissipate. The presidency was a kind of trap. Along with immense power and responsibility, the office meant curtailed movement and an incredible lack of privacy. Sam Houston Johnson, the president's eccentric brother, often referred to the presidency as a prison "sentence."[4] The ranch allowed Lyndon Johnson to regain a measure of the freedom of ordinary people. There he could attempt to elude the Secret Service, fully confident that other than the irritation of the agents there would be no negative consequences. The clouds in his psyche, the

enormous stress of his position brought on by the gravity of every decision, cleared away in the Texas hills, on the county roads, and along the
Pedernales River.

As the public changed its initially positive perception of the Johnson
administration and the popularity of the president began to decline, the
ranch became even more important to the president's peace of mind. In
1964 and 1965, Johnson and his policies were very popular with the public. Despite historian Eric Goldman's contention that as many people
voted against Barry Goldwater as for Johnson, Johnson's 1964 landslide
victory over Goldwater illustrated the warmth the American public felt
toward the man who had revived a distraught nation after the Kennedy
assassination. The Great Society programs were extremely popular, as
long as the nation retained both its prosperity and its basic historic optimism. But beginning late in 1965 and continuing throughout the remainder of the decade, the attitudes that had characterized the nation
during the twenty years following World War II began to change, and
Americans looked at their society and its institutions in a more critical
fashion than ever before.[5]

As the war in Vietnam became more and more of a quagmire, the positive achievements of the Johnson administration became increasingly obscure to an ever larger segment of the press and the public. Domestic
accomplishments, at the core of Johnson's vision for the United States,
were overshadowed by the specter of Vietnam. For Johnson, the war became, in the words of one scholar, "a personal as well as a national tragedy." Particularly after the Tet Offensive, in early 1968, which shattered
the illusion that the United States had entered a new and more positive
phase in the war, the approval rating of the Johnson administration plum-
meted, and with it the popularity of the president. "That bitch of a war,"
as Johnson once referred to Vietnam, took his time and energy away
from the Great Society programs close to his heart and eventually tore
the nation apart as it exacted a great price from Johnson on a personal
level. The children of his friends, such as Harold Woods, the superintendent of the LBJ State Park, went off to fight; Woods's son came home
wounded, and Johnson felt personally responsible. He even visited the
young man at the hospital in San Antonio. The war provided him with
his most painful moments and forced him to grapple with a gnawing
feeling that the war had diverted his presidency from its primary path. In
the end, Johnson came to hate the war and saw his political demise in it.

"The only difference between the Kennedy assassination and mine," Johnson lamented in 1968, was that "I am alive and it has been more torturous."[6]

For Lyndon Johnson, derailing his presidency on a foreign policy issue was a cruel turn of events. Even as he recognized that the honeymoon at the beginning of his presidency was a temporary situation, Johnson had reveled in it. A deep-seated need to be loved was a central feature of his character, and the early public response to his administration fulfilled that need. The positive response to the Great Society harkened back to the early days of the administration of Franklin D. Roosevelt, a parallel from which Johnson did not shy. But the warm relationship between the administration and the public did not last. Beginning in the summer of 1965, U.S. cities exploded in race riots. In Los Angeles, that summer with its Watts riot was only the beginning of a sequence of long, hot summers that rocked the positive attitude of the nation and led many to ask questions about the ramifications of the Civil Rights Movement. A backlash followed, as segments of the public that had been at best lukewarm to civil rights turned away from the movement. Their difficulty compounded by the problems of Vietnam and the domestic turmoil it spawned, the later years of the Johnson administration were a great burden for the president.

His ranch provided a consistency that did not exist for Lyndon Johnson in Washington, D.C. The Hill Country rhythms were his, instilled in him from his youth. From the ranch house, he could see the places important in his personal history—the Junction Schoolhouse, where he began his education, and a range of other places with great personal meaning. Johnson could think at the ranch, and he could see clearly what he often could not in the swirl of Washington, D.C. He could carry that clarity with him back to the nation's capital, just as he brought back the hot pork sausage made from the hogs on his ranch.[7] His memories were there in Texas, as was the strength that had first propelled him away yet later brought him back to purchase the old ranch as a testimony to his success. The rooted feeling of belonging in a place, of finally being able to call the difficult Hill Country his own, had great resonance for Johnson.

The ongoing returns to the ranch for holidays and personal events clearly illustrated this rootedness. Although Johnson kept an extremely busy schedule, he and Lady Bird always made it back to the ranch for important celebratory occasions. It often took a great effort to reach Texas in time for important events. At certain times, such as Christmas of 1966, they arrived at the last minute. When the Johnsons arrived after dark on December 24, a fire was burning in the hearth, and the house was decorated with balsam rope along the mantelpieces in the big living room and the den and along the stair rail. Mistletoe and holly hung from the light fixtures. A great bowl of eggnog and plates of cookies sat upon the sideboard in the dining room. Christmas carols were playing on the record player. Johnson invited in the Secret Service agents and the military personnel for eggnog. In a similar instance on Thanksgiving Day in 1967, Johnson stayed in his bed with his young grandson, Patrick Lyn Nugent, for part of the afternoon. The family followed that afternoon with a drive along the pastures to take a last look at the Hill Country's fall colors. Lady Bird remembered it as a day of "sheer contentment." Having Christmas that year at the ranch required an even greater effort than in previous years. Johnson returned from a trip around the world, which included a stop in Vietnam, on December 24, and after a day the tired president and the first lady departed for the ranch.[8] The soothing qualities of being in the family home at this important time of the year made even a worn Johnson willing to make one more trip home.

The ranch was also the place where both Johnsons became rejuvenated. The ranch offered rest and vacation as well as the camaraderie of old friends and guests, familiar surroundings, and a controlled environment. The nature of entertaining there was different; the Johnsons were far more familial with their old friends and neighbors from the Hill Country than they were with official visitors. Some Hill Country friends, such as Harold Woods, were considered part of the Johnson family, and there was always room for them at the Johnson table. Others felt at home at the ranch. Cactus Pryor's children "practically grew up at the ranch," he recounted. Charles Boatner only attended a few formal events at the ranch, but he and his sons were Christmas guests. Father Wunibald Schneider was another frequent dinner guest. At home, the nature of socialization changed from semiformal barbecues to relaxed dinners with family and friends, a level of personal interaction that the president highly valued. Even during his busiest times, Johnson always stopped to "visit," in Texas terms, with ranch workers. The ranch was his spread, and he reveled in the combined networks of sociability, kinship, and friendship there.[9]

Even when away, Lyndon Johnson felt renewed just thinking of the ranch. Its importance was clear from a number of his unorthodox actions. Chief among these was his near obsession with demanding daily weather reports from the Hill Country. When he was away from Texas, Johnson received reports of moisture—rain and snowfall. He also spoke almost daily with the ranch foreman, Dale Malechek, giving instructions and hearing what was new at the ranch. Such information reassured Johnson about the state of his ranch during his absences. From a distance, rainfall reports and daily work updates allowed the president to retain a feeling of control over activity at the ranch.[10]

Upon their return to the Hill Country, the Johnsons reveled in its familiarity. To them the region seemed more real than Washington, D.C., populated with authentic people instead of the stereotypically power-driven social climbers of the nation's capital. Because relaxation in a conventional sense was not Johnson's forte, the pace of life even in rural Texas remained frenetic, but for Lyndon Johnson even a fast-moving trip to the ranch was an experience he craved. He often returned to the ranch bedraggled and worn; after even a few days, he left inspired and full of the energy he and the nation needed.[11]

One manifestation of this was a pattern of inviting special friends to the ranch at particularly beautiful times of the year. Lady Bird Johnson proposed most such activities, carefully planning guest lists and selecting the time of year. Her staff came to refer to these as weekends of "sharing the ranch at a pretty time of the year with people we enjoy," as one memorandum on the subject was titled. These were informal affairs, loosely planned around the activities the Johnsons most enjoyed: driving around the ranch, watching the deer, spending time at the lake, and if a Sunday was included, attending church in Fredericksburg. Guest lists of fifteen to twenty people were typical. Visitors included Mary Lasker, who played an important role in Lady Bird Johnson's beautification program; stalwart friends and political supporters Arthur Krim, the president of United Artists Corporation, and his wife, Mathilde Krim, a faculty member at the Weizmann Institute in Israel; and others. Sometimes the Saturday night dinner would be expanded to include a number of Texas dignitaries. Personal, yet with characteristics of formality, these private events were prize moments for the Johnsons.[12]

"Off-record" weekends also accentuated the importance of the ranch to the president. These weekends were considered private, no press coverage permitted during them. Guests for these events were often new friends, and the informal atmosphere of the activities allowed for the development of camaraderie. One such weekend gathering occurred on August 2–4, 1968. The Johnsons invited a combination of close associates such as

McGeorge and Mary Bundy, Clark and Marny Clifford, and HEW Secretary Joseph Califano and his wife, Trudye; close friends such as A. W. and Mariallen Moursand and John and Nellie Connally; and important supporters such as Armand and Frances Hammer of the Occidental Petroleum Company and Edward J. Daly, chairman of World Airways, Inc. Beginning late on Friday afternoons, such events again showcased the ranch, allowed Johnson a comfortable environment in which to conduct business, and showed the president at his best on the personal level.[13] The ability of the ranch to soothe the president and greatly add to his vast charm was apparent.

For Lyndon Johnson personally, the ranch also had a tremendous recuperative effect. After his gall bladder operation in October, 1965, Johnson spent the better part of the next two months at the ranch, planning and relaxing while running the country by telephone and communications system. Even the demands of the presidency did not detract from the qualities of the ranch that Johnson so sorely needed to restore his health. The effect of the Hill Country was soothing, a trait often noted by Lady Bird Johnson. After the last guests and the press departed from the 1963 Erhard barbecue, the first ceremonial event of the new Johnson presidency, the Johnsons boarded a helicopter for the Moursands' house. As the sun began to sink low in the sky, the view was idyllic. "We saw deer outlined against the sky . . . leaping the fences in the pastures," silhouetted against the coming darkness, as Lady Bird Johnson recounted. They called Texas Governor John Connally and his wife, Nellie, and the Connallys came to the ranch. The group ended up in A. W. Moursand's hunting tower. Peering into the darkness in search of the little gleams of light that were the eyes of deer staring back at the tower, Lady Bird Johnson felt relaxed, out of the whirl for the first time since the assassination. In another instance, on one beautiful autumn day in October, 1965, the Johnsons began their day with breakfast together and went for a walk—"just the two of us," she wrote in her diary—past the dam and the birthplace, past the cemetery and the old Junction School, and on to the place where their daughters had met the school bus when the Johnsons first moved to the Hill Country in the early 1950s. Throughout the three-mile jaunt, they talked of the ranch and their plans for it. Later that evening, the Johnsons and A. W. Moursand drove to 3-Springs over what Lady Bird Johnson recalled as a "non-road that it was unbelievable a Continental could navigate" and arrived at the brink of a great bluff. There they sat on rocks above the river, and Johnson talked of

his youth and his childhood, of the dreams he held then and of their meaning in the present.[14] These were rare moments during the presidency; personal and intimate in ways characteristic of Johnson yet detached in an
atypical fashion from the concerns of the day.

Cathartic and in some ways epiphanic, such moments characterized the
meaning of the ranch for the president. Johnson could unburden himself
in Texas in ways that he could not in Washington, D.C., and those close to
him recognized the positive effect of the ranch on the increasingly tired
president. Observers such as Yolanda Boozer watched his physical condition improve as a result of little more than a tour across his land. He loved
to watch the sunset from a knoll near Llano, a small town about fifty miles
as the crow flies from Stonewall. Watching the sunset revitalized him, and
he "would lose his sense of fatigue," Boozer said. He loved to see the wild-
life, for it too took the years away from him. As the strain of the presidency
grew, he had a genuine need for such opportunities.[15]

As a result of Johnson's incessant mistrust of the press, most of these
occasions were private—witnessed and recorded only by Lady Bird Johnson,
his closest friends, and members of the Johnsons' staff. Yet such moments
paint a picture of a different Johnson, an accentuated version of the man
that even hostile reporters regarded as more personable during his Hill
Country stays. This Johnson exhibited a vulnerability that he did not cover
with bluster, as he so often did in front of television cameras and newspaper reporters in Washington, D.C. He seemed more genuine and less
mythic, more concerned with what was real than with an image. On these
occasions, Johnson had a personal and emotional depth that was not always apparent in his everyday communications with the media. Not self-
conscious and not on display, among his closest friends and family Lyndon
Johnson could express a broader range of his emotions and thoughts than
was possible under more conventional presidential circumstances.

The safe feeling that the ranch provided also allowed the president a
wider range of behavior than that in which he might otherwise have engaged. Johnson's fifty-eighth birthday at the ranch, on August 27, 1966,
revealed his level of comfort in the Hill Country. The rain that drummed
on the roof was the first of Johnson's birthday presents; nothing pleased
him more than a hard Hill Country rain. The press had arrived from San
Antonio by bus and were marooned in the hangar by the inclement weather.
In the hard rain, the characteristic milling around outside the house was
uncomfortable and pointless. Johnson dropped his characteristic guard

and invited the press into the house. Reporters occupied "every possible chair, [sat] on the hearth, the piano stool, or [stood] in the corners, around the bridge table," Lady Bird Johnson recounted. Lyndon Johnson sat in his big reclining chair, with Lady Bird beside him. The president spoke for an hour, his wife remembered, "counting blessings and finding them plentiful." The event was "a purely Johnsonian performance," one newsman wrote.[16] In it, Johnson exhibited both his feelings of security at the ranch and the control of events he craved. His hostility to the press—the feelings that sometimes made him uncooperative and blustering—disappeared in the environment of the ranch. No one could challenge Johnson here.

In this sense, the ranch became a magnet for the president. Lyndon Johnson believed in the power of the ranch, and this belief was the basis of a pattern that continued throughout his presidency. The ranch provided a kind of consistency for Johnson, and he returned to it many times in many ways. It pulled on him, brought him home, and he developed a pervasive faith in the recuperative powers of the place and the Hill Country around it.

A New Year's Day trip in 1966 to Enchanted Rock, about one hour's drive from the ranch, illustrated Johnson's relationship to the Hill Country. Even in the aftermath of Johnson's gall bladder surgery, efforts to begin a peace process to resolve the situation in South Vietnam had continued. On that New Year's Day, Thomas C. Mann, the former assistant secretary of state for inter-American affairs and the undersecretary of state for economic affairs, arrived at the ranch to report on the efforts of the five roving U.S. emissaries who had traveled to forty countries in an effort to pressure the North Vietnamese government to enter into peace negotiations. The Johnsons and Mann drove to Enchanted Rock with other officials, engaging in a conversation about the receptiveness of Mexican leaders to U.S. entreaties. The car telephone rang constantly, Joseph Califano and Bill Moyers calling repeatedly to report on the efforts of the peace-seekers. Each time the telephone rang, conversation in the car stopped until the president finished the call.[17]

When the party reached Enchanted Rock, the second largest granite outcropping in the United States after Stone Mountain, Georgia, the president and others climbed the great granite dome. Lady Bird Johnson worried about her husband's heart condition, but up the group went. When they finally reached the top, they found a National Geodetic Survey marker. The top of the dome offered a view of the world to the horizons. From the peak, Lady Bird Johnson felt "one owned the world in every direction!"[18] This feeling of being on top of the world captured the meaning of the Hill Country for the Johnsons.

The resolution and aftermath of the threatened steel strike of 1965 offered another example of the importance of the ranch to Johnson. In the middle of the 1960s, the production of steel remained an important U.S. industry, crucial to national defense and an important basis of the industrial economy. A strike deadline set for September 1, 1965, had the potential to disrupt the functioning of the U.S. economy. A 1959 strike in the industry had been a catalyst for the recession of 1960–61, a reprise of which Johnson desperately wanted to avoid. Negotiations between the United Steelworkers of America, headed by its new president, I. W. Abel, and the steel industry had ended. On the evening of August 17, Johnson met with Abel and Califano in the Oval Office to see how far apart the two sides really were. After his staff reviewed the documents, Johnson told Califano, "I'm afraid this one's going to end up here"—in the Oval Office, adjudicated by the president. According to Califano, Johnson did not fear being compelled to resolve the dispute; in fact, he "welcomed the challenge."[19]

A tense two weeks followed. The gulf between labor and management remained wide, and Johnson feared the prospect that any increase in wages would cause a larger increase in the price of steel. By August 25, a strike appeared even more likely. Abel had made promises to his constituency that he intended to keep, and management officials were prepared to battle to avoid concessions to labor. On August 26, Johnson laid down the terms he thought best in a meeting that included Secretary of Commerce John Connor, Secretary of Labor William Wirtz, Treasury Secretary Joseph Fowler, Chairman of the Council of Economic Advisors Gardner Ackley, and HEW Secretary Califano. Johnson directed Connor to advise industry representatives that a 3.2 percent increase in wages and benefits, equivalent to the 1964 numerical wage-price guidepost for economic growth, could be granted without a concomitant increase in the price of steel. Wirtz, who represented labor issues in the cabinet, thought that this would tie Abel's hands; Connor, a former Fortune 500 chief executive, had expressed private sympathy with the steel industry's claim that the 3.2 percent increase should include a rise in the cost of steel.[20]

Johnson left the next day for the ranch to celebrate his fifty-seventh birthday. Even in the midst of a major crisis with important ramifications for the U.S. economy, he left Washington, D.C., for this customary celebratory occasion. The communications infrastructure installed at the ranch to support the presidency made it possible for Johnson to be geographically distant and still remain current with any developments in the situation. During his three days in Texas, he kept in close touch, tracking the events through Califano and others.[21]

When Johnson returned from Texas for a Monday, August 30, breakfast meeting, he began to reveal his strategy to avert the strike. The politics of his approach were typical. He utilized the skills of the individuals involved, emphasizing the cost to them if they failed to find a resolution. When necessary, he cajoled people, reminding them that if they failed, the consequences would be vast. He intimated that if he was compelled to do so, he might use provisions of the Taft-Hartley Act, anathema to labor, to delay the strike for eighty days. He utilized the prestige of former President Dwight D. Eisenhower by inviting him to the White House, playing on Eisenhower's antipathy for both labor and the steel industry and subtly reminding the nation of the imperative of cooperation during wartime. The negotiating teams were made aware of Eisenhower's interest in the situation. Johnson even brought people with whom he had ongoing disagreements, in particular Senator Wayne Morse of Oregon, into the process, taking advantage of the political cachet they brought to the situation. As he entrusted the negotiations to Connor and Wirtz, telling them that he depended solely on them to resolve the issue, Johnson also opened a back channel between labor and management. Clark Clifford, a close advisor of Democratic presidents who had represented Republic Steel before joining the administration, and U.N. Ambassador Arthur Goldberg, who had negotiated on behalf of the steelworkers during his career as an attorney, bypassed the formal negotiations; Johnson told them that they too were his only hope for resolution of the dispute. By turning up the pressure from a range of sources and making leaders feel personally responsible for the situation, the president gave industry and labor two choices: either agree with each other or face a president determined to make both sides pay for pushing the nation to the brink of economic calamity.[22]

On August 30, labor and management representatives were sequestered in a room at the White House, given only the information that Johnson wanted them to receive, and told to get the negotiation process moving. There was only a little time left to secure an extension of the strike deadline. But within a few hours of the 1:00 P.M. beginning of the meeting, the parties agreed to an eight-day extension. The negotiations resumed, with

Johnson playing an expanding role. At one point, the president pulled Abel out of the meeting and told him that if labor put the national interest first in this case, Johnson would give labor's interests primacy when the opportunity arose. Despite such offers, the two sides seemed no closer to any resolution.

A week of strained meetings that lasted into the late evening and early morning hours followed. Johnson monitored the events closely as Congress debated and passed pieces of Great Society legislation. With the talks looking deadlocked, Johnson brought everyone involved back into his office and again pleaded with them, flattered them, and cajoled them. In one instance, Johnson used a personal entreaty to further negotiations. He wanted to be at the ranch with Lady Bird for the upcoming Labor Day weekend, he told the gathered officials. It was the last real weekend of summer. The chance to spend it at his ranch was so important to him that he would agree to invite them all to his next inauguration in 1969 if they reached an agreement in time for him to go to Texas for the holiday weekend.[23] This strategy involved both flattery and intimidation; the president needed them and simultaneously reminded them of his needs. Johnson surmised that both sides had come to rely on the cabinet secretaries for leadership in the resolution of the agreement. When Johnson found out through his back channel that Wirtz and Connor, the two cabinet members, could not agree, he forced an agreement. With this accomplished, the negotiations quickly came to a successful conclusion.[24]

On Friday, September 3, 1965, the beginning of the Labor Day weekend, word came to Lady Bird Johnson at about 4:00 P.M. suggesting that she turn on the television. Live on the national news, she saw her husband, "jubilant, calm, never looking stronger," she remembered, with Abel and R. Conrad Cooper, the chief negotiator for the steel industry, as the president announced the successful conclusion of the negotiations. The threat of the strike was over. When Lady Bird Johnson telephoned him, he said that by 7:00 P.M. he would be on his way to Texas for the Labor Day weekend.[25]

Strategic and necessary, Johnson's attachment to the ranch played a significant role in the steel negotiations. His wish to be in Texas came to represent his desires to the negotiators, reinforced by the trip he made to the ranch in the middle of the negotiations. His suggestion that they were denying him the last big weekend of the summer took the place of insisting that the strike had to be avoided for the good of the nation. Johnson

replaced the national interest with his personal needs, with something the
negotiators could understand and relate to their own desires. In his way,
Johnson told the negotiators that they had to resolve the issue quickly. His
need for a last summer trip to the ranch served as a catalyst for this understanding.

The weeks of the steel negotiations were among the most stressful of
the first two years of the Johnson presidency. In their aftermath, Johnson
rushed to the ranch to unwind. He announced the end of the strike on the
evening television news on all three national networks and within thirty
minutes was on his way to Texas. Johnson headed back to the place he
loved and needed, rewarding himself for the successful completion of a
difficult task. The ranch once again served as a haven, a place where he
could release the pressure of the White House and Washington, D.C.[26]

It was also the place where Johnson went to make his toughest decisions.
The most difficult choice he ever faced was the decision about running for
reelection in 1968. As the war in Vietnam worsened and opposition to it
grew, the popularity of the Johnson administration had precipitously declined. For a man who needed public approval as much as Lyndon Johnson,
this was a hard reality. Even though in 1964 and 1965 he had acknowledged
that he knew the postelection honeymoon of popularity could not last, he
was visibly shaken by the response to his policies. The chant "Hey, hey,
LBJ, how many kids did you kill today?" that came to permeate college
campuses was noxious, personally offensive, and insulting, but it was also a
reflection of changing public attitudes toward this president and ultimately
the presidency.[27] To Lyndon Johnson, who had spent his life seeking power
only to arrive at its pinnacle by a fluke, the reality of growing opposition
required him to rethink his personal objectives in light of the needs of the
nation.

In the setting that most relaxed him and where he felt he had the most
control, he made the decisions that mattered most. Johnson's big decision
about whether to run again became an ongoing conversation that lasted
from the middle of 1967 into early 1968. Prone to reflecting aloud, Johnson
sounded out his friends on a number of occasions before he decided to go
public with his decision to decline the nomination. The ranch was the
setting for much of this discussion; in the Hill Country, Johnson had the
people around him and the vistas he required for this, the toughest of
decisions. In one of many conversations about the subject of reelection,
Johnson drove around the ranch on September 8, 1967, with John Connally

and Congressman J. J. "Jake" Pickle for eight hours. In Lady Bird Johnson's recollection of the day, the Johnsons had already decided he would not to run again. As was typical for a politician of Johnson's skill and experience, the question had become how to announce his decision. Connally, a close confidante of the president who had recently stepped down from the governorship of Texas, knew the stresses and strains of high office. The Johnsons had discussed the issue of running for reelection with him throughout the summer, and Connally believed that Johnson had come to a decision to which he would stick. Lady Bird Johnson remembered that Pickle was amazed and refused to believe that Johnson would not run again.[28]

The conversation about Johnson's options continued throughout the winter of 1967–68. In another instance of the Hill Country serving as a setting for deep reflection, on January 4, 1968, Lyndon Johnson spent the entire day in his Austin office, speaking with R. Sargent Shriver; Charles Schultze, director of the U.S. Bureau of the Budget from 1965 to 1967; and Schultze's successor, Charles Zwick. After the discussions, the Johnsons and John and Nellie Connally drove back from Austin through a heavy fog, had dinner, and sat in Johnson's bedroom for more than three hours, where they again talked about whether Johnson should run for reelection. The Connallys offered sound advice, John Connally suggesting that Johnson should run only if he could look forward to being president again. Nellie Connally remarked that if Johnson decided not to run, he might feel that time had stopped, almost as if someone close to him had died. After that, she said, a wave of great relief would follow. This had been their experience after they decided John Connally would not seek the governorship of Texas again.[29]

At the ranch he loved, Johnson was able to see more clearly, to let down his guard more thoroughly. He felt older and more tired than he had before taking over the presidency, he told Lady Bird and the Connallys, and was not sure he could give the country what it needed and deserved. How would the servicemen in Vietnam respond? Johnson wondered. How would history would judge him if he chose to withdraw? How would his friends who believed in him regard the decision? Johnson, however, had already decided. "We went round and round," Lady Bird Johnson remembered, "finding no cool oasis, no definite time for an acceptable exit."[30]

Although the accounts of Johnson's decision not to seek reelection are few, they all reflect one salient feature. This was a decision discussed and made almost exclusively at the Texas White House and in the Hill Country. The people with whom Johnson discussed it were Texans, and the

subject was discussed in the manner of Texas. Johnson's White House staff
knew little of the president's intentions until a few days before the speech.
Everyone, friend and foe, expected Johnson to run again. On March 31,
1968, the day of the speech in which Johnson planned to announce his
decision to leave office, former North Carolina governor Terry Sanford
had a meeting with the president and left expecting to run his 1968 campaign. Even Johnson's close advisor Clark Clifford was stunned. "You could
have knocked my eyes off with a stick," the venerated statesman remembered his reaction to the news being, about four hours before Johnson
delivered the speech. "The weight of the day and the weeks and the months
had lifted," Lyndon Johnson remembered as the immediate aftermath of
the speech. The evening after the decision was announced, Johnson, looking as if "he'd been pulled through a wringer," was the host for a dinner
party at the ranch. Even then, he could muse about his administration, its
accomplishments and shortcomings.[31] Again the ranch held its recuperative qualities, its special ability to let the president be the human being he
was capable of being. Among friends and in a place in which he felt almost
complete control, Johnson could speak with a candor rarely possible elsewhere. The decision not to seek a second full term was Lyndon Johnson's
secret from the world, held closely with his many friends in the Hill Country he loved.

The decision not to seek reelection also had an impact on the ranch
house. Once the Johnsons were reasonably certain that they would return
home to the ranch in January, 1969, remodeling for the post-presidential
years began. Johnson's decision not to seek reelection and their determination to build master bedroom suites were, in Lady Bird Johnson's words,
"complementary and coincident." The Johnsons had great confidence in
their architectural team, led by Roy White and including landscape architect Richard Myrick and designer Herbert Wells, and this mitigated any
concerns they had about building at the ranch while they continued to
reside at the White House and could not regularly oversee the work.[32]

Two master bedroom suites, which Lady Bird Johnson called her "forever rooms," were the core of this development program. White was given
the task of designing the rooms. Lady Bird Johnson specified that her room
offer a good view to the east, lots of bookshelves, and a fireplace. Lyndon
Johnson could not get enough light for his suite. A domed skylight was
installed in his bathroom, and the entire suite had more light than was
needed. White recalled that once when he took a light-meter reading, the

"hand shot off the contraption and it almost blinded you." The president's bedroom was just as well lit.[33]

The construction of these new rooms during the presidency accentuated the haven-like characteristics of the ranch. The two bedroom suites were designed for the post-presidential needs of the Johnsons, another dimension of the control the president craved, and they reinforced the permanence of the Johnsons at the ranch. In the aftermath of the construction of these new rooms, the ranch—always home—was even more closely identified with the personal side of the Johnsons' lives. The never-ending process of making the ranch a home continued long after its status as homeplace was confirmed and widely accepted.

The ranch also served to lift the president's spirits during and after the cataclysmic events of 1968. The first of these events was the April 4, 1968, assassination of the Reverend Dr. Martin Luther King, Jr., in Memphis, Tennessee. In Memphis to lead a march in support of striking sanitation workers, King was killed by a sniper's bullet as he stood on a motel room balcony. At the White House, Johnson later wrote, "a jumble of anxious thoughts ran through my mind, including fear, confusion, and outrage." Johnson's thoughts quickly turned to the King family, and he telephoned Coretta Scott King, Martin Luther King's widow, to express his condolences. A few moments later, Johnson went on national television from the West Lobby and asked "every citizen to reject the blind violence that has struck Dr. King, who lived by nonviolence. . . . It is only by joining together and only by working together that we can continue to move toward equality and fulfillment for all people."[34]

Groups of people across the nation failed to heed his words. The ramifications of the assassination were instantaneous and immense; riots broke out in at least 125 U.S. cities, and in the African American sections of a number of American cities, turmoil followed. Washington, D.C., home to a large African American population, experienced considerable violence. More than seven hundred fires lit the night sky. By the next evening, the White House had become, in Lady Bird Johnson's words, "a fortress." As the rioting in the nation's capital became worse, Lyndon Johnson ordered four thousand National Guard troops into the capital to restore order. Within two days, the riots in Washington, D.C., ended, leaving at least 6 dead and as many as 350 injured.[35]

Johnson had close ties with the Civil Rights Movement, and in the aftermath of King's assassination he invited its leaders to the White House.

On the advice of the Secret Service and the Federal Bureau of Investigation, the president did not attend King's funeral, a decision that was widely criticized. "Once again," Johnson said, "the strange mixture of public and private capacities inherent in the Presidency prevented free action." As a private citizen, Johnson would have attended; as president, following the recommendations of his security staff, he could not. By bringing the civil rights leaders to the White House and seeking accommodation, however, Johnson could obviate criticism and avoid appearing insensitive in the aftermath of the tragic episode.[36]

By 1968, Lyndon Johnson had a strong track record as supporter of civil rights, and at the suggestion of his White House visitors, he planned to engineer another legislative victory. Since 1966, the Johnson administration had sought the passage of a law that forbid discrimination against home buyers and renters on the basis of race. Such a measure, typically referred to as an open housing law, would go a long way toward ending segregation in housing. The African American community supported the bill, but traditionally Democratic constituencies, particularly working-class European-American ethnic communities in large cities, were adamantly opposed to it. In the Senate, the powerful Everett Dirksen of Illinois led the opposition. The bill to end discrimination in housing had been stalled for two years.

Early in 1968, advocates of open housing suddenly found a more receptive climate. Senator Dirksen withdrew his opposition to the measure, and on March 11 the Senate passed the bill. The fate of open housing rested in the rules committee of the House of Representatives, a committee Johnson called "that graveyard of so much progressive legislation." The bill stalled there, becoming a weapon in the Republican effort to unseat Johnson in 1968; campaign literature promised to protect people from "LBJ's bureaucrats." When Johnson announced his decision not to run for reelection on March 31, 1968, chances of the bill's passage again improved.[37]

After the King assassination, Johnson felt that there was a small window during which the legislation could be passed, and he pressed for rapid action. The assassination generated tremendous sympathy for the Civil Rights Movement. For all of the efforts of J. Edgar Hoover and the Federal Bureau of Investigation to discredit King, he remained a monumental figure, the only person in the nation who had the stature to rely on moral suasion. His commitment to nonviolence and the clear and precise nature of the words he spoke resonated with the public. Johnson believed rapid action was essential to passage of the open housing bill, before a backlash from the rioting could turn sympathy into contempt, "normal compassion," as he said, "into bitterness, retaliation, and anger." Johnson seized the opportunity and channeled all his efforts into passage of open housing legislation. "He just put everything aside," recalled Robert C. Weaver. "This is it. This is the time. And he knew how to take advantage of the cards he had." On April 10, the House voted on the bill. In the final tally, 250 voted for the measure, while 171 opposed it. The next day, Johnson signed the Civil Rights Act of 1968 in the East Room of the White House, dedicating it to the memory of Martin Luther King, Jr.[38]

The assassination of King was a thunderous blow to the nation as well as a tragedy of immense proportions. King was perhaps the only person in the nation who could straddle the racial fissures of 1968, often the most reasonable voice in a nation seemingly gone mad. Johnson had had a volatile relationship with King. The two men, both dominant personalities, had trouble establishing a rapport. Both favored social change, but in different ways: Johnson was a tactician, using legislation and maintaining social order, while King favored direct, nonviolent action that disrupted social conventions. The two men needed each other, and for a time they worked together well, acquiring mutual respect if not always understanding. Even though Johnson remained closer to three other African American leaders—Roy Wilkins of the NAACP; Whitney Young of the Urban League; and A. Philip Randolph, the seventy-four-year-old venerated leader of the Brotherhood of Sleeping Car Porters who had merged the role of labor leader with that of independent civil rights advocate—and even though King's opposition to the war in Vietnam had strained their relations badly, the president recognized King's heroic qualities and retained tremendous respect for the slain civil rights leader.[39]

In a time of tragedy and after the signing of the new civil rights bill, Johnson sought the brief respite that only his ranch could provide. The day after the bill signing, Friday, April 12, he left for the ranch for the weekend before continuing to Hawaii on a trip that had been postponed because of the assassination. In this instance, in the aftermath of one of the most destructive weeks in U.S. history, the ranch was once again, in Lady Bird's words, "an island of peace and rest." On Saturday, the Johnsons took a typical driving trip that included the Green Mountain Ranch, the Davis Ranch, and the lake. At about 8:00 P.M., the Johnsons flew to the West Ranch and joined the Moursands for dinner. The president and

A. W. Moursand engaged in a domino game, full of "bluffing and teasing and as much talk as skill," Lady Bird Johnson remembered. The tension of the previous week melted in the Hill Country evening, and the importance of the place and the friendships forged there seemed great. Lady Bird Johnson felt this most strongly that night. "For longer than twenty years, I have enjoyed the hospitality of this house," she recorded in her diary. The Johnsons were home by eleven, in typical rural fashion. "What a good way to spend a day—that is, in contrast to those that have gone before," Lady Bird reflected. "This was the sort of day when time stood still and I was satisfied with the present and didn't reach for anything else."[40]

That ability to see the world healed and whole from the perspective of the Hill Country was the most important piece of the relationship between Lyndon Johnson and his ranch. The pace of Washington, D.C., and the frenetic demands made there never offered a moment during which to find perspective. The ranch provided that commodity in abundance. It was a place the president trusted, a place where he could be and see in a way he could not elsewhere. In Johnson's way of looking at the world, the ranch offered perspective and crucial distance. The presence of friends and the control he could exercise over the workings of the property not only allowed him elusive clarity and anchored him to his sense of what was right, but they also allowed him to express an incredible degree of candor. Such candor mostly came outside of conventional reporting channels, away from the pens and cameras of the press and among only the closest of the president's friends and associates, but its importance in the president's life cannot be overstated. For Lyndon B. Johnson, the ranch was haven from the world at large, from the difficult decisions he had to make, from the political and personal opponents with whom he daily dealt. There he could set the terms of even presidential existence and could control the interaction between the myriad facets of his responsibilities. This seeming mastery gave the president a kind of personal confidence that he never felt in Washington, D.C. It washed his doubts away, made him capable of reflection in broad and meaningful ways, and reinforced his basic beliefs. It was no wonder that even the most consistent of his adversaries in his own mind—the press—found him more personable along the Pedernales River.

CHAPTER 10

"Eight Hundred Yards up the Road"

The Ranch and Retirement, 1969–73

Lyndon B. Johnson's retirement remains the source of many of the stereotypes about the man and his ranch. After returning to the Texas Hill Country in the aftermath of Richard M. Nixon's electoral victory over Hubert Humphrey in the 1968 presidential election, Johnson found himself described as "a worn old man at sixty, consumed by the bitter, often violent five years" in the White House, a man who had been "swept down a hole of obscurity" into retirement. His "removal into irrelevancy" followed his departure from the White House, one reporter cruelly wrote.[1] This portrait—of a man exhausted by the Oval Office who resented his treatment by the press—contributed greatly to the popular view of Johnson as a man defeated by the presidency, someone who only surfaced occasionally and reluctantly during his retirement.

For the press, this characterization of Johnson served as retribution against the man whom they never understood but who many in the media felt betrayed them and the country in the quagmire of Vietnam. Always difficult to label, Johnson, in his decision to remain apart from public life after leaving the White House, allowed the press to fix upon him a stereotype of failure—in their terms, not in his. The man who had manipulated journalists throughout his career did not publicly respond to them now, for once deciding not to attempt to fashion a counterimage to negate the one put forward by his detractors. The result has been a popularly held and widely reinforced mischaracterization of Johnson's retirement as an admission of defeat on a personal as well as a political level.

With Lyndon Johnson, however, no transformation of this magnitude could be so simple. His return by choice to the ranch embodied much more than the public perception of a worn and tired old man. In his retirement, Johnson melded the various functions of the ranch in his life and career: the symbol, the haven, and the place he could control. Rather than flamboyantly display his retirement and beg for the attention of the world, as have many ex-presidents since, Johnson chose to live, for the first time in his adult life, on personal rather than public terms. He left the public scene, leaving a void behind him, and his attitude reflected his sense that he was, at last, home. "He was still a politician," long-time aide Yolanda Boozer remembered, "but he reverted more to a rancher-businessman type of person, more a father." His attention now focused on different issues than it had during his political career. Even in private, he rarely discussed matters of state or criticized the actions of his successor, except in the case of offering strategic advice to 1972 Democratic presidential candidate, Senator George McGovern. Johnson promised Lady Bird, he told one reporter, to "cultivate more small pleasures" in retirement, and he genuinely tried to do so.[2] With both Lynda and Luci and their children at the ranch or in Austin, Johnson had ample opportunity to exercise long-denied paternal instincts, to enjoy a life without the constant stress and maneuvering of politics.

To journalists and individuals still embroiled in the public world of Washington, D.C., his decision to give up the power and primacy of presidential status was incomprehensible; it reinforced their feeling of having never understood the man and, in some ways, accentuated their desire to mark him as defeated. Even Doris Kearns, who became a close confidante of the president during the preparation of his memoirs, tacitly accepted this perspective when she wrote that "after thirty-two years of public service, with the end of his presidential responsibility, a terrible, perhaps impossible transition to the hill country awaited him. . . . Whatever vestiges of power went with the retiring president . . . the real power was gone." Johnson had assumed a value system that the public world of journalism and politics could not fathom. Only writers such as Flora Schreiber of *Modern Maturity,* who represented a constituency of older Americans accustomed to such difficult transitions, appeared sympathetic to the president's desire to leave the public world; the mainstream political press regarded his desire to retire in a far more negative manner.[3] The resulting characterizations denigrated Johnson for being what he had become: a man of the country who had succeeded in the world of national politics but who turned his back on it after achieving the position, if not always the goals, he set for himself.

The lack of public appearances and media attention belied the typically more complicated nature of life at the ranch during Johnson's retirement. Always a hands-on administrator, Johnson still had many projects to occupy his time. He supervised the details of the construction of the LBJ Library on the University of Texas campus; dictated the sessions that became his book, *The Vantage Point: Perspectives of the Presidency, 1963–1969;* and managed his various properties in Texas and Mexico from the ranch on the Pedernales River. Johnson reveled in life at the ranch, escorting guests, checking his herd, and not "keeping to anyone's schedule but his own." He let his hair grow almost to shoulder-length, a visage that elicited comment when George McGovern visited the ranch during the 1972 presidential campaign. He traveled by Air Force helicopter and a personal turboprop airplane, using the military aircraft to check on progress on the library and the private airplane for longer trips. Each year on December 21, the Johnsons hosted a rollicking party at the Argyle Club in San Antonio, Texas, to celebrate their wedding anniversary.[4]

One of his biographers, Paul Conkin, detects an important change in Johnson during retirement. "For the first time since childhood," he notes, Johnson "was not tugged and pulled by ambition, not challenged by some new task." This "subdued, passive" former president had changed his scope and understanding of the world, and not withstanding his morbid sense of an early death, which was confirmed by an actuarial study he commissioned, he sought a different and more peaceful existence after leaving the presidency. According to Conkin, the public Johnson, the combative veteran of political wars, ceased to exist in 1968, and a new incarnation of the man, one focused on private rather than public affairs, lived on. This change was most apparent in his lack of public comment on political matters. According to Tom and Betty Weinheimer, Hill Country neighbors and friends, the only public comment on the Vietnam War Johnson offered from retirement was that he was "glad that it's someone else's problem." This attitude reflected his changed feelings about public life.[5]

The ranch was as central to this new private Johnson as it had been to the presidential Johnson. He had become, in the words of one urban, Ivy League–educated aide who typically could not understand the distinctions of rural life, "a goddamn farmer," albeit one who received foreign policy briefings from the staff of Nixon administration Secretary of State Henry Kissinger every Friday.[6] This conflicting picture, of a man at peace with self and place who could not resist keeping a hand in national affairs, defined the post-presidential years for Johnson. His ranch gave him the ability to do both, to be both. From it, he could—with only minor exceptions, such as the interviews by Walter Cronkite he allowed during retirement—control not only his world but also the outside world's knowledge of him and, through this, the way in which he was perceived. Johnson understood this, but again, as had been the case throughout his career, his desire to manage an image for the world conflicted with his essential character, formed and affirmed by the Hill Country. In retirement, as in the presidency, Lyndon Johnson remained paradoxically both a man of the world and a man of the Hill Country. In this sense he had traveled a great deal farther than the "eight hundred yards up the road"—a phrase some caustic locals used to describe Johnson's accomplishments—from his birthplace to the ranch.

Although Lyndon Johnson had left the presidency of his own volition, the approaching inauguration of Richard M. Nixon offered a permanent closure to his years in the White House. The final days in Washington, D.C., became a whirl of farewells and parties, while much official business remained unfinished. A farewell dinner for the cabinet on January 10 reflected the closeness of his staff, working together through difficult times. Although from anyone else such sentiments would seem hackneyed, Lady Bird Johnson best expressed the feelings in the room by quoting Charles Dickens: "It was the best of times, it was the worst of times," she began. "It's a rare unequaled feeling, a once-in-a-lifetime thing, and we are fortunate to have known it, to have shared it with you, and we are grateful," she told the people who comprised the cabinet.[7] The Vietnam War and domestic unrest had taken an enormous toll on the cabinet over the years, and the people in that room, including Vice President Hubert Humphrey and Dean Rusk, had shared difficult and trying times and made hard decisions together. Brought close by the trials of the Johnson presidency, they felt a kind of bond that stemmed from their experiences. Exchanges of gratitude and closeness marked the last weeks before the inauguration of Richard Nixon.

More public events and characterizations also reflected on the accomplishments of Johnson's years in the White House. For Lyndon Johnson, this was harder; it required coming to grips with a legacy of which he was not entirely proud. According to Conkin, Johnson's presidency "ran aground on Vietnam. On this, as on no other issue in his life, he failed. He knew it. He suffered intensely." This knowledge meant that there was a tone of apology in Johnson's final speeches, as well as a hint of defensiveness. During his final news conference at the National Press Club, Johnson echoed Winston Churchill when he told the assembled press corps that he did not think that his administration "had done enough in hardly any field." In telling a story long attributed to Churchill, Johnson quoted: "so little I have done, so much I have yet to do."[8]

Johnson's final State of the Union address, scheduled for January 14, 1969, took on significant personal meaning for the departing president. Johnson "invited" his grandson, eighteen-month-old Patrick Lyndon Nugent, to the speech, telling Lady Bird that she and their daughters could attend but that "it's my State of the Union speech and it's my last one and the only person I'm inviting is Patrick Lyndon." Seated in the gallery with his mother, the toddler behaved impeccably throughout the speech. At its conclusion, Democrats and Republicans cheered, and misty-eyed congressional leaders reflected on the Johnson presidency. The press reported that Lady Bird Johnson cried. She denied it, saying she was laughing at her grandson, the youngest listener ever to survive a State of the Union address. The baby "might not remember it," Lyndon Johnson said, "but I would."[9]

On their last night in Washington, D.C., the Johnsons threw a party for the White House staff and their families. As had much of the rest of the week, the evening offered memories and reminiscences, hopes for the future, and sadness at the parting of ways. It was a happy affair; the only sad moment came when a five-piece Marine band played "Hello, Dolly," with Johnson's staff changing the words to "Hello, Lyndon."[10] All the joy of the experience of working in the White House, all the tension and fear, were embodied in this welcoming song, set against imminent departure.[11]

The morning of the inauguration, January 20, dawned as a typical Washington, D.C., winter day: dreary, cold, and gray. The Johnsons planned to leave for Texas shortly after the inauguration. As they had throughout the presidency, military valets awakened Lyndon Johnson at 7:00 A.M. on the last morning of his term. Shortly after 10:00 A.M., Richard Nixon arrived at the White House, and by a little after noon, the United States had a new president. A lunch at the Clark Cliffords' followed; from there, the entire Johnson clan, including the two grandchildren, Patrick Lyndon Nugent and Lucinda Desha Robb, left for the airport. A huge crowd of well-wishers awaited, among them Congressmen George H. W. Bush, there, as he said, to "pay his respects" to "his president."[12]

At Bergstrom Air Force Base in Austin, Texas, five thousand people and a huge sign that read "WELCOME HOME MR. PRESIDENT AND FAMILY" greeted the Johnson entourage. Resplendent in its trademark orange, the University of Texas Longhorn band struck up "The Eyes of Texas" and "Ruffles and Flourishes." Dignitaries and friends dotted the crowd, and the mayor of Austin presented Lady Bird Johnson with a bouquet of early spring flowers. The ex-president gave a short speech, and the Johnsons boarded a Jetstar for the ranch.[13]

The ranch came in sight as darkness fell, and the Johnsons could see that a crowd had gathered to welcome them home. More than five hundred local people waited at the hangar, some of whom had known Lyndon Johnson his entire life. The former president greeted his friends and neighbors with a talk that emphasized how glad he was to be home. Leaving the hangar and walking into the warm, mild weather, the Johnsons went into their house. A "giant mound" of luggage awaited them in the kitchen. "For the first time in five years," Johnson remembered, "there were no aides to carry the bags inside to the rooms." Lady Bird began to laugh: "the coach has turned back into a pumpkin and the mice have all run away."[14] At last, the Johnsons were home.

The pile of luggage was a fitting beginning for their readjustment to private life. Although in the view of some the ranch had never been home to the Johnsons, in the minds of the former first family they were returning to their life, their place, and their people. The circumstances were different; at every level of public life, the Johnsons had experienced the intersection of their daily existence with senatorial, vice presidential, and presidential obligations. The transformation of the ranch into a remote White House during the presidency was an especially poignant example of this complex condition. But after January 20, 1969, the Johnsons were on their own on a ranch that they thought of as home but that they often had shared with federal officials charged with ensuring their welfare. Finding their baggage dumped in the middle of the kitchen floor was a reminder that after the presidency, life would be very different.

The most salient feature of the Johnsons' return to the ranch was a newfound privacy. Without the eternal glare of the press and with the absence of a vast staff, the Johnsons could regain some of the small pleasures of life. There were now solitude and darkness, things that the network of Secret Service searchlights shining away from the house to hamper anyone trying to see in had entirely obliterated. "Some nights, you couldn't even see the house for all the lights," bus driver M. W. Ivy said. Johnson had a number of habits typical of rural people in which he could not engage during the presidency. In particular, he liked to end his evening by urinating off the porch at the ranch, a habit he acquired from his father. Johnson enjoyed this practice but found that becoming president had limited his freedom. On the first night he was home after assuming the presidency, he had tried to sneak away from the Secret Service agents to engage in this nightly ritual. Johnson "eased out on the front porch, and . . . started," he recalled, "and right in the middle, this big floodlight hit me." Although Johnson remonstrated with the Secret Service agents, they insisted that his security was paramount. When he tried the next night, again Secret Service floodlights came on. After that, "I just decided to give it up," Johnson told William W. Heath, an Austin attorney whom Johnson appointed ambassador to Sweden in 1967. "The small pleasures in life you have to give up."[15] After Nixon's inauguration, he could again do as he pleased, a prospect that well suited the former president.

Nor were there pressing demands on the former first family. "We were living on our own time," Lady Bird Johnson recalled, thinking of the thirty-five years Johnson spent in a hurry during his political career. The pace of life slowed greatly, something the former president appreciated. For the first time in their married life, the Johnsons picked their social engagements based on their choice of friends rather than on political needs or requirements. "The people who the president saw during his retirement years were people he wanted to see," Jewell Malechek remembered, "not people he had to see." Everyone who came by the ranch was invited for lunch or dinner, for Johnson did not like to be alone. He kept a telephone by the table to call people: relatives of guests or perhaps old friends who were being discussed during the meal. Typically, lunch was followed by a nap, a luxury the presidency had not allowed. Johnson resumed his activities about 5:00 P.M., when dinner guests would arrive for a cocktail, a drive around the ranch, and the spectacular sunset. Even his sleep was better. "One of the things I enjoyed most was being able to go to bed after the ten o'clock news at night and sleep until daylight the next morning," Johnson recalled of the early days of his retirement. "I don't remember ever having an experience like that in the five years I was in the White House."[16]

Despite the pleasure that Johnson experienced when he returned to the Hill Country free of the burdens of public service, the beginning of his retirement did not go well. "The man didn't know how to enjoy retirement," George Reedy asserted, and the first months of 1969 amply demonstrated that observation. Johnson became depressed—ceasing the characteristic activities of a politician, such as attending funerals; failing to respond to the phone messages of former associates; and becoming something of a mystery. "He has remained invisible, a kind of non-presence," Marshall Frady, a southerner who oddly tried to recast Johnson's retirement in the terms of the South, wrote in *Harper's.* Lady Bird tried to find people to visit who could bring him out of this depression, but the transition was slow. According to Conkin, this attitude stemmed from Johnson's dissatisfaction with the activities he had set out for himself. Johnson "came home to be a real rancher," this biographer states, "a formerly idealized profession that in no way matched his talents or inclinations." Johnson was a politician, a people person, not the taciturn kind of person who typified the ranching profession. Johnson's expertise was with people, not animals. The president had also been worn down by the demands of the presidency, a situation that dampened the spirits of this typically energetic man. "It took him nearly a full year to shed the fatigue from his bones," former White House staffer Leo Janis recounted.[17]

The transition from the position of leader of the free world to that of gentleman rancher remained difficult, but after the feelings of gloom lifted, the former president found his ranch, as he had often said, a good place to walk. After his depression lifted and he began to adjust, Johnson enjoyed a period of good health and good spirits, and his primary interest remained the ranch. His land in the Hill Country had captured his heart long before retirement, and as he became accustomed to life in the Hill Country, the ranch became the center of his existence in a way it never before had been. At last, the ranch became a place to live, not merely one to visit.

In retirement, Johnson did exactly what was expected of a man of his energy and temperament. "What he did was go to work," reported W. Thomas Johnson, deputy press secretary and special assistant to the president, who moved to the executive staff of the Texas Broadcasting Corporation when Johnson retired. "He became one of us," ranch foreman Dale Malechek remembered. Johnson "just wanted to ranch" in retirement, Russell Thomas, a veterinarian who specialized in large and exotic animals and who consulted at the ranch, recalled. Despite his protests to the contrary, Johnson ran both the ranch and the Texas Broadcasting Company. Malechek reported to him daily, as did Jesse Kellam of his communications company. "I've got to go out and see about my [water] pipe. It's not working right," was a frequent Johnson refrain in retirement. Malechek remembered milking cows at 6:00 A.M. and finding Johnson standing behind him in pajamas and house shoes asking questions. Johnson "didn't know everything" about ranching, Father Wunibald Schneider remembered, but he paid close attention to its details. Whenever, as president, he returned from a trip, the first question he asked was, "What did I miss?"[18] The operation of the ranch, one of Johnson's primary interests during the presidency, occupied an even more central place in his life in retirement.

In particular, Johnson participated in the irrigation operation during his first year of retirement. He "hauled pipe," Malechek recalled, because "he wanted to get some exercise, and come spring, he got in and started helping us move pipe. . . . We let him have the light end . . . and he would carry that and do the site lining to line us up." In typical fashion, Malechek recalled, Johnson was "very cranky in wanting [the pipe] as straight as it could be . . . since he was hellbent on getting them as straight as can be, we gave him that chore" of siting. He engaged in laying pipe throughout the spring and summer of 1969, but ongoing heart trouble forced him to quit in 1970. In the summers, when the "cattle work" lasted until as late as 10:00 P.M., Johnson frequently watched and sometimes participated.[19]

As soon as he got into the rhythm of retirement, Johnson returned to the daily habits that had typified his public life. He remained a driven man and retained some of the great energy that had been characteristic of his political life. Johnson rose early and tended to ranch matters, and at about 8:30 or 9:00 A.M. he returned to his bed to read the newspapers and answer correspondence. He "never let a letter sit on his desk," Jewell Malechek recounted, answering them all the day they arrived.[20] This pattern allowed Johnson the sense of being involved so crucial to his well-being, the illusion of leisure that spending time in bed at 9:00 A.M. meant to a man such as Johnson, and the feeling of control that dictating correspondence from his pillows gave him. In this respect, retirement allowed Lyndon Johnson to be exactly who he wanted to be, albeit on a smaller scale. He had traded the limelight and power of national politics for the control of even the minuscule details of the ranch operation.

Johnson remained a social being, "the kind of person who liked people," in the words of the long-time editor of *The Blanco News,* J. N. "Jimmy" Houck. The Johnsons maintained a busy social life, particularly with people from the Hill Country. There was an ongoing stream of dinner and afternoon visitors from among their neighbors and friends, for the president craved the company of his Hill Country neighbors. As he had during the presidency, Johnson visited the Blanco Mill and the Blanco Nursing Home on a regular basis. He had "a way about him" that made him visit people, Houck recalled, and his neighbors reciprocated in the age-old manner of rural people.[21]

The Johnsons were much more selective about travel outside of the Hill Country during retirement. For every fifty invitations he received, Johnson told his staff, he accepted one. Still, these added up. By 1971, he had attended a parade of functions and hosted a number of others. Old colleagues and friends, such as Walter Heller and Henry Fowler, were hard to turn down; the president felt a responsibility to them. He attended a dinner for his old political colleague Representative Henry B. Gonzalez one Saturday early in the fall of 1971, followed shortly after by a dinner given by Mr. and Mrs. Stanley Marcus in Dallas.[22] Such occasions fulfilled social needs as well as the ex-president's desire to feel wanted.

Although his political activities were distinctly curtailed, Johnson did meet with a number of political candidates in his retirement. He tried "as hard as one man can to ignore politics," reporter Nicholas Chriss wrote in *The New York Times* of Johnson's retirement, but entirely disengaging was impossible for Johnson. By 1971, visitors to the ranch had included former vice president Hubert Humphrey, Senator Henry Jackson, and others. Members of Nixon's cabinet, including Henry Kissinger and Secretary of the Interior Rogers C. B. Morton, also came to the ranch. Many of these were courtesy calls, but some still sought the political advice of the sage former president.[23]

Retirement also accentuated characteristics of Johnson's personality that the stress and strain of five years in the White House had diminished. "He discovered play," his daughter Luci recalled, and his sense of humor returned with a vengeance. Johnson had many of the characteristics of a prankster during his public life, and retirement revived these traits. He always had a prank or a joke on hand in any social setting, and as was characteristic of him, some of them were biting. Johnson also developed his touch for ironic humor, which had been muted during his presidency. One day, Johnson and Doris Kearns were out in a boat on Lake LBJ. "It was a magic afternoon—the sky was blue, the water was blue, and the boat was magnificent," Kearns remembered. In this tranquil setting, Johnson turned to her and said: "Boy, I sure do miss the Middle East!"[24] This typical display of humor masked one aspect of his true feelings: his desire to remain part of the world of politics, even in a tangential way. It also reflected his joy at being back in his Hill Country.

Johnson clearly enjoyed his new status as a grandparent during retirement and took pleasure in his relationship with his grandchildren. He "loved his grandchildren," Father Wunibald Schneider recounted; "he would kneel down on the floor and play with them." As the first-born grandchild, Patrick Lyndon "Lyn" Nugent became the favorite, bouncing on his grandfather's knee. This allowed Johnson to experience some of the joy of parenting that he had missed with his own children as a result of his busy travel schedule and frequent absences from home. Although neither of the Johnson daughters ever expressed resentment about their father's absences, others have suggested that Johnson recognized that he missed out on important experiences and sought to make up for them with his grandchildren.[25]

Johnson was different in retirement, relaxed and relieved but engaged in defending his actions in the Oval Office. The large-scale entertaining ceased after he left the White House, but when small affairs were held, Johnson felt obligated to explain his presidential policies. On one such occasion, shortly after Johnson's retirement, Lady Bird Johnson invited people in the Stonewall area who had helped at various presidential functions to a small thank-you party. When Johnson addressed the group, his comments turned to Vietnam. "The pain of that memory was evident," Cactus Pryor, who attended the event, said. Johnson "was explaining to these farm people the political frustration of that episode and it hit me, the ghost was still there, the nightmare still existed. Here he was home with his neighbors, but the specter of that disaster was still plaguing him."[26] Yet this was a personal kind of justification and even perhaps absolution, different from the stoic refusal to comment on politics that he regularly offered the press.

Another manifestation of the changes in Johnson was a willingness to delegate responsibility for things close to him. Secret Service Special Agent Michael Howard, who had served the Johnson family since the vice presidential years, was stationed at the ranch during the former president's retirement. A Texan, Howard had developed a good relationship with Johnson that began when the agent served as his driver in Texas during the vice presidency. In 1970, Howard noticed that Johnson's horses were not being properly attended to on the ranch. Johnson was known, even feared, for requiring his staff in both Washington, D.C., and at the ranch to be on top of every detail all the time. When something as personally meaningful as his horses was not well cared for, it suggested that the president might be slipping. Howard asked about the horses, and Johnson placed them in the agent's care. "That's when I first started taking care of them," Howard said. "Any time he'd have guests come in after that, he'd call, and I'd saddle them and he'd come down and ride a little bit." By 1970, Johnson was debilitated by heart problems, and he did not ride for a very long time, "but he'd get up on there," Howard recounted, "and trot around a little bit." From the perspective of Father Wunibald Schneider, riding around the ranch renewed the former president. "He loved to see the cattle and the deer" from horseback.[27] Johnson had begun to step back from the obligations of public life and let others do some of the work while he enjoyed the benefits.

In retirement, the Johnsons traveled frequently. They visited Acapulco every February, staying in a villa owned by former Mexican president Miguel Alemán, one of Johnson's partners in the ranching business. As had been the norm when he was president, the trips were nearly spontaneous. Typically, Johnson invited people on one day's notice, and his flights to Mexico disgorged people, food, liquor, and bottled water. A cook accompanied the entourage, and Arthur Krim, Johnson's old friend, made sure that first-run movies were available for screening in the evenings.[28]

Life on these trips was vintage Johnson. Despite an array of important personages who came and went, the entire vacation party would follow Johnson's whims. He determined what would happen; if he wanted to go to the beach, everyone went to the beach. Golf was another common activity, with the president leading his entourage across the links. Some days, he sat down to breakfast, and he and the entire party conversed until lunch. Johnson especially enjoyed jaunts to Alemán's ranch, called Las Pampas, in the interior of Mexico. The stark beauty and isolation of the location touched Johnson, and he and his entourage could bask in the solitude of that magnificent setting.[29]

Excluding these trips to Mexico, travel outside of Texas was more infrequent after retirement. The president rarely went north at all, favoring the warmer climate of the South. Johnson appears to have made only three trips to Washington, D.C., each time to events hosted by President Nixon. Once he regained his emotional equilibrium, he resumed his time-honored practice of traveling to funerals of friends and colleagues. This symbolized his connection to politics, to the ways and activities of a politician. Johnson attended a Democratic Party dinner in Chicago, a park dedication in California with Lady Bird Johnson, and an Apollo moon launch in Florida. Besides these trips, he spent his time in Texas, occasionally leaving on private excursions to visit personal friends.[30]

Johnson became a devoted football fan and used his retirement to indulge this newfound passion. "Football became almost his life" in retirement, Cactus Pryor believed, and although on some occasions Johnson denied this, he became the leading fan of the University of Texas football team. He "really buried himself in the Texas football program," Pryor recounted, befriending players such as star halfback Jim Bertelsen. The president took his "football group," which included Lady Bird; Carroll Staley; Frederick Spurga, the vice president of the Securities State Bank in the Hill Country; Harold Woods, the LBJ State Park manager; Jesse Kellam; and the Malecheks as its nucleus, to all the Texas games, home and away. In 1969 and 1970, Coach Darrell Royal's Longhorns were the best team in the land, winning the mythical national collegiate championship both years with the last segregated teams at the university. Despite Johnson's commitment to civil rights, he and the racially intransigent Royal developed a friendship. Royal was a frequent guest at the ranch, and he was the kind of hard-boiled, successful man with whom Johnson had much in common. "Johnson related to Darrell [Royal] in a very personal way," Pryor said; he sought his company so often that the coach was sometimes forced to neglect other responsibilities. Johnson assisted Royal by inviting Texas football recruits to the ranch, where Johnson would deliver a pep talk. At home games, the president and his entourage were very visible in their fifty-yard-line seats, but "nobody sat with him in the stadium," Pryor quipped in his characteristic manner, "because he was mostly on his feet, shaking hands, playing the politician." Students at the campus, at least those involved in official organizations, loved him, making him an honorary member of the Silver Spurs, a prestigious student service organization. He reciprocated their affection and was quite comfortable in the fall in the excitement of Southwestern Conference football stadiums.[31] Again, pleasure and status were melded in retirement.

Johnson also engaged in other activities, when football was not in season. Golf became a passion for him in the spring and fall. "Sometimes he'd spend the whole morning playing golf," Jewell Malechek remembered. He typically played at either Fredericksburg or Kingsland, both relatively close to the ranch. The Johnsons often spent part of August at the Haywood Ranch, near the Kingsland golf course, and the Malecheks would join them in the evenings. Dale Malechek would drive back to the main ranch in the morning with the Malechek children, while Jewell Malechek remained with the president as he played golf. During one round, Johnson was observed tossing a ball he hit into the rough out onto the fairway; one Secret Service agent quipped that these were "LBJ rules." After rounds at Kingsland, the group would ride back to the LBJ Ranch in a helicopter, sometimes handling the president's correspondence on the way.[32] But as much as he enjoyed the game, golf was never the obsession that football became. Johnson never added a few holes or a putting green at the ranch, preferring the sport as a way to get off the property and out into the world. At the ranch, he preferred other activities.

From the ranch, Johnson engaged in a number of projects that he hoped would serve to highlight his legacy. Although Doris Kearns, who played an important role in constructing *The Vantage Point,* believed that "none of these projects really engaged Johnson," the president spent an enormous amount of time assuring that every detail fit his conception of each project. These were his statements for posterity in an actual and symbolic sense, and they allowed him to play the role that best defined him, that of the hands-on chief executive who attended to every detail. The evolution of this legacy consumed much of his energy during retirement.[33]

The first piece of the Johnson legacy was the Lyndon B. Johnson National Historic Site, authorized on December 2, 1969. Consisting of Johnson's original boyhood home in Johnson City and the reconstructed birthplace cottage near the ranch, the new historic site was the beginning of the legacy that the former president himself fashioned. The boyhood home in Johnson City was the subject of comprehensive renovation. At the former president's request, J. Roy White handled the project. Johnson "saw the house as something related to his youth, his times in the past in the area, and the home it always was," White remembered. "He felt he wanted to recreate it." Johnson's birthplace, near the ranch, was transferred to the National Park Service during the summer of 1970, and the president could not resist the chance to offer personal tours of the property. "He wanted people to see and enjoy the things that gladdened his heart," newsman and long-time aide Charles Boatner said. "He wanted to gladden their hearts.[34]

Johnson regarded the Lyndon B. Johnson Library and the Lyndon B. Johnson School of Public Affairs on the University of Texas at Austin campus as central to his legacy—important emblems of his impact on American society. During his presidency, Johnson had begun to plan the shape of his legacy. In 1965, he agreed to donate his papers and other historical materials to the University of Texas at Austin, and the plans for the library began. In December, 1966, the design for the eight-story structure was unveiled. Windowless, the nearly eleven million dollar project was referred to by some as "austere," by others as "architecturally forbidding," but Johnson believed it a fitting testimony to his accomplishments. At the dedication of the library in May, 1971, he expressed his views. "It's all here," he said from the podium, "the story of our time—with the bark off. There is no record of a mistake, nothing critical, ugly or unpleasant that is not included in the files here. We have papers from my . . . years of public service in one place for friend and foe to judge, to approve or disapprove." An enormous crowd of dignitaries, including President Nixon, Senator Barry Goldwater, former vice president Humphrey, Senator Edmund Muskie, and countless others, attended the ceremonies. Senator Philip Hart of Michigan best summed it up when he quipped, "I never thought I'd come to Austin, Texas, and know half the people I saw."[35]

Both the national historic site and the library attracted many visitors, in no small part because of Johnson's persistent promotional efforts. He demanded daily visitor traffic reports from both locations as religiously as he had insisted upon Hill Country weather reports in the White House. Johnson could often be found at the Johnson City house and at the birthplace, giving guided tours of the home, inviting passersby in to see what he claimed was the crib in which he rested as a baby, and selling *The Vantage Point* and other books. Yolanda Boozer recalled that when she needed the president and could not find him, a phone call to the boyhood home or the birthplace usually established his location. Johnson often helicoptered in to the library, both during construction and after its completion, and did everything he could to increase the number of tourists who came to see it. He signed books, encouraged visitation, and in one episode remarkable for its sheer audacity sought to persuade the announcer at nearby Memorial Stadium, where the Longhorns were in the middle of a football game, to invite the crowd of more than fifty thousand to the library to use the facilities and have a drink of water after the game. Fortunately, the announcer demurred. At the time, the library had one public drinking fountain and one set of public restrooms.[36]

At the ranch, Johnson also began to fashion his memoirs, a project of such enormity that it would have daunted even someone with the suitable temperament and skills. All accounts agree that Johnson was a poor candidate to accomplish such a task. Recognizing this, he assembled a team to assist him that included MIT professor and Kennedy and Johnson White House stalwart Walt W. Rostow, staff assistant Harry Middleton, speech writer Robert Hardesty, and a young Harvard University doctoral candidate in government named Doris Kearns. Johnson believed that his memoirs were his "last chance with the history books," Kearns reported Johnson telling her, and the project had to be done properly.[37]

The Vantage Point, as Johnson's memoir was titled, became a compendium of the efforts of his staff augmented by the staccato explosions of the former president. The project began slowly. "It soon became clear," Kearns recalled, "that [Johnson] would rather be doing anything else than working on his memoirs." In formal interviews for the book, Johnson remained his public self: stiff and even pedantic. As soon as the formal portion of each interview ended, he relaxed, and a colorful Lyndon Johnson, the powerful stump speaker and brilliant persuasive political leader, emerged. But Johnson regarded the memoir as a representation of the man he thought he should be, a "calm, almost cold man, sober fellow, with pinched energy; humble, earnest, and crashingly dull," as Kearns later wrote. He resisted the efforts of his writers to use material from the relaxed portions of the interviews. "What do you think this is," he shouted at Kearns one day, "the tale of an uneducated cowboy? It's a presidential memoir, damn it, and I've got to come off looking like a statesman, not some backwoods politician."[38]

Although in her account of this process Kearns borders on the melodramatic, the tension she portrays reflects the most difficult side of retirement for the still-energetic Johnson. A master at controlling everything around him, Johnson became frustrated by the self-imposed limits of retirement. Reflective by nature but fiercely impatient, the former president felt hamstrung by the prospect of time on his hands. In the haste of the presidency, Johnson could trust his finely honed instincts. The opportunity to reflect in retirement, which would have been good for most people, propelled him to question himself in unhealthy ways. It accentuated his doubts about himself and his position, about the choices he had made and the ways he could represent them to the world. The press, which he had long perceived in an adversarial fashion and sincerely believed denigrated and mocked him in retirement, became the focus of his attention.

Even in the peace and quiet of his ranch, Johnson retained bitterness about his treatment by the press. He displayed antagonism about the way in which he was quoted by reporters and about books that purported to show the decision-making process in the White House. A new book or article would engender a press release denouncing the work as filled with major inaccuracies. Johnson even attacked the demography of the journalism profession, claiming that he and other rural presidents, such as Herbert Hoover and Andrew Johnson, could not get fair treatment from the East Coast press.[39]

Much of Johnson's animosity towards the press predated his retirement, but a solid measure of his feelings emanated from press treatment of his retirement and from the series of interviews he did with CBS's Walter Cronkite, the beloved face of television news, after he returned to Texas. Johnson was upset by the editing of the early tapes, but he continued the interviews. Most of the taping was done in the Cedar Guesthouse, for the amount of lighting and camera equipment made it impossible to use the main house; one interview was done at the LBJ Library, and others occurred at various locations. Johnson liked and respected Cronkite, but the president was not always happy with the results of the broadcasts. He believed that his remarks were taken out of context.[40] Cronkite was a symbol of the American people, and in the president's view the newsman's fond ambivalence about the president reflected the nation's views. Johnson's tension with the media never subsided.

Johnson's physical condition soon became a major problem, for in his retirement, as in earlier periods of limited involvement in public affairs, his vaunted control disappeared and he became undisciplined. He stopped following his diet, gained weight, and in 1971 resumed smoking "like a fiend," as Abraham Feinberg, chairman of the executive committee of the American Trust Company, noted. One biographer, noting Johnson's history of heart trouble and the pattern of early death for males in his family, describes this as "insanity." He also experienced periods of intermittent depression. Biographer Paul Conkin states that despite the stress associated with the presidency, Johnson would have lived longer had he served a second full term.[41] Inactivity proved more dangerous to him than the intensity of public life.

Johnson's medical needs were a constant issue during most of his retirement, and they compelled a daily routine that provided supervision for the former president. Navy medical corpsman Thomas Mills, who after Johnson's retirement became the lone medical professional at the ranch, checked on Johnson first thing every morning. If the president seemed ill, Mills stayed close at hand. If not, he attended to other duties. Daily exercise for the former president was strongly encouraged; Johnson liked to swim when the weather was nice, and he usually went to the pool after he had returned to bed, watched the news, and read the newspapers. A plastic canopy over the pool allowed him to swim even in cold weather. This worked well "if you could get him to do it," Mills recalled. Mills began to eat lunch with Johnson during retirement and usually departed afterwards, returning to give Johnson an evening massage. Unlike during the White House years, when he accomplished his daily reading as the kinks were worked out of him, in retirement Johnson often fell asleep during the massages. Especially during the summer, when he kept a later schedule and ate his evening meal, called "supper" in rural Texas, quite late, Johnson's massages often began after 10:00 P.M.[42]

Johnson pushed himself even in retirement. "He was out there as long as anybody else," Mills recalled, a sentiment that Malechek echoed with evident consternation in his voice as he recalled enduring the president's constant involvement.[43] At his age and with his health problems, Johnson's insistence on carrying irrigation pipes and opening gates for cattle was a double-edged sword. It helped him feel vital, in control, and a part of the operation, but it taxed his weakened body.

Despite his chronic problems, Johnson "kept plugging ahead." Mills tried to get him to take a daily walk, "up and down the runway, anywhere, to get him more exercise than he did," Mills remembered. The Johnsons often walked together after their evening meal. Strictures on his diet increased in a largely unsuccessful effort to reduce his weight. "It seemed he

was always on a diet," Jewell Malechek remembered, and his weight fluc-
tuated dangerously. His salt intake was restricted, something Johnson ab-
horred. Johnson liked salt, pepper, spices, and sweets, and "he didn't want
to give up any of them," according to Mills. Fried foods, especially catfish,
were favorites, and Johnson liked to eat. When Lady Bird Johnson was
away, he always took an extra helping of dessert. Even when she was present,
he was known for sneaking a spoonful of dessert from someone else's plate.[44]

Although he knew well the dangers of overeating for a man with his
health problems, Johnson could not resist the opportunity to tweak authority even when rules were enacted in his own best interest. Nash Castro,
a National Park Service official who became a frequent guest at the ranch
and whom Lady Bird Johnson regarded as both an indispensable supporter
of her beautification efforts and a close friend, recognized this trait. On
one occasion, Johnson received a batch of homemade pecan cookies from
a neighbor as a group departed on one of his motorized safaris. After passing the cookies around, Johnson set them on the dashboard in front of
him, and "as we drove along," Castro recounted, "LBJ kept snitching cookies—quietly and unobtrusively." Lady Bird noticed this and said, "Lyndon,
if you eat another cookie, you will spoil your dinner." Lyndon Johnson
replied, "I've only had one, Lady Bird. Isn't that right, Nash?" As Johnson
turned toward Castro, he muttered "plus" under his breath.[45] He indulged
a passion while defying orders given to him.

This pattern led directly to new and greater health problems. A little
more than a year into his retirement, Johnson began to exhibit symptoms
of his most serious long-term malady, heart trouble. Since his first major
heart attack, in 1955, the specter of a reoccurrence had haunted Johnson.
Severe chest pains in March, 1970, sent him to Brooke Army Medical Center
in San Antonio, and angina pains were ever after a constant companion.
In the middle of 1971, he was again hospitalized in San Antonio, this time
with viral pneumonia.[46] Illness, added to his smoking and his refusal to
carefully monitor his diet, increased the risk of a serious coronary.

In the spring of 1972, Johnson experienced a major heart attack at Lynda
and Chuck Robb's house in Charlottesville, Virginia. Rushed to a hospital, he was in intensive care for three days. Certain he was going to die,
Johnson browbeat Lady Bird and his physicians until they grudgingly
allowed him to fly home in a few days. The hospital director opposed the
idea. Johnson insisted that when he departed life he do so from his beloved Texas and defied the leaders of the institution. Some accounts offer

the mythic scenario of the director of the Charlottesville Hospital rushing to prevent Johnson's departure only to find an abandoned wheelchair in the hospital parking lot. Although Johnson survived this episode, the remainder of his life was a pain-racked ordeal. Nitroglycerin tablets and an oxygen tank were necessities, and almost every afternoon Johnson had to stop his activities and lie down and gulp oxygen as sharp, racking chest pains hit him. After returning to Texas, Johnson again became ill and was flown by helicopter to Brooke Army Medical Center in San Antonio. Mills accompanied him and stayed in the hospital room, while an array of medical personnel attended to the president's needs. Lady Bird Johnson and a secretary also accompanied the president. "I'm hurting real bad," he confided to friends, and the pain remained throughout the rest of his life.[47]

This second major heart attack squarely focused Johnson's attention on his legacy. The national historic park was a "backwater park which LBJ did not take great interest in," as Edwin C. Bearss, long-time chief historian of the National Park Service, recalled, "until he has the [1972] heart attack. Then it goes on a fast track. The heart attack is in April; the superintendent's out of there in July," after disagreeing with Johnson's plans. The superintendent was "out of there" after he curtly refused a Johnson request to change the information in a leaflet. Shortly afterward, as Johnson became deeply interested in his park, the former president approached the National Park Service Director, George B. Hartzog, Jr., with a proposal to donate the entire Johnson ranch to the American people—to, in the words of Bearss, "make a real park. . . . Where they could tell the president's story from cradle to grave." Johnson had been rebuffed in a prior effort to acquire his grandfather's nearby ranch, then owned by a neighbor who resented him, but with the help of the National Park Service, the National Park Foundation, Bearss, and Richard Stanton, the chief land acquisition negotiator for the agency, the deal was secured. Shortly after, Bearss and Stanton arranged for the purchase of the Junction School and found themselves, as Bearss phrased it, "in high cotton with the president." With the two properties secured, only the ranch remained to complete a park of the stature that Johnson envisioned.[48]

On Labor Day weekend of 1972, as the Park Service prepared to celebrate the one-hundredth anniversary of the founding of Yellowstone National Park, a group of Park Service officials and planners descended upon the Johnson ranch. George Hartzog and his wife, Helen; their son, George; Bernard Meyer, the Department of the Interior solicitor assigned to National Park Service issues; Jay Bright, a planner from the Western Service Center in Denver; and Bearss all flew to the ranch. Johnson met them with the Lincoln Continentals for a tour of the ranch. Bearss found it "a little strange" when Hartzog ordered him into the lead car with Johnson, inverting the hierarchy within the agency; other Park Service officials present ranked more highly than he. The group drove around the ranch while the president indicated what he wanted to donate and on what terms. Johnson and Hartzog "[thought] big," Bearss remembered, "much bigger than the ranch," envisioning a larger park that included much adjoining land. The following day, they examined the Johnson ranch payroll and began to decide who would become a federal employee and who would stay with the Texas Broadcasting Company, Johnson pushing for the well-paying GS-12 for Dale Malechek, whose qualifications might not have been adequate in other circumstances. Everyone left the ranch but George Hartzog, Bright, and Bearss, the historian whom Hartzog had selected for this task as a result of his nearly total recall. After two days of wrangling, a plan was finalized. The Lyndon B. Johnson National Historical Park had become more than a dream. Congress would authorize it in 1980.[49]

Besides accelerating his interest in his legacy, chronic illness made Johnson grow more introspective. By the fall of 1972, his physicians had ordered him to give no more speeches, but he could not resist accepting some invitations, especially when old friends asked. He used the chance to speak to people in a way that some later remembered as preparing for his departure from life. His love of the Hill Country came through even more clearly as he thought his end neared. He referred to "the pleasure he got from riding around the property and seeing the sunset. . . . He was trying to get the most out of the land," Mills recalled.[50] It remained in him and became even more important as he grew older and more frail.

Even the debilitating effects of long-term illness did not deter Johnson from pursuing the causes closest to his heart. The last public affair Johnson hosted was a civil rights symposium on December 11 and 12, 1972, at the LBJ Library. It was the second in a series of symposia on public issues; the first, in January of 1972, had featured discussions about education policy issues. The civil rights symposium was supposed to begin with a reception at the ranch on the evening of December 10, but bad weather delayed visitors, including former Chief Justice Earl Warren and Hubert and Muriel Humphrey. It was one of the coldest and iciest spells in the history of Central Texas. The ranch was iced in, and for a while it appeared that

Johnson would not be able to attend the conference. His physician advised him not to make the trip, and Lady Bird Johnson begged him to stay home. "I was just heartsick at that," Harry Middleton, then director of the LBJ Library, recalled. "But then we got word that he was coming anyway, that he was at the wheel himself, that he got impatient with whoever was driving this snowmobile, and he took over and drove it." Resplendent in cowboy boots, Johnson was pleased to find that he had successfully negotiated seventy miles to reach the conference, while Elspeth Rostow, who lived four miles away from the library, had not yet arrived. Warren, Humphrey, and other guests were bused in from San Antonio. Warren quipped that he had expected to come to discuss civil rights but not actually to be bused in order to do it. With Johnson's surprise presence, the conference flourished.[51]

The strain of attending the conference was enormous, as Johnson's physicians had anticipated, but despite feeling poorly, the former president decided to give his scheduled keynote address. All the remaining major figures of twenty years of the Civil Rights Movement had assembled for the symposium, but in the aftermath of the 1968 assassination of the Reverend Dr. Martin Luther King, Jr., and with a Republican executive branch, there was no clear national leader for the cause of civil rights. On the last day of the conference, Johnson insisted that a group of demonstrators be given special podium time to offer their point of view over the objections of Tom Johnson, Harry Middleton, and event chairperson, Burke Marshall. The event coordinators felt that an addition to the program was unwarranted, but Johnson overruled them. He wanted everyone to have their say. The former president came quietly into the auditorium to hear the words of the demonstrators. Later he rose from his first-row seat to give his planned keynote speech. "I don't suppose anyone who saw him come up will ever forget it," Harry Middleton said. "He was very slow on those steps."[52]

The speech he made was one of his boldest and most poignant. As in his famous "nigra, nigra, nigra" speech in Baton Rouge in 1964, in which Johnson told Southerners that succumbing to race baiters at election time prevented them from receiving the quality of political leadership they deserved, Johnson now pushed far beyond his prior publicly stated positions on civil rights. Despite feeling so ill that he needed a nitroglycerin pill during his talk, Johnson articulated both the successes and the problems of American society regarding civil rights. He raised the issue of the level playing field, discussed with candor the problems of being black in a white society, and insisted that no one could delude themselves, despite the progress of the previous two decades, that real civil rights had been attained. "The progress has been much too small; we haven't done nearly enough," Johnson insisted. "I'm kind of ashamed of myself that I had six years and couldn't do more. . . . We know there's injustice. We know there's intolerance. We know there's discrimination and hate and suspicion. . . . But there is a larger truth. We have proved that great progress is possible. We know how much still remains to be done. And if our efforts continue, if our will is strong and our hearts are right . . . I am confident we shall overcome."[53]

The speech ended in applause, but some factions in the audience wanted to use the end of symposium to denounce the racial policies of the Nixon White House. Reverend Kendall Smith of the National Council of Churches and Roy Innes of the Congress of Racial Equality composed a statement that Reverend Smith delivered. It was highly critical of the Nixon administration, asserting that Republican policies had increased racism and insisting that the symposium had to devise a strategy that would combat the attack on the successes of the 1960s. "We demand an extension of today's agenda," Smith concluded.[54]

For a few brief moments, the old Lyndon Johnson returned. The fatigue, the weariness, the health problems all fell away, and an invigorated Johnson bounded back up the steps and delivered an impromptu speech that revealed once again his incredible persuasiveness. "The formal talk had ended," Middleton said; "now it was just Lyndon Johnson from the courthouse square." It was classic Johnson, full of emphasis on reason and communication, brimming with ideas about how to approach Nixon, how to sway him, and how to get both sides to work together. "Until every boy and girl born into this land, whatever state, whatever color, can stand on the same level ground," he closed, "our job will not be done!" The audience thundered its applause and crowded around, seeing the old Johnson magic again and feeling the energy and commitment of this veteran of national political and moral wars.

It was a fitting finale for the public career of the man from Texas, who had challenged local sentiments in his construction of national leadership and who had forced a reckoning between the South and the rest of the nation that has resounded through national politics since. Both in his formal speech and in his impromptu remarks that day, he showed the most important of his qualities: leadership, resolve, and vision. Only a man of Lyndon Johnson's stature and experience could have delivered the remarks he did that day; only a man at peace with himself and his role in the world, convinced of his own mortality, would have tried. Only someone with vision and hope would have attempted the brave reconciliation he offered in his last public words. The civil rights symposium showed Johnson at his best, at his most persuasive and charismatic, his most compassionate and skillful. For one brief instant, he was again the leader he had been in the Senate and in the first years of his presidency, the leader who could see the solution to any problem facing the nation. The day signaled an appropriate closure to Johnson's public career.

A little more than one month later, on January 22, 1973, Lyndon B. Johnson died. Stricken by a massive heart attack at 3:50 P.M., he called the ranch switchboard and asked for Secret Service agent Mike Howard. Howard was unavailable, and two other agents, Ed Newland and Harry Harris, rushed to the bedroom with a portable oxygen unit. Johnson was lying on the floor, unconscious and ashen faced. The agents tried to revive him, Newland giving mouth-to-mouth resuscitation, but their efforts were unsuccessful. Howard arrived a few minutes later and tried external heart massage; he too failed.[55] Lyndon B. Johnson, the thirty-sixth president of the United States, was dead.

After a state funeral, he was buried in the family cemetery by the Pedernales River, where he had always expected to be laid to rest. It was the place he had chosen, where he could join his ancestors and feel ever after the warm Pedernales River sun on the ground. The irrigated grass in the cemetery area is always green, rare in the Hill Country but vivid testimony to the fundamental optimism of the man laid there among his family.

At the burial, Johnson played one last trick on everyone. He had given specific instructions that he was to be buried between his mother's grave and his wife's future grave site, but according to custom his wife was to one day be buried to his right, the reverse of what Johnson had planned. Charles Boatner stopped the military grave diggers, persuading them to follow the president's wishes. About five feet down, the machine's digging bucket hit metal. It was a large irrigation pipe, running lengthwise down the center of Lyndon Johnson's grave. Boatner called Lawrence Klein, who came and cut the pipe and removed it. Boatner asked if Johnson was aware the pipe was there, and Klein replied that Johnson had located the line in the first place. "It's my firm belief," Boatner attested, "that one of the last little jokes that the president thought that he'd play on his staff was locating that line lengthwise to that grave and wondering how we would handle the digging of the grave when we hit that pipe."[56]

During his retirement, Johnson had finally been able to be his personal self, to do as he pleased outside of the public eye. He had chosen a public life, and he had lived most of his life on those terms, but retirement to the ranch allowed him a freedom from scrutiny that he had not previously experienced. Despite the claims of the press that Johnson was depressed or otherwise unhappy, Johnson appears to have been engaged by the activities of his retirement. He missed the limelight but enjoyed his newfound ability to choose—who to see, what to do—that had never been available to him as a public servant. Retaining the knowledge that Vietnam had turned into a debacle that destroyed his presidency and negatively affected his legacy but celebrating the accomplishments of his domestic programs, Johnson still believed in the moral righteousness of his cause, the Great Society. His retirement did not diminish him; Lyndon Baines Johnson was fortunate to spend the last years of his life doing what he most wanted to do: breathing the air of his beloved Hill Country how and when he chose.

Epilogue

Power and Place in

American Culture

"There's no other place, no Virgin Islands, no Miami coastline, no boat trips across the Atlantic that can do for me what this soil, this land, this water, this people, and what these hills, these surroundings can do. . . . They provide the stimulation and inspiration that nothing else can provide."[1] This was how Lyndon B. Johnson summed up the meaning of the Hill Country, the world from which he came and that his ranch came to represent to the world at large. The ranch provided him with something that no other place on the planet truly did: it helped his restless soul find peace. There this domineering man could fashion the kind of control he needed to feel secure. There the rhythms of life relaxed him and helped him see clearly. There he could be candid in a manner he could not elsewhere. The man; his genius for politics; the place that he chose to represent those politics; the meaning of that place; the way in which this meaning was transmitted to a public that first adored Johnson, then came to fear him, and finally left him shouldering the burden of its disappointment with the direction of American society— all these were intrinsically and inextricably wrapped up in the LBJ Ranch.

This ranch, known ever after as the Texas White House, receded from the public view after the ex-president's death in 1973. It remained a home to Lady Bird Johnson as well as the seat of the Johnson family cattle enterprise, but it receded from its central place in American political culture and became historic in its appeal. In accordance with Johnson's wishes, the ranch was incorporated into the Lyndon B. Johnson National Historical Park, comprised of his boyhood home in Johnson City, his birthplace, and the Texas White House. In effect, Johnson sought to take the meaning of the ranch, the symbolism he had developed for it, and make it an integral part of his legacy. This was one more way in which the dynamic former president could influence American history.

The Texas White House is a symbolic but anomalous place in the line of presidential residences. Many of these had iconographic features similar to those of the LBJ Ranch; others became more important as a result of changing technologies. George Washington's Mount Vernon and Thomas Jefferson's Monticello were the prototypes for presidential homes; rural, spacious, and evocative, they set a standard for the image of a president's home. Andrew Jackson's Hermitage in Tennessee had much in common with the Texas White House; it, too, was far from the nation's capital, a representative of a form of rural economy that had iconographic connotations. In Jackson's time, of course, the president could not easily commute from Washington, D.C., to his home and certainly could not conduct the business of his office from there. Dwight D. Eisenhower's Gettysburg farm served as a prototype for the way Johnson used his ranch. By the 1950s, air transportation had improved significantly, and Eisenhower could regularly commute to his farm. But the communications systems that Johnson installed at the Texas White House were unavailable at the Gettysburg farm. The Kennedy family estate at Hyannisport also shared characteristics with the Texas White House. Both locations had strong familial connotations, Kennedy's because of the direct line from his father and mother, Johnson's because of his aunt's and uncle's ownership of the property and his childhood memories of the ranch as the center of family holiday and celebratory activities.

Yet among presidential residences, only the Texas White House melded all these characteristics. It evoked sentiment about rural America, retained the family ties so important in expressing presidential identity, could be easily reached in the age of the jet airplane, and had the most sophisticated communications system in the world. The Texas White House became an extension of the White House, an office in a different setting. It served as a transition between an older American motif, the home-as-residence, and its modern counterpart, the home-as-extension-of-workplace. In this respect, Johnson's use of the Texas White House foreshadowed trends in larger American society, as more and more people began to work their longer hours from their homes.

Johnson's use of the Texas White House was also a precursor of the modern use of presidential homes. Richard M. Nixon's San Clemente, Ronald Reagan's ranch in the Santa Monica Mountains in California, and George H. W. Bush's Kennebunkport estate were successors to the Texas White House. All were personal residences that became presidential; all were equipped with the communications systems and technologies necessary to assure that the president was in contact with everyone he needed at all times. But only the Texas White House retained the immense cultural cachet that came with this status. As the first of a type, clearly identified with the president and his chosen way of life, visible in the media in constant and obvious ways, the Texas White House stood alone among presidential residences. It was mythic, while the others were merely real and important.

The Texas White House also served as a bridge between the different types of presidential residences, for it embodied characteristics of all the different homes. Like Jackson's Hermitage, it was a working place. The presence of Dale Malechek and his crews, the cattle in the pastures, and Johnson's predilection for showing the eastern press ranch activities made its functional attributes abundantly clear. Like San Clemente and Kennebunkport, the Texas White House was a place for leisure and recreation, a place where the Johnsons could be themselves and act as they chose. Johnson managed to maintain a measure of privacy and, indeed, idiosyncracy at the ranch that was possible only because it was his ranch. But the Texas White House also became a public symbol, as identifiably Johnson's as his vivid mannerisms and twangy speech.

The combination of media attention and the ranch's figurative and literal distance from urban life gave the Texas White House unequaled symbolic meaning and significance for the nation during the turbulent 1960s. The mythology of the ranch served to represent the transformative quality of American life, a symbolism that followed Franklin D. Roosevelt on his crutches during the New Deal, followed Harry Truman's common roots and the stories about his many failures. Johnson was not born to this ranch, the myth articulated; the dogtrot cabin nearby was his birthplace. He reached the ranch house by his own efforts, making the tale of his eight-hundred-yard journey up the road into a classic American "pull-yourself-up-by your bootstraps" story. Johnson fashioned the ranch as a symbol of plain speaking and plain living, of a rural America of networks of families and friends that was part of the mythic past for which Americans wistfully yearned. In this it became a representation of the best of American life, its simplicity, integrity, and purity.

The Texas White House also served as the backdrop for Johnson's remedies for the nation's social ills, his Great Society legislation and the many programs it fostered. Citing his experiences as a young man in rural Texas, Johnson made his personal experiences a cornerstone of the rationale for educational and social programs. The fictive poverty of his youth, to which he often referred, symbolized the need for these programs; the Pedernales River valley became the setting Johnson favored when signing these bills into law. The idyllic Hill Country fit nicely the president's views of the remedies for the nation's problems. Its beauty offered the promise shared in the social programs of the era; the setting harkened back to a preindustrial and fictive egalitarian past. As a setting for the enactment of important legislation, the Texas White House became a resonant symbol.

Johnson masterfully used the ranch to express contradictory sentiments. As well as acting as a symbol of his personal triumph, the ranch represented common American roots, ordinary and shared origins. Johnson presented himself as a man of the people during much of his career, and the ranch accentuated that pose. He also showed this ordinary side in the White House; of all post–Civil War presidents, only Johnson and possibly Harry Truman could have spoken of animals as "mortgage-lifters." Most presidents prior to Johnson had little experience with the travails of everyday life. They were closer to George H. W. Bush in his amazement at grocery store scanners during the 1992 campaign. Despite the wealth he amassed and the preternatural drive that separated him from the mass of people, Johnson and his ranch retained a dimension of rootedness with which millions identified.

For Johnson, the ranch was also a source of power. In his own view, it defined him as a man of stature, someone who belonged in the Senate and the White House as well as at home. The ranch was visible evidence of belonging, a characteristic important to Johnson. The ranch gave him sustenance and strength, stability and comfort. In his driving jaunts around the Hill Country, sitting on rocks watching the sun set or inspecting his herds, Johnson showed an emotional depth that he masked elsewhere. He could use the ranch and its environment as a means of renewal, a way to refresh himself for yet another of the endless political battles that dominated the life of the president.

But most importantly to Lyndon Johnson, he had control in the Hill Country. Unlike Washington, D.C., the pace and rhythm at the ranch followed his desires. On his ranch he could always assert his primacy and, in the process, behave in a magnanimous manner that endeared him to visitors and the press alike. It was his place, and he could use his knowledge of rural ways to play a game of "one-upmanship" with people who visited. At Johnson's ranch, he was never bested. During his years in the White House and in retirement, this helped him establish the hierarchies so important to the way he understood the world.

The Texas White House developed a unique symbolism that resulted from the image Johnson fashioned and from the way in which it was presented to the public. The ranch came to mean, first and foremost, national heritage; in an era when the Western movie dominated the national sense of identity and when the westward experience represented the nation, the ranch linked Johnson to what he and for a long time the public saw as the quintessential American experience. Such roots and the meaning they conveyed gave Johnson power to persuade, to cajole, to enunciate as authentic his goals and dreams for the nation. The ranch represented the reality of his feelings, made them more comprehensible and more believable as a result of their ties to the Hill Country.

The ranch also represented independence in an era that increasingly valued "doing your own thing." During the 1960s, individualism came to replace interdependence as a goal for American society. While the emphasis on personal independence had always been strong in American culture, the oppositional politics of the era accentuated it even further. Even his detractors gave Johnson credit for acting as an individual, albeit one operating with a value system entirely different from theirs. In the end, the people who refused him this distinction—the press and other commentators—were those most closely allied with the concept of individual expression.

In this way, Johnson's ranch became as anachronistic as the man himself. When he built the image of himself as a westerner, when he took the ranch and indeed Texas and made a claim for their place in the nation, Johnson played off of national myths that were rife in popular culture. Westerns such as John Ford's *The Searchers* reflected the importance of the idea of a homeplace, a concept broadly current in Texas literature and history. No less an eminence than John Graves, Texas's writer laureate, stubbornly affirmed the virtues of a homeplace—with all its drawbacks— throughout a long and beautifully prolific life. By the time Johnson left office, however, the nation had changed, its values shifting away from the kind of place-based emphasis so crucial to Johnson. Even the Western, the basis of the very mythology that Johnson had embraced and packaged for the public, had become something new. After *Little Big Man* in 1970 and especially with *Pat Garrett and Billy the Kid,* which debuted in 1973, the year of Johnson's death, the idea of the need for a place had been replaced by an emphasis on the need to wander. The hero had become an antihero, the place one to leave, not one to which to return. When Johnson needed the ranch most as a symbol, it had become an anachronism, a reflection of values that had receded from the national stage.

The ranch simultaneously represented a fusion of the modern world with traditional America. Its satellite dishes, communications apparatus, televisions, and telephones showed a rural world with modern accouterments, a melding of the agrarian image of Thomas Jefferson's view of the nation with the world of technology. This melding of different worlds was something to which Americans aspired: rural people sought the seeming luxury of modern communications systems, and urban people sought the peace and quiet of the country without leaving the tools of their trades behind. The ranch subtly became both—a simpler and relaxing rural locale to urban Americans and an up-to-date modern agricultural and ranching operation to rural people. That malleability characterized Johnson as well; it contributed to his success and ironically to his demise as well.

In the end, the ranch also represented a spirit, a feeling of knowing what was right not just for American society but for the world. The ranch became a symbol for being grounded, for having roots in a genuine world that differed from the head-turning pull of politics and high society. In that respect, the Texas White House represented common sense in a world that seemed increasingly devoid of it. The ranch was, over time, what Lyndon B. Johnson wanted it to be, both for the public and for himself. For the public it became the symbol of what was good about the nation, fashioned to the demands of the office of senator, vice president, and president. For Johnson, it became an articulation of his roots and his memories, the most special place on earth. Lyndon and Lady Bird Johnson's favorite name for the place, "our heart's home," was quite apt. It reflected what they felt about their place in the Hill Country; as they looked at the stars that shone above the shimmering Pedernales River, both Johnsons always knew that they were home.

NOTES

INTRODUCTION

1. Robert A. Caro, *The Years of Lyndon Johnson,* vol. 1, *The Path to Power* (New York: Alfred A. Knopf, 1982), 201.

CHAPTER 1. BUNTONS, BAINESES, JOHNSONS, AND THE HILL COUNTRY

1. John Graves, *Hard Scrabble: Observations on a Piece of Land* (New York: Alfred A. Knopf, 1974).
2. T. R. Fehrenbach, *Lone Star: A History of Texas and the Texans* (New York: Macmillan Publishing Company, 1968), 14–15; Elizabeth A. H. John, *Storms Brewed in Other Men's Worlds: The Confrontation of Indians, Spanish, and French in the Southwest, 1540–1795* (College Station: Texas A&M University Press, 1975), 166, 193, 279–83; Alfred W. Crosby, *Ecological Imperialism: The Biological Expansion of Europe, 900–1900* (Cambridge: Cambridge University Press, 1986), 200–39.
3. Ferhrenbach, *Lone Star,* 31–36; John, *Storms Brewed,* 215–19, 306–12.
4. Fehrenbach, *Lone Star,* 31–36; John, *Storms Brewed,* 258–303, 336–430. John Graves, *Goodbye to a River, A Narrative* (New York: Alfred A. Knopf, 1960), provides a wonderful literary exploration of the changing relationships in Texas.
5. David Hackett Fischer, *Albion's Seed: Four British Folkways in America* (New York: Oxford University Press, 1989), 605–781; John Mack Faragher, *Sugar Creek: Life on the Illinois Prairie* (New Haven: Yale University Press, 1986); John Perlin, *A Forest Journey: The Role of Wood in the Development of Civilization* (New York: W. W. Norton and Company, 1989).
6. Caro, *Path to Power,* 6–8; Paul K. Conkin, *Big Daddy from the Pedernales: Lyndon B. Johnson* (Boston: Twayne Publishers, 1986), 2; Robert Dallek, *Lone Star Rising: Lyndon Johnson and His Times, 1908–1960* (New York: Oxford University Press, 1991), 17–18; Ronnie Dugger, *The Politician: The Life and Times of Lyndon Johnson: The Drive for Power, from the Frontier to Master of the Senate* (New York: W. W. Norton, 1982), 25–31, 48–52.
7. Caro, *Path to Power,* 8, 15; Conkin, *Big Daddy,* 2–3; Dallek, *Lone Star Rising,* 14–15.
8. Caro, *Path to Power,* 8–26. Wallace Stegner, *Beyond the Hundredth Meridian: John Wesley Powell and the Second Opening of the West* (Boston: Houghton Mifflin Company, 1954), furnishes an excellent articulation of this situation and of the efforts of John Wesley Powell to transcend it. Another example of this problem is provided by H. Craig Miner, *West of Wichita: Settling the High Plains of Kansas, 1865–1890* (Lawrence: University Press of Kansas, 1986); see also Hal K. Rothman, "The Perceptual Trap: Climate and Perception in the Nineteenth-Century American West," *Halcyon: A Journal of the Humanities* 17 (1995), 127–44.

9. Conkin, *Big Daddy,* 8–10; Dallek, *Lone Star Rising,* 18–19.

10. Caro, *Path to Power,* 40–48; Conkin, *Big Daddy,* 3–5; Dallek, *Lone Star Rising,* 21–25.

11. Dallek, *Lone Star Rising,* 27–28; Conkin, *Big Daddy,* 6. This site is now the Lyndon Baines Johnson Birthplace, part of the Lyndon B. Johnson National Historical Park (LBJNHP).

12. Caro, *Path to Power,* 50–56; Conkin, *Big Daddy,* 6–7; Dallek, *Lone Star Rising,* 19–20, 28–29. The nature of Rebekah Johnson's feelings about the clan is the first of the infinite number of places in which Conkin, Dallek, and Caro disagree on the meaning of the circumstances of Johnson's life. Robert A. Divine, "The Maturing Johnson Literature," in Robert A. Divine, ed., *The Johnson Years,* vol. 3, *LBJ at Home and Abroad* (Lawrence: University Press of Kansas, 1994), provides an insightful discussion of the insights and flaws in all three approaches. See also Dugger, *Politician,* 61.

13. Conkin, *Big Daddy,* 20–25; Caro, *Path to Power,* 66–69; Dugger, *Politician,* 59–61; Dallek, *Lone Star Rising,* 33–34; Doris Kearns, *Lyndon Johnson and the American Dream* (New York: Harper and Row, 1976), 25. It is in Dallek's account that Rebekah Johnson emerges as a domineering and manipulative force in her son's early life.

14. Conkin, *Big Daddy,* 16–19; Caro, *Path to Power,* 66–72; Dallek, *Lone Star Rising,* 35; Kearns, *Lyndon Johnson and the American Dream,* 23–26.

15. Dallek, *Lone Star Rising,* 38–39, 46–47.

16. Albert Wierich, interview by Konrad Kelley, May 19, 1977, Southwestern Parks and Monuments Association (SPMA) Oral History Collection, LBJNHP, 291:1; Caro, *Path to Power,* 72–75; Dugger, *Politician,* 70–72; Dallek, *Lone Star Rising,* 36–38, 50–51.

17. Caro, *Path to Power,* 55–63; Merle Miller, ed., *Lyndon: An Oral Biography* (New York: G. P. Putnam's Sons, 1980), 9–12; Sam Houston Johnson with Enrique Hank Lopez, *My Brother Lyndon* (New York: Cowles Book Company, 1970), 18–24, 32–34; Kearns, *Lyndon Johnson and the American Dream,* 32–33, 39–41; Dallek, *Lone Star Rising,* 28–29, 36–40.

18. Albert Wierich, interview, 291:1; Caro, *Path to Power,* 71–72.

19. Conkin, *Big Daddy,* 25; Caro, *Path to Power,* 85–90; Dallek, *Lone Star Rising,* 55–57. For an analysis of the impact of World War I on American agriculture, see Donald Worster, *Dust Bowl: The Southern Plains in the 1930s* (New York: Oxford University Press, 1980), and Pete Daniel, *Breaking the Land: The Transformation of Cotton, Tobacco, and Rice Cultures Since 1880* (Urbana: University of Illinois Press, 1985).

20. Caro, *Path to Power,* 79. Dallek, *Lone Star Rising,* 36–37, dates the beginning of family problems to Rebekah Johnson's health problems, which followed the birth of children in 1914 and 1916 and were compounded by medical difficulties in 1917.

21. Dallek, *Lone Star Rising,* 38–39, 56–57; Caro, *Path to Power,* 96–97; Father Wunibald Schneider, interview by Konrad Kelley, March 31, 1976, SPMA Oral History Collection, LBJNHP, 242:3; Dugger, *Politician,* 90–93, 104–105.

22. Sam Houston Johnson, *My Brother Lyndon,* 25.

23. Ibid., 12–13, 21; Caro, *Path to Power,* 96–106; Dallek, *Lone Star Rising,* 46–47, 56–58. This is an aspect of Johnson's personality into which Conkin barely delves.

24. Caro, *Path to Power,* 111–12; Dallek, *Lone Star Rising,* 37–38, 45–46, 53; Kearns, *Lyndon Johnson and the American Dream,* 42.

25. Conkin, *Big Daddy,* 32–35; Caro, *Path to Power,* 121–29; Kearns, *Lyndon Johnson and the American Dream,* 24–25; Sam Houston Johnson, *My Brother Lyndon,* 20–24; Dugger, *Politician,* 100–103; Dallek, *Lone Star Rising,* 58–61.

26. Caro, *Path to Power,* 141–65; Conkin, *Big Daddy,* 37–47; Dugger, *Politician,* 108–14; Dallek, *Lone Star Rising,* 62–74.

27. Dugger, *Politician,* 123–24; Caro, *Path to Power,* 141–60; Dallek, *Lone Star Rising,* 68–69, 75–76.

28. Caro, *Path to Power,* 201. Dallek, *Lone Star Rising,* 61, is far more persuasive than Caro on this point. Dallek writes: "There was more to the mature Johnson than the sum of these parts. He was not simply an offshoot of his ancestors but a distinctive person with ambivalent feelings about his parents and heritage, which, combined with the influences of his environment, translated into contradictions that defy easy understanding. . . . As with all human beings, he exhibited patterns of behavior that repeated themselves throughout his life."

29. George Reedy, interview, AC 76-23, LBJ Library, Austin, 60.

30. Caro, *Path to Power,* 166–74; Dugger, *Politician,* 115–18; Dallek, *Lone Star Rising,* 77–80.

31. Caro, *Path to Power,* 169–70; Conkin, *Big Daddy,* 52–53; Dallek, *Lone Star Rising,* 77–80. This is another of the rare circumstances about which Caro and Conkin agree, albeit in a shortsighted manner; Dallek offers a more well-rounded perspective.

32. Caro, *Path to Power,* 172.

33. Ibid., 174–201; Conkin, *Big Daddy,* 53–56; Sam Houston Johnson, *My Brother Lyndon,* 26–29; Dugger, *Politician,* 118–20; Dallek, *Lone Star Rising,* 81–86.

34. Caro, *Path to Power,* 203; Conkin, *Big Daddy,* 59–60; Dugger, *Politician,* 122–23; Dallek, *Lone Star Rising,* 86–87.

35. Caro, *Path to Power,* 203; Conkin, *Big Daddy,* 59; Dallek, *Lone Star Rising,* 86–87.

36. Caro, *Path to Power,* 204; Dallek, *Lone Star Rising,* 89.

37. Caro, *Path to Power,* 204–14; Conkin, *Big Daddy,* 59; Dugger, *Politician,* 124–26; Dallek, *Lone Star Rising,* 88–92.

38. Caro, *Path to Power,* 214–31; Dallek, *Lone Star Rising,* 93–124; Conkin, *Big Daddy,* 60; Sam Houston Johnson, *My Brother Lyndon,* 43–44; Dugger, *Politician,* 127–29.

39. Caro, *Path to Power,* 221–22, 261–64; Dallek, *Lone Star Rising,* 119–22; Sam Houston Johnson, *My Brother Lyndon,* 44; Dugger, *Politician,* 128–29, 164–65.

40. Caro, *Path to Power,* 261–73; Dugger, *Politician,* 166–70.

41. Caro, *Path to Power,* 276–77; Conkin, *Big Daddy,* 70.

42. Caro, *Path to Power,* 281–85.

43. Dugger, *Politician,* 175–81; Dallek, *Lone Star Rising,* 115–21; Caro, *Path to Power,* 294–301; Kearns, *Lyndon Johnson and the American Dream,* 80–82; Sam Houston Johnson, *My Brother Lyndon,* 37–42; Bruce Schulman, *Lyndon Johnson and American Liberalism: A Brief Biography with Documents* (Boston: Bedford Books, 1995), 15.

44. Dallek, *Lone Star Rising,* 166; Caro, *Path to Power,* 306–40, 758–59; Conkin, *Big Daddy,* 73–74; Sam Houston Johnson, *My Brother Lyndon,* 37–39.

45. Caro, *Path to Power,* 325–40; Dallek, *Lone Star Rising,* 122–24.

46. Caro, *Path to Power,* 340–48; Dallek, *Lone Star Rising,* 125–56; Conkin, *Big Daddy,* 74–79; Sam Houston Johnson, *My Brother Lyndon,* 51.

47. Caro, *Path to Power,* 390–91; Dallek, *Lone Star Rising,* 145–54; Conkin, *Big Daddy,* 79–80; Sam Houston Johnson, *My Brother Lyndon,* 53–56.

48. Caro, *Path to Power,* 369–436; Dallek, *Lone Star Rising,* 157–60.

49. Caro, *Path to Power*, 448–59; Dallek, *Lone Star Rising*, 175–85; Sam Houston Johnson, *My Brother Lyndon*, 56–60.

50. Caro, *Path to Power*, 460–66; Dallek, *Lone Star Rising*, 175–79; Conkin, *Big Daddy*, 80–83.

51. Caro, *Path to Power*, 469.

52. Ibid., xiii–xviii, 476–84; Dallek, *Lone Star Rising*, 189–93; Conkin, *Big Daddy*, 98–99. Again the biographers disagree; for an analysis of their perspectives, see Divine, "Maturing Johnson Literature," 4.

53. Caro, *Path to Power*, 675–95; Dallek, *Lone Star Rising*, 207–24; Conkin, *Big Daddy*, 104–105; Sam Houston Johnson, *My Brother Lyndon*, 71–72.

54. Caro, *Path to Power*, 695–703.

55. Ibid., 704–14; Dallek, *Lone Star Rising*, 211–15; Conkin, *Big Daddy*, 104.

56. Caro, *Path to Power*, 718–40; Dallek, *Lone Star Rising*, 217–24; Conkin, *Big Daddy*, 105–106; Robert A. Caro, *The Years of Lyndon Johnson*, vol. 2, *Means of Ascent* (New York: Alfred A. Knopf, 1990), 3–5.

57. Caro, *Path to Power*, 760–68; Dallek, *Lone Star Rising*, 225–67; Conkin, *Big Daddy*, 106–12.

58. Caro, *Means of Ascent*, 143–302; Conkin, *Big Daddy*, 115–16; Sam Houston Johnson, *My Brother Lyndon*, 73–77.

59. Caro, *Means of Ascent*, 303–402; J. Evetts Haley, *A Texan Looks at Lyndon: A Study in Illegitimate Power* (Canyon, Tex.: Palo Duro Press, 1964), 21–55; Sam Houston Johnson, *My Brother Lyndon*, 77–79; Dugger, *Politician*, 295–341; Dallek, *Lone Star Rising*, 298–348; Conkin, *Big Daddy*, 116–18. For a critique of Caro's approach, see Divine, "Maturing Johnson Literature," 1–3.

60. Caro, *Means of Ascent*, 80–118; Dallek, *Lone Star Rising*, 347–66; Caro, *Path to Power*, xiii–xvi, 339–40; Dugger, *Politician*, 267–72.

CHAPTER 2. BUYING THE FAMILY RANCH

1. Caro, *Means of Ascent*, xxxii–xxxiv; Dallek, *Lone Star Rising*, 298–348; Eric Goldman, *The Crucial Decade—and After: America, 1945–1960* (New York: Random House, 1961), 4–5, 12–15; David McCullough, *Truman* (New York: Simon and Schuster, 1992).

2. Caro, *Means of Ascent*, 398–401; Conkin, *Big Daddy*, 121; Edwin C. McReynolds, *Oklahoma: A History of the Sooner State* (Norman: University of Oklahoma Press, 1954), 389–92.

3. Walter Jenkins in Miller, *Lyndon: An Oral Biography*, 141; Conkin, *Big Daddy*, 121; Dallek, *Lone Star Rising*, 380.

4. Caro, *Means of Ascent*, 80–118; Conkin, *Big Daddy*, 110–14; Dallek, *Lone Star Rising*, 246–52, 409–11.

5. Paul H. Douglas in Miller, *Lyndon: An Oral Biography*, 147; Conkin, *Big Daddy*, 119–21; Dallek, *Lone Star Rising*, 379.

6. Miller, *Lyndon: An Oral Biography*, 150; Conkin, *Big Daddy*, 129–31; Edwin C. Bearss, "Historic Resource Study: Lyndon B. Johnson and the Hill Country 1937–1963" (Santa Fe: National Park Service, 1984), Southwest Cultural Resources Center Professional Papers # 3, 51–53; Dallek, *Lone Star Rising*, 389–94.

7. Conkin, *Big Daddy*, 124; Caro, *Path to Power*, 477–92; Dallek, *Lone Star Rising*, 408–409.

8. Conkin, *Big Daddy,* 121–22.

9. Edwin C. Bearss, "Historic Structure Report: The Texas White House, Lyndon B. Johnson National Historical Park, Texas," (Santa Fe: National Park Service, 1986), Southwest Cultural Resources Center Professional Papers # 4, # 5; Mrs. Lyndon B. (Lady Bird) Johnson, interview by Elizabeth Hulett, February 3, 1993, NPS Oral History tape 457:1, Park Library, LBJNHP, 2; Dugger, *Politician,* 68–69; Dallek, *Lone Star Rising,* 33.

10. Lady Bird Johnson, interview, February 3, 1993, 3. Mrs. Johnson's account is a little more subdued than most of the others. In the 1993 interview, she suggests that Lyndon Johnson told her he wished to buy the house on the way back from the ranch. While she avers that his decision to buy it without consulting her was "no way to behave for a husband who wants peace and smooth sailing . . . when [she] saw how much he cared about it, [she] just couldn't raise a ruckus." See also Dugger, *Politician,* 46; J. Roy White, interview by Konrad Kelley and Edwin C. Bearss, June 6, 1978, SPMA Oral History Collection, LBJNHP, 315:1.

11. Conkin, *Big Daddy,* 123; Bearss, "Texas White House," 5; Dallek, *Lone Star Rising,* 408.

12. Conkin, *Big Daddy,* 123; Dallek, *Lone Star Rising,* 408–409.

13. Elizabeth "Liz" Carpenter, "The Story of the LBJ Ranch and Home," draft, n.d., White House Social Files (WHSF), Liz Carpenter's Files, Box 69, Lyndon Baines Johnson Library (LBJ Library), Austin; Liz Carpenter, "The Story of the LBJ Ranch and Home," cursive type, n.d., WHSF, Liz Carpenter's Files, Box 69, LBJ Library, Austin; "Deposition of R. G. Bouldin dated Feb. 12, 1904," Cause No. 773, *Elizabeth Power et. al.* vs. *A. M. Benner et. al.,* WHSF, Liz Carpenter's Files, Box 69, LBJ Library, Austin; Fehrenbach, *Lone Star,* 190–215, 247–67; David J. Weber, *The Mexican Frontier, 1821–1846: The American Southwest under Mexico* (Albuquerque: University of New Mexico Press, 1982), 176–79; 242–55. Bearss, "Texas White House," 1, gives the "Rachael" spelling for Means's first name.

14. Weber, *Mexican Frontier,* 158–62, 178; Carpenter, "Story of the LBJ Ranch," cursive type.

15. Fehrenbach, *Lone Star,* 298–302; Graves, *Goodbye to a River.*

16. Carpenter, "Story of the LBJ Ranch," cursive type; Elise Kowert, "Chain of Title to that Portion of Sur. No. 6, Rachel Means, Situated in Gillespie County, Texas," July 14, 1965, WHSF, Liz Carpenter's Files, Box 69, LBJ Library, Austin.

17. Carpenter, "Story of the LBJ Ranch," cursive type; Fehrenbach, *Lone Star,* 291–95; Dugger, *Politician,* 39–40.

18. Carpenter, "Story of the LBJ Ranch," cursive type; Bearss, "Texas White House," 1. For a more general description of backwoods Texas life, see Fehrenbach, *Lone Star,* 298–302, and Graves, *Hard Scrabble.* For a general view of the travails of preindustrial agricultural life, see John Ise, *Sod and Stubble: The Story of a Kansas Homestead* (New York: Barnes and Noble, 1938). For the impact on American agriculture, see Daniel, *Breaking the Land,* and Worster, *Dust Bowl.*

19. Bearss, "Texas White House," 2.

20. Carpenter, "Story of the LBJ Ranch," cursive type; Bearss, "Texas White House," 2. Bearss gives Mrs. Meier's name as "Wilhelmina," but the Meiers' daughter Clara is quoted in Carpenter referring to her mother as "Anna."

21. Bearss, "Texas White House," 2–3.

22. Ibid., 3.

23. Leonard Pitt, *The Decline of the Californios: A Social History of the Spanish-Speaking Californians, 1846–1890* (Berkeley: University of California Press, 1966); William E. DeBuys, *Enchantment and Exploitation: The Life and Hard Times of a New Mexico Mountain Range* (Albuquerque: University of New Mexico Press, 1985); Victor Westphall, *Mercedes Reales: Hispanic Land Grants of the Upper Rio Grande Region* (Albuquerque: University of New Mexico Press, 1983); Hal K. Rothman, *On Rims and Ridges: The Los Alamos Area Since 1880* (Lincoln: University of Nebraska Press, 1992); G. Emlen Hall, *The Four Leagues of Pecos: A Legal History of the Pecos Grant, 1800–1933* (Albuquerque: University of New Mexico Press, 1984); Arnoldo De León, *They Called Them Greasers: Anglo Attitudes Toward Mexicans in Texas, 1821–1900* (Austin: University of Texas Press, 1983); Fehrenbach, *Lone Star*, 283–84, 510–11.

24. Bearss, "Texas White House," 3–4.

25. Ibid., 4.

26. Ibid., 5.

27. Dallek, *Lone Star Rising*, 408; Dugger, *Politician*, 356–58; Conkin, *Big Daddy*, 123–24.

28. George Reedy, interview, AC 84-40, LBJ Library, Austin, 20–21; Bearss, "Texas White House," 7; Dallek, *Lone Star Rising*, 406–408; Conkin, *Big Daddy*, 123–24.

29. Dallek, *Lone Star Rising*, 408; Caro, *Path to Power*, 109–10, 149–53, 198–200, 449, 665–66. Caro, *Means of Ascent*, 9–10, 122–24, advances the professional son argument. Conkin, *Big Daddy*, does not really address this facet of Johnson's character in any detail.

30. Elspeth Rostow in Miller, *Lyndon: An Oral Biography*, 403; Caro, *Path to Power*, 334, 339, 423–44, 494, 704; Caro, *Means of Ascent*, 136–40,194–206; Conkin, *Big Daddy*, 146, 192; Dallek, *Lone Star Rising*, 155, 301–302, 406–407.

31. Lyndon Johnson to Rebekah Baines Johnson, August 1, 1958, Family Correspondence, Sam Houston Johnson, Box 2, LBJ Library, Austin; Adrian A. Spears to Senator and Mrs. Lyndon B. Johnson, September 5, 1953, Senate Political Files, 1949–61, Box 12, LBJ Library, Austin.

CHAPTER 3. THE SENATE YEARS: CREATING A MYTHIC PLACE
FROM AN ACTUAL ONE, 1951–60

1. Caro, *Means of Ascent*, 149–73, describes Stevenson's persona in detail; Divine, "Maturing Johnson Literature," 2–3, offers a balance to Caro's description of Stevenson's virtues. Haley, *A Texan Looks*, an anti-Johnson diatribe written in 1964, seems to exist to debunk the idea that Johnson was a "True Texan"; for elaboration, see Robert A. Divine, "The Johnson Literature," in Robert A. Divine, ed., *The Johnson Years*, vol. 1, *Foreign Policy, the Great Society, and the White House* (Lawrence: University Press of Kansas, 1987), 2–3.

2. William E. Leuchtenberg, "The Old Cowhand from Dixie," *The Atlantic* 270 no. 6 (December, 1992), 92–100; Sam Houston Johnson, interview by Konrad Kelley, February 7, 1976, SPMA Oral History Collection, LBJNHP, 225:5.

3. Fehrenbach, *Lone Star*, xii, 619–23, 650–55. For more on Hogg, see David F. Prindle, *Petroleum Politics and the Texas Railroad Commission* (Austin: University of Texas Press, 1981).

4. Richard Moorehead, *50 Years of Texas Politics: From Roosevelt to Reagan, From the*

Fergusons to Clements (Burnet, Tex.: Eakin Press, 1982); Sam Kinch and Stuart Long, *Allan Shivers: The Pied Piper of Texas Politics* (Austin: Shoal Creek Publishers, 1973).

5. Fehrenbach, *Lone Star,* 650–55; Dallek, *Lone Star Rising,* 95.

6. D. B. Hardeman in Miller, *Lyndon: An Oral Biography,* 203–204; Dallek, *Lone Star Rising,* 371.

7. Caro, *Path to Power,* 711–40; Caro. *Means of Ascent,* 302–84; Conkin, *Big Daddy,* 101–106, 115–18; Dallek, *Lone Star Rising,* 207–26, 295–346.

8. White, interview, 315:1; Bearss, "Historic Structure Report," 7–8; *Fredericksburg Standard,* November 14, 1951.

9. *Fredericksburg Standard,* November 14, 1951.

10. Caro, *Path to Power,* 86–90; Dallek, *Lone Star Rising,* 19, 55–58.

11. Bearss, "Historic Structure Report," 5, gives total acreage of the purchase as 243 acres.

12. *Fredericksburg Standard,* November 14, 1951; Bearss, "Historic Structure Report," 9.

13. Bearss, "Historic Structure Report," 8; Mary Rather, interview by Konrad Kelley, June 8, 1978, SPMA Oral History Collection, LBJNHP, 319:2.

14. Conkin, *Big Daddy,* 123–24.

15. A. W. Moursand to Lyndon B. Johnson, March 4, 1954; Lyndon B. Johnson to A. W. Moursand, March 10, 1954; A. W. Moursand to Lyndon B. Johnson, April 7, 1954; Lyndon B. Johnson to A. W. Moursand, April 23, 1954; A. W. Moursand to Lyndon B. Johnson, May 7, 1954; Lyndon B. Johnson to A. W. Moursand, May 13, 1954; A. W. Moursand to Lyndon B. Johnson, February 27, 1957; Lyndon B. Johnson to A. W. Moursand, March 4, 1957, LBJ Archives (LBJA), Selected Names, Box 27, LBJ Library, Austin.

16. Bearss, "Historic Structure Report," 8–9.

17. Ibid., 9, 14–16; Lady Bird Johnson, interview, February 3, 1993, 4.

18. Lady Bird Johnson, interview, February 3, 1993, 4.

19. Ibid.; Berniece Greider to Circulation Manager, September 25, 1953, Senate Political Files, 1949–1961, Box 12, LBJ Library, Austin.

20. Lady Bird Johnson, interview, February 3, 1993, 4.

21. Ibid., 5; White, interview, 315:1; Bearss, "Historic Structure Report," 9.

22. Lady Bird Johnson, interview, February 3, 1993, 5; White, interview, 315:1. For a discussion of vernacular architecture, see John Stilgoe, *The Common Landscape of North America, 1580–1845* (New Haven: Yale University Press, 1984).

23. Bearss, "Historic Structure Report," 9–13; White, interview, 315:1; Lawrence Klein, interview by Konrad Kelley, March 30, 1977, SPMA Oral History Collection, LBJNHP, 288:1A.

24. Lady Bird Johnson, interview, February 3, 1993, 6; Bearss, "Historic Structure Report," 16–17; Josepha Johnson to Lyndon Johnson, January 24, 1955, Family Correspondence, Josepha Johnson, Box 2, LBJ Library, Austin.

25. Bearss, "Historic Resource Study," 53–55; Rather, interview, 319:2; Kermit Hahne and Ohlen Cox, interview by Konrad Kelley, May 31, 1978, SPMA Oral History Collection, LBJNHP, 311:1; Dale Malechek, interview by Konrad Kelley, December 27, 1979, 365:22; Jewell Malechek, interview by Konrad Kelley, July 5, 1978, SPMA Oral History Collection, LBJNHP, 323:1.

26. Bearss, "Historic Resource Study," 55–56.

27. Ibid., 56.

28. For examples, see William O. Douglas to Lyndon Johnson, October 22, 1953;

Lyndon Johnson to Paul Rogers, October 26, 1953; Winston Taylor to Lyndon Johnson, November 22, 1953, Senate Political Files, 1949–1961, LBJ-Personal Miscellaneous (2 of 2), Box 12, LBJ Library, Austin. Also see Lyndon Johnson to Floyd McGowan, November 10, 1953, Senate Political Files, 1949–1961, Saturday Appointment, Box 15, LBJ Library, Austin.

29. Conkin, *Big Daddy*, 124.

30. Richard "Cactus" Pryor in Miller, *Lyndon: An Oral Biography*, 403–404.

31. Bearss, "Historic Resource Study," 57–59.

32. Miller, *Lyndon: An Oral Biography*, 150; Dallek, *Lone Star Rising*, 389–94.

33. Price Daniel in Miller, *Lyndon: An Oral Biography*, 151–56; Dallek, *Lone Star Rising*, 416–17.

34. Miller, *Lyndon: An Oral Biography*, 173–74; Dallek, *Lone Star Rising*, 430–31; Conkin, *Big Daddy*, 145.

35. Miller, *Lyndon: An Oral Biography*, 179–80; Conkin, *Big Daddy*, 146; Dallek, *Lone Star Rising*, 483–89.

36. Miller, *Lyndon: An Oral Biography*, 181; Cecil Presnell, interview by Konrad Kelley, July 27, 1978, SPMA Oral History Collection, LBJNHP, 327:1.

37. Miller, *Lyndon: An Oral Biography*, 182; Rather, interview, 319:2; Yolanda Boozer, interview by Konrad Kelley, July 11, 1978, SPMA Oral History Collection, LBJNHP, 324:5.

38. Miller, *Lyndon: An Oral Biography*, 183.

39. Liz Carpenter, interview by Konrad Kelley and Edwin C. Bearss, June 7, 1978, SPMA Oral History Collection, LBJNHP, 316:1; Willard Deason in Miller, *Lyndon: An Oral Biography*, 183–84; Bearss, "Historic Resource Study," 66–67.

40. Carpenter, interview, 316:1; Bearss, "Historic Resource Study," 68–69; Dallek, *Lone Star Rising*, 488–89.

41. Dallek, *Lone Star Rising*, 491–94; Miller, *Lyndon: An Oral Biography*, 184–86.

42. Miller, *Lyndon: An Oral Biography*, 184–85; Bearss, "Historic Resource Study," 68–69.

43. Bearss, "Historic Resource Study," 70–72; Miller, *Lyndon: An Oral Biography*, 192–93.

44. Miller, *Lyndon: An Oral Biography*, 191–93; Dallek, *Lone Star Rising*, 489. Miller, *Lyndon: An Oral Biography*, 213–14, describes Johnson's recruitment of Tully.

45. George Reedy, interview, AC 84-50, LBJ Library, Austin, 74–76; Miller, *Lyndon: An Oral Biography*, 191–93.

46. Bearss, "Historic Resource Study," 72.

47. White, interview, 315:1; Hahne and Cox, interview, 311:1; Bearss, "Historic Structure Report, 18–19.

48. Boozer, interview, July 11, 1978, 324:1; Dale Malechek, interview with Konrad Kelley and Edwin C. Bearss, June 1, 1978, SPMA Oral History Collection, LBJNHP, 313:1; Bearss, "Historic Structure Report, 20.

49. Dale Malechek, interview, June 1, 1978, 313:1; Bearss, "Historic Structure Report," 20–22.

50. George Reedy, interview, AC 84-53, LBJ Library, Austin, 49; Miller, *Lyndon: An Oral Biography*, 174; Dallek, *Lone Star Rising*, 473–76.

51. Miller, *Lyndon: An Oral Biography*, 143. Dallek, *Lone Star Rising*, 367–68, puts Johnson in a better light. Dallek emphasizes Johnson's support for the concept of civil rights at the expense of the methods of 1950s advocates.

52. For different takes on the postwar growth of the West, see Gerald Nash, *World War II*

and the West (Albuquerque: University of New Mexico Press, 1993), and Donald Worster, *Rivers of Empire: Aridity and the Growth of the American West* (New York: Oxford University Press, 1985).

53. Miller, *Lyndon: An Oral Biography,* 144–45; Dallek, *Lone Star Rising,* 369.

54. George N. Fenin and William K. Everson, *The Western, From Silents to Cinerama* (New York: Orion Press, 1962); John H. Lenihan, *Showdown: Confronting Modern America in the Western Film* (Urbana: University of Illinois Press, 1980, 1985).

55. Nicholas Lemann, *The Promised Land: The Great Black Migration and How it Changed America* (New York: A. A. Knopf, 1991); Herbert Gutman, *The Black Family in Slavery and Freedom, 1750–1925* (New York: Vintage Books, 1976); Lerone Bennett, *Before the Mayflower: A History of Black America,* 4th ed. (Chicago: Johnson Pub. Co., 1969) Taylor Branch, *Parting the Waters: America in the King Years, 1954–1963* (New York: Simon and Schuster, 1988), 1–31, 112–25; William Chafe, *The Unfinished Journey: America Since World War II,* 2nd ed. (New York: Oxford University Press, 1991), 146–76.

56. Caro, *Path to Power,* 166–73; Miller, *Lyndon: An Oral Biography,* 148.

57. Miller, *Lyndon: An Oral Biography,* 187–88; Conkin, *Big Daddy,* 141; Branch, *Parting the Waters,* 185–86. At the Democratic nominating convention later in 1956, three southern senators put their names forward for national office: Johnson, Kefauver, and Gore, the three who refused to sign the manifesto.

58. Conkin, *Big Daddy,* 140–41; Miller, *Lyndon: An Oral Biography,* 204–205.

59. Conkin, *Big Daddy,* 140–41; Miller, *Lyndon: An Oral Biography,* 206–12.

60. Conkin, *Big Daddy,* 140–41; Miller, *Lyndon: An Oral Biography,* 204–205; Branch, *Parting the Waters,* 222–24.

61. Mary L. Vaughn, "Even Honey Jars Have LBJ Brands," *Austin American,* October 23, 1960; Miller, *Lyndon: An Oral Biography,* 208; Dugger, *Politician,* 144–45.

62. Lyndon B. Johnson, "Cattle Industry Needs Greater Public Understanding," *The Cattleman* (May, 1957); Branch, *Parting the Waters,* 112; Bennett, *Before the Mayflower.* See also Dallek, *Lone Star Rising,* photo section following 464, for a shot of Johnson on horseback at the ranch, waving a Stetson, with the family beside him.

63. Bearss, "Historic Resource Study," 59–60; Lyndon B. Johnson to Zephyr Wright, September 21, 1957, Lyndon B. Johnson Subject File, 60E, LBJ Library, Austin; Dallek, *Lone Star Rising,* 408–409; Lyndon Johnson and Lady Bird Johnson, interview, September 18, 1972.

64. LBJ Ranch Guest House Register, 1956–1961, AC 661/3, 6K46, LBJ Library, Austin.

65. Conkin, *Big Daddy,* 147; Miller, *Lyndon: An Oral Biography,* 14; Bearss, "Historic Resource Study," 78, 80–81.

66. George Reedy, interview, AC 85-23, LBJ Library, Austin, 24–25; Mary Margaret [Wylie] to Lyndon Johnson, August 28, 1959, U.S. Senate, 1959, Lopez Mateos Visit, Box 675, LBJ Library, Austin; Dallek, *Lone Star Rising,* 542; Bearss, "Historic Resource Study," 84–85.

67. From the Desk of Earl Deathe, n.d.; From the Desk of Earl Deathe, n.d.; From the Desk of Charles Howell, n.d.; Lyndon B. Johnson to My dear Friend, December 13, 1957; Memorandum to Mr. Kellam, from Lloyd Hand, n.d.; Lloyd N. Hand to [Jesse] Kellam, July 21, 1958; Jesse C. Kellam to Lloyd Hand, July 26, 1958; Lloyd Hand to Senator Johnson, August 16, 1958, LBJA Subject File, Box 31, LBJ Library, Austin. Also see Richard S. "Cactus" Pryor, interview by Paul Bolton, September 10, 1968, University of Texas Oral History project, LBJ Library, Austin.

68. Stuart Long, "Texans Put on Bull," *San Antonio Light,* October 11, 1959; "LBJ's Ranch Ready to Host a President," *Austin Statesman,* October 15, 1959; Margaret Meyer, "Lady Bird Calmly Awaits Visitors," *Dallas Times-Herald,* October 18, 1959; Memorandum, Mary Margaret to Senator Johnson, August 28, 1959; Mildred [ ], "Resume of Telephone Conversation from Mr. Edward Cale, of the American Embassy in Mexico City, September 29, 1959; George E. Reedy, Jr., to Arthur Diggie, September 30, 1959; I. W. "Stormy" Davis to Warren Woodward, October 8, 1959; Memorandum, George Reedy to Senator Johnson, October 10, 1959, U.S. Senate File, Subject Files, 1959, Box 675, LBJ Library, Austin.

69. Office of the Chief of Protocol, Visit of his Excellency Adolfo Lopez Mateos, President of the United Mexican States, October 18, 1959, LBJA Subject File, Box 93, LBJ Library, Austin; Bearss, "Historic Resource Study," 84–85.

70. Wes Izzard, "Party on the Pedernales," *The Amarillo Daily News,* October 20, 1959; Bearss, "Historic Resource Study," 84–85; Dallek, *Lone Star Rising,* 542; "The Program, Visit of President Adolfo Lopes Mateos, October 18, 1959," LBJA Subject File, Box 93, LBJ Library, Austin.

71. Bearss, "Historic Resource Study," 84–85; Lloyd Larrabee, "Go With Us on a Drive Through Lyndon's Ranch," *Houston Press,* October 19, 1959; "Johnson Host to Lopez Mateos, HST at Texas Ranch Barbecue," *Arizona Republic,* October 19, 1959, 27; Sam Kinch, "Guests Sneak Politics into Neighborly Party," *Fort Worth Star Telegram,* October 19, 1959; Charles Guptill, "Lopez Mateos Will Visit With Daniel Informally," *Abilene Reporter News,* October 19, 1959; "President Mateos Feted at LBJ Ranch Barbecue Sunday," *The Fredericksburg Standard,* October 21, 1959.

72. "Lopez Mateos Calls Trip Big Success," *San Antonio Light,* October 20, 1959; Lorraine Barnes, "Warmth Conquers Language Barriers," *The Austin American,* October 19, 1959; Dawson Duncan, "Mexico's First Family Visiting Sen. Johnson," *Dallas Morning News,* October 19, 1959; Robert C. Hill to George Reedy, October 29, 1959; Robert C. Hill to Lyndon B. Johnson, October 29, 1959; Harry S. Truman to Lyndon and Ladybird Johnson, October 27, 1959; Lyndon B. Johnson to "My dear Mr. President" (Harry S. Truman), November 4, 1959, U.S. Senate, 1949–1961, Subject Files, 1959, Box 675, LBJ Library, Austin.

73. Conkin, *Big Daddy,* 145–46; Dallek, *Lone Star Rising,* 559–61.

74. Bearss, "Historic Resource Study," 86–87; "Presidente Adolfo Lopez Mateos (Listing of persons who assisted in visit)," November 11, 1959, U.S. Senate, 1949–1961, Subject Files, 1959, Box 675, LBJ Library, Austin; "Revised Ranch Housing Plan, October 16, 1959," U.S. Senate, 1949–1961, Subject Files, 1959, Box 676, LBJ Library, Austin.

75. Bearss, "Historic Structure Report," 27.

CHAPTER 4. THE VICE PRESIDENT'S RANCH

1. Miller, *Lyndon: An Oral Biography,* 235; Caro, *Path to Power,* 100, 535, 759. Caro, *Means of Ascent,* xxviii, 3, 81, is the leading advocate of the idea that Johnson spent his life expecting to run for and win the presidency; Conkin, *Big Daddy,* and Dallek, *Lone Star Rising,* reject this idea. For the best analysis of the three perspectives, see Divine, "Maturing Johnson Literature."

2. Conkin, *Big Daddy,* 149–50; Dallek, *Lone Star Rising,* 493–507; Bearss, "Historic Resource Study," 73–76; Miller, *Lyndon: An Oral Biography,* 235–36.

3. Conkin, *Big Daddy,* 152; Dallek, *Lone Star Rising,* 555–82; Bearss, "Historic Resource Study," 77–78; Miller, *Lyndon: An Oral Biography,* 236–37, 240.

4. Conkin, *Big Daddy,* 152; Dallek, *Lone Star Rising,* 569–72; Bearss, "Historic Resource Study," 87–89; Miller, *Lyndon: An Oral Biography,* 241–43.

5. Conkin, *Big Daddy,* 152–54; Dallek, *Lone Star Rising,* 577–83; Bearss, "Historic Resource Study," 87–89. Miller, *Lyndon: An Oral Biography,* 246–62, offers the best minute-by-minute account of the 1960 convention.

6. David Halberstam, *The Powers That Be* (New York: Alfred A. Knopf, 1979), makes a form of this argument; see also Daniel Boorstin, *The Image: A Guide to Pseudo-Events in America* (New York: Harper and Row, 1961).

7. Theodore H. White, *The Making of a President, 1960* (New York: Athaneum, 1961); Halberstam, *Powers That Be,* 315–41.

8. Halberstam, *Powers That Be,* 315, 428–31; David Culbert, "Johnson and the Media," in Robert A. Divine, ed., *The Johnson Years,* vol. 1, *Foreign Policy, the Great Society, and the White House* (Austin: University of Texas Press, 1981), 214–32.

9. Miller, *Lyndon: An Oral Biography,* 262–63.

10. Elizabeth Rowe in Miller, *Lyndon: An Oral Biography,* 264.

11. Conkin, *Big Daddy,* 155–56; Dallek, *Lone Star Rising,* 584–88; Bearss, "Historic Resource Study," 95–96; Miller, *Lyndon: An Oral Biography,* 264, 266–72. See also Theodore H. White, *Making of a President,* and George Brown Tindall with David E. Shi, *America: A Narrative History,* vol. 2, 3rd ed. (New York: W. W. Norton, 1992), 1334, for a breakdown of the results of the election of 1960.

12. Conkin, *Big Daddy,* 156–58; Dallek, *Lone Star Rising,* 578–89; Miller, *Lyndon: An Oral Biography,* 272–73.

13. Miller, *Lyndon: An Oral Biography,* 273–74.

14. "LBJ Gets Ready for Kennedy's Visit," *San Antonio Light,* November 13, 1960; Bo Byers, "Kennedy, Lyndon Hunt Deer in Hill Country," *Houston Chronicle,* November 17, 1960; Richard Lyons, "Johnson to Have Important Role, Kennedy Says After Conference," *The Washington Post,* November 18, 1960; "Kennedy Goes Deer Hunting with Johnson," *The Chicago Daily Tribune,* November 18, 1960; Joseph R. L. Sterne, "Johnson Role Emphasized," *The Baltimore Sun,* November 18, 1960; Miller, *Lyndon: An Oral Biography,* 302.

15. Byers, "Kennedy, Lyndon Hunt Deer"; Douglas B. Cornell, "Johnson Welcomes Kennedy," *Abilene Reporter-News,* November 17, 1960; Sam Fore, Jr., "President-Elect Kennedy Gets a Warm Texas Welcome to LBJ Ranch; Thrills Rural Guests With Cordiality," *Floresville Chronicle-Journal,* November 18, 1960; Bo Byers, "Kennedy and Johnson Consider Poage as Agriculture Secretary," *Houston Chronicle,* November 18, 1960; Cecil Presnell, interview by Konrad Kelley, July 28, 1978, SPMA Oral History Collection, LBJNHP, 327:1.

16. Bicknell Eubanks, "LBJ Ranch Calms Down After Top-Level Bustle," *The Christian Science Monitor,* November 19, 1960; Margaret Mayer, "Johnson's Ranch Back to Normal," *The Dallas Times-Herald,* November 18, 1960.

17. Conkin, *Big Daddy,* 156–57; W. H. Lawrence, "Kennedy Expects Johnson to Press Campaign Goals," *The New York Times,* November 18, 1960; Robert J. Donovan, "Kennedy, Johnson Map Roles," *The New York Herald Tribune,* November 18, 1960.

18. White, interview, 315:2; Bearss, "Historic Structures Report," 27–28. Although they were built in 1961, Bearss refers to these rooms as the "Lopez Mateos addition."

19. Miller, *Lyndon: An Oral Biography,* 280–81; Bearss, "Historic Resource Study," 99.

20. Miller, *Lyndon: An Oral Biography,* 281; Bearss, "Historic Resource Study," 99; Dugger, *Politician,* 92.

21. Walter Jenkins in Miller, *Lyndon: An Oral Biography,* 285. Johnson had similar experiences almost everywhere he traveled. Miller, *Lyndon: An Oral Biography,* 292–94, describes an analogous experience in Turkey.

22. Miller, *Lyndon: An Oral Biography,* 285; Bearss, "Historic Resource Study," 101–102.

23. Miller, *Lyndon: An Oral Biography,* 286.

24. Office of the Chief of Protocol, "Administrative Arrangements for the Departure from Washington of his Excellency Dr. Konrad Adenauer, Chancellor of the Federal Republic of Germany, April 16, 1961"; Office of the Chief of Protocol, "Informal Visit of His Excellency, Dr. Konrad Adenauer, Chancellor of the Federal Republic of Germany"; Office of the Chief of Protocol, "Administrative Arrangements for the Arrival at Austin, Texas of his Excellency Dr. Konrad Adenauer, Chancellor, Federal Republic of Germany"; Office of the Chief of Protocol, "Passenger List for Flight from Bergstrom Air Force Base to LBJ Ranch"; Office of the Chief of Protocol, "LBJ Ranch, Stonewall Texas, Room Directory for the Visit of His Excellency Dr. Konrad Adenauer, Chancellor, Federal Republic of Germany, April 16–17, 1961"; Office of the Chief of Protocol, "Informal Visit of His Excellency, Dr. Konrad Adenauer, Chancellor of the Federal Republic of Germany, Members of the Chancellor's Party Staying at the Nimitz Hotel, April 16–17, 1961," LBJA Subject File, Box 90, LBJ Library, Austin; Father Wunibald Schneider, interview; Miller, *Lyndon: An Oral Biography,* 281; Bearss, "Historic Resource Study," 99–100.

25. Pryor, interview, September 10, 1968, 2–3; Thomas Mills, interview by Konrad Kelley, January 17, 1979, SPMA Oral History Collection, LBJNHP, 346:1; Bearss, "Historic Resource Study," 100. Pryor gives the number of the people in the tent as about one hundred.

26. Pryor, interview, September 10, 1968, 4–5; "Dinner List, LBJ Ranch, April 16, 1961, Honoring Chancellor Adenauer"; GER (George E. Reedy) to "Mr. Vice President," n.d., accompanying "Memorandum: Press Arrangements for Visit of Chancellor Adenauer," LBJA Subject File, Box 90, LBJ Library, Austin; Bearss, "Historic Resource Study," 100; Liz Carpenter, *Ruffles and Flourishes: The Warm and Tender Story of a Simple Girl Who Found Adventure in the White House* (Garden City, N.Y.: Doubleday and Company, 1969), 6.

27. Pryor, interview, September 10, 1968, 4–5; Bearss, "Historic Resource Study," 100–101.

28. "Welcome to Texas!, July 15, 1961"; "Housing Schedule for LBJ Ranch Party, Saturday, July 15–Monday July 17, 1961," LBJA Subject File, Box 91, LBJ Library; Bearss, "Historic Resource Study," 103.

29. "Dinner List, LBJ Ranch, July 15, 1961"; Lyndon B. Johnson to Edgar Perry, August 7, 1961, LBJA Subject File, Box 91, LBJ Library, Austin; Pryor. interview, September 10, 1968, 6–7; Bearss, "Historic Resource Study," 102.

30. Memorandum to Cliff [Carter] from Walter, July 10, 1961; [Guest List for Ayub Khan Barbecue] n.d., LBJA Subject File, Box 91, LBJ Library, Austin; Pryor, interview, September 10, 1968, 7–8; Bearss, "Historic Resource Study," 103.

31. Elizabeth (Liz) Carpenter, Oral History, AC 74-193, LBJNHP, 14.

32. Carpenter, Oral History, 12; Hamilton McCaughey to Mohammed Ayub Khan, June 28, 1961; Hamilton McCaughey to Vice President Lyndon Johnson, July 13, 1961, LBJA Subject File, Box 91, LBJ Library, Austin; Pryor, interview, September 10,

1968, 8; Bearss, "Historic Resource Study," 103; Miller, *Lyndon: An Oral Biography,* 286.

33. Dale Malechek, interview, January 22, 1979, 313:2; Bearss, "Historic Resource Study," 104–105.

34. Bearss, "Historic Resource Study," 104–105; Carpenter, Oral History, 12.

35. "The Poems, Parable, and Proverbs, of Bashir Ahmad [*sic*], The Camel Driver from Karachi," LBJA Subject File, Box 91, LBJ Library, Austin; Miller, *Lyndon: An Oral Biography,* 286; Bearss, "Historic Resource Study," 105.

36. "Poems, Parable, and Proverbs"; Bearss, "Historic Resource Study," 105–106.

37. Bearss, "Historic Resource Study," 106; Miller, *Lyndon: An Oral Biography,* 286.

38. Mohammed Ayub Khan to Lyndon B. Johnson, August 25, 1961; Mohammed Ayub Khan to Lyndon B. Johnson, October 26, 1961; Capt. Wesley B. Shull to Frank Kuest; Frank Kuest to Elizabeth Carpenter, LBJA Subject File, Bashir Ahmed, Box 91, LBJ Library, Austin; Carpenter, Oral History, 13.

39. Office of the Vice President, "Guests Latin American Ambassadors at Ranch Barbecue—Oct. 12, 1962," LBJA Subject File, Invitations from LBJ, Box 91, LBJ Library, Austin; Bearss, "Historic Resource Study," 111–12.

40. Pryor, interview, September 10, 1968, 8–9; Carpenter, Oral History, 12; Bearss, "Historic Resource Study," 118–19.

41. Pryor, interview, September 10, 1968, 9–10.

42. White, interview, 315:4; Bearss, "Historic Structure Report," 30–32.

43. Bearss, "Historic Resource Study," 112–14.

44. Ibid., 115–26.

CHAPTER 5. CREATING THE FIRST REMOTE WHITE HOUSE

1. Miller, *Lyndon: An Oral Biography,* 309–42; Conkin, *Big Daddy,* 170–73.

2. Miller, *Lyndon: An Oral Biography,* 337.

3. Dale Malechek, interview by Konrad Kelley, December 13, 1978, SPMA Oral History Collection, LBJNHP, 341:3.

4. William Robbins, *Colony and Empire: The Capitalist Transformation of the American West* (Lawrence: University of Kansas Press, 1994), makes a case for Iowan Herbert Hoover as a western president. David McCullough, *Truman,* notes the southernness of Truman's background and his roots in a slave state, but despite occasional narrowness, Truman emerges as an archetypical free stater. See Carl Abbott, *The Metropolitan Frontier* (Tucson: University of Arizona Press, 1994), for an articulation of the persistent and long-standing urban characteristics of the Sun Belt and the West.

5. Caro, *Means of Ascent,* 211–34; Dallek, *Lone Star Rising,* 298–348.

6. Maj. James U. Cross, interview by Arthur J. Mayer, May 15, 1970, LBJ Library, Austin, 30.

7. Miller, *Lyndon: An Oral Biography,* 340; Reedy, interview, AC 76-23, 47; George Reedy, interview, AC 84-54, LBJ Library, Austin, 10.

8. I. W. "Stormy" Davis, interview by Konrad Kelley, March 19, 1977, SPMA Oral History Collection, LBJNHP, 285:1; Bearss, "Historic Structure Report," 60; I. W. "Stormy" Davis, "Vice President Lyndon B. Johnson LBJ Ranch Stonewall, Texas," ca. 1961, LBJNHP.

9. I. W. "Stormy" Davis, interview, 285:1; Bearss, "Historic Resource Study," 60.

10. Bearss, "Historic Resource Study," 60; I. W. "Stormy" Davis, "Vice President Lyndon B. Johnson."

11. I. W. "Stormy" Davis, interview, 285:1; Bearss, "Historic Structure Report," 60–61.

12. I. W. "Stormy" Davis, "Vice President Lyndon B. Johnson."

13. Bearss, "Historic Structures Report," 44.

14. C. Phyll Horne to Rosel H. Hyde, October 31, 1966; Rosel H. Hyde to W. Marvin Watson, November 10, 1966; Col. Jack A. Albright to Marvin Watson, December 14, 1966, PP 13-2/Texas, Box 97, LBJ Library, Austin.

15. Col. Jack A. Albright, Memorandum for W. Marvin Watson, Subject: Communications in Texas, March 7, 1967; Col. Jack A. Albright, Memorandum for W. Marvin Watson, Subject: Communications in Texas, March 22, 1967; Col. Jack A. Albright, Memorandum for W. Marvin Watson, Subject: Communications in Texas, April 4, 1967, PP 13-2/Texas, Box 98, LBJ Library, Austin; Col. Jack A. Albright, Memorandum for W. Marvin Watson, Subject: Communications in Texas, May 2, 1967, Presidential File, 1963–1969, WH 12, Box 22, LBJ Library, Austin.

16. Col. Jack A. Albright, Memorandum for W. Marvin Watson, Subject: Communications in Texas, April 4, 1967; Thomas L. Johns, Memorandum for Marvin Watson, April 3, 1967, Ex WH 121-1, Box 23, LBJ Library, Austin.

17. Cross, interview, May 15, 1970, 12–16; Rather, interview, 319:2; Kermit Hahne and Gus Ohlen, interview by Konrad Kelly and Edwin C. Bearss, May 31, 1978, SPMA Oral History Collection, LBJNHP, 311:1; Bearss, "Historic Structure Report," 55; Bearss, "Historic Resource Study," 98–99; Caro, *Means of Ascent,* 209–67.

18. Bearss, "Historic Structure Report," 55–56.

19. I. W. "Stormy" Davis, interview, 285:2; Bearss, "Historic Structure Report," 58.

20. Bearss, "Historic Structure Report," 61.

21. I. W. "Stormy" Davis, interview, 285:2; Bearss, "Historic Structure Report," 61.

22. Ibid.

23. Jack Valenti to Lyndon B. Johnson, December 18, 1963; Memorandum for Captain Shepard, December 19, 1963, PP 13-2/Texas, Box 96 #3, LBJ Library, Austin; Bearss, "Historic Structure Report," 62.

24. C. V. Clifton, Memorandum for Marvin Watson, April 21, 1965; I. W. Davis to Marvin Watson, May 7, 1965; RGM to MW, 5/13/65; C. V. Clifton, Memorandum for Jack Valenti, June 8, 1965, PP 13-2/Texas, Box 97, LBJ Library, Austin; Col. Jack A. Albright, Memorandum for W. Marvin Watson, November 10, 1965, EX WH 12-1, Box 23, LBJ Library, Austin; Bearss, "Historic Structure Report," 62.

25. Cliff Carter, Memo to the President, December 12, 1963, PP, Box 96, LBJ Library, Austin; Texas Highway Department, Minute Order, Gillespie County, District 14, December 19, 1963; Clifton C. Carter to Dewitt C. Greer, January 2, 1964, Papers of Lyndon B. Johnson—President, Gen HI 2/ST 42, Box 5, LBJ Library, Austin.

26. Harold Woods, interview by Konrad Kelley, August 2, 1979, SPMA Oral History Collection, LBJNHP, 359:2; Larry Megow to President L. B. Johnson, December 12, 1966, PP, Box 3, LBJ Library, Austin.

27. United Press International, Wire Report (Demonstration), December 23, 1965, President 1963–1969, Local Government EX LG/SAN, Box 11, LBJ Library, Austin.

28. United Press International, Wire Report (Demonstration); "Group of Telegrams Filed, January 5, 1996"; Nell Yates to Jake Jacobsen, December 23, 1965, Cite: WH50632, "The Following are Three Telegrams . . . ," President 1963–1969, Local Government EX LG/SAN, Box 11, LBJ Library, Austin.

29. John Chancellor to David Wat[t]ers, February 15, 1964; "Mr President," February 17, [1964], PP 13-2/Texas, Box 96, LBJ Library, Austin; Houston Harte to George Reedy, April 5, 1965; "Mr. President," April 7, [1965]; George Reedy to Houston Harte, April 9, 1965; Jack Valenti to Mr President, July 7, 1965, PP 13-2/Texas, Box 97, LBJ Library, Austin.

30. Douglass Cater to the President, November 19, 1964, PP, Box 97, LBJ Library, Austin.

31. Cross, interview, May 15, 1970, 23; Bearss, "Historic Structure Report," 55; Conkin, *Big Daddy,* 178.

32. N. E. Halaby, FAA Administrator, Memorandum for the President, Subject: Aircraft Operations at the Ranch, n.d.; Maj. James U. Cross, Memorandum for the President, January 7, 1965, PP 13-2/Texas, Box 97, LBJ Library, Austin.

33. Cross, interview, May 15, 1970, 30.

34. White House Communications Agency to Marvin Watson, August 9, 1965; "Military Personnel Movements Between Texas and Washington, D.C., August 27–30, 1965," PP 13-2/Texas, Box 97, LBJ Library, Austin.

35. Memorandum, from Maj. James Cross, (as dictated to Mildred over telephone), November 28, 1963; George G. Burkley, M.D., Memorandum for Walter Jenkins, December 6, 1963; Tazewell Shepard, Jr., Memorandum for the President, December 10, 1963, PP 13-2/Texas, Box 96, LBJ Library, Austin; Horace Busby, Memorandum for Marvin Watson, June 15, 1965, "Trip of the President to the LBJ Ranch, January 14–17, 1965," PP 13-2/Texas, Box 97, LBJ Library, Austin.

36. "Total Number of Separate Trips to LBJ Ranch Since November 1963," n.d., PP 13-2/Texas, Box 98, LBJ Library, Austin.

37. Pierre Salinger to E. W. Morrison, January 8, 1964; Jack Albright to Marvin Watson, August 24, 1965; Marvin Watson to Lyndon Johnson, December 24, 1965, PP 13-2/Texas, Box 97, LBJ Library, Austin.

38. Conkin, *Big Daddy,* 178; Peter Lisagor, "This House is More than a Home," *Chicago Daily News,* December 22, 1963; Jack A. Albright, Memorandum for Joseph A. Califano, Jr., August 4, 1965, White House Administration, EX WH 12-1, Box 23, LBJ Library, Austin.

39. White House Correspondents' Association, Garnett D. Horner, Secretary, Telegram to the President, December 28, 1964, PP 13-2/Texas, Box 97, LBJ Library, Austin.

40. Garth Jones to George Christian, October 11, [1964], EX WH 12-1, Box 23, LBJ Library, Austin; George Christian, interview by Joe B. Frantz, December 4, 1969, AC 74-196, LBJ Library, Austin, 6.

41. Christian, interview, 6–7.

42. John Kobler, *Capone: The Life and World of Al Capone* (New York: G. P. Putnam's Sons, 1971), 306–307; Miller, *Lyndon: An Oral Biography,* 314–15.

43. Albert Wierich and Olivia Wierich, interview by Konrad Kelley, May 19, 1977, SPMA Oral History Collection, LBJNHP, 291:4.

44. Bearss, "Historic Structure Report," 56.

45. Lady Bird Johnson, *A White House Diary* (New York: Holt, Rinehart, and Winston, 1970), 19; Father Wunibald Schneider, interview.

46. Lt. Col. James U. Cross, Memorandum for All Military Personnel Assigned or Attached for White House Duty, Subject: Military Activities at the LBJ Ranch, October 15, 1965; Lt. Col. James U. Cross, Memorandum for All Military Personnel Assigned or Attached for White House Duty, Subject: Military Activities at the LBJ

Ranch, January 14, 1966; Lt. Col. James U. Cross, Memorandum for the President,
January 20, 1966, PP 13-2/Texas, Box 97, LBJ Library, Austin; Col. Jack A. Albright,
Memorandum for W. Marvin Watson, Subject: Weather Wire Service, May 24,
1967, EX WH 12-1, Box 23, LBJ Library, Austin.

47. Arthur Hoppe, "The President and His Roots," *The San Francisco Chronicle,* December 9, 1966.

CHAPTER 6. THE PRESIDENT'S PALACE: THE RANCH
DAY-TO-DAY, 1963-69

1. Lady Bird Johnson, *White House Diary,* 27.
2. Daniel J. Holder, comp., "Year at a Glance, Johnson at the Ranch," a listing of
   when Johnson was at the ranch from 1955 to 1968.
3. Charles W. Bailey, "A Visit to the LBJ Ranch—a Working Place," *The Minneapolis
   Sunday Tribune,* April 12, 1964; Hahne and Cox, interview, 311:1.
4. Bailey, "Visit to the LBJ Ranch;" Dale Malechek, interview by Konrad Kelley and
   Jim Brandenberger, November 22, 1978, SPMA Oral History Collection, LBJNHP,
   339:1; Dale Malechek and Jewell Malechek, interview by Konrad Kelley and Jim
   Brandenberger, November 9, 1978, SPMA Oral History Collection, LBJNHP, 337:1;
   Mills, interview, 346:1; Dale Malechek, interview by Konrad Kelley and Barry
   Gates, January 22, 1979, SPMA Oral History Collection, LBJNHP, 347:1; Rather,
   interview, 319:2.
5. Dale Malechek and Jewell Malechek, November 9, 1978, interview, 337:1; Dale
   Malechek, interview, January 22, 1979, 347:1.
6. Dale Malechek and Jewell Malechek, interview, November 9, 1978, 337:1
7. Bailey, "Visit to the LBJ Ranch."
8. Ibid.; Dale Malechek, interview, December 13, 1978, 347:1; Dale Malechek, interview, June 1, 1978, 313:2; "LBJ: Hereford Breeder," *Hereford Journal* (February 1,
   1964).
9. Dale Malechek, interview, November 9, 1978, 337:1.
10. Dale Malechek and Jewell Malechek, interview, December 8, 1978, 339:2.
11. Dale Malechek, interview, January 22, 1979, 347:2; Dale Malechek and Jewell
    Malechek, December 20, 1978, 341:3.
12. Dale Malechek, interview, January 22, 1979, 347:2.
13. Ibid.
14. Bailey, "Visit to the LBJ Ranch."
15. Ibid.
16. Dale Malechek, interview, December 13, 1978, 341:3, 347:3.
17. Ibid., 347:3; Juanita Roberts to Lyndon B. Johnson, September 14, 1964, PP 13-2/
    Texas, Box 96, LBJ Library, Austin; Memorandum for the Record, February 15,
    1964, PP 13-2/Texas, Box 97, LBJ Library, Austin; "April 15, 1967," White House
    Press Office Files, PSNC #803A, Box 13, LBJ Library, Austin.
18. Carpenter, *Ruffles and Flourishes,* 175; Bailey, "Visit to the LBJ Ranch."
19. Carpenter, *Ruffles and Flourishes,* 175;
20. Dale Malechek and Jewell Malechek, interview by Konrad Kelley, December 13,
    1978, SPMA Oral History Collection, LBJNHP, 341:3., 341:3; Otto Schumann,
    interview by Konrad Kelley, December 27, 1978, SPMA Oral History Collection,
    LBJNHP, 344:3; Tom Weinheimer and Betty Weinheimer, interview by Konrad

Kelley, March 10, 1977, SPMA Oral History Collection, LBJNHP, 282:1; Rather, interview, 319:2; Lady Bird Johnson, *White House Diary,* 696.

21. Miller, *Lyndon: An Oral Biography,* 407.

22. Dale Malechek, interview, December 13, 1978, 341:3; Michael Howard, interview by Konrad Kelley, June 6, 1977, SPMA Oral History Collection, LBJNHP, 292:1; I. W. "Stormy" Davis, interview, 286:3.

23. Lady Bird Johnson, *White House Diary,* 27.

24. Maj. James U. Cross, interview by Konrad Kelley, October 22, 1978, SPMA Oral History Collection, LBJNHP, 333:1; Russell Thomas, interview by Konrad Kelley, November 8, 1978, SPMA Oral History Collection, LBJNHP, 336:1; Lady Bird Johnson, *White House Diary,* 27.

25. Jack Valenti to Lyndon Johnson, December 12, 1964, PP 13-2/Texas, Box 97, LBJ Library, Austin; Walter Heller, interview, AC 83-9, 83-10, LBJ Library, Austin; Lady Bird Johnson, *White House Diary,* 27.

26. Lady Bird Johnson, *White House Diary,* 27, 201–202, 206–208.

27. "The Following Will be Accompanying the President . . ," December 20, 1964, PP 13-2/Texas, Box 97, LBJ Library, Austin; Eric Goldman, *The Tragedy of Lyndon Johnson,* 70 (New York: A. A. Knopf, 1969); Lyndon B. Johnson, *The Vantage Point: Perspectives of the Presidency, 1963–1969* (New York: Holt, Rinehart, and Winston, 1971), 270, 278–80, 464.

28. Yolanda Boozer, interview by Konrad Kelley, June 7, 1978, SPMA Oral History Collection, LBJNHP, 317:1.

29. Jack Valenti to Marvin Watson, October 30, 1965, PP 13-2/Texas, Box 97, LBJ Library, Austin; Lady Bird Johnson, *White House Diary,* 334–36.

30. Woods, interview, August 2, 1979, 359:1; Dale Malechek, interview, November 22, 1978, 339:1; Dale Malechek, interview by Konrad Kelley, January 30, 1980, SPMA Oral History Collection, LBJNHP, 365:1; Carpenter, interview, 316:3; Reedy, interview, AC 84-50, 81; Jewell Malechek, interview by Konrad Kelley and Edwin C. Bearss, June 9, 1978, SPMA Oral History Collection, LBJNHP, 320:5; Miller, *Lyndon: An Oral Biography,* 406.

31. Miller, *Lyndon: An Oral Biography,* 405.

32. Heller, interview; Miller, *Lyndon: An Oral Biography,* 361–62.

33. Christian, interview; Reedy, interview, AC 85-23, 24; Miller, *Lyndon: An Oral Biography,* 405.

34. Christian, interview, 6.

35. Lady Bird Johnson, *White House Diary,* 571–72.

36. Ibid.

37. Reedy, interview, AC 84-53, 49.

CHAPTER 7. A SLICE OF REAL AMERICA: SHOWCASING THE RANCH DURING THE PRESIDENCY

1. W. D. Taylor, "On LBJ Ranch Menu: Barbecue, Diplomacy," *The New York Herald-Tribune,* November 13, 1964; Horace Busby to Bess Abell, September 28, 1964, Files of Bess Abell, Ranch Visit, Diaz Ordaz, Box 7, LBJ Library, Austin.

2. Idealized, rural living was more a goal than a practice of some elements of the counterculture; few succeeded in actually living off the land although the imagery spread far and wide. The film *Easy Rider* (1969) showed a struggling commune,

modeled after the famous Taos Commune of the late 1960s. William deBuys and Alex Harris, *River of Traps* (Albuquerque: University of New Mexico Press, 1992), 43–44, offers a more realistic view of the experience of some late 1960s and early 1970s communes.

3. George Reedy, interview, AC 84-42, LBJ Library, Austin, 27; Caro, *Path to Power*, 376–78, 469.

4. Pryor, interview, September 10, 1968; Schumann, interview, 344:3.

5. Lloyd Hand to Lyndon Johnson, September 16, 1958, LBJA Subject File, Box 81, Invitations from LBJ, LBJ Library, Austin; "List of People Who Assisted at Lopez Mateos Barbecue," November 11, 1959, U.S. Senate 1959, Lopez Mateos Visit, Box 675, LBJ Library, Austin; Office of the Vice President to Archives, October 12, 1962, LBJA Subject File, Box 60, Invitations from LBJ, LBJ Library, Austin; "For Release to A.M. Papers," November 12, 1964, Social Files, Bess Abell, Diaz Ordaz Ranch Visit, Box 7, LBJ Library, Austin.

6. Graves, *Goodbye to a River*, 25–26; Fehrenbach, *Lone Star*, 446–52; Pryor, interview, September 10, 1968.

7. Among the examples of such letters are Mrs. Fred McConnell to Bess Abell, June 6, 1964; C. Lynn to Bess Abell, January 28, 1965; G. L. Roberts to Bess Abell, May 7, 1965; Charles Bjernold to Bess Abell, August 1, 1965; Mrs. Philip Breseau to Bess Abell, April 27, 1967, WHSF, LBJ Ranch-B, Box 1345, LBJ Library, Austin.

8. Richard C. Wald, "Johnson and Erhard Face Decision Hour," *The Philadelphia Inquirer*, December 27, 1963; "Johnson and Erhard: Why Weekend's Talks are Important to the President," *The Wall Street Journal*, December 27, 1963.

9. Lady Bird Johnson, *White House Diary*, 22–23; "Visit to the United States of His Excellency Dr. Ludwig Erhard Chancellor of the Federal Republic of Germany, Accommodations at the LBJ Ranch, December, 28–29, 1963," Social Files, Liz Carpenter, Subject Files, Box 1, LBJ Library, Austin.

10. Lady Bird Johnson, *White House Diary*, 21–22.

11. Transcript, News Conference # 51, December 15, 1963, White House Press Office Files, Press Secretary News Conference, PSNC #47-55, Box 1, LBJ Library, Austin; Culbert, "Johnson and the Media," 214–16.

12. Lady Bird Johnson, *White House Diary*, 22.

13. Ibid.

14. "Tentative Program for the Visit to the United States of His Excellency Dr. Ludwig Erhard, Chancellor of the Federal Republic of Germany, December 27–29, 1963," Revision # 1, December 10, 1963; Stewart Davis, "Fredericksburg Plans German Gala to Honor Erhard," *The Houston Chronicle*, December 29, 1963; Maryrice Brogan, "Johnson, Erhard Land at Flag-Draped Ranch," *The Houston Chronicle*, December 29, 1963; "Dinner at LBJ Ranch, Saturday, December 28, 1963 at 7:30 o'clock," Social Files, Liz Carpenter, Subject Files, Box 1, LBJ Library, Austin; Lady Bird Johnson, *White House Diary*, 23–24; Pryor. interview, September 10, 1968, 15–16.

15. Lady Bird Johnson, *White House Diary*, 24; Houston Harte, "The Texas Hill Country," draft column, n.d., Social Files, Liz Carpenter, Subject Files, Box 1, LBJ Library, Austin.

16. Lady Bird Johnson, *White House Diary*, 24; Carpenter, *Ruffles and Flourishes*, 184; Pryor, interview, September 10, 1968, 18.

17. Walter Jetton to Bess Abell, December 13, 1963; "Barbecue List," December 17,

1963, Social Files, Bess Abell, Chancellor Erhard, Box 1, LBJ Library, Austin; Carpenter, *Ruffles and Flourishes,* 184; Pryor, interview, September 10, 1968; Lady Bird Johnson, *White House Diary,* 27.

18. Marta M. Miller, "Memo to Liz and Bess on My Conversations with Cactus Pryor," n.d., Social Files, Liz Carpenter, Subject Files, Box 1, LBJ Library, Austin; Carpenter, *Ruffles and Flourishes,* 184–85; Pryor, interview, September 10, 1968, 18.

19. Walter Jetton to Bess Abell, December 13, 1963; "State Officials, December 17, 1963"; "Barbecue at LBJ Ranch, Sunday, December 29, 1963, at One o'clock"; Mrs. Sterling R. Maddox to Bob Goolrick, March 18, 1964, Social Files, Liz Carpenter, LBJ Library, Austin; Harte, "Texas Hill Country"; Pryor, interview, September 10, 1968, 17; "Barbecue List," December 17, 1963; "Master List of Guests at LBJ Ranch for Erhard," December 29, 1963, Social Files, Bess Abell, Chancellor Erhard, Box 1, LBJ Library, Austin; Lady Bird Johnson, *White House Diary,* 26–27.

20. "Erhard Gets Texas Hat and Big Welcome," *The New York Times,* December 30, 1963; Pryor, interview, September 10, 1968, 18; Carpenter, *Ruffles and Flourishes,* 186.

21. Philip Potter, "Texas Talent to Entertain Erhard While at LBJ Ranch," *The Baltimore Sun,* December 28, 1963; Lady Bird Johnson, *White House Diary,* 26–27; Pryor, interview, September 10, 1968, 18.

22. Carpenter, *Ruffles and Flourishes,* 185; Pryor, interview, September 10, 1968.

23. "Building Bridges at LBJ's Ranch," *The New York Herald-Tribune,* December 30, 1963; Pryor, interview, September 10, 1968.

24. Harte, "Texas Hill Country"; "Text of Joint Communique by Johnson and Erhard," *The New York Times,* December 30, 1963, 8; Tom Wicker, "Erhard Pledges to Join Johnson in Peace Effort," *The New York Times,* December 30, 1963.

25. George McGhee, interview, AC # 74-153, LBJ Library, Austin.

26. Carpenter, *Ruffles and Flourishes,* 186–87.

27. "In View of the Poor Physical State . . . ," Social Files, Liz Carpenter, Subject Files, Box 13, LBJ Library, Austin.

28. Pryor, interview, September 10, 1968, 22–23; Christian, interview; "Guest List for Latin American Ambassadors' Barbecue," April 1, 1967, Social Files, Bess Abell, LBJ Ranch (Barbecue), Box 20, LBJ Library, Austin; "Dear Ambassador," March 17, 1967; "Schedule of Events for Latin American Ambassadorial Visit to Texas," March 30, 1967, WHSF, Social Entertainment, 4-1-67 Barbecue at Ranch, Box 90, LBJ Library, Austin.

29. Pryor, interview, September 10, 1968, 23; "Meal Arrangements," May 31, 1967, Social Files, Bess Abell, LBJ Ranch (Barbecue), Box 20, LBJ Library, Austin; Christian, interview.

30. "Friendship Fiesta, Not for Release," May 31, 1967; "Acceptance List," April 1, 1967, Social Files, Bess Abell, LBJ Ranch (Barbecue), Box 20, LBJ Library, Austin; "Schedule of Events for Latin American Ambassadorial Visit to Texas," March 30, 1967; "List of Ambassadors and Wives," March 30, 1967; "List of Texas Guests," March 30, 1967, WHSF, Social Entertainment, 4-1-67 Barbecue at Ranch, Box 90, LBJ Library, Austin; Pryor, interview, September 10, 1968, 23–25.

31. Lyndon B. Johnson, *Vantage Point,* 349–51. Walter LaFeber, "Latin American Policy," in Robert A. Divine, ed., *The Johnson Years,* vol. 1, *Foreign Policy, the Great Society, and the White House* (Austin: University of Texas Press, 1981), 85, argues that "the Alliance for Progress—both Kennedy's and Johnsons's version of it—had failed."

32. "The President and Mrs. Johnson Invite You to Barbecue Honoring President-Elect

and Mrs. Diaz Ordaz," November 6, 1964, PP 13-2/Texas, Box 97, LBJ Library, Austin; "Barbecue at the LBJ Ranch, Thursday, November 12, 1964, at one o'clock," Social Files, Liz Carpenter, Box 13, LBJ Library, Austin; "Fact Sheet on Barbecue of President and Mrs. Lyndon Johnson Honoring President-Elect of Mexico and Mrs. Gustavo Diaz Ordaz, at 1:00 P.M., Thursday, November 12, 1964, at the LBJ Ranch"; Horace Busby to Mrs. Bess Abell, September 28, 1964, Social Files, Bess Abell, Ranch Visit—Diaz Ordaz, Box 7, LBJ Library, Austin; Social Secretary, "The President and Mrs. Johnson invite you to barbecue [sic] honoring President-elect and Mrs. Diaz Ordaz, Thursday, November 12, at 1:00 P.M., LBJ Ranch, Stonewall, Texas. Formal Invitation Follows. RSVP," November 6, 1964, PP 13-2/Texas, Box 97, LBJ Library, Austin.

33. Pryor, interview, September 10, 1968, 19–20; Frank Holeman, "LBJ Treats Next Mexican President," *The New York Daily News*, November 13, 1964; Douglas Kiker, "On LBJ Ranch Menu: Barbecue, Diplomacy," *The New York Herald-Tribune*, November 13, 1964; Untitled, November 12, 1964, Social Files, Liz Carpenter, Mexican President, Box 13, LBJ Library, Austin.

34. "Limited Official Use, Memorandum for Jack Valenti, Meeting with Diaz Ordaz at the LBJ Ranch, November 12–13," November 2, 1964, PP 13-2/Texas, Box 97, LBJ Library, Austin.

35. Marie Smith, "Diaz Ordaz, LBJ Agree on Aims," *The Washington Post*, November 13, 1964; Douglas Kiker, "Johnson, Diaz Ordaz at Odds on Cuba," *The Philadelphia Inquirer*, November 14, 1964; Marie Smith, "LBJ, Diaz Ordaz Call Talk 'Highly Successful,'" *The Washington Post*, November 14, 1964; "Important Visitor From Mexico," *The Philadelphia Inquirer*, November 14, 1964. For Lake Powell, see Marc Reisner, *Cadillac Desert: The American West and Its Disappearing Water* (New York: Viking Penguin, 1986), 255–59, and Worster, *Rivers of Empire*.

36. George Christian, "Memorandum for the President," January 7, 1968, PP 13-2/Texas, Box 98, LBJ Library, Austin; "Room Assignments, [Eshkol Visit]," n.d., WHSF, LBJ Ranch D, Box 1346, LBJ Library, Austin.

37. Miriam Eshkol to President and Mrs. Johnson, February 9, 1968, White House Alpha File, Box 758, LBJ Library, Austin; Reedy, interview, AC 84-42, 20–21.

38. Miller, *Lyndon: An Oral Biography*, 403.

39. Hugh Davis Graham, "The Transformation of Federal Education Policy," in Robert A. Divine, ed., *The Johnson Years*, vol. 1, *Foreign Policy, the Great Society, and the White House* (Austin: University of Texas Press, 1981), 155–84; Lyndon B. Johnson, *Vantage Point*, 209–12, 380.

40. Miller, *Lyndon: An Oral Biography*, 407; Reedy, interview, 84-42, 27.

41. Miller, *Lyndon: An Oral Biography*, 408–12; Joseph A. Califano, Jr., *The Triumph and Tragedy of Lyndon Johnson: The White House Years* (New York: Simon and Schuster, 1991), 70–71; Graham, "Transformation of Federal Educational Policy," 157–63; Lyndon B. Johnson, *Vantage Point*, 206–12.

42. Lady Bird Johnson, *White House Diary*, 257–58; Charles Boatner, interview by Konrad Kelley, June 5, 1979, SPMA Oral History Collection, LBJNHP, 356:3; Cross, interview, October 22, 1978, 333:4.

43. Lady Bird Johnson, *White House Diary*, 258–59; Lyndon B. Johnson, *Vantage Point*, 212; Edwin C. Bearss, interview by Hal K. Rothman, June 2, 1994.

44. Lady Bird Johnson, *White House Diary*, 258–59; Lyndon B. Johnson, *Vantage Point*, 212; Cross, interview, October 22, 1978, 333:4.

CHAPTER 8. EASTERN MEDIA AND THE MAN FROM TEXAS: THE
RANCH AS A CROSS-CULTURAL EXPERIENCE

1. Culbert, "Johnson and the Media," 214.
2. Ibid., 214–15.
3. Miller, *Lyndon: An Oral Biography,* 408; Lyndon B. Johnson, *Vantage Point,* 28–29.
4. Tom Weinheimer and Betty Weinheimer, interview, 282:4; Merriman Smith, "Will
   LBJ Visit Ranch Often? Hill Country Like a Vitamin Pill," *The Houston Press,* January 6, 1964; Nan Robertson, "The First Lady Takes Huge Guest Lists in Her
   Stride," *The New York Times,* January 4, 1964; Tom Wicker, "With Johnson on the
   Ranch," *The New York Times,* January 5, 1964; Douglas Kiker, "Lyndon Baines
   Johnson—A Measure of the Man," *The New York Herald-Tribune,* January 6, 1964.
   Merriman Smith was the United Press International (UPI) White House reporter.
   His report appeared in hundreds of newspapers across the nation and around the
   world.
5. Wicker, "With Johnson on the Ranch"; Kiker, "Measure of the Man."
6. Lyndon Johnson to Dave Cheavens, October 1, 1953, Senate Political Files, LBJ Per-
   sonal Miscellaneous, Box, LBJ Library, Austin; Nathaniel Schneider to Lyndon
   Johnson, August 14, 1964, PP13-2/Texas, Box 96, LBJ Library, Austin; Conkin, *Big
   Daddy,* 185.
7. Conkin, *Big Daddy,* 185; Dugger, *Politician,* 20–21.
8. Goldman, *Tragedy of Lyndon Johnson,* 409–10; Culbert, "Johnson and the Media,"
   223–24; Kearns, *Lyndon Johnson and the American Dream,* 302–303. Halberstam,
   Powers That Be, 514, indicates that Johnson watched the CBS report live in the
   White House; Culbert demonstrates otherwise, 225–26.
9. Harold Woods, interview by Konrad Kelley, August 8, 1979, SPMA Oral History
   Collection, LBJNHP, 360:1; Boatner, interview, 256:4; Carpenter, interview, 316:2.
10. News Conference #808A, Transcript, April 15, 1967; News Conference #830A, Tran-
    script, May 8, 1967, White House Press Office Files, Press Secretary, News Confer-
    ences, #PSNC 808A–#PSNC 903A, Box 13, LBJ Library, Austin; Carpenter, inter-
    view, 316:2.
11. Lady Bird Johnson, *White House Diary,* 331–33.
12. Jewell Malechek, interview, July 5, 1978, 323:4; Lady Bird Johnson, *White House
    Diary,* 331–32; Robert A. Divine, "Lyndon B. Johnson and the Politics of Space," in
    Robert A. Divine, ed., *The Johnson Years,* vol. 2, *Vietnam, the Environment, and Sci-
    ence* (Lawrence: University of Kansas Press, 1987), 247–48.
13. Goldman, *The Tragedy of Lyndon Johnson,* 409–17, offers an account of Johnson's
    problems of credibility. Goldman is at once credible and tainted by his own politi-
    cal sympathies. He articulates the genuine problems of communication between the
    presidency and the press but lays too much of the blame on Johnson for this cross-
    cultural lack of communication. In effect, on this issue Goldman engages in
    "twenty-twenty hindsight."
14. Reedy, interview, AC 76-23, 60.
15. Culbert, "Lyndon Johnson and the Media," 214–25; Goldman, *The Tragedy of
    Lyndon Johnson,* 411–13; Sam Houston Johnson, *My Brother Lyndon,* 193.
16. Halberstam, *Powers That Be,* 3–18, 428–37. Halberstam notes that Johnson's resis-
    tance to television and his refusal to hold press conferences hurt him, for " ironi-
    cally [television] would have been the perfect format for him; the questioning of a

few intelligent journalists would have evoked the sheer force and above all the incredible knowledge of government that Lyndon Johnson possessed" (434).

17. Christian, interview, 4–5; M. W. Ivy, interview by Konrad Kelley, October 25, 1978, SPMA Oral History Collection, LBJNHP, 334:1.

18. George Reedy, interview, AC 84-25, LBJ Library, Austin, 11; Christian, interview, 22. Conkin, *Big Daddy,* 184–86, offers the most reasoned explanation of this phenomenon.

19. Culbert, "Lyndon Johnson and the Media," 214–26, describes some of the ways in which the press had an impact on Johnson; Conkin, *Big Daddy,* 184–86, and Kearns, *Lyndon Johnson and the American Dream,* 246–49, describe Johnson's philosophy and some of his actions. Kearns's unflattering portrayal is consistent with the image of Johnson that emerges from her work, but it assesses only the president's culpability, not that of all the involved parties, when attempting to dissect this relationship.

20. Reedy, interview, AC 84-25; Ivy, interview, 334:2; Miller, *Lyndon: An Oral Biography,* 541–42; Culbert, "Lyndon Johnson and the Media," 220.

21. Marshall Frady, "Cooling Off With LBJ," *Harper's* (June, 1969), 66; Sam Houston Johnson, *My Brother Lyndon,* 193.

22. Frady, "Cooling Off With LBJ," 66–67.

23. Culbert, "Lyndon Johnson and the Media," 220–23; Halberstam, *Powers That Be,* 435–37.

24. Lady Bird Johnson, *White House Diary,* 333.

25. Carpenter, *Ruffles and Flourishes,* 173.

26. Christian, interview, 7.

27. Ibid.; John Chancellor to David Waters, February 17, 1964, PP 13-2/Texas, LBJ Library, Austin.

28. Sam Houston Johnson, *My Brother Lyndon,* 193–96; Carpenter, *Ruffles and Flourishes,* 168.

29. Carpenter, *Ruffles and Flourishes,* 177–78; Father Wunibald Schneider, interview; Lewis L. Gould, *Lady Bird Johnson and the Environment* (Lawrence: University Press of Kansas, 1988), 29–75; Sam Houston Johnson, *My Brother Lyndon,* 193.

30. Carpenter, *Ruffles and Flourishes,* 178.

31. Ibid., 176–77; Mills, interview, 346:1.

32. Klein, interview, March 30, 1977, 288:3; Culbert, "Lyndon Johnson and the Media," 214–16. See also Sam Houston Johnson, *My Brother Lyndon.*

33. Miller, *Lyndon: An Oral Biography,* 405; Kiker, "Measure of the Man."

34. Kiker, "Measure of the Man"; Mills, interview, 346:1.

35. Miller, *Lyndon: An Oral Biography,* 404; Conkin, *Big Daddy,* 179.

36. Reedy, interview, AC 84-54, 10.

37. For histories of hunting as a social ritual, see William Cronon, *Changes in the Land: Indians, Colonists, and the Ecology of New England* (New York: Hill and Wang, 1982); John Mack Faragher, *Daniel Boone: The Life and Legend of an American Pioneer* (New York: Henry Holt, 1992); and Stuart Marks, *Southern Hunting in Black and White* (Princeton: Princeton University Press, 1992).

38. John Reiger, *American Sportsmen and the Origins of Conservation* (Norman: University of Oklahoma Press, 1975); Thomas L. Altherr and John Reiger, "Hunting and Historians," *Environmental History Review* 19, no. 3 (fall, 1995), 39–58; Merriman Smith, "Will LBJ Visit Ranch Often?"

39. Merriman Smith, "Will LBJ Visit Ranch Often?"

40. J. O. Tanner, interview by Konrad Kelley and Buddy Hughes, February 19, 1976, SPMA Oral History Collection, LBJNHP, 228:1.

41. Rather, interview, 319:4.

42. Mills, interview, 346:2; Dale Malechek, interview, December 27, 1979, 365:2; Klein, interview, March 30, 1977, 288:3; Dale Malechek and Jewel Malechek, interview, December 13, 1978, 341:3.

43. Lyndon Johnson to Sam Houston Johnson, November 17, 1957, Family Correspondence, 1950–1959, Box 2, LBJ Library, Austin; Juanita Roberts to Cliff [Carter], November 23, 1962, Vice Presidential Papers, Box 183, Science-Space and Aeronautics-Astronauts, LBJ Library, Austin; Juanita Roberts to Ewel Stone, November 2, 1964; Ralph Dungan to Jack Valenti; Lyndon Johnson to Walter McDonald, November 29, 1964, PP 13-2/Texas, Box 97, LBJ Library, Austin; Jim Jones to Lyndon Johnson, December 29, 1967, PP 13-2/Texas, Box 98 #4, LBJ Library, Austin; James Davis, interview by Michael L. Gillette, November 3, 1983, LBJ Library, Austin, 7; Heller, interview, 42–44.

44. Father Wunibald Schneider, interview; Albert Wierich and Olivia Wierich, interview, 291:2.

45. James Davis, interview, 9–10.

46. Ibid.; Boatner, interview, 356:3.

47. Howard, interview, 292:1; James Davis, interview; Miller, *Lyndon: An Oral Biography,* 405.

48. Miller, *Lyndon: An Oral Biography,* 404.

CHAPTER 9. THE RANCH AS A HAVEN

1. Miller, *Lyndon: An Oral Biography,* 406.

2. Reedy, interview, AC 84-40, 19; Boozer, interview, June 7, 1978, 317:1.

3. Miller, *Lyndon: An Oral Biography,* 406; Boozer, interview, June 7, 1978, 317:3; Everee Wade, interview by Konrad Kelley and Edwin C. Bearss, June 9, 1978, 322:3; Holder, "Year at a Glance."

4. Sam Houston Johnson, *My Brother Lyndon,* 1–5.

5. Goldman, *Tragedy of Lyndon Johnson,* 411–12; Chafe, *Unfinished Journey,* 273–360.

6. Woods, interview, August 2, 1979, 359:1; Lloyd Gardner, "Lyndon Johnson and Vietnam: The Final Months," in Robert A. Divine, ed., *The Johnson Years,* vol. 3, *LBJ at Home and Abroad* (Lawrence: University Press of Kansas, 1994), 198–202; George C. Herring, "The War in Vietnam," in Robert A. Divine, ed., *The Johnson Years,* vol. 1, *Foreign Policy, the Great Society, and the White House* (Austin: University of Texas Press, 1981), 27.

7. Dale Malechek and Jewell Malechek, interview by Konrad Kelley, November 27, 1979, SPMA Oral History Collection, LBJNHP, 365:8.

8. Lady Bird Johnson, *White House Diary,* 464–65; 590, 605–607; Holder, "Year at a Glance."

9. Rather, interview, 319:1; Woods, interview, August 2, 1979, 359:2; Dale Malechek, interview, November 22, 1978, 339:2; Ohlen Cox and Edward Maier, interview by Konrad Kelley, March 31, 1977, SPMA Oral History Collection, LBJNHP, 290:1; Richard S. "Cactus" Pryor, interview by Konrad Kelley, August 29, 1979, SPMA Oral History Collection, LBJNHP, 363:1; Boatner, interview, 356:2; Father Wunibald Schneider, interview, 242:1.

10. Juanita Roberts to Lyndon Johnson, September 14, 1964, PP 13-2/Texas, Box 96, LBJ Library, Austin; Memorandum for the Record, February 15, 1964, PP 13-2/Texas, Box 97, LBJ Library, Austin; Jack Albright to Marvin Watson, May 24, 1967, EX WH 12-1, Box 23, LBJ Library, Austin; Dale Malechek, interview, November 22, 1978, 339:2; Carpenter, *Ruffles and Flourishes*, 175, 184.

11. Father Wunibald Schneider, interview, 242:1; Miller, *Lyndon: An Oral Biography*, 406; Conkin, *Big Daddy*, 177-78.

12. "Memorandum for Mrs. Johnson, Re: Your weekend of 'sharing the ranch at a pretty time of the year with people we enjoy'," March 19, 1968; "Room Arrangements for the Ranch—April 19-21"; "Menus for April 19, 20, 21," Social Files, Bess Abell, Ranch Weekend, 4/19-4/21/68, Box 25, LBJ Library, Austin.

13. "*Off Record*, Dinner at the LBJ Ranch, Saturday, August 3, 1968 at seven o'clock"; Mrs Lyndon B. Johnson to Mr. and Mrs. [Edward J.] Daly, July 26, 1968, Social Files, Bess Abell, Ranch Weekend, 2-8/4/68, Box 27, LBJ Library, Austin.

14. Lady Bird Johnson, *White House Diary*, 22-23, 329-30.

15. Boozer, interview, June 7, 1978, 317:2; Sam Houston Johnson, interview, 225:4.

16. Lady Bird Johnson, *White House Diary*, 415-16; Hahne and Cox, interview, 311:2.

17. Lady Bird Johnson, *White House Diary*, 345; Califano, *Triumph and Tragedy*, 284-86, 326-28.

18. Lady Bird Johnson, *White House Diary*, 346.

19. Califano, *Triumph and Tragedy*, 87-88.

20. Ibid., 88-90.

21. Ibid., 90-91; Holder, "Year at a Glance."

22. Califano, *Triumph and Tragedy*, 90-91; Dallck, *Lone Star Rising*, 473-76.

23. Califano, *Triumph and Tragedy*, 92.

24. Ibid., 93-94.

25. Ibid.; Lady Bird Johnson, *White House Diary*, 316-17; Holder, "Year at a Glance."

26. Lady Bird Johnson, *White House Diary*, 317; Holder, "Year at a Glance."

27. Culbert, "Lyndon Johnson and the Media," 214-17.

28. Lady Bird Johnson, *White House Diary*, 565-66; J. J. "Jake" Pickle, interview by Konrad Kelley, January 2, 1975, SPMA Oral History Collection, LBJNHP, 203:2; Father Wunibald Schneider, interview.

29. Lady Bird Johnson, *White House Diary*, 611-12.

30. Ibid., 612.

31. Frady, "Cooling Off with LBJ," 66; Miller, *Lyndon: An Oral Biography*, 511. Conkin, *Big Daddy*, 288, writes that "even his closest White House aides knew about the carefully guarded secret ending of his [March 31, 1968] speech only a day before he delivered it."

32. Bearss, "Historic Structure Report," 33; Lady Bird Johnson, interview by Alec Gould, John Tiff, and Edwin C. Bearss, August 12, 1978, SPMA Oral History Collection, LBJNHP; White, interview, 315:1; Lawrence Klein, interview by Konrad Kelley, Edwin C. Bearss, and Libby Huitt, May 31, 1978, SPMA Oral History Collection, LBJNHP, 310:3; Jewell Malechek, interview, June 9, 1978, 320:2.

33. Bearss, "Historic Structure Report," 33-35; White, interview.

34. Lyndon B. Johnson, *Vantage Point*, 174; Califano, *Triumph and Tragedy*, 273-76.

35. Lady Bird Johnson, *White House Diary*, 660-62; Miller, *Lyndon: An Oral Biography*, 514; Califano, *Triumph and Tragedy*, 275.

36. Lyndon B. Johnson, *Vantage Point*, 173-76.

37. Ibid., 177–78; Miller, *Lyndon: An Oral Biography,* 515. Not everyone shared Johnson's view of the situation. According to U.S. District Court Judge Thomas "Barefoot" Sanders, in the aftermath of the assassination "yeas and nays canceled each other out," negating any gains in support for the legislation; for more, see Steven F. Lawson, "Civil Rights," in Robert A. Divine, ed., *The Johnson Years,* vol. 1, *Foreign Policy, the Great Society, and the White House* (Austin: University of Texas Press, 1981), 104–106. Lawson suggests that more study is needed before the real impact of the assassination on the subsequent passage of the legislation can be determined.

38. Lyndon B. Johnson, *Vantage Point,* 178–79; Miller, *Lyndon: An Oral Biography,* 515.

39. Steven F. Lawson, "Mixing Moderation with Militancy: Lyndon Johnson and African-American Leadership," in Robert A. Divine, ed., *The Johnson Years,* vol. 3, *LBJ at Home and Abroad* (Lawrence: University Press of Kansas, 1994), 83–90. For more on the transformation of King's thinking and the problems this precipitated with Johnson, see David Arrow, "From Reformer to Revolutionary," in David J. Arrow, ed., *Martin Luther King, Jr., and the Civil Rights Movement* (Brooklyn: Carlson Publishing, 1989), 427–36, and Adam Fairclough, *To Redeem the Soul of America: The Southern Christian Leadership Conference and Martin Luther King, Jr.* (Athens: University of Georgia Press, 1987), 380–85.

40. Lady Bird Johnson, *White House Diary,* 664.

CHAPTER 10. "EIGHT HUNDRED YARDS UP THE ROAD": THE RANCH AND RETIREMENT, 1969–73

1. Leo Janis, "The Last Days of the President: LBJ in Retirement," *The Atlantic* (July, 1973), 35–41; Frady, "Cooling Off with LBJ," 66.

2. Flora Rheta Schreiber, "When L.B.J. Retires," *Modern Maturity* (December–January, 1969), 11; "Notes of President Johnson's meeting with George Christian, Neal Spelce, and Tom Johnson, Friday, October 1, 1971," Post-Presidential Name File, George Christian, Box 27, LBJ Library, Austin; Boozer, interview, June 7, 1978, 317:2; Father Wunibald Schneider, interview.

3. Kearns, *Lyndon Johnson and the American Dream,* 353, 359; Schreiber, "When L.B.J. Retires."

4. Janis, "Last Days of the President," 37, 41; Kearns, *Lyndon Johnson and the American Dream,* 353; Miller, *Lyndon: An Oral Biography,* 549–50; Conkin, *Big Daddy,* 291.

5. Tom Weinheimer and Betty Weinheimer, interview, 282:2; Conkin, *Big Daddy,* 287–88; Janis, "Last Days of the President," 35. Miller, *Lyndon: An Oral Biography,* 548, describes this sentiment as being responsible for reports that Johnson was "massively depressed."

6. "Notes of President Johnson's meeting with George Christian, Neal Spelce, and Tom Johnson"; Miller, *Lyndon: An Oral Biography,* 545–46; Conkin, *Big Daddy,* 293; Janis, "Last Days of the President," 37.

7. Lady Bird Johnson, *White House Diary,* 762.

8. Conkin, *Big Daddy,* 243; Miller, *Lyndon: An Oral Biography,* 527.

9. Miller, *Lyndon: An Oral Biography,* 528–29.

10. Ibid., 529.

11. Carpenter, *Ruffles and Flourishes,* 334; Miller, *Lyndon: An Oral Biography,* 530.

12. Miller, *Lyndon: An Oral Biography,* 530; Carpenter, *Ruffles and Flourishes,* 336–37.

13. Lady Bird Johnson, *White House Diary,* 782.

14. Ibid., 782; Miller, *Lyndon: An Oral Biography,* 530; Boozer, interview, July 11, 1978, 317:2; Carpenter, *Ruffles and Flourishes,* 338–39.

15. Miller, *Lyndon: An Oral Biography,* 539–40.

16. Jewell Malechek, interview, June 9, 1978, 320:5; Reedy, interview, AC 85-23, 27; Nicholas C. Chriss, "LBJ A Mellowing Sideliner," *The New York Times,* October 18, 1972; Janis, "Last Days of the President," 37.

17. Rather, interview, 319:2; Frady, "Cooling Off with LBJ," 66; Miller, *Lyndon: An Oral Biography,* 406; Conkin, *Big Daddy,* 291; Janis, "Last Days of the President," 35.

18. Miller, *Lyndon: An Oral Biography,* 544–46; Thomas, interview, 336:1; Father Wunibald Schneider, interview.

19. Dale Malechek, interview, November 9, 1978; Mills, interview, 346:1.

20. Mills, interview, 346:1; Jewell Malechek, interview, June 9, 1978, 320:5.

21. J. N. "Jimmy" Houck, interview by Konrad Kelley, March 31, 1979, SPMA Oral History Collection, LBJNHP, 355:3; Jewell Malechek, interview, June 9, 1978; Boozer, interview.

22. Chriss, "LBJ A Mellowing Sideliner"; "Notes of President Johnson's meeting with George Christian, Neal Spelce, and Tom Johnson."

23. "Notes of President Johnson's meeting with George Christian, Neal Spelce, and Tom Johnson."

24. Miller, *Lyndon: An Oral Biography,* 544.

25. Father Wunibald Schneider, interview.

26. Pryor, interview, August 29, 1979, 363:1.

27. Howard, interview, 292:1.

28. Miller, *Lyndon: An Oral Biography,* 548.

29. Jewell Malechek, interview, June 9, 1978, 320:5; "Notes of President Johnson's meeting with George Christian, Neal Spelce, and Tom Johnson"; Miller, *Lyndon: An Oral Biography,* 548; Janis, "Last Days of the President," 37.

30. Conkin, *Big Daddy,* 293.

31. Pryor, interview, August 29, 1979, 363:1; Jewell Malechek, interview, June 9, 1978, 320:5; "Notes of President Johnson's meeting with George Christian, Neal Spelce, and Tom Johnson"; Conkin, *Big Daddy,* 293. In 1972, fullback Roosevelt Leaks became the first African American football player at the University of Texas. He went on to a decade-long career in the National Football League.

32. Jewell Malechek, interview, June 9, 1978, 320:5; "Notes of President Johnson's meeting with George Christian, Neal Spelce, and Tom Johnson"; Janis, "Last Days of the President," 37.

33. Miller, *Lyndon: An Oral Biography,* 549–50; Kearns, *Lyndon Johnson and the American Dream,* 353.

34. Bearss, interview; Boatner, interview, 356:5; White, interview, 315:1; Lawrence Klein, interview, May 31, 1978; Boozer, interview, 317:2; Carpenter, Oral History, 22–23; Miller, *Lyndon: An Oral Biography,* 549.

35. Richard Dudman, "In Johnson Land," *The New Republic* 155 no. 25 (December 17, 1966), 11–12; Horace Busby to Lady Bird Johnson, November 14, 1966; Tom Johnson to Mr. President, December 12, 1966, PP 13-2/Texas, Box 98, LBJ Library, Austin; Miller, *Lyndon: An Oral Biography,* 549–50.

36. Miller, *Lyndon: An Oral Biography,* 549–50; Conkin, *Big Daddy,* 290; Boozer, interview, June 7, 1978, 317:2; Cross, interview, October 22, 1978, 333:4.

37. Kearns, *Lyndon Johnson and the American Dream,* 14, 355–58; Conkin, *Big Daddy,* 291;

38. Kearns, *Lyndon Johnson and the American Dream,* 14, 357.

39. Frady, "Cooling Off with LBJ," 69; Kearns, *Lyndon Johnson and the American Dream,* 356.

40. Jewell Malechek, interview, July 5, 1978, 323:1; Walter Cronkite, "LBJ: Why I Chose Not to Run," CBS News Special Broadcast, December 27, 1969, Oral History, Lyndon B. Johnson, AC 79-69, LBJ Library, Austin.

41. Conkin, *Big Daddy,* 294; Miller, *Lyndon: An Oral Biography,* 544.

42. Mills, interview, 346:1.

43. Dale Malechek, interview, November 9, 1978; Mills, interview, 346:1.

44. Mills, interview; Bearss, interview; Jewell Malechek, interview, 320:5; Chriss, "LBJ A Mellowing Sideliner"; Janis, "Last Days of the President," 40.

45. Nash Castro, "The LBJ I Remember," June 18, 1977, Papers of Nash Castro, Box 2, LBJ Library, Austin; Lewis L. Gould, *Lady Bird Johnson and the Environment,* 81.

46. Janis, "Last Days of the President," 39; Conkin, *Big Daddy,* 294; Homer F. Cunningham, *The Presidents' Last Years: George Washington to Lyndon B. Johnson* (Jefferson, N.C.: McFarland and Company, 1989), 302.

47. Mills, interview; Chriss, "LBJ A Mellowing Sideliner"; Janis, "Last Days of the President," 41; Miller, *Lyndon: An Oral Biography,* 551; Cunningham, *Presidents' Last Years,* 391.

48. Bearss, interview.

49. Ibid.; Mackintosh, *Shaping the System,* 77.

50. Mills, interview; Miller, *Lyndon: An Oral Biography,* 547.

51. Miller, *Lyndon: An Oral Biography,* 559–61; Lawson, "Civil Rights," 113.

52. Miller, *Lyndon: An Oral Biography,* 560–61.

53. Ibid., 561–62.

54. Ibid., 562.

55. Ibid., 556.

56. Boatner, interview, 54–55; Klein, interview.

EPILOGUE: POWER AND PLACE IN AMERICAN CULTURE

1. Miller, *Lyndon: An Oral Biography,* 406.

INDEX

HAL K. ROTHMAN is a leading historian of the American West, especially of the environment in the West. Holding a Ph.D. in American Studies from the University of Texas, he teaches at the University of Nevada, Las Vegas. He has served as editor of the journal *Environmental History* and has written many books and articles on western and environmental history. His book *Devil's Bargains: Tourism in the Twentieth Century American West* received the Western Writers of America's Spur Award for Best Contemporary Non-Fiction in 1999.